STUDIES IN MODERN ART 5

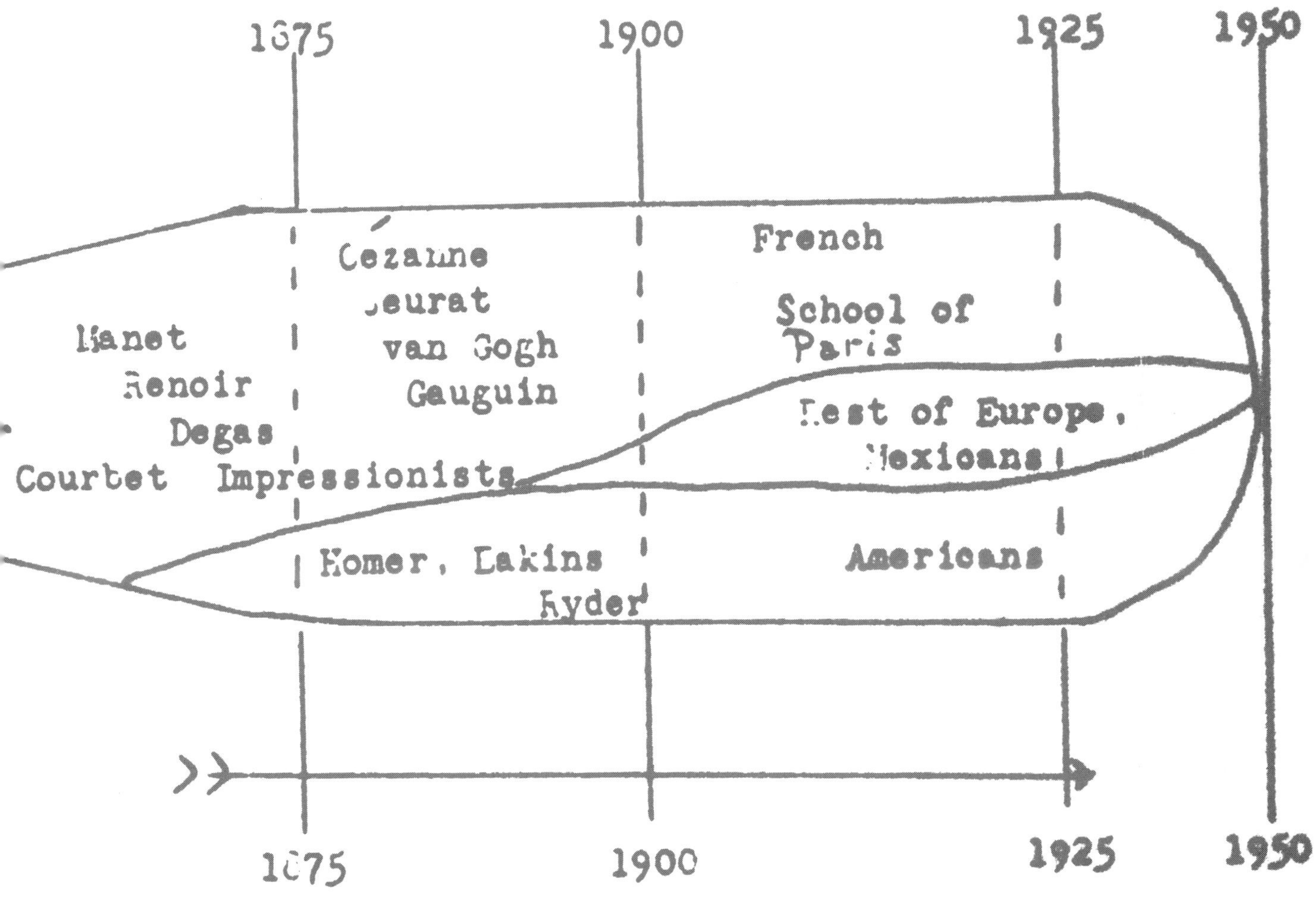

STUDIES IN MODERN ART 5

The Museum of Modern Art at Mid-Century

Continuity and Change

THE MUSEUM OF MODERN ART, NEW YORK

Distributed by Harry N. Abrams, Inc., New York

Studies in Modern Art is prepared by the Research and Scholarly Publications Program of The Museum of Modern Art, which was initiated with the support of a grant from the Andrew W. Mellon Foundation. Publication is made possible by an endowment fund established by the Andrew W. Mellon Foundation, the Edward John Noble Foundation, Mr. and Mrs. Perry R. Bass, and the National Endowment for the Humanities' Challenge Grant Program.

Produced by the Department of Publications,
The Museum of Modern Art, New York
Osa Brown, Director of Publications
Edited by Barbara Ross
Design and typography by Charles Davey *design lab* and Jean Garrett
Production by Marc Sapir
Printed by Science Press, Ephrata, Pennsylvania
Bound by Acme Bookbinding Company, Inc., Charlestown, Massachusetts

Studies in Modern Art, no. 5

Library of Congress Catalog Card Number 95-081119
ISBN 0-87070-128-2 (The Museum of Modern Art and Thames and Hudson Ltd.)
ISBN 0-8109-6153-9 (Harry N. Abrams, Inc.)
ISSN 1058-997X

Published annually by The Museum of Modern Art,
11 West 53 Street, New York, New York 10019

Distributed in the United States and Canada by
Harry N. Abrams, Inc., New York, A Times Mirror Company

Distributed outside the United States and Canada by
Thames and Hudson, Ltd., London

Contents

Preface

Studies in Modern Art 5, like the preceding issue it is designed to accompany, is devoted to The Museum of Modern Art's own history in the period around mid-century, and mainly during the 1950s.

We chose as the focus of the preceding issue the contrast and relationship between the Museum's national and its international activities. As such, it included two articles on programs that were largely national in scope, Edgar S. Kaufmann, Jr.'s Good Design project and Dorothy Miller's series of "Americans" exhibitions; two on topics primarily of international significance, the Museum's International Program and revisionist histories of this and other Museum programs; and one on an exhibition, Edward Steichen's "Family of Man," that was presented both at home and abroad. The issue concluded with excerpts, relevant to the period under discussion, reprinted from a "Chronicle of the Collection of Painting and Sculpture," written in the 1970s by the Museum's Founding Director, Alfred H. Barr, Jr. Barr's "Chronicle" comprises the principal link between the previous issue and this one, which addresses selective topics relating to Museum policies and departmental programs, and to conceptual as well as practical aspects of the Museum's collections, exhibitions, and publications, in the mid-century period.

To say, as we do in the subtitle of this issue, that its focus is continuity and change within The Museum of Modern Art may seem to be saying no more than would be true of any institution at any given point in its history. But this antimony is probably more telling a characterization of the Museum's own evolution in the period around mid-century than in any other, except, perhaps, the current end-of-century period, which is why what appears in this volume has even greater historical relevance.

A broad outline of why this particular period is of such crucial importance to the Museum's history is contained in the preface to the preceding volume, and for that reason such an overview is not attempted here. It should be repeated, however, that the mid-century period saw the culmination of long-standing debates within the Museum concerning the aims and intended scope of the collection of painting and sculpture, particularly with regard to the balance between art we now call contemporary but was then called "modern," and art we now call modern but was then called "classic." The outcome of these debates was a contractual agreement made with The Metropolitan Museum of Art in 1947 (but cancelled six years later) to transfer to that museum selected works which both museums agreed had passed from the category of "modern" to that of "classic." Barr's aforementioned "Chronicle" offers few details of that agreement and, for the most part, cites only officially promulgated documents pertaining to the wider issues. These issues, as well as the inter-museum agreement and its impact on the Museum's collection policy, are newly considered here by Kirk Varnedoe, Chief Curator of the Department of Painting and Sculpture. Through detailed study of archival materials, some of which had not been examined previously, he has composed a radically different picture of what was a particularly vexing issue for the Museum.

It is clear from Barr's "Chronicle" that a special relationship between The Museum of Modern Art and the Metropolitan Museum, modeled after that between the Musée Luxembourg and the Musée du Louvre in Paris, had been envisaged by Barr and others within the Museum when the Modern was founded in 1929. It is also clear from the "Chronicle" that such an arrangement might easily have been considered when the Museum in fact had no collection. What does not appear in Barr's account, however, is that discussions with the Metropolitan on this subject began almost immedi-

ately upon the Modern's founding and continued with increasing urgency through the mid-1930s as its collection was being formed. At that time, it is now established, a consensus did exist within the Museum as to the wisdom of its not maintaining a permanent, and ultimately historical, collection.

And yet, Barr had already begun to consider the implications of such a policy. From this consideration emerged, in 1933, his famous "torpedo report," which imagined the Museum Collection "as a torpedo moving through time, its nose the ever advancing present, its tail the ever receding past." That this missile, in Barr's description, is uncharacteristically elastic appears to have passed without comment at the time. There was no reason why it should have been remarked upon, given Barr's accompanying suggestion: that works more than fifty years old should be transferred to the Metropolitan. In 1933, this plan effectively preserved the Modern's collection of Post-Impressionist paintings—for the time being. In 1947, when negotiations with the Metropolitan, which had stalled in the mid-1930s, were resumed with alarming haste, this was no longer the case. Although the end of the story is well known, its details are not, and they reveal as much of pragmatism as of the idealism that is constantly evoked in descriptions of the Museum's pioneering years. It would be unfair to reveal any more here, except to say that, but for a decision nearly made and left unmade, the Museum's collections might well now begin with Jasper Johns.

The Museum's understanding and representation of itself as devoted to the history of modern art since the 1880s, and of things contemporary as continuous with that history, does not date to the period around mid-century, but a new awareness of these things does. Varnedoe's article makes this explicitly clear. It is no mere coincidence, of course, that such a stance was taken at the same time, in the 1950s, that the Museum engaged in proselytizing missions for its various programs, seeking to attract broader audiences for modern art. Articles in the preceding issue of *Studies in Modern Art,* especially those on exhibitions mounted by the Photography and Architecture and Design departments and on the activities of the International Program, described how popularism as well as popularity were among the Museum's primary aims at mid-century. The article in this issue by Mary Lea Bandy, Chief Curator of the Department of Film and Video, shows that what was originally called the Film Library dealt with issues of popular taste and broad audience appeal from its very inception.

There were, of course, other concerns, principal among them the need "to create a consciousness of tradition and of history within the new art of film"—the founding manifesto of the Film Library's first curator, Iris Barry. Thus, issues concerning the relationship of old and new comparable to those being debated elsewhere in the Museum marked Barry's agenda, too. They did so, moreover, with a particular urgency. When Barry was appointed in 1935, there were a few film societies in the United States, but film collections, programs, schools, festivals, repertory theaters, and the like simply did not exist. At her retirement from the Film Library in 1951, all of these, and more, existed in abundance throughout the country. Bandy's article addresses the period of Barry's tenure as curator and, later, director of the Film Library, and details how this remarkable woman contributed decisively to that change by creating for film its curatorial apparatus. That it was in principle the same as for any other medium—"the analysis and conservation of the object itself and its placement historically and critically through exhibition and publication," in Bandy's description—takes nothing away from the achievement; rather, it only confirms how securely the medium of film was thus attached to museology.

Essential to Barry's success was Alfred Barr's own enthusiasm for film and that of John Hay ("Jock") Whitney, Chairman of the Film Library's Trustee Committee from its founding until 1955. Whitney, a celebrated collector of Post-Impressionist and Fauve paintings, had found a filmic parallel to his painterly interests in the new three-color process of Technicolor, in which he became an investor in 1933; this involvement led to his partnership in Selznick International Pictures, which six years later would produce *Gone with the Wind.* Whitney was instrumental in making contact for Barry with Hollywood in 1935; she returned with its endorsement of the Museum's film program, and soon had in place a landmark agreement with the major studios allowing the Museum to make prints of their films for preservation and study.

From this, everything else followed. By 1940, the Film Library had sixteen hundred titles, including numerous acquisitions made in the international arena. Whatever their sources, however, Barry made no bones about the fact that she was interested in film as both art and entertainment. Unsurprisingly, there was opposition at first within the Museum, but it could not have hurt that a member of the Film Library Committee named Erwin Panofsky agreed with her. Barry's tenure at the Museum, let us remember, roughly coincided with the period defined by Panofsky's *Studies in Iconology* (1939) and *Meaning in the Visual Arts* (1955). How the textual source of a picture determines its meaning was necessarily high on Barry's agenda, and she discovered that meaning in Disney as well as Eisenstein.

When Barry screened Disney cartoons at Columbia University and the polemical films of Eisenstein before broad audiences at the Museum, she was following the founding principles of her institution. Its original charter had been granted by the Education Department of New York State in 1929 "for the purpose of encouraging the study of modern arts and the application of such arts to manufacture and practical life, and furnishing popular instruction. . . ."[1] Thus, when other Museum departments became more actively involved in expanding their programs to attract wider audiences, they were not redefining the Museum's original mission but, rather, more strenuously attempting to implement it.

In 1944, Barr restated that mission in a more succinct and "user-friendly" way: "The primary purpose of the Museum is to help people enjoy, understand and use the visual arts of our time." To this, he added a telling conclusion:

Obviously, these three activities—enjoying, understanding, using—should be thought of as interdependent. Each confirms, enriches, and supports the other. Together they indicate the Museum's primary function, which is educational in the broadest, less academic sense.[2]

In light of this statement, it is not surprising that the mid-century period saw the redefinition of the Museum's specifically educational programs. What happened to these programs demonstrates most clearly the extent to which the Museum's popularism was carried, and the extent of its collapse as well.

The People's Art Center (the name telling all of this story's first part) and associated educational initiatives of the 1950s are the subject of the article by Carol Morgan, formerly Acting Director of the Museum's Department of Education. This center, its classrooms and offices, occupied three floors of the Museum's newly renovated building at 21 West 53 Street, which opened in 1951. As Morgan's article points out, this was a very large allocation of space and resources to educational programs. The Center was directed by Victor D'Amico, who had been appointed by Barr in 1937 as the Museum's first Director of the Department of Education. A proponent of John Dewey's theories of creative self-expression, known under the rubric "progressive education" when popularized in the 1950s, D'Amico had established a national Committee on Art Education in the war years; this organization and the People's Art Center were the mediums through which he sought to advance art education beyond what he perceived to be the limitations of the disciplines of art history and art criticism.

Morgan's story has parallels to the subjects of several articles in the preceding issue of *Studies in Modern Art:* Her description of D'Amico's Museum classes for children and their parents, for teenagers, and for adults reminds us that this was the era of Steichen's "Family of Man" exhibition; his opposition to military-like conformity and use of the mass media to publicize that fact recall Kaufmann's ecumenical, antimachinist, but media-aware Good Design program; and the successful re-creation of his famous Children's Art Carnival has correlations to the activities of the International Program. Morgan herself associates D'Amico's ideas of creative self-expression with the contemporaneous work of the Abstract Expressionists, which the Museum only recently had begun to exhibit and collect. Popularist but also nonconformist; aware of a mass audience and mass communications yet antitechnological; internationalist but issuing from American initiatives—these are but some of the varied descriptions of the Museum's programs at mid-century.

As Morgan explains, D'Amico's programs gradually lost institutional support in the second half of the 1950s, and in 1960 the independent Institute of Modern Art was incorporated under his direction to assume responsibility for a number of them. The People's Art Center would finally be closed in 1970, a year after D'Amico retired. Newer, discipline-based practices of education had become the order of the day. Similarly, Kaufmann's popularist program ended, giving way to the emphasis on design theory and corporate (and curatorial) professionalism that would mark Arthur Drexler's tenure. And "The Family of Man" was the end of its line, too: Steichen's successor described it in the previous issue of this publication as the product of "noble ambitions" but "a heroic failure." Many would apply his words to the Museum's other popularist programs around mid-century as well.

When the 1950s began, Barr was no longer the Museum's director; that post had been assumed by René d'Harnoncourt (himself more of a popularist than Barr) in 1949; Barr subsequently devoted his time to acquisitions and exhibitions of painting and sculpture, and to writing. This latter activity is the subject of the contribution to this volume by James Leggio, formerly Senior Editor in the Museum's Department of Publications and now holding that same title at the publishing house of Harry N. Abrams.

Barr's art-historical prose is so often celebrated for its detachment and objectivity that it would seem immune from topical concerns. It is the premise of Leggio's article, however, that this is not the case; rather, that Barr's writing can be called allegorical in its purposeful deployment of metaphor in the

discussion of works of art, and that the allegories used in his texts tell of contemporary events and issues even as they frame such events and issues in archetypal terms. Barr's writings, Leggio observes, make frequent use of personification, and one of its applications is to abstract and machine forms in art, thus to humanize them. More broadly, Barr's methods of narrative are seen to be millenialist, almost Biblical, with artists as "prototypes" who prepare the ground for others—the "archetypes" who fulfill their prophesies—and with revelatory events in the form of artistic breakthroughs. And yet, because the modern artist was, for Barr, akin to a scientist or an inventor, the myth of Icarus is also evoked, and with it the specters of hubris, failure, and tragedy.

Leggio considers these and other metaphorical references in Barr's writings in a literary context, and also in the contexts of social and political events, most notably world War II and the advent of the Nuclear Age. Thus, he traces the emergence of a "typology of Armageddon" in the texts he analyzes, observing a chastened tone in the writer who, more than anyone else, had promulgated, through the institution he helped found, a confident, optimistic picture of classic modernism. Perhaps social and aesthetic progress were not to be believed in anymore. Barr, like his Museum, went through crisis and reexamination in the period studied in this volume.

The full consequences of the Museum's ideological transformation would not be felt until Barr and the whole of his founding generation had passed on the implementation of Museum policy to their successors. It hardly requires a Freudian to tell us that this new generation of curators would rebel against its inheritance. But it does require historians, like those who have contributed to this and the preceding volume, to tell us that its rebellion was mainly against how the Museum's stated mission had been transformed during their predecessors' tenures. Knowing this allows us to ask questions—the right questions—about what may be learned and made use of from this history.

In conclusion, it should be stressed that what happened subsequent to the mid-century period was not, of course, a reimagination of the Museum as it was before. It would be simplistic to argue that continuity won out over change; the latter, inevitably, had altered the meaning of the former. Besides, the personalities had indeed changed. As a reminder of that fact, we decided to close this volume with excerpts from an unpublished autobiography, preserved in the Museum Archives, by James Thrall Soby, an art historian, critic, collector, and curator who was among the most important members of the founding generation of the Museum. It is unnecessary to set the stage here for this fascinating, and at times hilarious, memoir, since that task has been admirably fulfilled by Rona Roob, the Museum's Archivist, in her introductory essay and extensive annotation of the memoir itself; she has also contributed a complete bibliography of Soby's published writings. All that needs saying is that these excerpts afford a unique, personal view of the art world, and of the Museum's place in it, during the period examined in these volumes, and that they surely demonstrate how lightly erudition may be worn.

It remains only to say two things before extending our thanks to those who helped make this volume possible. First: This publication, taken together with the previous issue, offers a fuller view of the Museum at mid-century than has previously existed in print, in part because more extensive and careful use of the Museum Archives has allowed for expansion upon, and frequently correction of, previously published accounts. It needs stressing, however, that certain topics of great importance remain to be examined, from the development of curatorial programs in the mediums of photography, drawing, and printmaking to the critical and little-known role in the Museum of René d'Harnoncourt, Director from 1949 to 1968; that the programs and policies examined in these two volumes represent only a part of the work of those departments and the individuals responsible for them; and that the institutional allegiances of the authors who study their predecessors' programs and policies inevitably must bias their accounts, however subtly. Second, and consequent upon the last point: Notwithstanding either their professional affiliations or unrestricted access to the Museum's records, the authors collectively offer not an official institutional history but an anthology of individual views on the Museum's past.

Like the preceding issue, this has been an exacting publication to prepare. We are grateful to the authors for submitting to its demands, as well as for the quality of their contributions. Beatrice Kernan, Executive Editor of *Studies in Modern Art,* supervised all the detailed scholarly and editorial procedures and made innumerable substantial contributions in this process. She, especially, deserves our thanks. These are also extended to Sharon Dec for her support, which included but far exceeded her administrative responsibilities. Rona Roob and her staff in the Museum Archives, particularly Leslie Heitzman, were critical to this enterprise, for obvious reasons. Christel Hollevoet, Ramona Bannayan, and interns Jasmine Moorhead and Gaele Broze are also to be thanked for their valuable research assistance.

We are deeply indebted to Barbara Ross, who, with

exemplary skill, performed the highly demanding task of editing this volume while also contributing significantly to the research that supports its contents. The issue was designed by Charles Davey and Jean Garrett, under the supervision of Jody Hanson, and its production overseen by Marc Sapir, all of whom we thank for the quality of what they have achieved. And we are most grateful to the members of the Advisory and Editorial boards of *Studies in Modern Art* for their advice and support, and to the anonymous readers who offered pertinent criticisms of the articles in draft form.

Finally, let me inform new readers and remind old ones that the purposes of *Studies in Modern Art* are described in my preface to previous issues, most completely in that to the first,published in 1991. These are, in brief, to encourage study of the Museum's collections and programs, primarily but by no means exclusively by members of the Museum's staff. And let me take this opportunity to thank Richard E. Oldenburg, who retired as Director of The Museum of Modern Art as this publication was being written, for it was with his encouragement and support that *Studies in Modern Art* was founded; and Glenn D. Lowry, the Museum's new Director, for his unhesitating endorsement of the purposes of this series of publications.

John Elderfield
Editor-in-Chief
Studies in Modern Art

Notes

1. Alfred H. Barr, Jr., "Chronicle of the Collection of Painting and Sculpture," in *Painting and Sculpture in The Museum of Modern Art, 1927–1969* (New York: The Museum of Modern Art, 1977), p. 620.
2. Ibid., p. 629.

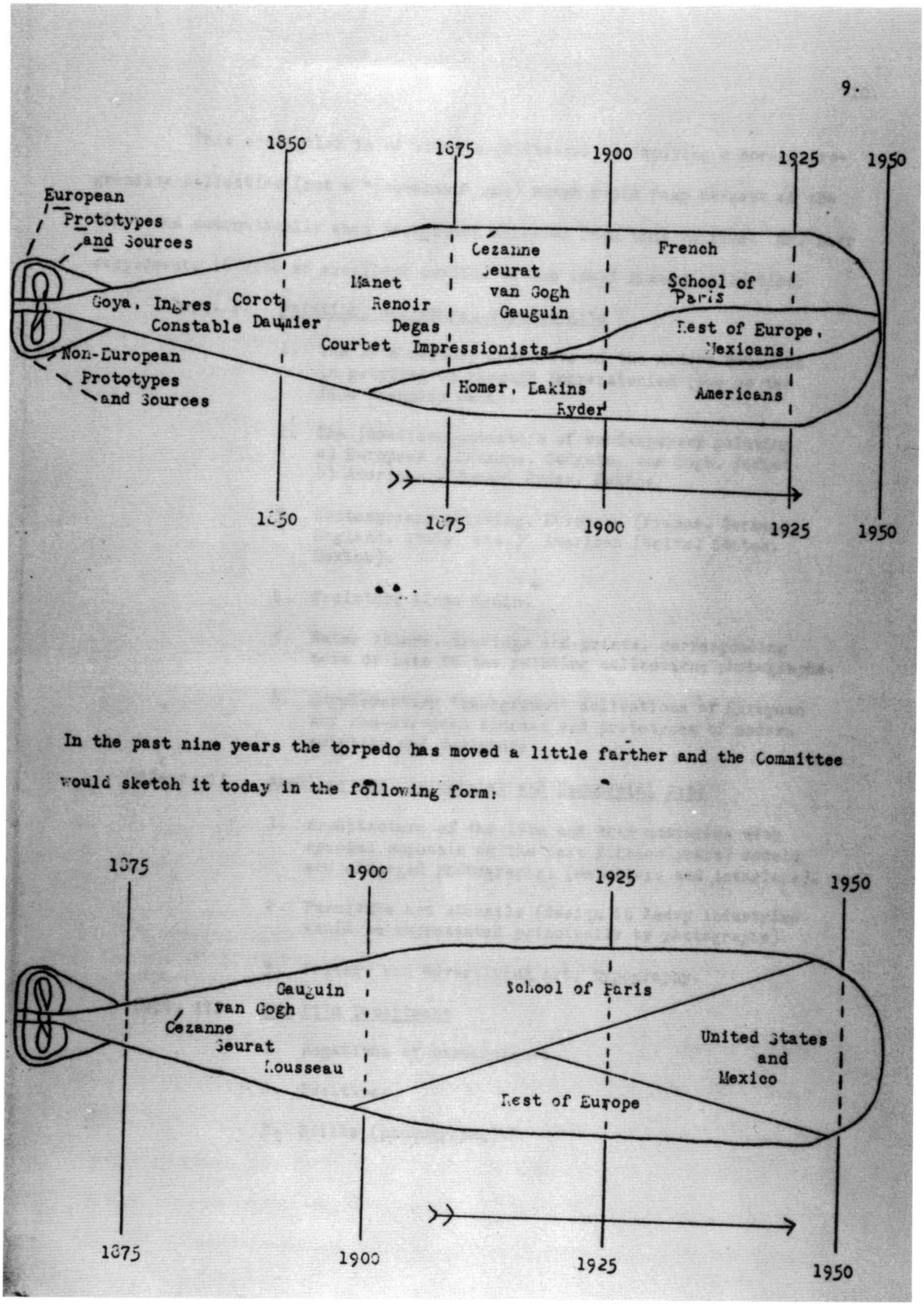

"Torpedo" diagrams of the ideal permanent collection of The Museum of Modern Art, as advanced in 1933 (top) and in 1941 (bottom); prepared by Alfred H. Barr, Jr., for the "Advisory Committee Report on Museum Collections," 1941

The Evolving Torpedo: Changing Ideas of the Collection of Painting and Sculpture of The Museum of Modern Art

Kirk Varnedoe

The Museum collections as exhibited should be for the public the authoritative indication of what the Museum stands for in each of its departments. They should constitute a permanent visible demonstration of the Museum's essential program, its scope, its canons of judgment, taste and value, its statements of principle, its declarations of faith.

—Alfred H. Barr, Jr. (1944)[1]

Never having agreed when modernity begins, people lately argue whether it has ended. In a college course, "modern" history might as plausibly start with the Italian Renaissance as with the French revolution, and "modern" art as logically with David as with Manet. The adjective formerly had at least the agreed-upon meaning of "relevant to today," but now believers in a *post*modern culture insist just the opposite; and with their fresh contentions about dating its demise, debate over the parameters—and meaning—of the "modern" only seems to become more confused.

If any source should be clear on these issues, however, it should be The Museum of Modern Art. The Museum's collection of painting and sculpture embodies a cumulative proposal, more than thirty-three hundred objects strong and sixty-five years in the making, about the nature of modern art. The selective installation of that collection's highlights in the Museum galleries has rightly been taken as a declaration of what this institution is about in the most literal sense (see Alfred Barr's affirmation, in the epigram above).

As currently presented, this wordless manifesto affirms that modern art, and thus the Museum's just purview, starts with Cézanne around 1880 and extends to today. This is a credo that implies an argument, which (as organizer of the present installation) I might sketch as follows: In the late nineteenth and early twentieth centuries, primarily in Europe and America, a watershed occurred in the visual arts, in which a new set of questions about the purposes and parameters of representation was essayed and a new set of social arrangements regarding the producers, promoters, and

publics of art was forged. No rift of equal profundity and scope has occurred in the visual arts since. The questions raised and options opened in that formative period, by artists as diverse as Picasso, Duchamp, Cézanne, Malevich, and Kandinsky, among many others, still dominantly inform the parameters of innovation in contemporary art. We can therefore broadly link the avant-garde art of 1980 or 1990 to basic premises and alternatives already present in 1930 or 1940, with much the same general solidarity that links, say, the art of the 1850s to the art of the early 1800s—while we *cannot* similarly group the art of 1920 with that of 1870, because of the vast differences of conditions, concepts, and formal means that intervened in *that* half-century.

This idea of the inception and ongoing continuity of the "modern" in art serves to justify the viability of the Museum of Modern Art today, and to explain why it maintains its policy of collecting and exhibiting both works of the last turn of the century and those of the approaching one. Not surprisingly, I believe the idea is not merely convenient but true. At the same time, however, I recognize that it differs in important ways from the vision of the "modern" on which the Museum was founded in 1929, and that, as a matter of institutional policy, this more current definition has arisen far less from reasoned decisions about history than from a patchwork of pragmatic accommodations and particular contingencies.

The story of how the Museum came to embrace the present notion of its collection and its responsibilities vis-à-vis the "modern" is relatively easily discovered in its major outlines. The "Chronicle of the Collection of Painting and Sculpture," written by the Museum's Founding Director, Alfred Barr, has recounted the main points of this story, and other aspects have been covered in writings by Calvin Tomkins, Russell Lynes, and Helaine Messer.[2] Yet there remains a great deal to say and to think about this history, both through examination of previously unpublished documents and through fresh interpretation; and now—as the Museum approaches the end of the twentieth century and stands poised to enter a new phase of its existence—seems an ideal time to revisit its major episodes.

We need to recall that the Museum's founders first conceived of a collection that would "metabolically" discard older works as it acquired newer ones, to honor the spirit of "modern" as meaning of the present, and ever-changing; then to explain how the Museum in fact once formally arranged to sell off older works to The Metropolitan Museum of Art, in order to stay focused only on the present and recent past; and, finally, to understand why in 1953 it renounced this arrangement and decided to retain a permanent group of masterworks. It was this last decision that opened the door to "freezing" the select group of Post-Impressionist works in the collection, such as Cézanne's *The Bather* (ca. 1885; see p. 35) and van Gogh's *The Starry Night* (1889; p. 35). By effectively renouncing the earlier idea of eliminating such "classics" as time moved on, the 1953 decision was the key step in the Museum's eventual framing of "modern" in its present usage—as an epoch or a tradition with a fairly clear beginning around 1880, but with an open-ended prospect for the present and future.

From its inception, the Museum was imagined as having a collection, and one that would include later nineteenth-century works. *A New Art Museum,* the advance brochure that appeared in the summer of 1929 before the Museum opened its first show, stated in its second paragraph that the institution's "ultimate purpose will be to acquire, from time to time, either by gift or by purchase, a collection of the best

modern works of art," and further on specified that among its many functions the Museum would "First of all . . . attempt to establish a very fine collection of the immediate ancestors, American and European, of the modern movement."[3] A trustee-staff Committee on Gifts and Bequests was established before the opening,[4] and it seems clear that they were not seeking only current works as donations; Barr was already trying that fall to raise money to acquire Georges Seurat's *Parade* of 1887–88.[5] The brochure also made much of the presence in other world capitals of museums or public galleries devoted especially to the art of the day, and noted, "In these museums it is possible to gain some idea of the progressive phases of European painting and sculpture during the past fifty years."[6] The founders of The Museum of Modern Art apparently envisioned presenting a similar opportunity to the New York public.

Beyond the issue of its scope, the related question raised by mention of a collection was that of its permanence. The foreign institution most prominently cited as a precedent for The Museum of Modern Art was the Musée de Luxembourg in Paris, a state collection of work by living artists that had long served as a kind of provisional waiting room from which, in time, worthy pieces were passed on to the Musée du Louvre. The brochure explicitly evoked this precedent by saying that "The Museum of Modern Art would in no way conflict with the Metropolitan Museum of Art, but would seek rather to establish a relationship to it like that of the Luxembourg to the Louvre."[7] The press seized on that proposed parallelism, which gave the fledgling enterprise a reassuring pedigree and forestalled suspicions about its hostility or competitiveness toward the city's premier historical museum.[8] The idea of "the American Luxembourg" brought with it, though, a clear implication for the works the new museum would acquire: That in time they (or at least the best of them) would be transferred to the bigger, older institution.

Of course, in the summer of 1929 such future cessions were entirely hypothetical, since The Museum of Modern Art as yet owned no art. This changed swiftly: A few donations were accepted during the winter of 1929–30, and as spring approached the Museum was anticipating the receipt of a massive gift that would powerfully shape its future direction. Lillie P. Bliss, one of the three original founders of the Museum, died on March 12, 1930, and bequeathed the Museum her valuable collection of paintings by Cézanne, Gauguin, Seurat, and others—*on condition that* within three years the institution raise enough money to ensure its ongoing viability.[9] With this challenge in view, and with a very positive public response to their initial exhibitions behind them, the staff and trustees moved in the year that followed to declare the experiment they had launched a success, and to transform their initial ideals into a stable institution with a better-defined set of long-range goals. Not least, they began to plot simultaneously a plan for increasing the collection and a principle for winnowing it.

The ambition was to attain a "permanent collection" with a fixed scope but changing contents. Its character was spelled out in a prospectus drawn up (presumably, largely by Alfred Barr) in April 1931, in anticipation of a massive fundraising drive. As an answer to the fundamental question "What is Meant by 'Modern Art'?," this publication answered: "'Modern Art', as referred to in this statement, is a relative, elastic term that serves conveniently to designate *painting, sculpture, architecture, and the lesser visual arts, original and progressive* in character, produced especially within the last three decades but including also 'pioneer ancestors' of the 19th

Installation view of "Memorial Exhibition: The Collection of the Late Lillie P. Bliss," The Museum of Modern Art, New York, 1931. From left to right: Henri de Toulouse-Lautrec, *May Belfort* (1895); Pablo Picasso, *Woman in White* (1923); Edgar Degas, *After the Bath* (1885); Paul Cézanne, *Portrait of Mme Cézanne* (1885–87); and the Coptic textile *Child with Bird*

Century."[10] Later in the same document, under the rubric *Permanent Collection,* an account of the current (very small) holdings was offered,[11] and then a more detailed prospect was proposed:

The permanent collection (of which a nucleus is already formed) must be planned along most flexible lines since capacity for change *is an essential element in the Museum's program. The permanent collection will be formed during the next few years largely through gifts. Any gifts or purchases are accepted by the Museum only upon the condition that they may be retired from exhibition whenever that may seem desirable to the trustees. Such disposal would if possible take the form of gift or sale to museums of historic art in New York or other cities. The collection should include the following divisions:*

(1) Painting *which might include three general periods:*

(a) The 19th century ancestors of the modern movement up through Impressionism (to be represented by only one or two fine examples each).

(b) The immediate ancestors of contemporary painting to include such painters as Gauguin, van Gogh, Toulouse-Lautrec, Cézanne, and Seurat, by five or six works each.

(c) Contemporary painting to include a carefully selected collection of works by painters and sculptors of France, America, Germany, Mexico, Italy, and other countries in such proportion as may seem valuable and appropriate to students and the general public.

(2) Contemporary Sculpture *since Rodin. . . .*[12]

Regardless of the appeal of this clear vision, the prospectus was essentially stillborn, since fundraising ambitions had to be trimmed severely in light of the worsening economic depression. But more focused solicitations, and the solidification of ideas regarding a Museum collection, continued.

In May 1931, the Bliss collection first went on view at the Museum, in a show that lasted into the fall.[13] Impressive though it was, this group of predominantly Post-Impressionist canvases doubtless raised concerns among the more progressive supporters of the Museum: A trove of fifty-year-old treasures would inevitably threaten the Museum's identity as a champion of the present and the future, especially if it were to be maintained for decades to come. Meanwhile, Barr was finding that his commitment to building a Museum collection and keeping it on view seemed increasingly at odds with the wishes of A. Conger Goodyear, the President of the Board of Trustees, to continue emphasizing loan exhibitions;[14] Barr's plans for the ongoing disposal of older pictures raised still other worries. When he wrote to Mrs. Rockefeller in March 1931 to urge budgeting for a space in which the collection could be shown on a steady basis, she replied that, of all the questions surrounding his plans, the "part that distresses me most is how we are going to remain modern and at the same time satisfy donors that the pictures they give us will not be disposed of in a manner that would be objectionable to them."[15]

Mrs. Rockefeller's concern for the sensitivities of donors regarding the disposition of the older part of the collection was astute, and prescient. Yet such worries presumably might be allayed by a "Luxembourg–Louvre" relationship with the Metropolitan, if such an accord could be made official and public. The acquisition of the Bliss Collection gave the new, young museum fresh credibility—and a desirable asset—when it approached the Metropolitan with an eye to such a compact.

The Museum of Modern Art was seeking, however, more than just a future repository for the older parts of its collection; its other interests must have become clear in the discussions Goodyear held with his counterpart at the Metropolitan, William Sloane Coffin, beginning in 1931.[16] The younger museum wanted to define a chronological division of "territory" between the two collections, in order to forestall any potential competition for purchases and donations. To further its ambitions in acquiring new works, the Modern also wanted to be able to exploit the Metropolitan's Hearn Fund, a bequest designated exclusively for the purchase of works by living American artists.[17] The Metropolitan had long been criticized for its too-timid and too-infrequent use of this fund, and in informal talks Coffin (apparently without asking the Metropolitan's Board of Trustees) seems to have been amenable to a contract by which The Museum of Modern Art would indeed become involved in selecting and showing Hearn Fund purchases[18]—and thus relieve the older museum from the pressure of such complaints. In return, the Metropolitan eventually would receive the pictures the younger museum, in order to maintain its focus on current art, put behind it as years went by. This kind of reciprocity involved something less one-directional than the Luxembourg–Louvre model, and the agreement proved accordingly hard to reach.

At the close of 1931, Goodyear published an article in *Creative Art* that seemed to offer the clarifications of policy his own internal constituency had been demanding, and that pointed directly to the sister institution uptown. The questions concerning the permanency of the Modern's collection, and of its eventual disposition, were directly addressed: "The permanent collection will not be unchangeable," Goodyear insisted. "It will have somewhat the same permanence a river has. With certain exceptions, no gift will be accepted under conditions that will not permit of its retirement by sale or otherwise as the trustees may think advisable. Even assum-

Alfred Barr, Conger Goodyear, and Cornelius Bliss, as The Lillie P. Bliss Bequest is officially deeded to The Museum of Modern Art in 1934; behind them is Picasso's *Woman in White*, included in the bequest

ing one hundred per cent omniscience in original selection, as time goes on some works once necessary will no longer be desirable." He also proposed that "The Museum of Modern Art should be a feeder primarily to the Metropolitan Museum, but also to museums generally throughout the country. There would always be retained for its own collection a reasonable representation of the great men but where yesterday we might have wanted twenty Cézannes, tomorrow five would suffice." Goodyear promised a future in which rigorous attention to quality, in conjunction with constant weeding and disposal, would keep the collection "within the limits of a small museum."[19]

With the bequest of the Bliss collection and other developments, though, the "small museum" was already in an expansion mode. The same article announced that The Museum of Modern Art was trying to lease a townhouse at 11 West Fifty-third Street; within months it had already begun its move. For a radio broadcast to celebrate the opening of the Museum's new quarters, on May 7, 1932, Coffin of the Metropolitan was invited to speak, and the agenda of his on-air speculations could not have been clearer: "When the so-called 'wild' creatures of today are regarded as the conservative standards of tomorrow," he said, "is it too much to hope that you will permit some of them to come to the Metropolitan Museum of Art, leaving space on your walls for the new creations of the new day?"[20] In his response Barr encouraged the idea of noncompetitive friendship, but he also sounded a cautionary note that specifically rebutted Goodyear's article in one key phrase. "No other institution includes so wide a public as the Metropolitan," he affirmed, "and to it should go ultimately the finest works of the foremost modern artists. . . ." Then he added, with the stiffened spine of independence the Bliss pictures afforded him: "We do not,

however, wish merely to become the feeder to other museums. To live we need the bone and sinew of a permanent collection which has strength and vigor, which looks toward the future but retains the support of the recent past."[21]

As these corrective remarks suggest, Barr may have been more than a little at odds with some of his trustees, attempting to moderate their concessions to the Metropolitan in order to maintain the integrity of the collection he was hoping to build at the Modern. Goodyear, in a letter to Paul Sachs in December 1932, indicated that he was moving fast toward an agreement, and that in this progress he was untroubled by the notion of, essentially, signing away future rights to the Modern's collection without receiving much in return:

You may be glad to know that we are at the point of making a definite agreement with the Metropolitan. . . . On the face of it, it would seem that the Metropolitan gets everything and gives little. However, I am convinced that the happiest life for an institution or an individual is not to be troubled with too many possessions, and this scheme should result in keeping the Museum of Modern Art a living active institution abreast of its time.[22]

At center: The Museum of Modern Art building at 11 West Fifty-third Street, New York, 1932

Goodyear's enthusiasm apparently was shared by Stephen C. Clark, a prominent collector of Post-Impressionist and other modern masterworks and a member of the Modern's board who was appointed to the board of the Metropolitan as well in 1933. In January of that year, only shortly after Goodyear's letter to Sachs, Clark wrote to Coffin affirming his support for the pact, while only gently suggesting that the Metropolitan might make the arrangement a little more palatable for the Modern:

I have discussed this matter with Conger Goodyear and he feels as I do that the Museum of Modern Art should cooperate in every way possible with the Metropolitan, and that, although the Museum of Modern Art should preserve its independence and, of course, finance itself, it should be willing to turn over to the Metropolitan any works of art that might be given to it. The Metropolitan on its side might be willing to give to the Museum of Modern Art the custody of the pictures bought from the Hearn Fund, and a participation in their selection.

Both Goodyear and I feel very strongly that the main interest of the Museum of Modern Art should lie in the exhibition of modern art, and that any collection which the Museum of Modern Art might acquire would lose most of its value after a comparatively short period—say twenty years.[23]

Near this time Goodyear in fact drafted a plan for cooperation that called for, among other things, the transfer to the Metropolitan of any work in the collection of The Museum of Modern Art that was twenty or more years old.[24] The address Coffin gave to the American Association of Museums that June was an evident attempt to lobby on behalf of such a deal. "A modern museum cannot form a permanent collection," he warned, "without incurring the risk of eventually becoming permanently congested with examples of the taste of its early friends. It would seem ten or twenty years should be the limit of modernity. At the end of this fixed period each object should be transferred by gift or sale to the collections of other museums, or sold at auction." Anticipating a concern he must have known would be raised by

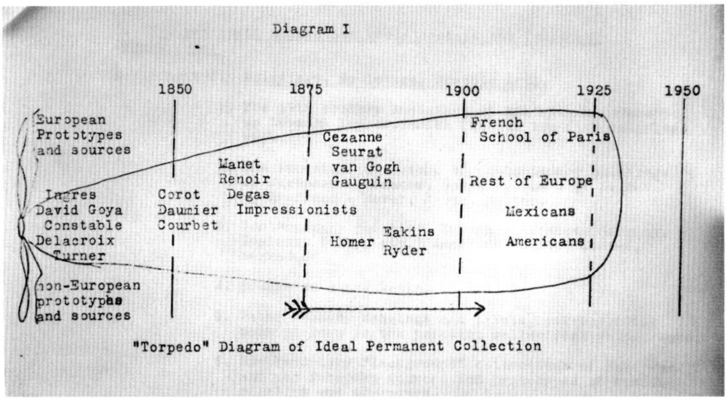

"Torpedo" Diagram I, outlining The Museum of Modern Art's ideal permanent collection

Diagrams prepared by Barr to illustrate his "Report on the Permanent Collection," November 1933

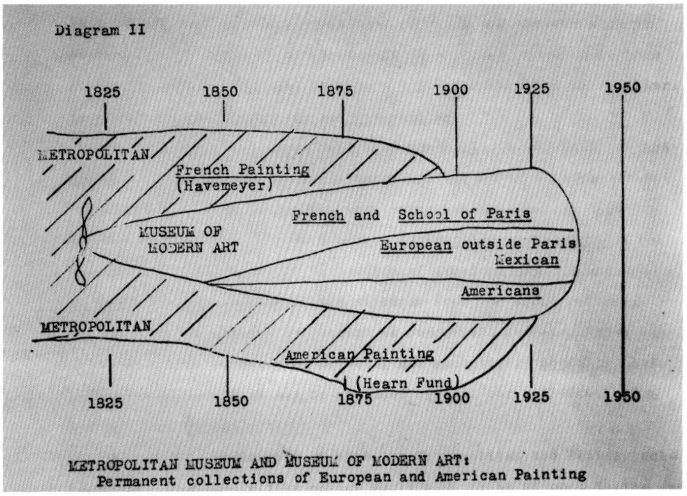

"Torpedo" Diagram II, outlining The Museum of Modern Art's ideal collection as it related to the Metropolitan's holdings

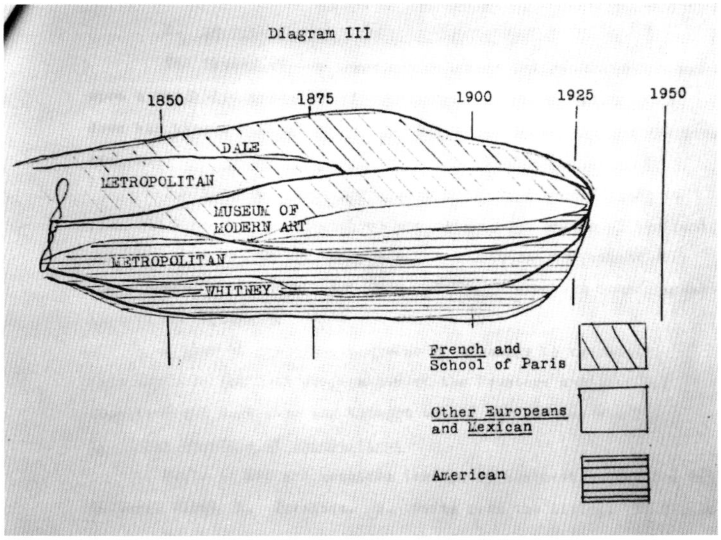

"Torpedo" Diagram III, outlining The Museum of Modern Art's ideal permanent collection as it related to other New York collections

Barr's desire that The Museum of Modern Art's holdings should elucidate the roots of the modern movement, Coffin added that in order to "illustrate contrast and evolution, modern museums can borrow from the collections of other institutions."[25]

Amidst the pressures of these initiatives (which under one construal would have ceded the gems of the Bliss collection to the Metropolitan immediately), Barr drafted that fall a definitive statement as to the character and role he thought the Museum's collection should have. In his "Report on the Permanent Collection," submitted in typescript in November 1933, he argued that, until a representative collection showing the origins and history of modern art could be kept on view year-round, the Museum would not have fulfilled one of the prime purposes for which it was founded. This document is familiarly known within the institution as the "torpedo report," for the telling metaphor Barr (an amateur of military history) coined to visualize that potential collection's scope and destiny. "The Permanent Collection may be thought of," he wrote, "as a torpedo moving through time, its nose the ever advancing present, its tail the ever receding past. . . ."[26]

Barr diagrammed this analogy (somewhat falsely, since torpedoes are not in fact tapered from front to rear, but tubular for virtually their entire length) in a series of drawings: one representing the collection alone, and two presenting it moving through the "seas" shared with other New York collections (see opposite). The sections of the collection marked in the drawings echoed the divisions described in the 1931 fundraising document (see p. 15 above), with the notable addition of two small collections as the propeller blades of the missile. The accompanying text reads:

One of these collections would be a group of fine paintings representing those phases of the older European traditions which seem most significant <u>at present</u> [underlined by hand on the typescript]: for instance, a Fayum portrait, a Byzantine panel, Romanesque miniatures, Gothic woodcuts, a Giotto school piece, a Florentine panel of the XVth century, a follower of Masaccio or Piero della Francesca, a Venetian XVIth century figure composition (Titian or Tintoretto), a Bruegel school piece, a Rubens, a Poussin, a Greco, prints by Rembrandt, Blake, Pirenesi [sic], etc.

The second "Background" collection would be composed of a small group of non-European works of art, Coptic textiles, Scythian bronzes, Japanese prints, Chinese painting, African and pre-Columbian objects.

The purpose of these two supplementary collections is educational: 1) to epitomize the character, variety, and continuity of the European tradition. 2) To show what non-European traditions have influenced European and American art in the past fifty years. 3) To destroy or weaken the prejudice of the uneducated visitor against non-naturalistic kinds of art.[27]

Barr's missionary fervor, vivid in this last line, has often been remarked upon. Less widely celebrated is his matching skill at discerning what the Museum had to do, practically and pragmatically, to make its way in a real world of limited resources and competing interests. "Building up a permanent collection should not be left to chance," he cautioned in this same report. "Most museum collections are largely the result of accident, and they show it. . . . A plan of campaign, a system of strategy is necessary."[28] He saw that displaying the collection on a regular basis would serve, for

example, not only educational purposes but also acquisition efforts, by helping attract gifts. He was careful to map the relationship of the potential Museum collection to existing private collections in New York, some of whose owners he thought might well be courted for future participation. He was shrewd, too, in insisting on the pitfalls inherent in depending on his own trustees for gifts of works of art, and he objectively weighed the advantages and risks involved in slanting collecting policy toward stringent discrimination on the one hand or greater permissiveness on the other. While committed to the ideal of a rationally planned collection of the highest quality, Barr said, "It is better to face realistically the fact that compromise will doubtless enter into the Museum's acceptance of gifts," and he saw that a "rigidly high standard of acquisition . . . practically . . . may prove a boomerang for the more guesses one makes the more chance there is of being right ten years from now—and the mistakes of an acquisition committee will then be readily forgiven providing they are on the side of commission and not of omission. Mediocre acquisitions can be stored, sold, given away, or circulated. But fine works not acquired are often irremediably lost."[29] (This pragmatic wisdom is, like its author's idealism, still constantly evoked at the Museum today.)

Not surprisingly, when Barr turned to the pressing case of the Museum's possible relationship with the Metropolitan, his assessment was particularly strategic. Acknowledging the "fundamental paradox that as time goes on 'great' [quotation marks added by hand to the typescript] modern pictures become more important to the Metropolitan but less important to the Museum of Modern Art,"[30] he tried to chart a course toward his philosophical and aesthetic ends that would allow for the political and financial realities of the situation:

The present scope of the Metropolitan's permanent collection of European painting suggests the following policy in relation to our permanent collection. The Metropolitan's collection stops with the Impressionist generation, that is, about fifty years ago. Fifty years ago makes a convenient date for the beginning of the bulk of our collection. At present we would wish to have one or two paintings, preferably small but typical, by earlier 19th century masters such as Delacroix, Corot, Courbet, Daumier, Manet, Renoir, and Degas. Cézanne who might form a transition between the two collections is at present extensively represented both in the Metropolitan and the Bliss collection. Our European collection proper would then begin with Seurat, van Gogh, Gauguin, Toulouse-Lautrec, Redon, Rousseau, none (?) of whose paintings is owned by the Metropolitan.

It is of great importance that we come to some agreement with the Metropolitan about the dividing line of the two collections with a view to adjusting future gifts to the two institutions. If it comes to bargaining our Museum is in a strong position only if the collections of our Trustees are considered as potentially ours more than they are the Metropolitan's. The fifty year period might be taken as a starting point. Paintings over fifty years old would then be under the control of the Metropolitan; paintings less than fifty years old would be under ours, irrespective of ownership—this arbitrary age limit to be adjusted by a committee drawn from the Trustees and Staff of each institution. This arrangement would obviate, temporarily at least, the problem of capital loss and gain through change of ownership—"capital" in this case implying prestige as well as money value. . . .

This arrangement might be active for a trial period of five or ten years. Then if it worked successfully the question of ownership, i.e. transfer of "capital" assets, might be considered.[31]

This idea for "shared custody" may not have been proposed as such to the Metropolitan, for the talks Clark and Goodyear held with the larger museum during 1933 seem to have foundered instead on the issue of The Museum of Modern Art's proposed access to the Hearn Fund, and on the Metropolitan's general reluctance to enter a binding agreement.[32] Undaunted, Nelson Rockefeller renewed discussion of an inter-museum accord early the next year, as the Modern made the final push to endow itself sufficiently and thus satisfy the terms of Miss Bliss's will. In the same month (March 1934) in which the requisite sum was finally raised and the Bliss collection secured, the Board of Trustees of The Museum of Modern Art resolved to accept the Metropolitan's suggestion that a joint committee be formed "to consider some form of regular relation between the Metropolitan Museum of Art and The Museum of Modern Art," and to be comprised of the three men—Clark, Rockefeller, and Cornelius N. Bliss (the brother of Lizzie Bliss)—who were trustees of both institutions as well as two additional trustees from each.[33] Yet when the group finally met, in November 1934, old problems reappeared and no substantive progress was made; the Metropolitan apparently continued to shy both from committing the Hearn Fund and from locking itself into a fixed division of collecting territory.[34] Despite polite expressions of interest in exploring broader areas of cooperation, the first meeting of the joint committee was also its last. Having gathered so much momentum within the Modern's first five years, impetus toward a formal two-museum accord then collapsed into a stall for the next five years, not to be revived until 1941 and not to be seriously pushed forward again until after World War II.

Within The Museum of Modern Art, though, discussion about the appropriate contents and limits of the collection only intensified in these same years, and especially during the war, when the Museum's regular programs were suspended and its resources sharply curtailed.[35] These analyses were frequently spurred by the Advisory Council, whose recommendations to the trustees regularly reemphasized the importance they attached to more rational planning and more extensive showing of the permanent collection. Their ambitions were allied with those of Barr, who, in the face of a space- and time-consuming exhibition program, still felt continually obliged to argue (as he had to Mrs. Rockefeller in 1931) for a proper policy of collection enhancement and display. Despite the rapidly increasing scale and richness of the Museum's holdings in painting and sculpture, no definitive commitment to these basic principles had yet been established.

Already in 1935, the Advisory Committee produced a report on the "Aims and Future Functions of The Museum of Modern Art" that supported Barr's 1933 concept of a collection of historic masterworks bearing on the modern movement, with changing contents yet constant display. Every work in the collection, the report asserted, should be disposable at any time at the discretion of the trustees; any work kept for twenty years should then be subject to formal review and disposed of unless it were judged sufficiently important to retain. In addition, enough space and time should be allotted to allow the display of this collection to be in balance with the

Left:
Aerial view of the new Museum of Modern Art building at 11 West Fifty-third Street, New York, 1939. Photograph by Andreas Feininger

Right:
Installation view of "New Acquisitions: Modern Primitives, Artists of the People," The Museum of Modern Art, New York, 1941–42. On freestanding wall at left: Joseph Pickett, ***Manchester Valley*** (1914–18). On far wall: John Kane, ***Self-Portrait*** (1929), left; and Henri Rousseau, ***The Sleeping Gypsy*** (1897)

program of loan exhibitions.[36] Yet even after the gallery space of the Museum tripled, when it moved into its new building on 11 West Fifty-third Street in May 1939, the same principles had to be fought for again. In 1940, the Advisory Committee set out formally to ask the trustees to reconsider some of the basic questions:

Should the present Permanent Collection remain intact? . . . Should the works of art be passed on after they have ceased to be active influences and sources of contemporary art to a museum of a definitely permanent character? . . . Should pictures be sold in order to purchase new acquisitions? . . . Should the temporary exhibitions be limited in the future as to size so as to allow a major part of the Permanent Collection to be on view at all times?[37]

The Advisory Committee memorandum for discussions prior to preparation of this report (which the trustees actually received in April 1941) suggests that they wanted above all to focus attention on keeping the collection more dynamic and up-to-date by making new acquisitions, and that the complementary idea of selling off "unnecessary" works to raise funds to buy contemporary art was a not-so-hidden agenda. Barr later recalled that he "worked with the Committee and was in general agreement with the report"; among other suggestions, he encouraged their questioning of the very term "Permanent Collection" (since "by far the major part" of the collection was to be "dynamic"), which led to the use of the less restrictive term "Museum Collection" in the final version of the report.[38] "What we are really studying," the document stated, "is *purchasing* policy," and at the end of a string of questions to be considered, summed up: "In other words, should the center of gravity of the collection be shifted to a more nearly contemporaneous point?"[39]

Such concerns about the proportional emphasis on contemporaneity in the collection, already raised by the Bliss Bequest, can only have grown more pointed as major acquisitions and gifts of early modern works accelerated in the years just before the war. In 1935 and again in 1939, Mrs. Rockefeller had given large groups of paintings and sculptures from her collection. As the 1930s ended, Picasso's *Demoiselles d'Avignon* of 1907 had been acquired, in part by selling a Degas pastel

from the Bliss Bequest, and the Museum had purchased as well several examples of "degenerate" German art (including Ernst Ludwig Kirchner's *Street, Dresden,* 1907) that the Nazis had confiscated from state museums and put up for sale. Mrs. Solomon Guggenheim had also begun her invaluable patronage of major masterworks sought by the Museum's curators, by funding the purchase of Picasso's relatively recent *Girl Before a Mirror* (1932) and Rousseau's more venerable *The Sleeping Gypsy* (1897).

With the luxury of such works to show, the Museum could afford to pursue more aggressively the divestment of lesser holdings; this process promised to dovetail neatly with the need to have more purchasing power for recent art. In a 1941 report on the collection, Barr devoted a section to "Disposal" that reaffirmed the principle of "gradually adding new works and disposing of old ones," and noted: "So far the Museum has done much of the former and little of the latter. Now in its second decade it should increase its metabolism, should dispose more rapidly of works which it does not need."[40]

Barr and everyone else recognized, however, that there was an economic problem built into any prospect of sale: Inevitably, the objects that would bring significant funds if sold were precisely those few the Museum would most want to keep, while the greater number it would be prepared to discard would likely be little sought after by others. These latter works would "have to be sold at a loss or given away."[41] Other problems (surprisingly downplayed or ignored in the reports that sought to stimulate the casting-off of unwanted works) centered on the potential unhappiness of donors who had originally given spurned works—the factor Mrs. Rockefeller had worried about from the outset—and on the possible negative reaction of a broader public to what we now euphemistically call deaccessioning. The dream of some arrangement with the Metropolitan Museum still seemed to Barr the ideal solution to these problems; it would be all the more attractive if it could on the one hand make money for the Modern that could then be used to buy new works, and if it could on the other preclude conflicts in regard to buying art and courting donors.

In the years since the original Luxembourg–Louvre idea had been broached, however, the key players who would negotiate for each party had begun to change. In 1941, the Metropolitan named a new director, Francis Henry Taylor, who—despite a personal dislike for progressive art that was unconcealed to say the least[42]—saw that reviving the long-dormant discussions with The Museum of Modern Art could serve the interests of his institution. In 1940, published attacks against the Metropolitan for its conservative rejection of modern art had flared up intensely, and Taylor seems early in his tenure to have recognized that securing an accord with the Modern might be one way to dampen this criticism.[43] In his first summer on the job, he expressed to The Museum of Modern Art's President, John Hay Whitney, "the hope that these two institutions may in the near future draw closer and closer to each other."[44] Barr, privy to a copy of this note, had written Taylor to say, "I want to tell you, perhaps superfluously, how much I agree . . . and how much I look forward to realizing what we both want: namely, to work out a sensible, intelligent and friendly cooperation."[45]

By the end of that year, however, Barr had become suspicious that Taylor might also be planning competition while he talked cooperation; he warned Stephen Clark that the specter of the Metropolitan making inroads into the terrain of the

younger museum added a new urgency to attempts to define firm boundaries between their spheres of interest. Barr noted that the two institutions were then in competition for a particular painting; that "the Metropolitan is now exhibiting 20th Century foreign pictures as well as American"; that recent purchases of living American artists by the Metropolitan overlapped acquisitions he and his curators had planned to make; and, finally, that Taylor—wholly out of character, given his aesthetic prejudices—had even taken the time to pay a flattering and solicitous call on Alfred Gallatin, owner of one of the choicest collections of modern European paintings.[46]

Despite such incentives and interests on both sides, no substantive progress toward an accord could be made during the war years. James Johnson Sweeney, a former director of the Department of Painting and Sculpture, told Russell Lynes that in the early 1940s "We [at The Museum of Modern Art] cooked up a deal whereby the Hearn Fund at the Met could be spent by the Modern, and the Met would eventually get the pictures. But Mrs. Rockefeller said to me, 'Jim, I've been talking to Nelson and he'd prefer to wait until he returns after the war.' And I guess that was the end of that."[47] In any event, the terms of such a "deal" became much more problematic when, following the death of Gertrude Vanderbilt Whitney in 1942, the Whitney Museum of American Art and the Metropolitan worked out a plan to merge the Whitney into the larger museum—with a partial coalescence of staff and trustees, and a new wing built onto the Metropolitan to house the Whitney's collection. This plan was tentatively approved by both boards in 1943,[48] and the semiformal institutional liaison that then ensued gave the Whitney virtual dominion over the Hearn Fund, all but removing a key dividend The Museum of Modern Art had sought to negotiate from the Metropolitan. Also in 1943, Barr was asked to resign as Director of the Department of Painting and Sculpture, and was replaced in this post by James Thrall Soby, a trustee and member of the Committee on Painting and Sculpture. This disruption in leadership (even though Barr stayed on in a lesser post, and worked well with Soby) doubtless further clouded any inter-museum discussions.

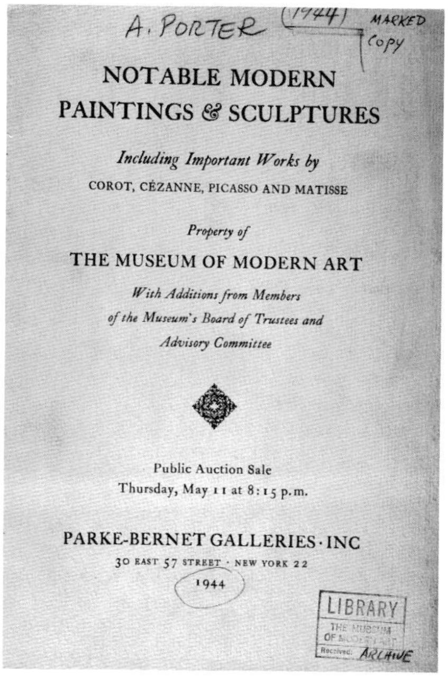
A. PORTER (1944) MARKED COPY

NOTABLE MODERN PAINTINGS & SCULPTURES

Including Important Works by
COROT, CÉZANNE, PICASSO AND MATISSE

Property of
THE MUSEUM OF MODERN ART

With Additions from Members of the Museum's Board of Trustees and Advisory Committee

Public Auction Sale
Thursday, May 11 at 8:15 p.m.

PARKE-BERNET GALLERIES · INC
30 EAST 57 STREET · NEW YORK 22
1944

Cover of *Notable Modern Paintings & Sculptures*, the catalogue of works from The Museum of Modern Art's collection that were auctioned at the Parke-Bernet Galleries, New York, May 11, 1944

In need of purchase funds and with no "Luxembourg–Louvre" accord visible anywhere on the horizon, the trustees of The Museum of Modern Art then essayed an alternative method of cleaning out the collection and raising money from it. Overriding the reluctance of both Soby and Barr,[49] they obliged the Museum staff to mount an auction sale of "Notable Modern Paintings and Sculptures" at the Parke-Bernet Galleries on May 11, 1944. The auction was dominated by works from the Museum's collection, including several from the Bliss bequest, but also included art donated by trustees and members of the Advisory Committee. The catalogue's opening statement held that the Museum was "selling certain nineteenth century works of art"—Cézannes and Seurats among them—"to provide funds for the purchase of twentieth century works, chiefly by living artists," and pleaded that "proceeds from the sale of these particular works will be spent with the utmost care, for modern art of exceptional quality."[50] It similarly explained that the more recent works put on the block, including Picasso and Matisse paintings of the 1920s, were redundant with others that would be kept. Yet in spite of such self-justifications, and such potentially appealing objects, the sale produced not only unsatisfying financial results but ill will among friends, and bad public relations in general.[51]

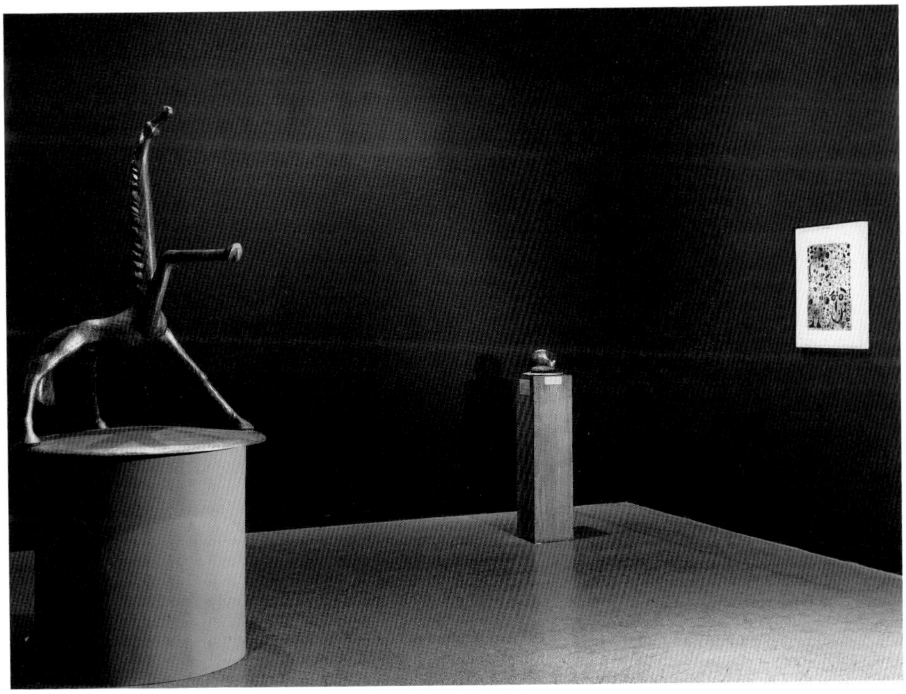

Installation view of the exhibition "Recent Acquisitions," The Museum of Modern Art, New York, February 1945. From left to right: Mary Callery, *Horse* (1944); Constantin Brancusi, *The Newborn* (1915); and Joan Miró, *The Beautiful Bird Revealing the Unknown to a Pair of Lovers* (1941)

Doubtless the failure of this approach renewed for those associated with the Modern the appeal of striking an agreement with the Metropolitan; when the war ended, talks resumed with greater intensity. The world had changed, though, and the background to these negotiations was markedly different from that of the 1930s. The Museum of Modern Art now had richer holdings and, given constraints of space, a pressing need to winnow them (a situation underlined for the trustees by the first show of the full collection in a dozen years, organized by Alfred Barr and curator Dorothy C. Miller in January 1945[52]). It also felt itself under pressure to renew its early dynamism in a postwar world, and to this end was as hungry for cash as it was heavy with older art.[53] The Metropolitan, on the other hand, had begun to take a far greater and more active interest in modern art, especially as regards earlier phases such as Post-Impressionism, and was more eager than before to strengthen its holdings in areas where it might overlap with the smaller museum. The confrontation was therefore no longer between a junior "feeder" and an established but wary senior institution, within a relatively disinterested notion of planning for the future; now it brought to the table an ardent, well-supplied seller and a more ready buyer, in a climate of incipient competitiveness and pointed immediacy of opportunity.

Shifts on the Metropolitan's board in the early 1940s had helped open the way to more substantial cooperation with the Modern, as Taylor made clear in confidential discussions with Barr at the very end of 1945. Clearly, Taylor was prepared to see an accord struck, even if for tactical reasons he was reluctant to raise the idea himself,[54] and in 1947 he found an enthusiastic advocate of the prospect in the new President of the Metropolitan's Board of Trustees, Roland L. Redmond. Wanting finally to sew up the still-pending merger with the Whitney as one of his first pieces of board business, Redmond saw the possibility of tying this into a possible agreement with the Modern. If a three-museum accord could be struck, it seemed it

might help rationalize the larger cultural situation in New York City, by defining and separating each institution's areas of specialization.

Discussions may have been initiated in 1946, but the first flurry of concentrated activity in this new phase seems to have begun in the late winter and early spring of 1947. Between April and September, when a three-museum pact was finally signed and publicly announced, the terms of the agreement were intensely debated within and between the Metropolitan and the Modern, and went through profoundly consequential revisions. At the outset, what was proposed was a wholesale and swift transfer of the early part of the collection of The Museum of Modern Art to the Metropolitan. Barr, until then the constant champion of an inter-museum accord, was obliged to mount a vigorous defense against this accelerated version of the idea; eventually, in part through his and Soby's resistance and in part because of hesitations on the part of the Metropolitan, the terms were made more modest.

In early April, Nelson Rockefeller asked Barr for a figure that would indicate the aggregate value of all works of art thus far purchased for the Museum's collection.[55] Thus forewarned that something large was afoot, Barr still seems to have been shocked by the proposal that was presented to the Executive Committee of the Modern at the end of April.[56] On receiving a draft of this blueprint for cooperation (initiated by Redmond and partly altered in conversations with Soby and John Hay Whitney), he wrote immediately to Rockefeller, arguing that since "certain very fundamental questions of policy concerning our Collection" were at stake, all members of the Committee on the Museum Collections should be immediately consulted.[57] Barr was particularly concerned about the reactions of Stephen Clark and Samuel A. Lewisohn, two members of the Committee whose collections of Post-Impressionist masterworks he coveted, and he took the further step of writing Clark directly to signal "the many questions and misgivings" he had about the plan.[58]

The first item Barr found alarming was the date—1910—proposed as a boundary line between the Modern's area of focus and that of the Metropolitan. That demarcation would have emptied the Modern of the Post-Impressionist treasures it had thus far amassed, and ruled out Barr's ever acquiring the gems of Clark's or Lewisohn's holdings (including the Seurat *Parade,* which Clark had bought after Barr's 1929 efforts at purchase had failed). Soby shared Barr's horror at these prospects, and also quickly wrote to Rockefeller:

If we agree to let the Metropolitan take over the work of deceased artists "whose work was substantially completed before 1910," we will give them late nineteenth and early twentieth century works which are of the greatest importance for our own purposes—as historical background for more recent paintings and sculpture. We will give them the period whose drawing power for the public is far greater than any other: the period of the great Post Impressionists, Cezanne, Seurat, Van Gogh and Gauguin. The public's interest in these men is nowhere near spent. . . .

I am worried, too, about the effect of such an arrangement on the important collectors who might be interested in leaving their collections to our Museum. On the other hand, I agree profoundly in working out some agreement with the Metropolitan, and your efforts in this direction have been the greatest possible encouragement to those of us who have worked on the Museum Collections. Can't we persuade the Metropolitan to accept 1880 as the dividing date? I do very much hope so.[59]

The longer Barr studied the new plan, the more his dismay increased, and on April 30, 1947, he drew up a "Highly Simplified Analysis of the Metropolitan Proposal" that emphasized how much The Museum of Modern Art stood to lose. The Redmond proposal covered the Modern's entire collection of painting and sculpture, then and for the future, in three categories: all "classic" works, including those of Cézanne, van Gogh, Gauguin, and Seurat, were to be transferred right away to the Metropolitan; all "modern" works that had been purchased (not including those bought from sales of gifts and bequests) would be ceded immediately in title of ownership, but The Museum of Modern Art would keep possession of them until such time as they became "classic"; and, finally, all "modern" works that had been given or bequeathed would be held both in title and in actuality by the Modern until they reached "classic" status, at which time they would be deeded and transferred to the Metropolitan. Among all this bounty, the Metropolitan was to pay only for the "modern" works that had been previously purchased by The Museum of Modern Art. As a sweetener of sorts, though, the Metropolitan did propose to make available, over ten years, a fund with which the Modern could buy new works, which would stay on Fifty-third Street until they entered the "classic" category, and then be transferred uptown; it further offered to put on deposit with the Modern certain "modern" works from its own collection.

As Barr's analysis showed, this prospect looked disastrous for his institution. Allowing that the money involved might be useful to have, he also acknowledged that The Museum of Modern Art might gain "perhaps, some satisfaction and public approval for having come to an understanding with the Met., and thereby solving our problems of remaining 'modern' and the Met's problems of building up its historic or classic collection of recent art." The losses, though, would be staggering: Gone would be all the nineteenth-century masters, "worth nearly half the total value of the Collection and of importance to us for prestige, popular interest and educational background"; lost, too, would be "the prestige of a great independent collection with the possibility of discouraging gifts and bequests, particularly of post-impressionist pictures which would probably go directly to the Met."[60]

Still, Barr was obliged to move ahead in good faith; during May, he was charged to write a preamble to the agreement that would describe the respective functions and missions of the Metropolitan, the Modern, and the Whitney, and to prepare for discussion three principal lists: Schedule A, which would deal with works the Metropolitan would deposit with the Modern; Schedule B, which would list works which would be sold to the Metropolitan at a twenty-percent discount off estimated market price (this was divided into B-1, works of nineteenth-century artists, and B-2, "Selection of 20th Century Painting and Sculpture, Principally by Older Artists"; see App. 2, 3); and Schedule C, of works to be given to the Metropolitan.[61] There was further discussion about the date that might be fixed to divide the Metropolitan's activities from the Modern's, and in this area, as in the question of collecting contemporary American art, Barr sought (not always successfully) to bring key trustees into accord on his position.[62] By early June, however, when the first drafts of the lists were ready, both sides had agreed simply to dodge this ticklish problem by ceasing to pursue any fixed date that might globally separate "classic" art from "modern."[63] This concession seemed at the time just a provisory gesture to expedite the general discussion; but it appears, significantly, to mark

Pablo Picasso. *La Coiffure*. 1906. Oil on canvas, 68⅞ x 39¼" (174.9 x 99.7 cm). The Metropolitan Museum of Art, Wolfe Fund, 1951; acquired from The Museum of Modern Art, Anonymous Gift (53.140.3.). Added by The Metropolitan Museum of Art to the list of works proposed for future transfer, as reflected in documents dated June 5–9 and July 9, 1947 (see App. 3a–b, 5a–b, 6)

Pablo Picasso. *Woman in White*. 1923. Oil on canvas, 32 x 23¼" (81.3 x 59.1 cm). The Metropolitan Museum of Art, Maria DeWitt Jessup Fund, 1951; acquired from The Museum of Modern Art, Lillie P. Bliss Collection (53.140.4.). Added by The Metropolitan Museum of Art to the list of works proposed for future transfer, as reflected in documents dated June 5–9 and July 9, 1947 (see App. 3a–b, 5a–b, 6)

Henri Matisse. *Piano Lesson*. 1915–16. Oil on canvas, 8' ½" x 6' 11¾" (245.1 x 212.7 cm). The Museum of Modern Art, New York. Mrs. Simon Guggenheim Fund. Removed by The Metropolitan Museum of Art from the list of works proposed for future transfer, June 5, 1947 (see App. 3a–b)

Pablo Picasso. *Portrait of Gertrude Stein*. 1906. Oil on canvas, 39⅜ x 32" (100 x 81.3 cm). The Metropolitan Museum of Art, Bequest of Gertrude Stein, 1946 (47.106). Confirmed for future transfer to The Museum of Modern Art, as reflected in Schedule A of the formalized agreement (App. 8)

the last time the parties seriously tried to define a border that could officially separate their historical areas of interest. Instead, subsequent negotiations centered more on "the bottom line" of determining which works would be delivered to the Metropolitan, when, and at what cost.

At a key meeting on June 9 of trustees and staff from both museums (the Whitney was not represented), the whole early part of the collection of The Museum of Modern Art (that is, works from ca. 1865–ca. 1925) was under consideration for possible disposal, and the Metropolitan sought to pick and choose (see App. 2, 3a–b). It judged insufficiently desirable a considerable number of items on the list of works The Museum of Modern Art proposed to sell; Matisse's *Piano Lesson* (1915–16), for example, was deleted, along with several other items by artists such as Charles Despiau, Aristide Maillol, and John Kane "principally because the Metropolitan did not wish to buy so many works by these artists, or because certain works seemed duplicates." On the other hand, Redmond felt that, in light of the Metropolitan's proposition to deposit with the Modern the 1906 *Portrait of Gertrude Stein* by Picasso, which it had received as a bequest of the sitter, it might in turn be given the opportunity to purchase work by Picasso—so that, he argued, the public would not get the impression that the Metropolitan simply did not care for this artist. Barr balked strongly at this suggestion, but in the long run two relatively conservative Picassos, *La Coiffure* of 1906 and *Woman in White* of 1923, were added to Schedule B (see App. 5a).[64]

Writing to Nelson Rockefeller two days later, Barr professed himself content: "I thought the meeting went very well indeed . . . altogether the procedure and the results seemed to be very satisfactory. A few paintings were too cheap, a few too dear, but I think the list averaged out very fairly." The account he attached with the letter concluded: "Throughout the meeting, which lasted three hours, the discussion was markedly amiable and cooperative. The spirit prevailing augured well for the future relations between the two institutions."[65] The Metropolitan's curators had even shown, separately, a new but apparently sincere eagerness to acquire the folk art previously given to The Museum of Modern Art by Abby Aldrich Rockefeller—a proposed free transfer on Schedule C in which little interest had previously been visible.[66]

Amid all this good feeling, though, no firm timetable for the implementation of the agreement had yet been determined, and this turned out to be a crucial point of contention. The Metropolitan was proposing to pay in installments over a number of years, and the Modern also envisioned its own delay, between contractual sale and actual delivery—an aging period during which, regardless of titular ownership, works would remain on view at the Modern until they attained "classic" status and were thus no longer deemed relevant to the presentation of contemporary art. When the Metropolitan's board reviewed the proposed agreement on June 18, the seeming open-endedness of this wait for actual possession caused—as Redmond had feared it would[67]—strong reservations. The board members worried that, lacking any clear criteria for determining when a work might pass from "modern" into "classic" status, the Modern would be able to keep anything it wanted for as long as it wanted, regardless of the sale agreement.[68]

As Barr confided to Rockefeller on learning of the objection, this dispute was bound to happen; and, for reasons he had raised before—combining educational

philosophy with the pragmatics of courting donors—the Modern was obliged to defend itself against giving up its treasures too soon:

. . . I was afraid that the question of the date of delivery of the Metropolitan's purchases in the light of the definition of 'classic' would almost certainly land us in debate eventually, if not now. It seems to be now.

I keep wishing that we could do away entirely with the classic-modern definition and simply face the fact that we will probably want to keep some of the pictures longer than the Metropolitan wants to let us. This is not only a matter of the usefulness of the late 19th century pictures to us, but of the feelings of Mr. Lewisohn and Mr. Clark, both of whom I gather are inclined to look at van Gogh, Gauguin, Seurat and certain Cézannes as modern, so that they might prefer to have their collections—filled with magnificent works by these artists—come to the Museum of Modern Art without the feeling that they were already too old for our purposes.

This is a problem which I feel we should have pretty clearly in our own minds before our team meets with the Metropolitan's champions.[69]

Soby, equally unsurprised that this problem had arisen, nevertheless wrote to Barr, "I wonder whether we'll get anywhere by abandoning the definitions of 'classic' and 'modern'. I should think their Board would be more likely to accept the deal if there were an upset figure mentioned—the 100 year limit we originally had" (a reference to the notion that no work might remain in the Museum collection more than one hundred years past the date of its creation). He continued, "I should think that otherwise their worry would be that we'd hang on forever. . . . [It] would seem a clearer [legal] title to the pictures (for them) if a date were specified when they'd *have* to be delivered. Naturally, the more open the matter is left the better for us, but it would be a pity if the agreement collapsed now. Maybe specify 75 years and 100 years as the two extremes?" (the latter referring, presumably, to works on Schedules B-1 and B-2, respectively).[70]

Working with the draft press release Redmond had given them on June 18, Clark, Barr, and Soby suggested amendments they hoped would calm the Metropolitan's fears while protecting their own prerogatives. If this amended release had been given to the press as planned in July, it would have described the purchase arrangement as follows:

The Metropolitan Museum has agreed to advance to the Museum of Modern Art certain sums of money, payable in equal annual installments, over a period of ten years. When these payments are completed, ten years hence, the Metropolitan will acquire title to certain works of art (specified on a list now agreed upon), although the Museum of Modern Art will retain possession of these works of art until they become "classic art". The term "classic art" as defined in this agreement shall be deemed to include "any painting, drawing, print or sculpture which has ceased to be significant in the contemporary movement of art and has become part of the cultural history of humanity." The artists whose works are included in this part of the agreement comprise Bellows, Bonnard, Cézanne, Davies, Despiau, Du Bois, Eilshemius, Ensor, Gauguin, van Gogh, Hart, Kane, Kolbe, Kuhn, Maillol, Matisse, Nolde, Picasso, Pickett, Prendergast, Redon, Rouault, Rousseau, Seurat, Signac, Speicher, Vuillard.

The ultimate date by which each of the works by these artists will pass from the Museum of Modern Art to the Metropolitan Museum will vary from five to thirty years hence according to the character of the work in question. Not all of the works in the Museum of Modern Art by the leading artists listed are involved in the present agreement. Others may be added when the agreement is renewed ten years from now, along with the works of artists not yet listed.

With the funds received from the Metropolitan Museum, under the terms of this agreement, the Museum of Modern Art will be able to buy, to a greater extent than before, the works of distinguished artists in both the American and foreign fields and of younger artists whose reputations are not yet established. These purchases will take the place of the works of older artists which, under the terms of this agreement, will gradually fall into the category of 'classic art' and pass along to the Metropolitan Museum.[71]

The stipulation of "five to thirty years" was likely intended to offer the Metropolitan some comfort, but Barr knew that Redmond wanted to set ten years as a maximum delay, and he was worried both about the pressure that might be exerted to advance the dates of delivery and about the effect this would have on some of his patrons. He was particularly concerned that highly valued and generous older trustees would not take kindly to the possibility of losing the collection's "classics"; when he explained the agreement to Mrs. Simon Guggenheim (who had given, among other works, Rousseau's *Sleeping Gypsy*), she seemed to him

preoccupied about our giving up certain pictures before they had fulfilled their term of usefulness here.

I explained to her the plan as it now stood, and she repeated that she thought we would lose a great deal of prestige if the principle [sic] works in the Bliss Collection were to pass on the Metropolitan in the next few years. . . .

From her, I understood more clearly how people in her generation feel. To them modern art which they like and believe in was produced in the generation of Cézanne, van Gogh, Seurat, Rousseau, etc., with earlier works by Matisse and Picasso coming along as a less important sequel. It is hard for them to think of our collection without those famous pioneers of the modern movement. She, Mr. Clark, and Mr. Lewisohn seem willing to accept the logical necessity of passing on some pictures, but it is clear that they want to postpone that moment well beyond the decade which the Metropolitan agreement stipulates as the minimum.

In the light of Mr. Redmond's recent conversation and letter, it was impossible for me to reassure her that we would not be under strong pressure to deliver a good number of things ten years from now, and possibly some of them sooner. I wish we could persuade the Metropolitan to look on this transaction as a kind of insurance or annuity policy. If they could take the long view of the matter, they could let us keep these important works which are so close to the hearts of our older trustees until the passage of time makes it possible for us to pass them on without creating misgivings.[72]

It was, however, clearly impossible to conclude the agreement without some specific understanding, if not about the chronological division between "classic" and "modern" in general, then at least about a firm date at which The Museum of Modern Art would be ready to yield possession of the pictures it was proposing to

sell. In early July, Barr and Nelson Rockefeller met with Redmond, and together they agreed that a way out of the impasse might be found if a range of dates could be fixed on a picture-by-picture basis.[73] Barr and Soby then set to work to define exactly when they expected that each individual work—van Gogh's *Starry Night,* Cézanne's *Bather,* and many, many more—would no longer be relevant to contemporary art, and hence disposable to The Museum of Modern Art. Their timetables are revealing and often surprising in retrospect: Soby's proposal, for example, would have kept the Cézanne *Bather,* Rouault's *Christ Mocked by Soldiers* (1932) and Vuillard's *Mother and Sister of the Artist* (ca. 1893) for twenty-five years, until 1972, longer than any other paintings; while he would have yielded Matisse's *Interior with a Violin Case* (1918–19; see p. 42), Picasso's *Woman in White,* and the Cézanne *Still Life with Ginger Jar, Sugar Bowl, and Oranges* (1902–06) and *Still Life with Apples* (1895–98) after only ten years, in 1957. His determinations were not based on a simple calculation of the age of a given object but on a more complex scheme that tried to take into account how radically forward-looking each work was, as well as its level of quality.[74]

When Soby presented such an item-by-item schedule (see App. 5a–b) to key trustees of the Modern on July 10, he met with general approval;[75] when Barr took the revised proposal to Mrs. Guggenheim, he also found her more receptive.[76] Barr then sent the new timetable to Redmond, proposing a meeting for discussion and also explaining the reasoning behind some of the varying dates. "I think we can all agree," he wrote, "that excellent representation of the leading modern masters should eventually be included in the Metropolitan's collection after they have served an appropriate period here. My own feeling is that we should not keep paintings longer than 50 or 60 years after they were painted and perhaps considerably less." But then, euphemistically understating the difficulties he faced in translating this abstract principle into an actual stripping of his walls, he noted: "Our problem is to put this procedure in motion with due regard to the status quo."[77] From that latter "problem" devolved a list which showed The Museum of Modern Art keeping several of its best paintings on view eighty or ninety years after they were painted, and—of more immediate interest—twenty-five or more years after their proposed sale to the Metropolitan.

Redmond was unpersuaded, by this letter or by a subsequent meeting with Barr, that his board would be understanding enough to tolerate such long delays in taking possession.[78] Late in July he therefore proposed that, for the purposes of getting the present agreement more easily and swiftly concluded, negotiations should be confined only to those works for which The Museum of Modern Art would be prepared to promise delivery in ten years or less.[79] This idea was accepted, and the lists accordingly cut; the major Post-Impressionist works were taken out of consideration (see App. 7). It is of course easy to see why this was readily agreeable to both sides: The Metropolitan no longer had to suffer with long delays, and several voices at The Museum of Modern Art readily welcomed putting off to some unspecified future the hardest sacrifices;[80] but it is also clear that when this decision was taken a critical juncture was passed. Had the Metropolitan been willing, in July 1947, to take a leap of faith and invest for the long term, it would very likely have come into possession of almost all the Post-Impressionist masterworks in the Modern's collection—the Rousseau *Sleeping Gypsy,* the van Gogh *Starry Night,* and so on—in the early 1970s (when their greatly increased value would have more than justified the

Henri Rousseau. *The Sleeping Gypsy*. 1897. Oil on canvas, 51" x 6' 7" (129.5 x 200.7 cm). The Museum of Modern Art, New York. Gift of Mrs. Simon Guggenheim. Proposed for transfer to The Metropolitan Museum of Art in 1972, as reflected in a list dated July 9, 1947 (App. 5a–b) but not included in the formalized agreement

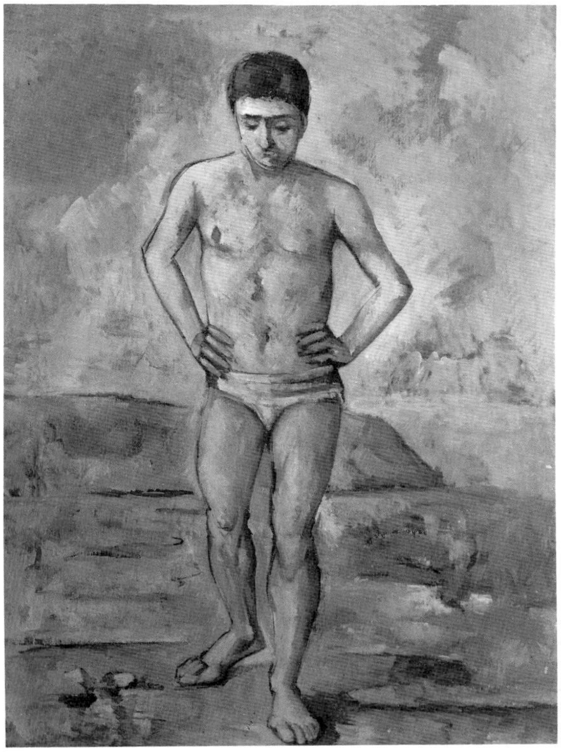

Paul Cézanne. *The Bather*. ca. 1885. Oil on canvas, 50 x 38⅛" (127 x 96.8 cm). The Museum of Modern Art, New York. Lillie P. Bliss Collection. Considered for transfer to The Metropolitan Museum of Art in 1972 and 1962 by James Thrall Soby and Alfred Barr, respectively (see App. 4a–b). Proposed for transfer in 1962 (see App. 5a–b) but ultimately removed from the final list by Soby and Barr (see App. 7)

Vincent van Gogh. *The Starry Night*. 1889. Oil on canvas, 29 x 36¼" (73.7 x 92.1 cm). The Museum of Modern Art, New York. Acquired through the Lillie P. Bliss Bequest. Considered for transfer to The Metropolitan Museum of Art in 1962 and 1977 by James Thrall Soby and Alfred Barr, respectively (see App. 4a–b) but ultimately not included in the formalized agreement

Edouard Vuillard. *Mother and Sister of the Artist*. ca. 1893. Oil on canvas, 18¼ x 22¼" (46.3 x 56.5 cm). The Museum of Modern Art, New York. Gift of Sadie A. May. Considered for transfer to The Metropolitan Museum of Art in 1972 and 1967 by James Thrall Soby and Alfred Barr, respectively (see App. 4a–b) but ultimately not included in the formalized agreement

early expenditure). The Museum of Modern Art, in turn, by giving real teeth to the idea of "modern" with which it had begun eighteen years before, would have set a very different course for its future. That course would logically have led to its selling off, for example, all its pre-1950 Matisses and Picassos by the year 2000, and its poured Pollock canvases shortly after; as of this writing, Robert Rauschenberg's *Bed* (1955) and Jasper Johns's *Flag* (1954–55) would be the historical anchors of the collection, poised for transfer uptown. Additionally, the Modern would not have experienced such a relentlessly increasing need for greater space to show its collection—a need that has driven two substantive expansions since World War II (in 1964 and 1980–84), and that now presses the Museum once again to enlarge its collection galleries. As it was, however, the final three-museum agreement (for which press releases were already being prepared when the list was revised) promised much less eventual benefit to the Metropolitan, provided a much smaller cash flow to The Museum of Modern Art, and left in the realm of rhetoric the whole ideal of a noncompetitive division of territory. Here again, the search for expedient relief from contention wound up shrinking the ambition of the agreement, and eagerness to settle its particulars seems to have sapped its larger spirit.

For the remainder of the summer, haggling continued over details. Among other revisions, the Metropolitan reduced the list of purchases even further by asking that all the contemporary American paintings be deleted, apparently out of deference to their relationship with the Whitney.[81] Nelson Rockefeller also decided that the folk art material formerly in his mother's collection should be sold, not given, to the Metropolitan.[82] Such revisions, especially of the list of works for sale, apparently continued until days before the inter-museum agreement was finally signed on September 15.[83] Finally, only twenty-six works of art (see App. 9) were contracted to be sold by the Modern to the Metropolitan; they were to be paid for in installments over five years, and collected in no more than ten.

The accord stated "the expectation . . . that this agreement will be renewed from time to time on similar terms and that the ultimate result of the continued renewal thereof will be that the Metropolitan Museum will eventually have the opportunity to acquire any paintings, drawings, prints and sculpture now owned or hereafter acquired by Modern Museum. . . ."[84] Such optimism, if sincere, was ill-founded; the era of good-spirited cooperation the agreement should in principle have inaugurated was almost absurdly short-lived.

The beginning of the end of the *entente* came in mid-February 1948 at a dinner at the Brook Club, called by Redmond and Francis Taylor to discuss among the three museums "the coordination of exhibitions in accordance with the terms of the agreement. . . ."[85] A large part of the meeting was taken up by Redmond and Taylor aggressively attacking the exhibition and acquisitions policies of both the Whitney and the Modern. The representatives of the Metropolitan criticized the other two institutions' vision of contemporary art as being too biased toward a narrow avant-garde, and out of touch with a broader range of current developments, especially in American locales outside New York City. As best one can judge from Barr's letter to Redmond a week later,[86] the issues seem to have been similar to those involved in the attack on "modern" art launched by the Institute of Modern Art in Boston. On that very day—February 17—the Institute issued an announcement denouncing the art that had come to parade under the rubric "modern," endorsed a more eclectic

and ultimately conservative view of the art of the day, and ceremoniously changed its name to The Institute of Contemporary Art in explicit defiance of its "parent," The Museum of Modern Art.[87] Nineteen forty-eight was a year of broad, often publicly clamorous reassessment of the modern movement in America, including a roundtable discussion of curators, scholars, critics, and artists sponsored by *Life* magazine in June, and a witheringly contemptuous article in December, denouncing modern tendencies, by none other than Francis Taylor.[88] The blast that Barr, Soby, and the Whitney representatives (Lloyd Goodrich and Herman More) received until 2 A.M. at the Brook Club was only a foretaste, clearly signaling that the Metropolitan would be essentially in the enemy camp, rather than an ally, in the fray ahead. Barr wrote to Nelson Rockefeller on February 28, 1948, to say that "...the Metropolitan is trying to bring pressure to bear so that our purchases and the Whitney's whole policy would be transformed to the taste of the older institution."[89]

It was, in any event, enough to convince the Whitney—which was the most restricted and the least rewarded of the signees of the three-way agreement—that its affair with the Metropolitan was over. The early dreams for a new wing had long since faded, a casualty of New York City Parks Commissioner Robert Moses's sterner attitude toward public financing of the Metropolitan in the postwar years. The Whitney's director, Juliana Force, had ceased advising the Metropolitan on the Hearn Fund, in displeasure that her recommendations were not being heeded.[90] Hospitalized for cancer, Force would die before 1948 ended; but when word of the Brook Club encounter was brought to her, she lent her authority to the movement that led the Whitney's trustees, on October 1, 1948, to issue a press announcement of their withdrawal from the three-museum agreement and in particular their definitive split with the Metropolitan.[91] As the representatives of the Whitney and of The Museum of Modern Art had joined together at the Brook Club dinner in opposing the Metropolitan's criticisms, so in the years that followed these two institutions would draw closer in spirit and even in location (the Whitney Museum announced plans to establish a new location adjacent to The Museum of Modern Art in 1949[92]).

If the Whitney had a problem with the Metropolitan's conservatism, however, the Modern saw trouble coming from its adventurism. Though the Metropolitan and the Modern reconfirmed their continuing two-way accord in fall of 1948 following the Whitney's withdrawal, the supposedly "classic" institution's growing intrusions into the "modern" area began to make it clearer and clearer that the 1947 document would do nothing to protect The Museum of Modern Art against competition from its uptown neighbor. On the occasion of the split from the Whitney, the Metropolitan had announced that it would begin developing its own ambitious program of exhibitions and acquisitions in contemporary American art; shortly it hired a new curator, Robert Beverly Hale, whose pursuit of that goal led him to engage directly with the work of advanced New York School artists such as Jackson Pollock.

The Metropolitan was publicly urged to pursue this expansive attitude even further, in a series of "Open Letters" from James N. Rosenberg (a retired lawyer, representational artist, and member of the Metropolitan) to Roland Redmond, published in *The New York Times* at intervals throughout January 1949. These letters denounced the pact signed in 1947 and exhorted the Metropolitan to "sever your ties with The Museum of Modern Art, and thereby regain and exercise complete free-

dom over the whole domain of art, 'modern' as well as 'classic'."[93] While Rosenberg may have come across as somewhat of a crank, such opinions that the Metropolitan should not delimit itself or leave the modern field only to others doubtless had wider currency. The Metropolitan was sensitive to the critique, and did in fact begin to move in the recommended direction; one of its first moves was to request the loan of the objects it was purchasing from The Museum of Modern Art, so that it could mount an exhibition that would counter the criticism that it had been neglecting modern European art.[94]

The coming "modernization" of the Metropolitan's collection was then made substantially more evident in the course of 1949 by gifts—Georgia O'Keeffe donated half of the Alfred Stieglitz collection, partly in pique at The Museum of Modern Art[95]—and by purchases. In July, an article in the *New York Herald Tribune* noted the recent acquisition by the Metropolitan of two van Gogh canvases, and commented:

Interest has been lately focussed on the declaration of the Metropolitan Museum of Art in favor of developing a program for contemporary American art exhibitions commensurate with the importance and authority of the Museum as a living influence in the community. Another aspect of the museum's activities which is being watched also with interest is the latter's consideration of its collections of contemporary art. It is not for the moment proposed to recall the availability of the Hearn Fund . . . but rather the recent progress shown in the collecting of work in related branches of modern painting, notably the work of modern old masters.[96]

Clearly, attitudes and ambitions were shifting within the Metropolitan, and Barr observed this, warily.[97] Other changes, also affecting the inter-museum agreement, were in progress at The Museum of Modern Art. Yet, when in retrospect we watch the accord between these two museums eroding toward failure in the late 1940s and early 1950s, we are also obliged to think beyond specific institutional matters of competitive programming and personalities, and consider a broader background. The whole status of modern and contemporary art as a focus of cultural and political concern was being reconsidered in this period. Before World War II, the kind of art The Museum of Modern Art supported was still commonly dismissed by many as a fringe avant-garde movement of interest largely to oversophisticated Europeans or trendy bohemians. With the defeat of Hitler's Germany, however, the antipathy between modern art and totalitarianism gave such art new stature as the embodiment of principles of individual freedom. This larger humanistic appeal, which could be slanted to more specifically political purposes, would become more and more touted as the Cold War intensified.[98]

The Cold War intruded on relations between the Metropolitan and the Modern in at least one very concrete instance as well. Both institutions were preoccupied by the question of protecting their collections against a hypothetical bombardment of New York, conceivably by atomic weapons, and they discussed the possibility of sharing bombproof storage facilities outside the city. Barr wrote Nelson Rockefeller: "We gather that full-scale war is unlikely for a couple of years but we cannot assume this. . . . Korea suggests . . . that an atomic Pearl Harbor is possible."[99] An immediate question involved deciding whose vault would hold the twenty-six

paintings the Metropolitan was still in the process of buying; but a more unhappy problem arose when the Metropolitan appeared to be luring one of the Modern's trustees into its camp by offering this collector space for her collection in their shelter—after having begrudged the Museum itself only a small portion of the storage room.[100]

In broader terms, though, the postwar climate of competition with the Soviet Union seems to have helped convince the Metropolitan—over and above its desire for certain collections—that the Museum's involvement in modern and contemporary art was now a more appropriate part of its mission. In these terms, even the redoubtable Francis Taylor was prepared to make a case for modern experiments (up to a point); he had written of a postwar world in 1945:

More than ever before, the American Museum will be called upon to fulfill a social function. . . . The Museum must become . . . the liberal arts college. . . . New disciples will flock to those masters who sit, not in any ivory tower with their vision fixed on a bygone day. . . . The same liberty which we seek to derive from art must be . . . guaranteed to the creative artists of our time. It is not for us to judge too hastily . . . they have freed themselves from the pre-war introspection of an hysterical and defeated Europe and are looking for strength in the ample American landscape. . . . We must consider our responsibilities in terms of Twentieth Century America.[101]

Taylor's curator, Hale, extended this line of reasoning more wholeheartedly in 1950, writing on the "American Painting Today—1950" exhibition he had just mounted at the Metropolitan—a show dominated by abstract art. He argued that "the vast majority of our artists [has] ceased to be conservative. . . . What has happened, of course, is that the United States, like the rest of the world outside the iron curtain, has succumbed to the aesthetic revolution largely promoted in Paris at the turn of the century."[102] Since Picasso's embrace of Communism and related developments in European artistic circles made many Americans uneasy, it must have seemed more important than ever to ground the contemporary American avant-garde in a longer modern tradition, with a less problematic French (and explicitly not German, Italian or Russian) ancestry that reached back into the late nineteenth century. The question of a lineage of modern masters became a matter not simply of formal evolutions but also of an inherited moral authority that affirmed the rights of individual freedom in opposition to the demands of totalitarianism, or indeed, in opposition to all pressures toward social collectivism and mass conformity. In this key sense the term "modern" was now required to carry added baggage; beyond denoting an up-to-date experimentalism, it was used more extensively, by advocates such as Hale, to designate a specific, sanctioning tradition as well.

The Museum of Modern Art had been instrumental in promoting the idea of that tradition and in defining its history; now the Museum would find itself the victim of its own success in two senses. First, historical institutions such as the Metropolitan were aware that it was not only appropriate but virtually indispensable that they align themselves with modern art in some fashion, if only via works of the late nineteenth and early twentieth centuries; and what had been the more-or-less exclusive province of the Modern became a domain of competition. Second,

within The Museum of Modern Art itself the idea of disposing of the Post-Impressionist pictures—and thereby dismantling the institution's unrivaled representation of the roots of the modern tradition in order to give more exclusive focus to the present and recent past—seemed, inexorably, to become less practicable. Ironically, as Barr's torpedo continued to advance through the years, it seemed to have a greater, not lesser, need for its tail-end connection to the late nineteenth century.

The more The Museum of Modern Art began to work actively to acquire postwar art, the more Barr found that some of the coveted collectors he had sought to mollify were becoming restive. Samuel Lewisohn resigned from the Museum's Board of Trustees in 1950 and transferred his allegiance to the Metropolitan, where he had been named a trustee the year before; most of the great Post-Impressionist works in his collection, which Barr had longed for, were then bequeathed to the Metropolitan when Lewisohn died in 1951.[103] Stephen Clark resigned from the Committee on Museum Collections in January 1951, having seen the purchase of a bronze *Chariot* (1950) by Alberto Giacometti as surpassing his tolerance for the avant-garde; and Conger Goodyear followed suit, because of a Rothko (*Number 10,* 1950), the next year. (Goodyear apparently was unappeased by Barr's idea that he, Clark, and other "special cases who have been uneasy" might be named to a special subcommittee to insulate them from ventures into contemporary art.[104]) Since it was clearer than ever that the Metropolitan was competing for the affections (and gifts) of such collectors, Barr must have felt under still greater pressure to keep these people connected to the Modern, in part by insuring that the early part of the collection conformed to their tastes. In the same regard, it must have seemed increasingly self-defeating for the Museum to retain its tie with the Metropolitan: Donors who saw that their gifts would wind up at the Metropolitan in any event might logically begin giving there directly and ignoring the Modern altogether.

In large part to address this latter issue, The Museum of Modern Art began investigating, in the summer of 1951, how it might form a truly permanent collection of masterworks without violating the 1947 accord (which looked forward to every picture at the Modern sooner or later passing to the Metropolitan). The Museum's legal counsel, James W. Husted, advised Nelson Rockefeller on July 5 that: "It is the word permanent that creates the difficulty under our agreement with the Metropolitan. There is nothing to prevent us from keeping any painting which is still significant in the contemporary art movement as long as we want and I suppose, therefore, we could maintain a Collection of Masterpieces indefinitely as long as it was not known as a permanent collection."[105] Rockefeller, d'Harnoncourt, and Barr continued to discuss the problem over the summer. Once they had decided that a permanent nucleus of masterpieces was what they wanted, and that the agreement with the Metropolitan stood in the way of this, the pact was definitively doomed.[106]

On September 28, 1951, The Metropolitan Museum of Art sent to the Modern its final installment payment for the twenty-six paintings it had agreed to buy; in sending the check, the Metropolitan's Treasurer was gracious enough to say that his institution was in no particular hurry to take possession of the items still on display at the Modern—works that were not scheduled to be released until 1957.[107] Shortly after this final payment arrived, The Museum of Modern Art moved in earnest to begin the process of cancelling the agreement, which in principle had five years left to run. At the meeting of the Museum's Board of Trustees on March 13,

1952, John Hay Whitney announced that he had already discussed such an annulment with Redmond of the Metropolitan, and that Redmond had already obtained the agreement of the Executive Committee of his own board—"provided that delivery is made immediately of some, if not all, of the works they have purchased."[108] Whitney obtained the authorization of the Modern's board to negotiate the official termination of the agreement,[109] and within a week Barr had produced an evaluation of the pictures that had been contracted for sale, commenting on which losses would be most damaging to the collection in light of expected delivery dates.[110]

By the June board meeting, Whitney was able to report that the full board of the Metropolitan had agreed to the termination, and that it had been determined when the pictures now owned by the Metropolitan would be delivered to them. He also reported, however, that Barr had been successful in buying back from the Metropolitan two Matisse paintings that had been sold to it under the agreement: *Gourds* (1916; see p. 42); and *Interior with a Violin Case,* the latter a piece from the original Bliss bequest.[111] (Actually, Whitney's announcement was premature about this recouping: Barr and Theodore Rousseau of the Metropolitan engaged in a long and testy negotiation as to the correct price to be paid for the two Matisses, and the matter was not finally resolved until late October.[112])

There can be little doubt of the direct linkage between the move to cancel the 1947 agreement and the Museum's desire to protect the possibility of future donations of early modern paintings in general, and to cement the loyalty of certain patrons in particular. In March, near the time when the proposed cancellation of the agreement was first announced to the board, Barr had also suggested that a committee be formed to develop a new acquisitions policy based on the idea of retaining certain masterworks permanently; the committee was to include, not surprisingly, Clark, Goodyear, and Mrs. Guggenheim.[113] At the June 12 board meeting, Whitney immediately followed his statement regarding the termination of the inter-museum agreement with another aiming in this direction:

Inasmuch as the Museum is not ready to dispose of further works from the Collection, and in view of the fact that the public is more keenly aware of the whole modern period and its prototypes and our exhibitions receive a larger audience than ever before, it is the feeling of certain members of the Board that a policy statement vis-à-vis the permanency of the Collection should be prepared for the consideration of the Trustees and it is suggested that a whole meeting in the autumn be devoted to a discussion of that subject.[114]

True to his word, Whitney turned to this subject at length at the board meeting in December. He began with a long preamble that reminded everyone of the founding idea of the Museum collection as impermanent and fluid, and revisited the origins and demise of the agreement with the Metropolitan. Noting that the Metropolitan since 1947 had taken a much more active interest in exhibiting and acquiring "progressive work" and "works by some of the most advanced artists," he also related that in the same period The Museum of Modern Art "became acutely aware of the need for retaining and increasing its collection of important masterpieces of the pioneers of modern art in order to enable its public to appreciate and study the movement as a whole." In view of all these considerations, Whitney "recommended for consideration by the Board of Trustees the following declaration of policy":

Paul Cézanne. *Dominique Aubert, the Artist's Uncle* [Man in a Blue Cap]. ca. 1866. Oil on canvas, 31⅜ x 25¼" (79.7 x 64.1 cm). The Metropolitan Museum of Art, Wolfe Fund, 1951; acquired from The Museum of Modern Art, Lillie P. Bliss Collecion (953.140.1). Sold to the Metropolitan, as reflected in Schedule B of the inter-museum agreement (see App. 9, 10)

Henri Matisse. *Interior with a Violin Case*. 1918–19. Oil on canvas, 28¾ x 23⅝" (73 x 60 cm). The Museum of Modern Art, New York. Lillie P. Bliss Collection. Sold to the Metropolitan, as reflected in Schedule B of the inter-museum agreement (see App. 9, 10). Reacquired by the Modern in 1952, before the work's release

Left:
Henri Matisse. *Gourds*. 1915–16; dated 1916. Oil on canvas, 25⅝ x 31⅞" (65.1 x 80.9 cm). The Museum of Modern Art, New York. Mrs. Simon Guggenheim Fund. Sold to the Metropolitan, as reflected in Schedule B of the inter-museum agreement (see App. 9, 10). Reacquired by the Modern in 1952, before the work's release

The Museum of Modern Art believes now, as it always did, that the principle of fluidity is valid for the major portion of its collection. It believes that in acquiring recently produced work it must attempt to cover all significant aspects of today's artistic production and cover every trend that holds promise. Such policy must lead inevitably to an accumulation of works which, while essential for the representation of today's work, is bound to be unwieldy once it becomes a review of yesterday. Elimination of works of art in the light of experience from extended holding will therefore always be an integral part of the Museum's policy and procedure. The important departure from the Museum's past policy and practice suggested below deals with outstanding works of art only.

Therefore, Mr. Whitney stated, the Museum proposes the establishment of a highly selective permanent collection of modern masterworks within the larger frame of its more fluid and extensive general collection. This collection of masterworks, he said, would be assembled by selection from the important works of art already in the Museum's collection and by acquisition or gifts. Ultimately this collection should become the outstanding collection of great works of the modern movement. The scope and policy would be determined by a special committee to be appointed for this purpose.[115]

The announcement of this new policy was made on February 15, 1953:

The Museum has come to believe that its former policy, by which all the works of art in its possession would eventually be transferred to other institutions, did not work out to the benefit of its public. It now believes it essential for the understanding and enjoyment of its entire collection to have permanently on public view masterpieces of the modern movement, beginning with the latter half of the nineteenth century. The Museum plans to set aside special galleries for this purpose and to transfer to them, from its collections, outstanding paintings and sculptures which it considers have passed the test of time, and to acquire additional works of art of equal excellence for permanent retention.[116]

When Barr first envisioned the scope of this new core collection, he thought that the gallery space available might limit it to one hundred works, of which only about fifty could be shown at any one time.[117] He also thought that the ability to promise permanency would give him a newly powerful aid in enticing gifts to the collection. Clearly, the emphasis in forming the masterworks group was not on honoring those pictures such as the Cézanne *Bather* that had already, *de facto,* become permanent fixtures, but on bonding present donors to the Museum and on luring new donations.[118] In this regard it seems more than coincidental that, at the same moment when the first designations for the masterworks list were made, the first proposal was being made for a plaque in the Museum honoring "Patrons of the Museum Collections" who had given over $10,000 to the institution.[119] Also, while the committee was making its initial considerations, new plans were being proposed for the Museum's twenty-fifth anniversary in 1954: Instead of mounting a review of the collection already assembled, it was suggested that a major exhibition of the year be "a very impressive show of masterworks, including pictures loaned or pledged by individuals,"[120] to complement the display of the collection. The intention seems clearly to have been to build the "masterworks" list largely from this field of prospective acquisitions.[121]

The committee designated to study a new collecting policy met for the first

Aristide Maillol. *The Mediterranean.* 1902–05. Bronze (cast ca. 1951–53), 41 x 45 x 29¾" (104.1 x 114.3 x 75.6 cm), including base. The Museum of Modern Art, New York. Gift of Stephen C. Clark, 1953. One of three works in the Modern's collection accorded masterwork status in May 1954

Henri Matisse. *The Morroccans.* 1915–16. Oil on canvas, 71⅜" x 9' 2" (181.3 x 279.4 cm). The Museum of Modern Art, New York. Gift of Mr. and Mrs. Samuel A. Marx, 1955. One of three works in the Modern's collection accorded masterwork status in May 1954

Henri Rousseau. *The Dream.* Oil on canvas, 6' 8½" x 9' 9½"(204.5 x 298.5 cm). The Museum of Modern Art, New York. Gift of Nelson A. Rockefeller, 1954. One of three works in the Modern's collection accorded masterwork status in May 1954

time on April 7, 1953, and resolved, first, that the board needed to make it rigidly clear—perhaps by a change in the institution's by-laws—that works designated as "Masterworks" would never leave the Museum; second, that "the date at which the Masterworks collection ought to begin should be 1875—the date at which the present Museum collection commences"; and, finally, that "the Museum should make as early as possible a list of masterworks anywhere in this country that should be appropriate and desirable for the collection."[122] The first official "masterworks" were not named until more than a year later, in May 1954. In light of the history we have seen, it is not surprising that one was a work given by Stephen Clark, Maillol's *The Mediterranean* (1902–05); that another was a recently promised gift, Matisse's *The Moroccans* (1916), by donors the Museum wanted greatly to encourage, Samuel and Florene Marx; and that a third was a Post-Impressionist work, Rousseau's *The Dream* (1910), given by Nelson Rockefeller. Additionally, in response to an invitation issued to the entire board, three trustees had submitted to the committee a list of their intended bequests to the Museum. The committee anointed one work from each of these lists: John Marin's watercolor *Lower Manhattan* (1920), from the collection of Philip L. Goodwin; Cézanne's *Château Noir* (1904–06), from the collection of Mrs. David M. (Adele) Levy; and Picasso's *Seated Woman* (1927), from the collection of James Thrall Soby.[123] Much more surprising, though, is the list drawn up for future consideration.

After studying photographs, the Policy Committee drew up a list of seven "desiderata" to be pursued, from private collections unconnected to the Museum: Cézanne's *The Black Clock* (1872, then in the Edward G. Robinson collection), his *Boy in a Red Vest* (1890–95, then in the Jakob Goldschmidt collection), Corot's *L'Italienne* (1872, Robinson collection), van Gogh's *Dr. Gachet* (1890, then belonging to Mrs. Siegfried Kamarsky), Picasso's *Dancer* (1907, then in the collection of Walter P. Chrysler, Jr.), Rouault's *Old Clown* (1917, Robinson collection), and Rousseau's *Carnival Evening* (1886, then in the Louis B. Stern collection).[124] Beyond the almost complete nineteenth-century slant of the list, it is striking to see that—with Barr's participation and guidance—the Policy Committee could still, in 1954, imagine the collection including not only Cézannes of the 1860s (even though they had sold an 1860s Cézanne portrait to the Metropolitan in the agreement) but also paintings by Corot. In fact, as late as 1957, Barr still offered the masterwork designation for a Manet still life (*Des Huitres,* ?1862) in hopes of securing its donation.[125]

At the close of 1954, Barr finally called the Policy Committee for the Museum's Permanent Collection of Masterworks to focus more directly on works already in the Museum collection. In a memorandum of December 27, 1954, and in the context of an exhibition of paintings from the Museum collection then on view, he reminded the committee "to make a study of the current exhibition of the Museum's own collection of paintings with a view to choosing which canvases should be added to the 'masterworks' list."[126] Adding was also to be connected to removing; on the same day, his memorandum to the larger Committee on the Museum Collection asked for help in triage:

If you could find the time I would very much appreciate your going through the show in order to pick out what seems to you the best twenty or thirty paintings in the col-

lection, or at least those which seem most valuable to the Museum. (While you are picking the best, it would also be interesting and entertaining to have your list of the twenty-five worst, or to put it more kindly, the least valuable.)

This is not simply a matter of making value judgments; the Committee will, in the not too distant future, be faced with the problem of eliminating works from the collection so that some study of the presumably better half of the collection should provide a valuable preparation for surgery.[127]

During the following year, the Policy Committee moved to present a formal resolution, to be approved by the full Board of Trustees, that would establish in detail the policy regarding the permanency within the Museum of works designated as masterworks. Drafting this document proved a ticklish task. Negative admonishments and restrictions were to the fore; the drafters wanted to include explicit assurances, for example, that *only* those select few works designated as masterworks need be retained, without prejudice to the disposability of the rest of the collection; that masterworks could be designated only by the Board of Trustees; and that, "generally speaking, the Masterworks collection shall not include works executed prior to the mid-19th Century." Of special concern was the binding nature of the masterwork categorization and the accompanying pledge not to sell. In order to leave an opening that would keep the Museum's hand somewhat free while reassuring potential donors, the drafters proposed that two successive votes by three-quarters of the trustees, a year apart, would be needed to affirm that "new conditions not foreseen by the donors or the Museum" had made a change in the masterworks policy necessary. It was further stipulated that any masterwork which might be deaccessioned in these unforeseeable circumstances would only be sold or given to another museum that would accept the work for its permanent collection.[128]

The trustees of The Museum of Modern Art did not officially confirm the masterworks concept, or define its scope and the rules that governed it, until a formal resolution was passed in May 1956.[129] That fall, the policy was used in negotiating with Nate Springold (four of his potential donations were prevoted as acceptable for masterwork status in December 1956[130]), and also figured in Nelson Rockefeller's acquisition of Picasso's *Girl with a Mandolin* (1910) from Roland Penrose, for eventual inclusion in the masterworks collection at the Museum.[131] Perhaps even more tellingly, though, members of the Policy Committee began to see that, in opening up the concept of guaranteed permanency, they had created a desirable category within the collection that would result in its steady expansion. They seemed prepared to admit this, and to move still further away from the all-inclusive elimination policy that had driven the inter-museum agreement. In their meeting of November 30, 1956, they reviewed the list of masterworks thus far officially designated—only four, now including the Cézanne *Boy in a Red Vest* (1888–90) in David Rockefeller's collection—and proposed eleven works from the existing collection for elevation to masterworks status, including, notably, Picasso's *Demoiselles d'Avignon.*[132] A proposal by Springold to give a group of works to the Museum on the condition that they remain permanently "raised a question not hitherto faced by the Policy Committee as to whether works of art not accepted for the Masterworks Collection should nevertheless be retained permanently by the Museum and the donor so assured." Recalling the original 1953 statement of "An Important Change in Policy,"

Paul Cézanne. *Boy in a Red Vest*. 1888–90. Oil on canvas, 32 x 25⅝" (81.2 x 65 cm). The Museum of Modern Art, New York. Fractional gift of David and Peggy Rockefeller. The fourth work in the Modern's collection to be accorded masterwork status, by November 1956

and the May 2, 1956, resolution of the Board of Trustees regarding masterworks, the committee showed a willingness to move further:

The intentions of these two statements (1953 and 1956) were kept in mind during the discussion which followed. Most of the members expressed the belief that the Museum's stated policy should be changed to accommodate donors who desired permanence, even though their gifts did not qualify for the Masterworks Collection, at least at the time of the gift. Mr. Goodwin questioned changing a policy which would tend to make the Museum's Collection more static. However, in general the Committee felt that the Museum would have little to lose by increasing the number of permanently owned works. If in the end the works seemed superfluous, they could, unless the donor had otherwise stipulated, be lent to other institutions or at the very worst occupy storage space. To maintain the Museum's present policy might well result in the loss of a good many highly desirable works. . . . The Committee concluded that it would be wise to consider establishing a third category of works of art which while not included in the Masterworks Collection would nevertheless be given the status of permanence if the donor so stipulated. . . . The Committee accepted the suggestion that this new category might be established by an amendment to the Trustees' resolution of May 2, 1956.[133]

Even though exceptions to the rule were beginning to proliferate (and in this sense the handwriting was on the wall with regard to permanently pinning down the tail of the torpedo) Barr clearly wanted to maintain the ideal of a dynamic, fluid collection that would be constantly winnowed as well as constantly kept abreast of the times. Responding to an attack by the critic Hilton Kramer in the January 1957 issue of *ARTS Magazine,* Barr wrote:

After characterizing some of the recent European painting accessions as "execrable", Mr. Kramer goes on to ask whether one can "seriously believe that those works . . . have passed into the permanent *collection of the . . . museum." Let him be reassured. None of the works in this exhibition has as yet passed into the "permanent" collection.*

As a matter of declared policy, the Museum had no permanent collection until four years ago. At that time, it was announced that an extremely limited number of works of art would be selected as a "Permanent Collection of Masterworks" while the vast bulk of the collection would remain, as before, an active testing ground rather than a repository. Of over 1350 works in the Museum's painting and sculpture collection, only four have so far been accepted for a permanent *collection. The rest are still on trial and these include all the recent accessions. We have often suggested that of our guesses nine out of ten would eventually prove mistaken.*[134]

This exchange between Barr and Kramer invites a reflection on the way some things seem not to change in the life of this Museum. Many of the historical factors that shaped the story sketched here, for example, are still very clearly operative today. The need to court financial support and donations of art, the constraints of space, the force of certain key personalities, questions of prestige and institutional identity, the gap between ideals and practical requirements—all of these concerns are recognizable to anyone working at The Museum of Modern Art today as grounds of affinity between their own situation and that of the early staff and leaders of the

institution. Within these continuities, however, real change has taken, and still does take, place, with profound consequences for the Museum; it has occurred not simply at points of official resolution such as the signing and renouncing of the intermuseum agreement but in less visible and more gradual accumulations of practice and unspoken code.

The masterworks policy, for example, is now an historical artifact, virtually forgotten within the Museum. In terms of its originating ambitions, it seems to have been a failure; aside, perhaps, from one or two of the initially designated works, we cannot readily point to any art that was lured into the collection because of this policy, and the major collectors it was intended to attract—notably, Clark and Goodyear—almost all bequeathed their art elsewhere. Yet it was clearly the leading wedge of what has become a general inversion in thinking about the Museum's collection. Now the concept of permanency within the collection is dominant; disposal is a far more infrequent, and much altered, part of the Museum's practice. From the Collection of Painting and Sculpture, we currently sell works only in direct exchange for the purchase of new works, not to secure funds for future buying. Moreover, the unwritten codes that now guide these transactions are diametrically opposite to Barr's idea of using the sale of the oldest works in the collection to fund experimental buying in the contemporary field. Instead, there has been in recent years a self-imposed prohibition against selling "classic" modern works to fund contemporary acquisitions; added to the injunction against selling the work of living artists, this stricture means that deaccessioning is now viewed primarily as a means of refining the older part of the collection, and efforts are made to exchange "like for like"—to select for sale works that are as close as possible in type or date to the new acquisition.[135]

These procedures have devolved from the greater fact that the Museum's responsibility to maintain a large and complex collection of modern art from 1880 onward is now accepted as a central part of its identity as both an historical repository and a contemporary institution. We believe (and are aware that many artists, historians, and critics also believe) that the presence in this institution of its great historical collection of modern art gives The Museum of Modern Art a special framework through which to view, explicate, and comment upon contemporary art. Conversely, we also believe that, by staying actively involved in contemporary creativity, we are constantly challenging our viewers to reassess the still-evolving meanings and consequences of the earlier modern works in the collection. The Modern is now and always has been torn between opposing forces that exhort it to concentrate its energies in only one area, either on the tradition of the "classics" such as Cézanne, Matisse, and Picasso, or more exclusively on the art of today. The institution seems to draw its very life energy from this tension, and will prosper as a special entity to the degree that it can continue to resist resolving the dilemma.

This means that those who steer The Museum of Modern Art today, and who revere Alfred Barr, also judge that he was wrong in one significant aspect of his historical view. Barr is often carelessly associated by inattentive writers with a "formalist" view of modernism, of the kind that argued for modern art's attainment of a set of necessary, universally valid formal structures. In some obvious respects, though, his plan for the collection suggests the opposite: a thoroughgoing historicism in which value in art is a factor of relevance to a moment in time. The original "metabolic" strategy proposed that the value of modern art would not be fixed but self-

renewing, in a continuous, open-ended process of rejuvenation. In this version of "modern," the founding masterpieces would always be dispensable in the future, because there would be new founding masterpieces to replace them, as innovation followed upon innovation. The befuddlement and alienation that greeted the first modernist revolutions would wane as those innovations—Cubism, say, or early abstraction—became more familiar and better understood; with these battles won, the Museum would thus no longer need to explain or defend these "classics" but could instead continually shift its energies to promoting the newer innovations—and to assuaging the new alienations and befuddlements—the future would inevitably bring.

History, however, played havoc with these ideals, not simply through the pragmatic realities of donors and their desire for permanency for their pictures but in more basic ways. On the one hand, Cubism and early abstract art, for example, remain intractably difficult and misunderstood for a very broad audience; age, understanding, and acceptance have not advanced in synchrony. On the other hand, pioneering the new in art is an option only rarely available, and historical moments of profound innovation (such as occurred in early modern art) may not be so easily sustained or replicated in kind. For all these and many other reasons, having Pollock or Johns does not turn out to efface our need or desire to have Picasso or Duchamp in the same collection. The tail of the torpedo has been pinned now to 1880, but the engine still runs and the vessel moves forward, to the immense benefit of The Museum of Modern Art and all who visit it. We believe it is profoundly in Barr's spirit to learn from history, and to affirm that a better understanding of the origins and development of modern art—and of its institutions—can be an effective springboard to innovation, and to finding the new or newly altered forms appropriate to one's own time. In 1945, Barr wrote, "No comprehensive collection of modern art . . . can possibly assume a rigid or final character. And this was never the intention of the men and women who have given so generously of their money and faith"—and we might add, honoring Barr, curatorial vision—"to make the collection possible."[136]

Appendix

March 6, 1941

Ideal Collection, Museum of Modern Art

Rooms 1-2-3 19th Century European

	We would need:
Monet or Pissarro	An impressionist painting as a point of departure and a clarification of the term "impressionism".
Renoir	1 late figure painting
Degas	1 late pastel
Cézanne	Uncle Dominic (Bliss) Oranges (Bliss) Apples (Bliss) Pines and Rocks (Bliss) A great landscape A great figure composition 3 watercolors (Bliss) 1 print (bathers - Bliss)
Seurat	1 important composition Landscape (Bliss) 3 drawings (Bliss) 2 drawings
Gauguin	(Bliss) 1 important painting 2 prints (Bliss)
Lautrec	1 good painting 2 lithographs or drawings
van Gogh	1 landscape 1 figure 1 still life or flowerpiece or interior 3 drawings (1 early)
Rousseau	Sleeping Gypsy 1 portrait 1 important jungle picture
Redon	Silence (Bliss) Flowerpiece (Bliss) 2 lithographs
Ensor	St. Anthony 3 prints
Munch	1 ~~print~~ painting (before 1900) 2 prints (before 1900)

(Early Vuillard, Bonnard, Rouault, etc. are considered 20th century)

1. "Ideal Collection, Museum of Modern Art," March 6, 1941

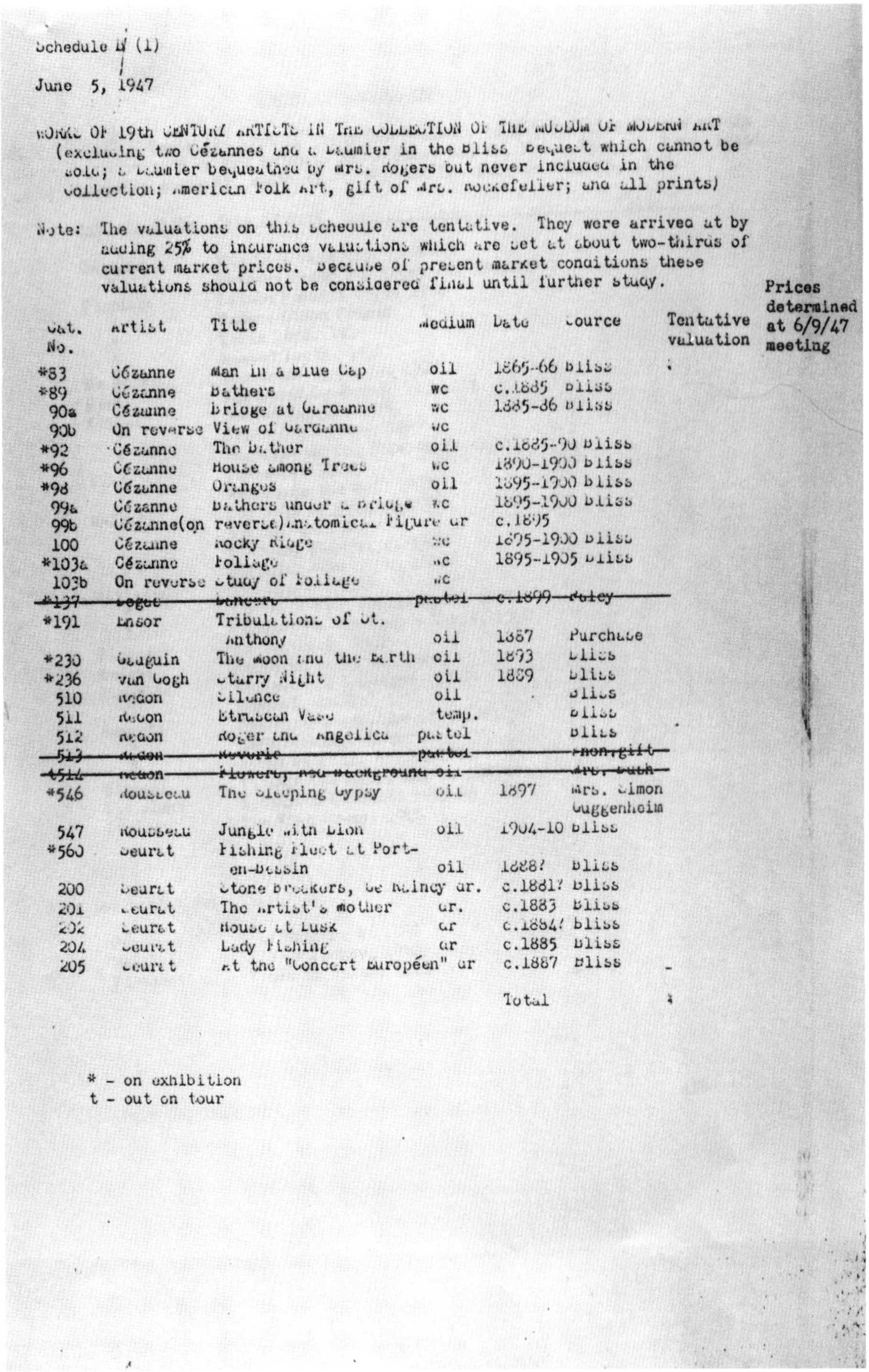

Schedule B (1)

June 5, 1947

WORKS OF 19th CENTURY ARTISTS IN THE COLLECTION OF THE MUSEUM OF MODERN ART
(excluding two Cézannes and a Daumier in the Bliss bequest which cannot be sold; a Daumier bequeathed by Mrs. Rogers but never included in the collection; American Folk Art, gift of Mrs. Rockefeller; and all prints)

Note: The valuations on this schedule are tentative. They were arrived at by adding 25% to insurance valuations which are set at about two-thirds of current market prices. Because of present market conditions these valuations should not be considered final until further study.

Cat. No.	Artist	Title	Medium	Date	Source	Tentative valuation	Prices determined at 6/9/47 meeting
*83	Cézanne	Man in a Blue Cap	oil	1865-66	Bliss		
*89	Cézanne	Bathers	wc	c.1885	Bliss		
90a	Cézanne	Bridge at Gardanne	wc	1885-86	Bliss		
90b	On reverse	View of Gardanne	wc				
*92	Cézanne	The Bather	oil	c.1885-90	Bliss		
*96	Cézanne	House among Trees	wc	1890-1900	Bliss		
*98	Cézanne	Oranges	oil	1895-1900	Bliss		
99a	Cézanne	Bathers under a Bridge	wc	1895-1900	Bliss		
99b	Cézanne(on reverse)	Anatomical Figure	dr	c.1895			
100	Cézanne	Rocky Ridge	wc	1895-1900	Bliss		
*103a	Cézanne	Foliage	wc	1895-1905	Bliss		
103b	On reverse	Study of Foliage	wc				
~~*137~~	~~[illegible]~~	~~[illegible]~~	~~pastel~~	~~c.1899~~	~~[illegible]~~		
*191	Ensor	Tribulations of St. Anthony	oil	1887	Purchase		
*230	Gauguin	The Moon and the Earth	oil	1893	Bliss		
*236	van Gogh	Starry Night	oil	1889	Bliss		
510	Redon	Silence	oil		Bliss		
511	Redon	Etruscan Vase	temp.		Bliss		
512	Redon	Roger and Angelica	pastel		Bliss		
~~513~~	~~Redon~~	~~Reverie~~	~~pastel~~		~~non-gift~~		
~~t514~~	~~Redon~~	~~Flowers, red background~~	~~oil~~		~~Mrs. [illegible]~~		
*546	Rousseau	The Sleeping Gypsy	oil	1897	Mrs. Simon Guggenheim		
547	Rousseau	Jungle with Lion	oil	1904-10	Bliss		
*560	Seurat	Fishing Fleet at Port-en-Bessin	oil	1888?	Bliss		
200	Seurat	Stone Breakers, Le Raincy	dr.	c.1881?	Bliss		
201	Seurat	The Artist's Mother	dr.	c.1883	Bliss		
202	Seurat	House at Dusk	dr	c.1884?	Bliss		
204	Seurat	Lady Fishing	dr	c.1885	Bliss		
205	Seurat	At the "Concert Européen"	dr	c.1887	Bliss		
				Total		$	

* - on exhibition
t - out on tour

2. Schedule B-1, "Works of 19th Century Artists in the Collection of The Museum of Modern Art," June 5, 1947, reflecting deletions made by representatives of The Metropolitan Museum of Art at their meeting with the Modern's representatives on June 9

Appendix

Appendix

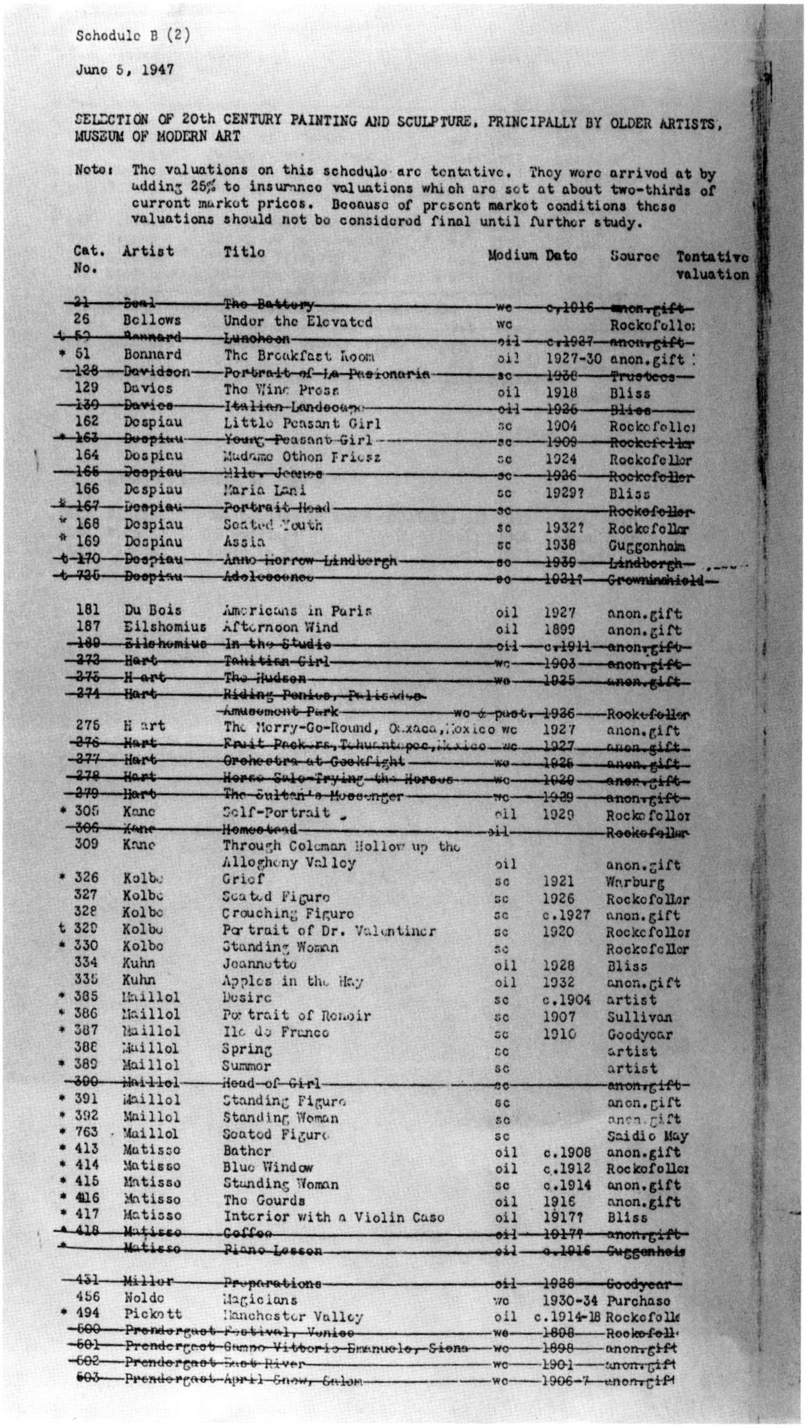

Schedule B (2)

June 5, 1947

SELECTION OF 20th CENTURY PAINTING AND SCULPTURE, PRINCIPALLY BY OLDER ARTISTS, MUSEUM OF MODERN ART

Note: The valuations on this schedule are tentative. They were arrived at by adding 25% to insurance valuations which are set at about two-thirds of current market prices. Because of present market conditions these valuations should not be considered final until further study.

Cat. No.	Artist	Title	Medium	Date	Source	Tentative valuation
~~21~~	~~Beal~~	~~The Battery~~	~~wc~~	~~c.1916~~	~~anon.gift~~	
26	Bellows	Under the Elevated	wc		Rockefeller	
~~t 52~~	~~Bonnard~~	~~Luncheon~~	~~oil~~	~~c.1927~~	~~anon.gift~~	
* 51	Bonnard	The Breakfast Room	oil	1927-30	anon.gift	
~~128~~	~~Davidson~~	~~Portrait of La Pasionaria~~	~~sc~~	~~1938~~	~~Trustees~~	
129	Davies	The Wine Press	oil	1918	Bliss	
~~139~~	~~Davies~~	~~Italian Landscape~~	~~oil~~	~~1926~~	~~Bliss~~	
162	Despiau	Little Peasant Girl	sc	1904	Rockefeller	
~~* 163~~	~~Despiau~~	~~Young Peasant Girl~~	~~sc~~	~~1909~~	~~Rockefeller~~	
164	Despiau	Madame Othon Friesz	sc	1924	Rockefeller	
~~165~~	~~Despiau~~	~~Mlle. Jeanne~~	~~sc~~	~~1926~~	~~Rockefeller~~	
166	Despiau	Maria Lani	sc	1929?	Bliss	
~~* 167~~	~~Despiau~~	~~Portrait Head~~	~~sc~~		~~Rockefeller~~	
* 168	Despiau	Seated Youth	sc	1932?	Rockefeller	
* 169	Despiau	Assia	sc	1938	Guggenheim	
~~t 170~~	~~Despiau~~	~~Anne Morrow Lindbergh~~	~~sc~~	~~1939~~	~~Lindbergh~~	
~~t 725~~	~~Despiau~~	~~Adolescence~~	~~sc~~	~~1921?~~	~~Gwenn Shield~~	
181	Du Bois	Americans in Paris	oil	1927	anon.gift	
187	Eilshemius	Afternoon Wind	oil	1899	anon.gift	
~~189~~	~~Eilshemius~~	~~In the Studio~~	~~oil~~	~~c.1911~~	~~anon.gift~~	
~~272~~	~~Hart~~	~~Tahitian Girl~~	~~wc~~	~~1903~~	~~anon.gift~~	
~~273~~	~~Hart~~	~~The Hudson~~	~~wc~~	~~1925~~	~~anon.gift~~	
~~274~~	~~Hart~~	~~Riding Ponies, Palisades Amusement Park~~	~~wc & past.~~	~~1936~~	~~Rockefeller~~	
275	Hart	The Merry-Go-Round, Oaxaca, Mexico	wc	1927	anon.gift	
~~276~~	~~Hart~~	~~Fruit Packers, Tehuantepec, Mexico~~	~~wc~~	~~1927~~	~~anon.gift~~	
~~277~~	~~Hart~~	~~Orchestra at Cockfight~~	~~wc~~	~~1926~~	~~anon.gift~~	
~~278~~	~~Hart~~	~~Horse Sale-Trying the Horses~~	~~wc~~	~~1929~~	~~anon.gift~~	
~~279~~	~~Hart~~	~~The Sultan's Messenger~~	~~wc~~	~~1929~~	~~anon.gift~~	
* 305	Kane	Self-Portrait	oil	1929	Rockefeller	
~~306~~	~~Kane~~	~~Homestead~~	~~oil~~		~~Rockefeller~~	
309	Kane	Through Coleman Hollow up the Allegheny Valley	oil		anon.gift	
* 326	Kolbe	Griof	sc	1921	Warburg	
327	Kolbe	Seated Figure	sc	1926	Rockefeller	
328	Kolbe	Crouching Figure	sc	c.1927	anon.gift	
t 329	Kolbe	Portrait of Dr. Valentiner	sc	1920	Rockefeller	
* 330	Kolbe	Standing Woman	sc		Rockefeller	
334	Kuhn	Jeannette	oil	1928	Bliss	
335	Kuhn	Apples in the Hay	oil	1932	anon.gift	
* 385	Maillol	Desire	sc	c.1904	artist	
* 386	Maillol	Portrait of Renoir	sc	1907	Sullivan	
* 387	Maillol	Ile de France	sc	1910	Goodyear	
388	Maillol	Spring	sc		artist	
* 389	Maillol	Summer	sc		artist	
~~390~~	~~Maillol~~	~~Head of Girl~~	~~sc~~		~~anon.gift~~	
* 391	Maillol	Standing Figure	sc		anon.gift	
* 392	Maillol	Standing Woman	sc		anon.gift	
* 763	Maillol	Seated Figure	sc		Saidie May	
* 413	Matisse	Bather	oil	c.1908	anon.gift	
* 414	Matisse	Blue Window	oil	c.1912	Rockefeller	
* 415	Matisse	Standing Woman	sc	c.1914	anon.gift	
* 416	Matisse	The Gourds	oil	1916	anon.gift	
* 417	Matisse	Interior with a Violin Case	oil	1917?	Bliss	
~~* 418~~	~~Matisse~~	~~Coffee~~	~~oil~~	~~1917?~~	~~anon.gift~~	
~~*~~	~~Matisse~~	~~Piano Lesson~~	~~oil~~	~~c.1916~~	~~Guggenheim~~	
~~431~~	~~Miller~~	~~Preparations~~	~~oil~~	~~1928~~	~~Goodyear~~	
456	Nolde	Magicians	wc	1930-34	Purchase	
* 494	Pickett	Manchester Valley	oil	c.1914-18	Rockefeller	
~~500~~	~~Prendergast~~	~~Festival, Venice~~	~~wc~~	~~1898~~	~~Rockefeller~~	
~~501~~	~~Prendergast~~	~~Campo Vittorio Emanuele, Siena~~	~~wc~~	~~1898~~	~~anon.gift~~	
~~502~~	~~Prendergast~~	~~East River~~	~~wc~~	~~1901~~	~~anon.gift~~	
~~503~~	~~Prendergast~~	~~April Snow, Salem~~	~~wc~~	~~1906-7~~	~~anon.gift~~	

3a. Schedule B-2, "Selection of 20th Century Painting and Sculpture, Principally by Older Artists, Museum of Modern Art," June 5, 1947, reflecting deletions and additions made by representatives of The Metropolitan Museum of Art at their meeting with the Modern's representatives on June 9

Schedule B (2) cont'd

Cat. No.	Artist	Title	Medium	Date	Source	Tentative valuation
~~504~~	~~Prendergast~~	~~Landscape~~	~~wc~~		~~anon.gift~~	
~~*~~	~~Prendergast~~	~~Acadia~~	~~oil~~		~~purchase~~	
* 539	Rouault	Woman at a Table	wc	1906	Bliss	
540	Rouault	Portrait of Lebasque	oil	1917	purchase	
t 541	Rouault	Man with Spectacles	wc	1917	Rockefeller	
t 544	Rouault	Funeral	gouache & pastel	1930	anon.gift	
* 545	Rouault	Christ Mocked by Soldiers	oil	1932	anon.gift	
568	Signac	Harbor of La Rochelle	wc	1922	Bliss	
569	Signac	Village Festival	wc		anon.gift	
579	Speicher	Katharine Cornell as Candida	oil	1925-6	Cornell	
~~585~~	~~Steer~~	~~Sandwich Bay~~	~~wc~~	~~1901~~	~~anon.gift~~	
~~612~~	~~Vivin~~	~~Church of St. Laurent and the Gare de l'Est~~	~~oil~~		~~Saidie May~~	
* 614	Vuillard	Mother and Sister of the Artist	oil	c.1900	Saidie May	
~~617~~	~~Wallis~~	~~Cornish Port~~	~~oil~~	~~c.1932-33~~	~~Nicholson~~	
				Total		

Added at meeting of June 9

681	Matisse	The Bouquet on the BambooTable	oil	1902	Mrs. Bush
478	Picasso	La Coiffure	oil	1906	anon.gift
487	Picasso	Woman in White	oil	1923	Bliss

* - on exhibition
t - out on tour

3b. Schedule B-2 (continued)

Appendix

Appendix

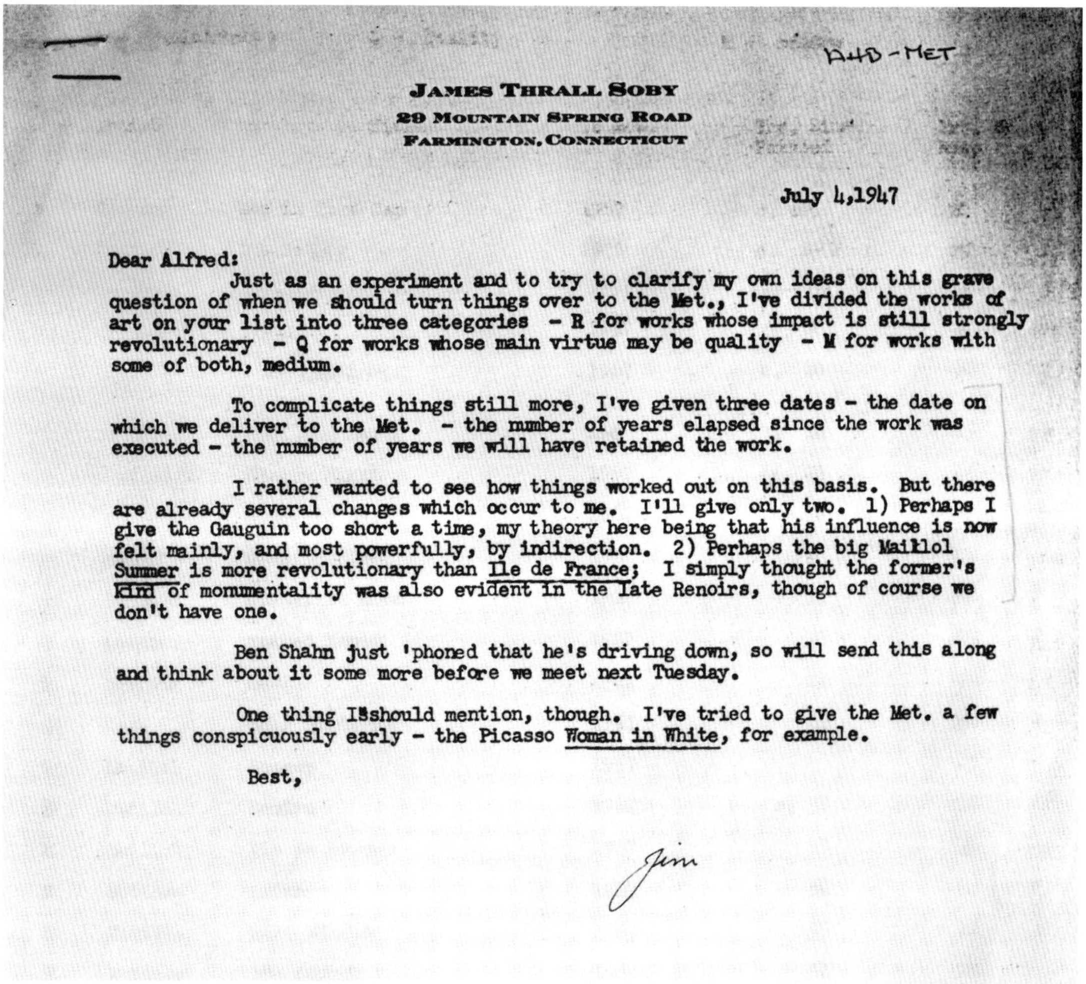

AHB - MET

JAMES THRALL SOBY
29 MOUNTAIN SPRING ROAD
FARMINGTON, CONNECTICUT

July 4,1947

Dear Alfred:

Just as an experiment and to try to clarify my own ideas on this grave question of when we should turn things over to the Met., I've divided the works of art on your list into three categories - R for works whose impact is still strongly revolutionary - Q for works whose main virtue may be quality - M for works with some of both, medium.

To complicate things still more, I've given three dates - the date on which we deliver to the Met. - the number of years elapsed since the work was executed - the number of years we will have retained the work.

I rather wanted to see how things worked out on this basis. But there are already several changes which occur to me. I'll give only two. 1) Perhaps I give the Gauguin too short a time, my theory here being that his influence is now felt mainly, and most powerfully, by indirection. 2) Perhaps the big Maillol Summer is more revolutionary than Ile de France; I simply thought the former's kind of monumentality was also evident in the late Renoirs, though of course we don't have one.

Ben Shahn just 'phoned that he's driving down, so will send this along and think about it some more before we meet next Tuesday.

One thing I should mention, though. I've tried to give the Met. a few things conspicuously early - the Picasso Woman in White, for example.

Best,

Jim

4a. Letter from James Thrall Soby to Alfred Barr, July 4, 1947, to which the list of works he proposed for transfer to The Metropolitan Museum of Art was attached (see opposite)

evolutionary Q - Quality M - medium

	Artist	Title	To Met.	Yrs. Since Painted	Yrs. Keep	
	Cezanne	Man in Blue Cap	1967	c. 100	20	15
R	Cezanne	The Bather	1972	c. 85	25	15
Q	Cezanne	Oranges	1957	c. 75	10	30
Q	Cezanne	Apples	1957	c. 60	10	15
R	Cezanne	Blue Landscape	1967	c. 70	20	30
M	Gauguin	Moon and Earth	1962	c. 80	15	20
R	van Gogh	Starry Night	1962	73	15	30
R	Rousseau	Sleeping Gypsy	1967	70	20	25
R	Seurat	Fishing Fleet	1962	74	15	20
Q	Bonnard	Breakfast Room	1967	c. 37	20	20
Q	Despiau	Seated Youth	1962	30	15	20
Q	Despiau	Assia	1962	29	20	20
Q	Kane	Self Portrait	1957	28	10	25
Q	Maillol	Summer	1957		10	20
M	Maillol	Desire	1962	c. 58	15	20
M	Maillol	Ile de France	1967	57	20	20
R	Matisse	Bather	1967	58	20	25
R	Matisse	Blue Window	1967	55	20	25
R	Matisse	The Gourds	1967	51	20	25
M	Matisse	Interior with Violin	1957	40	10	25
Q	Pickett	Manchester Valley	1962	c. 46	15	25
Q	Rouault	Lebasque	1962	45	15	25
R	Rouault	Christ Mocked	1972	40	25	25
Q	Speicher	Katharine Cornell	1957	31	10	5
R	Vuillard	Mother and Sister	1972	72	25	20
R	Picasso	La Coiffure	1962	56	15	20
Q	Picasso	Woman in White	1957	34	10	30

4b. List of works proposed for transfer to The Metropolitan Museum of Art by James Thrall Soby, July 4, 1947. Alfred Barr added his own figures for the number of years each work should be retained at the Modern in the handwritten column at far right

Appendix

Appendix

Artist, title, date of work	Date of delivery to Met.	Number of years from now	Total years we will have had	Age of work when delivered
Bellows: Under the Elevated.wc.c.1915	1967	20	32	c.52
Bonnard: Breakfast Room. 1927-30	1967	20	26	37
Cézanne: Man in a Blue Cap. 1865-66	1962	15	28	c.96
" Bathers. wc. 1885	1962	15	28	c.77
" Bridge at Gardanne.wc.1885-86	1977	30	43	c.96
" The Bather. c.1888	1962	25	38	95
" House Among Trees.wc.1890-1900	1977	30	43	c.77
" Oranges. 1895-1900	1977	30	43	c.77
" Bathers Under a Bridge.wc. 1895-1900	1977	30	43	c.77
" Rocky Ridge. wc. 1895-1900	1977	30	43	c.77
" Foliage. wc. 1895-1905	1977	30	43	c.72
" *Still Life with Apples.1890-1900	1962	15	28	c.62 - a.H.B
" *Pines and Rocks. 1895-1900	1977	30	43	c.77
Despiau: Little Peasant Girl. 1904	1952	5	12	48
" Madame Othon Friesz. 1924	1952	5	13	28
" Maria Lani. 1929	1957	10	27	28
" Seated Youth. 1932	1957	10	18	25
" Assia. 1938	1967	20	28	29
Du Bois: Americans in Paris. 1927	1957	10	22	30
Eilshemius: Afternoon Wind. 1899	1967	20	26	68
Ensor: Tribulations of St.Anthony. 1887	1972	25	32	85
Gauguin: The Moon and the Earth. 1893	1972	25	38	79
van Gogh: Starry Night. 1889	1972	25	31	83
Hart: The Merry-Go-Round.wc.1927	1957	10	22	30
Kane: Self Portrait. 1929	1972	25	33	43
Kane: Through Coleman Hollow.c.1932	1972	25	31	40
Kolbe: Grief. 1921	1967	20	28	46
" Seated Figure. 1926	1957	10	18	31
" Crouching Figure. 1927	1957	10	18	30
" Portrait of Dr. Valentiner.1920	1952	5	12	32
" Standing Woman. c.1922	1967	20	28	45
Kuhn: Jeanette. 1928	1952	5	18	24
" Apples in the Hay. 1932	1957	10	21	25
Maillol: Desire. c.1904	1967	20	37	63
Maillol: Portrait of Renoir. 1907	1957	10	18	50
" Ile de France. 1910	1967	20	37	57
" Spring. c.1920	1952	5	22	c.32
" Summer. c.1920	1967	20	37	c.47
" Standing Figure. c.1920	1957	10	18	37
" Standing Woman. c.1920	1957	10	18	37
" Seated Figure. c.1930	1967	20	25	37
Matisse: Bather. c.1908	1972	25	36	64
" Blue Window. c.1912	1972	25	33	60
" Standing Woman. sc. c.1914	1972	25	33	58
" The Gourds. 1916	1962	15	37	46
" Interior with Violin Case.1917	1967	20	33	50
" Bouquet on the Bamboo Table.1902	1957	10	15	55
Nolde: Magicians. wc. 1930-34	1972	25	33	38
Picasso: La Coiffure. 1906	1972	25	35	66
" Woman in White. 1923	1977	30	43	54
Pickett: Manchester Valley. c.1914-18	1972	25	33	54
Redon: Silence. c.1890	1972	25	38	c.82
" Etruscan Vase. c.1890	1962	15	28	c.72
" Roger and Angelica. c.1900	1972	25	38	c.72
Rouault: Woman at a Table. wc. 1906	1972	25	31	66
" Portrait of Lebasque. 1917	1972	25	33	55
" Man with Spectacles.wc. 1917	1972	25	37	55
" Funeral. 1930	1972	25	31	42
" Christ Mocked by Soldiers.1932	1972	25	31	40
Rousseau: The Sleeping Gypsy. 1897	1972	25	33	75
" Jungle with Lion. 1904-10	1972	25	38	c.60
Seurat: Fishing Fleet at Port-en-Bessin 1888	1972	25	38	84
" Stone Breakers. dr. c.1881	1977	30	43	96
" The Artist's Mother. dr. 1883	1962	15	28	79

5a. "Paintings and sculptures on Schedule B (two Cezannes added) with suggested terminal dates of delivery," July 9, 1947 (detail)

Appendix

- 2 -

Seurat:	House at Dusk. dr. c.1884	1962	15	28	78
"	At the "Concert Europeen" dr. c.1887	1972	25	38	85
Signac:	Harbor of La Rochelle.wc.1922	1967	20	33	45
"	Village Festival.wc.c.1920	1952	5	17	32
Speicher:	Katharine Cornell. 1925-6	1952	5	14	26
Vuillard:	Mother and Sister of the Artist. c.1900	1967	20	33	67
Davies:	The Wine Press. 1918	1952	5	18	34

Note - *To be given eventually, not sold, to the Metropolitan under the terms of the Lillie P. Bliss bequest.

5b. "Paintings and sculptures on Schedule B (two Cezannes added) with suggested terminal dates of delivery" (continued)

Appendix

7/9

Summary

Cezanne: We keep 15 years more except for 2 of smaller late oils and several watercolors which are less "important" but valuable to us as sources of cubism and abstract art. Mrs. Soby feels we should also keep the big Bather.

Generation of Auguin, van Gogh, Seurat, Ensor, Redon, dating mostly from 1880s: We keep 25 years more to serve as background to expressionism and fantastic art. Except for redon, we have only one painting by each otherwise some could go much sooner.
Exceptions: several of the best Seurat drawings and the Redon flower piece could go sooner, maybe in 15 years.

Rousseau: Keep 25 years for influence on cubists and surrealists.

Pickett, Kane: Original "primitives" of great quality. Keep as long as Rousseau, 25 years.

Bonnard, Vuillard, Signac: Keep 20 years, unless we acquire more paintings by them.

Matisse, Rouault, Nolde - the Expressionist generation - now dead or approaching 80 years of age

Keep most important works 25 years, though certain works should go earlier, especially if we increase our collection.

Speicher: Large conservative painting of good quality but little relevance to us. Pass on as soon as possible - 5 years? -immediately?

Kuhn, du Bois, Hart, Davis:
Somewhat more modern than Speicher, but less so than late Cezanne, and with very little influence on American painting. Keep 10 years or less.

Picasso: Coiffure (1906) early work, fairly traditional; keep 20 years as part of Picasso group.
Woman in White, important as our only example of Picasso's revolutionary post-cubist neo-classicism - Keep 30 years unless we acquire others.

Maillol, Despiau, Kolbe:
Keep one large figure, one small figure and possible a head by each for 20 years as a point of departure for more recent sculpture. Other can go in 5 or 10 years.

July 9, 1947

A. H. B., Jr.

6. Summary of information contained in App. 5a–b, prepared by Alfred Barr on July 9, 1947

MUSEUM OF MODERN ART

CONFIDENTIAL - Tentative list of works for delivery to Metropolitan Museum within 10 years, discussed by Mr. Redmond, Mr. Whitney and Mr. Barr, July 22, 1947, based upon discussion among Mr. Redmond, Mr. Moe and Mr. Barr on July 14, 1947.

Artist, title, date of work		Value
Cézanne	Man in a Blue Cap. 1865-66	
"	Bathers Under a Bridge. wc. 1895-1900	
Despiau:	Little Peasant Girl. 1904	
"	Madame Othon Friesz. 1924	
"	Maria Lani. 1929	
"	Seated Youth. 1932	
De Bois:	Americans in Paris. 1927	
Hart:	The Merry-Go-Round. wc. 1927	
Kolbe:	Seated Figure. 1926	
"	Crouching Figure. 1927	
"	Portrait of Dr. Valentiner. 1920	
Kuhn:	Jeanette. 1928	
"	Apples in the Hay. 1932	
Maillol:	Portrait of Renoir. 1907	
"	Spring. c. 1920	
"	Standing Figure. c. 1920	
"	Standing Woman. c. 1920	
Matisse:	The Gourds. 1916	
"	Interior with Violin Case. 1917	
"	Bouquet on the Bamboo Table. 1902	
Picasso:	La Coiffure. 1906	
Redon:	Etruscan Vase. c. 1890	
Rouault:	Portrait of Lebasque. 1917	
"	Funeral. 1930	
Seurat:	The Artist's Mother. dr. 1883	
"	Lady Fishing. 1885	
"	House at Dusk. dr. c. 1884	
Signac:	Village Festival. wc. c. 1920	
Speicher:	Katharine Cornell. 1925-26	
Davies:	The Wine Press. 1918	

Also possibilities:

Cézanne:	The Bather. c. 1888
Maillol:	Ile de France. 1910
Picasso:	Woman in White. 1923

July 22, 1947

AHB

Appendix

7. "Tentative list of works for delivery to the Metropolitan Museum within 10 years," prepared by Alfred Barr on July 22, 1947

Appendix

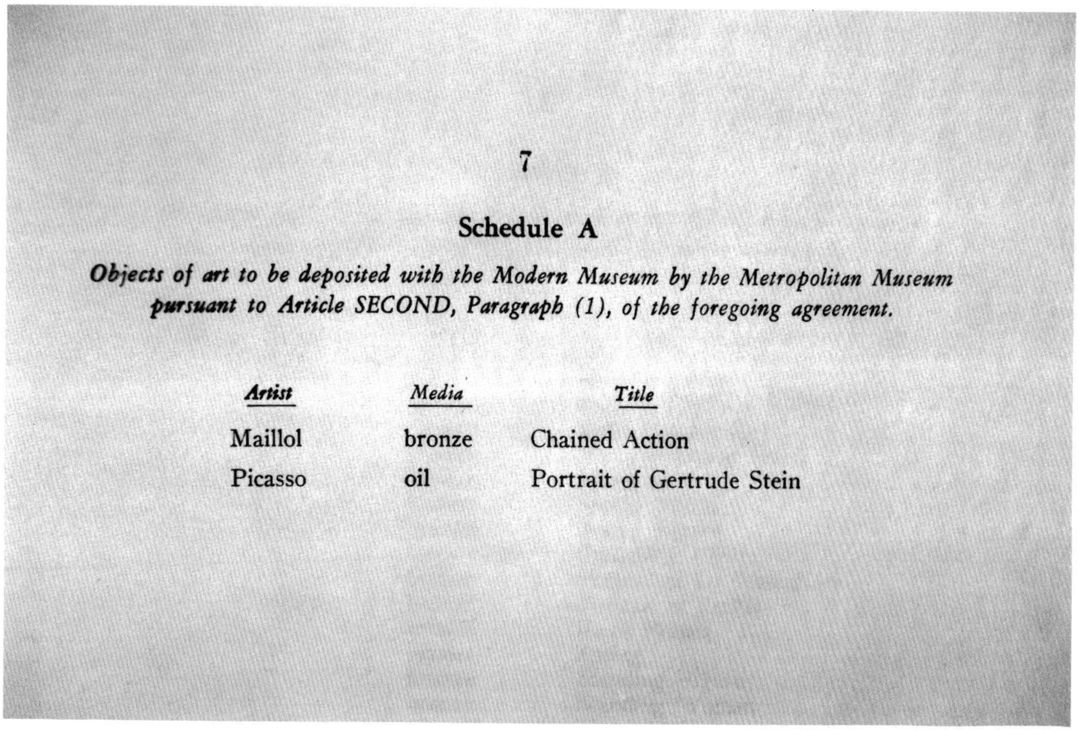

7

Schedule A

Objects of art to be deposited with the Modern Museum by the Metropolitan Museum pursuant to Article SECOND, Paragraph (1), of the foregoing agreement.

Artist	*Media*	*Title*
Maillol	bronze	Chained Action
Picasso	oil	Portrait of Gertrude Stein

8. Schedule A of the formalized inter-museum agreement, September 15, 1947

8

Schedule B

Objects of art to be sold by Modern Museum to the Metropolitan pursuant to Article THIRD, Paragraph (2), of the foregoing agreement.

Artist	Media	Title
Cezanne	oil	Man in a Blue Cap
"	wc	Bathers Under a Bridge
Despiau	plaster	Little Peasant Girl
"	plaster	Madame Othon Friesz
"	bronze	Maria Lani
"	bronze	Seated Youth
Kolbe	bronze	Seated Figure
"	terra cotta	Crouching Figure
"	bronze	Portrait of Dr. Valentiner
Maillol	bronze	Portrait of Renoir
"	bronze	Ile de France
"	plaster	Spring
"	bronze	Standing Figure
"	bronze	Standing Woman
Matisse	oil	The Gourds
"	oil	Interior with Violin Case
"	oil	Bouquet on the Bamboo Table
Picasso	oil	La Coiffure
"	oil	Woman in White
Redon	tempera	Etruscan Vase
Rouault	oil	Portrait of Lebasque
"	gouache, etc.	Funeral
Seurat	dr	The Artist's Mother
"	dr	Lady Fishing
"	dr	Seurat—House at Dusk
Signac	wc	Village Festival

American Folk Art

Artist	Media	Title
Hicks	oil	The Residence of David Twining
"	oil	The Peaceable Kingdom
Unknown	oil	Baby in Red Chair
"	wc	Glass Bowl with Fruit
"	oil	The Quilting Party
"	wood	Eagle
"	wood	Henry Ward Beecher
"	copper	Weathervane-Fish
"	iron	Weathervane-Horse
"	oil	Child with Dog
"	"fractur"	Crucifixion
"	dr	Deer
"	dr	Horse
"	wood	Seated Woman

9. Schedule B of the formalized inter-museum agreement, September 15, 1947

Appendix

Appendix

7

SCHEDULE B

Objects of art to be sold by Modern Museum to the Metropolitan pursuant to Article THIRD, Paragraph (2), of the foregoing agreement.

Artist	Media	Title
Cezanne	oil	Man in a Blue Cap — delivered
"	wc	Bathers Under a Bridge
Despiau	plaster	Little Peasant Girl
"	plaster	Madame Othon Friesz
"	bronze	Maria Lani
"	bronze	Seated Youth - delivered
Kolbe	bronze	Seated Figure
"	terra cotta	Crouching Figure
"	bronze	Portrait of Dr. Valentiner
Maillol	bronze	Portrait of Renoir delivered
"	bronze	Ile de France delivered
"	plaster	Spring
"	bronze	~~Standing Figure~~ Woman Arranging her Hair
"	bronze	Standing Woman
Matisse (purch'd by us)	oil	The Gourds
"	oil	Interior with Violin Case
"	oil	Bouquet on the Bamboo Table - delivered
Picasso	oil	La Coiffure — delivered
"	oil	Woman in White — "
Redon	tempera	Etruscan Vase "
Rouault	oil	Portrait of Lebasque — "
"	gouache, etc.	Funeral
Seurat	dr	The Artist's Mother not ret'd to us from Met.
"	dr	Lady Fishing
"	dr	Seurat—House at Dusk
Signac	wc	Village Festival

(not yet delivered to Met.)

AMERICAN FOLK ART

Artist	Media	Title
Hicks	oil	The Residence of David Twining
"	oil	The Peaceable Kingdom
Unknown	oil	Baby in Red Chair
"	wc	Glass Bowl with Fruit
"	oil	The Quilting Party
"	wood	Eagle
"	wood	Henry Ward Beecher
"	copper	Weathervane-Fish
"	iron	Weathervane-Horse
"	oil	Child with Dog
"	"fractur"	Crucifixion
"	dr	Deer
"	dr	Horse
"	wood	Seated Woman

(delivered to Met. Nov. 10, 1950)

10. Schedule B of the amended agreement between The Metropolitan Museum of Art and The Museum of Modern Art, September 15, 1947, which outlined the main points of the arrangement exclusive of the involvement of the Whitney Museum of American Art; annotated January 1957 with regard to the ultimate disposition of works

Notes

I would like to thank Fereshteh Daftari for invaluable initial research assistance on this article, and Victoria Garvin for subsequent help; their initiatives helped bring to light a great deal of relevant material. Their efforts and mine were given tremendous support by Rona Roob, Museum Archivist. Thanks also to Alice Buchanan for her assistance, and to John Elderfield and Beatrice Kernan for encouragement and timely suggestions. My most important debt of gratitude is to Barbara Ross, who undertook the complex tasks of editing this piece and of verifying sources in various archives; she located and collated some of the most important supporting documentation in the notes, and worked with scrupulous devotion to the ideal of making the history as clear, as solid, and as thoroughly researched as possible.

The designation *MoMA Archives* refers to The Museum of Modern Art Archives, New York. *Painting and Sculpture archive* indicates uncatalogued source material in the files of the Museum's Department of Painting and Sculpture.

1. Alfred H. Barr, Jr., "The Museum Collections: A Brief Report," typescript, January 15, 1944, p. 3. MoMA Archives: Reports and Pamphlets, Box 4/14.
2. See Alfred H. Barr, Jr., "Chronicle of the Collection of Painting and Sculpture," in *Painting and Sculpture in The Museum of Modern Art, 1929–1967* (New York: The Museum of Modern Art, 1977), pp. 619–50; Calvin Tomkins, *Merchants and Masterpieces: The Story of the Metropolitan Museum of Art* (New York: E. P. Dutton, 1970); Russell Lynes, *Good Old Modern: An Intimate Portrait of The Museum of Modern Art* (New York: Atheneum, 1973); and Helaine Messer, "MoMA: Museum in Search of an Image," Ph.D. thesis, Columbia University, New York, 1979.
3. *A New Art Museum,* 1st ed. (New York: The Museum of Modern Art, [August] 1929), n.p. MoMA Archives: Alfred H. Barr, Jr., Papers, 1.9B.
4. The committee, appointed October 25, 1929, consisted of Conger Goodyear, Paul J. Sachs, and, "ex officio, the Director" (Barr, "Chronicle," p. 620).
5. Barr began pursuing the Seurat *Parade* in early 1929, when the work was offered for sale by Reid and Lefevre, London. On May 7, 1930, he wrote to Cornelius Sullivan, expressing his hope that the Seurat might serve as a foundation for a future permanent collection at the Modern: "Buildings may be had for money, but such a painting as this if it should go to the Tate or to some other museum could never again be had or even its equivalent." The Museum, in need of a more permanent home, had already begun negotiating with John D. Rockefeller, Jr., to lease the townhouse he owned at 11 West 53 Street. With this expenditure looming, the Board of Trustees was unwilling to commit to raising the funds necessary for the purchase of *Parade.*

Georges Seurat. *Circus Sideshow (Parade).* 1887–88. Oil on canvas, 39¼ x 59" (99.7 x 149.9 cm). The Metropolitan Museum of Art, Bequest of Stephen C. Clark, 1960 (61.101.17)

In late May 1931, Barr approached trustee Stephen C. Clark with the suggestion that he purchase the painting, undoubtedly with the idea that it would eventually find its way into the Modern's collection. Clark responded on May 22: "I have received your letter of May 21st and am sorry to say that I am not interested in the purchase of the Seurat. Incidentally, the picture is here in New York and not in London" (Barr was apparently unaware that the painting had been acquired from Reid and Lefevre by M. Knoedler & Co. in January 1929). MoMA Archives: Barr Papers, Personal Correspondence, filing unit 3.

Clark later reconsidered Barr's proposal, purchasing *Parade* from Knoedler in November 1932; surviving correspondence does not indicate whether he acquired the work with the express intent of later giving it to the Modern. *Parade* would ultimately enter the collection of The Metropolitan Museum of Art as part of the Clark Bequest in 1960. See also n. 118 below.
6. *A New Art Museum,* 2nd ed. (New York: The Museum of Modern Art, [September] 1929), n.p. MoMA Archives: Barr Papers, 1.9A.
7. *A New Art Museum* (August 1929), n.p.
8. For a cross-section of editorial comment on the proposed coalition, see Appendix O, "Quotations from Newspapers and Periodicals Concerning the Museum," in "An Effort to Secure $3,250,000.00 for The Museum of Modern Art," Official Statement, The Museum of Modern Art, New York, April 30, 1931, pp. 88–103. MoMA Archives: Barr Papers, 1.9A.
9. Article V, subsection *s* of Bliss's will, dated August 16, 1930, specifically states that the works cited in her bequest would become "the absolute property" of the Museum once it had been established "to the full and complete satisfaction" of the Museum's Trustees "that the Museum of Modern Art is sufficiently endowed and is in the hands of a competent Board. . . ." MoMA Archives: Public Information Scrapbooks, 12A.

Bliss's will also stipulated that two Cézanne still lifes—*Still Life with Ginger Jar, Sugar Bowl, and Oranges* (1902–06) and *Still Life with Apples* (1895–98)—and Daumier's *The Laundress* (?1863) "shall only be delivered to and allowed to remain in the possession of" the Modern "subject to the condition that said pictures shall never be sold or otherwise disposed of," and that, should these conditions not be met, they would become "the sole and absolute property of The Metropolitan Museum of Art." The Daumier—deemed "to be more appropriately a part of the collection of the older institution" ("Revision and amplification of the tentative release given by Mr. Redmond to Mr. Barr, June 18 [1947]," p. 3)—was transferred to the Metropolitan in late 1947 as part of the inter-museum agreement.
10. "An Effort to Secure $3,250,000.00 for The Museum of Modern Art," p. 5.
11. Ibid. "Because of lack of space the Museum has been up till the present reluctant in accepting actual gifts of works of art although it has continually attempted to interest collectors who might eventually give part or all of their collections to the Museum. In spite of this reluctance the Museum has already received eight works by French and German sculptors, seven works by American and French painters, together with prints and drawings. . ." (p. 21).
12. Ibid., pp. 25–26.
13. "Memorial Exhibition: The Collection of Miss Lizzie P. Bliss," May 17–October 6, 1931.
14. See Goodyear–Abby Aldrich Rockefeller correspondence, letters dated June 23 and 30, 1933. In his letter of the 23rd, Goodyear wrote: "[T]he Museum has accomplished so much in the four years now nearly completed that we should not . . . consider any curtailment of our exhibition activities. . . .

"Alfred's inclination to a fewer number of exhibitions is passed on two considerations,— one, his determination to make our exhibitions completely representative and the other the feeling that he could not stand the physical strain of four exhibitions a year." MoMA Archives: Barr Papers, 10A.64b.ii.
15. Letter, Abby Aldrich Rockefeller to Barr, March 14, 1931; written in reply to Barr's letter of March 6, in which he stated that "we must have or we must budget sufficient funds . . . to pay for space for a beginning of the permanent collection or at least a collection borrowed from our friends which might be of a rotating nature. I do not believe that we could continue the quality of our past exhibitions even at four a year and that we ought to have a supplementary exhibition of more or less permanence." MoMA Archives: Barr Papers, 7.5.
16. See Coffin–Goodyear correspondence, letters dated August 28, October 8, October 13, October 14, October 29, and November 6, 1931. The Metropolitan Museum of Art Archives.

Goodyear, in a memorandum to members of the Modern's Executive Committee, September 1, 1931, indicated that the initial proposal was made by Coffin: "Mr. W. S. Coffin, Acting President of [The] Metropolitan Museum of Art, has made a very interesting suggestion in regard to a possible relation between that institution and our own. The income from the Herne [sic] Fund to the Metropolitan Museum amounts to about $15,000 a year. Mr. Coffin suggests that purchases from this fund should be made by a committee on which the Museum of Modern Art and the Metropolitan should be jointly represented.

"The pictures purchased from the fund, he proposes, should be hung in the Museum of Modern Art for a period of ten years, after which, at the option of the Metropolitan, they can be transferred to the Metropolitan or sold to other museums. . . .

"There will be no definite proposals possible until the next meeting of the Board of the Metropolitan Museum, which will come in October. I feel that this is a very interesting suggestion, however, and talking it over with Mr. Coffin, I discussed futher the possibility of a more general relation between the two institutions, an arrangement which both he and Mr. [Bryson] Burroughs [the Metropolitan's curator of paintings] decidedly approve. . . ." MoMA Archives: Barr Papers, Personal Correspondence, filing unit 3.

17. The Hearn Fund was established in 1906 by retailer George A. Hearn with an initial gift of $125,000 (he increased the Fund by an additional $125,000 in 1911). Hearn, a trustee of the Metropolitan from 1903 until his death in 1913, stipulated that the fund was "to be expended for paintings by persons now living, who are, or may be at the time of purchase, citizens of the United States of America or by those hereafter born who may at the time of purchase, have become citizens thereof." The Metropolitan Museum of Art Archives.

Hearn also explicitly authorized sales and exchanges. According to Tomkins, Robert de Forest and other members of the Metropolitan's board reinterpreted the terms of the gift after Hearn's death: "Hearn had said that the income should be used to buy paintings by 'living' American artists. Rather cleverly, de Forest suggested that this could be construed to mean works by artists *living at the time of the gift* in 1906" *(Merchants and Masterpieces,* p. 296).

18. See Coffin–Goodyear correspondence, The Metropolitan Museum of Art Archives, letters dated October 29 and November 6, 1931.

19. A. Conger Goodyear, "The Museum of Modern Art," *Creative Art* 9, no. 6 (December 1931), pp. 456–57 ff.

20. Quoted in Tomkins, *Merchants and Masterpieces,* p. 305.

21. Quoted in Lynes, *Good Old Modern,* p. 97.

22. Letter, Goodyear to Sachs, n.d. [December 1932]. The Metropolitan Museum of Art Archives.

23. Letter, Clark to Coffin, January 10, 1933. The Metropolitan Museum of Art Archives.

24. See minutes of the meeting of the Executive Committee of The Museum of Modern Art, January 25, 1933. MoMA Archives: A. Conger Goodyear Papers.

25. A transcript of Coffin's address to the AAM is housed in The Metropolitan Museum of Art Archives.

26. Alfred H. Barr, Jr., "Report on the Permanent Collection," typescript, November 1933, p. 3. MoMA Archives: Barr Papers, 1.9A.

27. Ibid., p. 4.

28. Ibid., p. 13.

29. Ibid., p. 19.

30. Ibid., p. 15.

31. Ibid., pp. 7–8. In the same discussion, Barr also devised four hypothetical situations to show how the plan might work:

"1) In 1935 Seurat's *Port en Bessin* in the Bliss collection will be fifty years old. There will be little question about the permanent value of Seurat or the importance to the Metropolitan of owning eventually a fine group of works by this great artist. The committee will then have to decide whether it is more valuable to the public to keep the Seurat for five or ten years more in our Museum or transfer it immediately to the Metropolitan. 2) If our Museum should be given an Ingres figure composition it would be transfered [sic] immediately to the Metropolitan which needs such a picture badly. 3) If our Museum were given a Courbet landscape the committee might easily permit it to remain in our gallery where two good Courbets would be valuable. The Metropolitan which is already rich in Courbets would not need it. 4) If the Metropolitan were to be given a Picasso it would ordinarily be transferred to our galleries as would a Lehmbruck or a Matisse" (p. 8).

32. See Coffin–Clark correspondence, letters dated January 10, January 13, January 31, February 9, March 9, and March 17, 1933. The Metropolitan Museum of Art Archives.

33. Minutes of the meeting of the Board of Trustees of The Museum of Modern Art, March 26, 1934. MoMA Archives: Board of Trustee Minutes, V.2. The additional committee members were Osborn and George Blumenthal, from the Metropolitan; and Goodyear, from the Modern. The identity of the Museum's second non-trustee committee member, if appointed, is unknown.

34. In a memorandum to Osborn of December 4, 1934, Winlock comments that the Metropolitan's trustees did not like "those difficult, dangerous proposals of Mr. Goodyear's." The Metropolitan Museum of Art Archives.

35. As Barr noted in his "Chronicle," "Many of the proposals and policies effected between 1929 and 1939 were reconsidered and debated during the period from 1940 to 1946, particularly since certain intentions of the previous decade had gone unfulfilled" (p. 628).

36. From "An Account of the Advisory Committee of the Museum of Modern Art, 1931–1938" (1938), p. 5: "In April 1935, a sub-committee was formed to bring in a report on the Permanent Collection policy of the Museum. The report follows:

"Report of the Committee appointed to consider the Aims and Future Functions of The Museum of Modern Art"

"The Committee recommends:

"1. A Permanent Collection

"The permanent collection should comprise primarily works of art of historic importance having a bearing on the development of the modern movement. Works of art in the possession of the Museum may be disposed of at any time at the discretion of the Director and Trustees. However, after a specific object has been in the Museum twenty years, formal consideration should be given [to] it and unless it is felt that the importance of the object warrants its being retained in the Permanent Collection, it should then be disposed of. As a general rule all objects which the Museum feels should no longer be kept in its collection should be offered first to the Metropolitan Museum and then to the various museums throughout the United States. No gifts should be accepted by the Museum unless they are free from restrictions of any kind. . . .

"2. The Museum should endeavor to have adequate space to show satisfactorily the Permanent Collection and the changing Loan Exhibitions. It is essential that the Museum should have this objective and work towards its accomplishment." MoMA Archives: Committee Minutes, Box 1.

37. Cited in "An Account of the Advisory Committee of the Museum of Modern Art, November 1938–May 1941" (1941), p. 5. MoMA Archives: Committee Minutes, Box 1.

38. Barr, "Chronicle," p. 628.

39. "Preliminary Memorandum for Discussion at First Meeting to be held July 23, 1940," May 1940, pp. 1, 6. In answer to the basic question "Should the Museum Have a Permanent Collection and of What Shall It Consist?," the memorandum alternates practical with idealistic concerns:

"Broadly speaking, the present collection and future purchases can be divided into objects of generally accepted importance and significance which are of correspondingly high price, and objects which are not so accepted and are thus comparatively cheap. We have many of the former in our collection.

"It has been suggested that the Museum build up a collection of such examples whose 'historic importance and influence given them a lasting position' which would form a condensed history of the development of Modern Art—this collection to be on permanent display, possibly in a separate building. Is this a sound idea? If so, should these pictures and objects be selected primarily for their significance in the history of art (as distinct from supreme esthetic value)? Should objects of importance in the present collection which are not necessary to such a 'condensed history' be sold? . . .

"Are a large number of 'great pictures' (pictures accepted as great by the general public) necessary in the permanent collection to assure large attendance, publicity, and hence income? Should new acquisitions of a frankly experimental character be made with the idea of encouraging talent and making the collection more representative of contemporary trends?

"In other words, should the center of gravity of the collection be shifted to a more nearly contemporaneous point?" (pp. 5–6). Painting and Sculpture archive.

40. On April 10, 1941, Barr wrote to William A.M. Burden, then Chairman of the Advisory Committee, saying "here's a rough draft of my piece"—the "piece," dated March 12, 1941, having the general title "The Collection of The Museum of Modern Art." Barr began the document by complaining that the permanent collection, though now large and valuable, was not enough on view; and he noted that, after the then-current exhibition of Native American art would close, "plans have been made to give over half the gallery space to curatorial departments primarily for the purpose of showing the Museum collection." Then, under the subheading *Functions of the Collection* (pp. 1–2), Barr reasserted the founding faith:

"The primary function of the collection is to

provide the Museum's public with a well chosen and carefully presented permanent exhibition of the modern arts—'permanent', to use Mr. Goodyear's phrase, 'as a stream is permanent'—with an everchanging content. Right from its very beginning the Museum assumed the responsibility of forming such a collection which over a period of years would be sifted and tested by time until finally the best things would be passed on to the Metropolitan or to some other museum somewhat as the Luxembourg transfers after a given period its finest possessions to the Louvre. In the meantime the Museum's collection would present the latest half century with at least the same thoroughness as the Metropolitan presents older periods."

Under the subheading *Disposal* (p. 6), Barr reasserted these principles in more specific terms:

"The Museum is concerned with modern art; therefore its collections cannot be permanent but must change gradually adding new works and disposing of old ones. So far the Museum has done much of the former and little of the latter. Now in its second decade it should increase its metabolism, should dispose more rapidly of works which it does not need. Such works would include:

"1. Works too old to be useful.

"2. Works which are more or less duplicates (some of which were originally accepted for exchange)

"3. Works which may be beneath the standard of travelling and school exhibitions." MoMA Archives: Barr Papers, 1.9A.

41. Ibid., p. 6. Barr continued: "In theory many of the Museum's purchases may decline in value but a few will greatly increase so that after a period of years 10 percent may be worth 10 times as much and 90 percent 1/10th as much. Naturally it is the 10 percent that other museums will want, while the 90% will have to be sold at a loss or given away.

"Under such circumstances it seems only fair that the Museum should try to maintain its capital by obtaining a reasonable payment for its 'good guesses' from those museums receiving them, after they have matured. Such payments would furnish capital for the purchases of new pictures. In this way the headwaters of the stream of our collection may be fed while at the other end of its course water is flowing over the dam into the filtered reservoirs of the historic museums or, in greater quantity, the sea."

42. On Taylor's antipathy to progressive art, and his tendency to refer to The Museum of Modern Art as "that whorehouse on Fifty-third Street," see Tomkins, *Merchants and Masterpieces,* p. 309.

43. For criticism of the Metropolitan's policy toward American art in this period, see Tomkins, pp. 299–301.

44. Letter, Taylor to Whitney, July 1, 1941. Painting and Sculpture archive.

45. Letter, Barr to Taylor, July 2, 1941. Painting and Sculpture archive.

46. Letter, Barr to Clark, December 4, 1941. Barr concludes this account as follows: "I dislike extremely the development of bad feeling between our two institutions and I always urged that some clear, though not necessarily rigid, division of field should be made, since not only are purchase policies and exhibition policies involved, but also potentially the question of gifts and bequests of 20th Century paintings." Painting and Sculpture archive.

47. Lynes, *Good Old Modern,* p. 287.

48. Minutes of the meeting of the Board of Trustees of The Metropolitan Museum of Art, March 3, 1943. The Metropolitan Museum of Art Archives.

49. For Soby's views on the 1944 auction, which he attended, see his excerpted memoir, "The Changing Stream," p. 208 of the present volume.

50. *Notable Modern Paintings and Sculptures, Including Important Works by Corot, Cézanne, Picasso and Matisse: Property of The Museum of Modern Art, With Additions from Members of the Museum's Board of Trustees and Advisory Committee* (New York: Parke-Bernet Galleries, 1944).

51. Press reports had in common a certain skepticism, if not outright mistrust, of what was seen as a growing tendency among American museums in general toward deaccessioning. Emily Genauer made these remarks in the *World-Telegram* several days before the auction: "Now there's nothing new in a museum's consigning its stuff to the auction block. Most institutions do it anonymously, and the works they sell [are] usually [either] . . . the white elephants they have had to accept from patrons more generous than discriminating . . . or objects which, interesting enough in their time, have simply gone out of fashion.

"The Museum of Modern Art sale is different. In the first place, the name of the institution is given. . . . In the second, the works to be auctioned include items that, instead of being old-fashioned, are of prime importance, like Cézanne's Portrait of Madame Cézanne, Matisse's Girl in Green, Picasso's Guitar and Fruit, all to be sold . . . because they 'are duplicated in the collection by other works of the same kind. . . .'"

"The works slated for auction are to be sold, the museum says, 'to provide funds for the purchase of 20th Century works, chiefly by living artists.' This opens the way to all sorts of provocative speculation. How come this institution established 15 years ago as 'a permanent public museum which will acquire from time to time collections of the best modern works of art,' and supported to the tune of millions of dollars by assorted Rockefellers, Whitneys et al., should not have had long available a sizeable endowment fund for the purchase of pictures, and not now be forced to sell some works from its 'permanent' collection in order to buy others?

"Furthermore, the museum's purchase policy has been under fire for years. The art world waits with bated breath to see what it will do with the money realized from the sale, and just what it considers 'modern art of exceptional quality,' which is what it says it will buy with the proceeds.

"One other aspect of the auction is of notable interest. Why shouldn't the museum have made public the fact that some of the paintings whose source is identified in the auction catalog as 'Museum of Modern Art' and consequently bear a certain cachet of importance, were never, strictly speaking, part of the museum's permanent collection. They were presented to it by a number of trustees with the idea that they be resold to realize additional purchase funds" ("All about Auctions—Museum Sale and WPA 'Junking,'" *World-Telegram,* May 6, 1944).

Leila Mechlin, in "Art Season Breaks Records as Sales Top $6,000,000"(*Washington Star,* July 30, 1944), observed that the "sale of paintings from the supposedly permanent collections of American art museums has caused much discussion among artists and donors during the past season. The Albright Gallery, Buffalo, was one of the first to take this aggressive step, shortly followed by an art institution in the Middle West which preferred to remain anoymous [sic] and later still by the Museum of Modern Art, New York. The purpose, it is claimed, was to increase standard[s], to better a choice none too wise, perhaps, and keep abreast of the times. But a delicate situation is thus created. To sell the works of a living artist cannot fail to be detrimental to reputation—to sell at all is at the same time acknowledgement of loss in value, error in choice. . . ."

"The Metropolitan Museum of Art was perhaps the first to inaugurate this custom, which now threatens to become habitual. The method employed was quite different. The works disposed of were not by living artists, and before any work was offered for sale the donors or their heirs were communicated with and willingness expressed to return the gift if so desired. Overfull museum cellars must in time be cleared—but better still would it be to keep them as empty as possible. To be sure, the overplus of a collection[could] be offered to smaller institutions on loan. . . ." MoMA Archives: Public Information Scrapbooks, General L.

52. According to Barr, this private exhibition was organized in direct response to the "Report of the Committee on Policy" submitted the previous year, so that the trustees could reflect on the issues it raised in regard to the actual works on hand. Barr and Miller prepared a ten-page guide to the exhibition, which emphasized the question of opposing emphases in collecting policy—between a desire for breadth and historical, educational inclusiveness on the one hand, and a search for masterpieces of singular quality on the other. In the course of the exhibition, on January 25, 1945, Barr and Soby cosigned with Sweeney a statement sent to each member of the Board of Trustees. They quoted one of the key questions that had been posed by the report, and responded to it:

"The issue to be resolved by the Trustees . . . is the following: If the Museum collections are limited to major works, the collections will be deficient as teaching instruments by reason of the lack of supplementary minor works. If the collections be developed with an emphasis on work primarily historical in character, the collections will be deficient in major works of quality. What is the Museum's best policy for this situation? . . .

"It is generally agreed that quality is of primary importance; that quality is to be found in a great variety of works, large and small, in different media and of different, even diametrically opposed schools. . . .

It is quality, too, that is the primary factor in making a work of art historically important or educationally valuable" (quoted in Barr, "Chronicle," p. 631).

53. Based on her conversations with Barr, Messer has stated that a major impetus behind the inter-museum agreement of 1947 was trustee ambition: "Barr was under pressure from Nelson Rockefeller and John Hay Whitney, who had both recently returned to Museum affairs from the war, to take steps to insure that the Modern's collection would never contain works more than fifty years old. This was part of their post-war plan to revitalize the Museum" ("MoMA: Museum in Search of An Image," pp. 261–62).

54. In a file memorandum of December 28, 1945, Barr provided a handwritten and then typed version of what Taylor had said to him in a recent conversation; the elisions are Barr's own:

"To sum up in the words of [Taylor]

"'We're ready to be had, but I am not putting forth any temptation.'

"'Tactically I think the best procedure would be to have N. [Nelson Rockefeller] make the proposal from the floor at one of the Trustee meetings at the Metropolitan. In view of all that has been said about me I am not anxious to make the proposal. But I will play ball.'

"'Now that Mr. ________ is dead I think the matter should be reproposed to the Trustees of the Metropolitan—but by a Trustee, not by me. I would suggest Nelson R. because he is a Trustee of both institutions. The committee for considering the matter should be reconstituted under the chairmanship of Nelson R. I would suggest Nelson Rockefeller and Cornelius Bliss and Henry Allen Moe as members—Rockefeller and Bliss as Trustees of both institutions and Moe as a lawyer to draw up the terms of the agreement.'

"'We have more than we can handle right now—'

"'To tell the truth I've just been sitting tight and doing nothing about it. I am not anxious to be accused of swallowing any more canaries, but I do feel bad about seeing the city's interests neglected by an unwillingness to get together merely on personal grounds.'

"'I would certainly like to have someone else make the mistakes and avoid situations like the [Adelaide] de Groot collection.'

"'It should be on a business basis we buy nothing we do not want; you sell nothing you want to keep—'

"'It should be merely an arrangement available for use in case both parties wish to make use of it—'

"'You need the money; you also need to get rid of accumulations.'

"(Elimination to make room for new acquisitions only basis on which a living organization can keep alive.)

"'Possessions entail the need to defend possessions.' (Monument—academicism, not live exploration.)

"'No Met Trustees which would be hostile to the plan now that ______ is dead and ______ has resigned. Only I will not launch the idea. I will go along with it.'"

Barr's memorandum closes with notes on Taylor's discussion of the funds available at the Metropolitan for possible purchases from the Modern. Taylor is reported to have said that the Hearn Fund generates about $12,000 and now has reserves of $60–70,000; he sees using it to buy American things from MoMA. He also discussed the Whitney Fund and other unrestricted funds totalling $250,000, of which Taylor wants to spend about ten percent a year on modern European art. Painting and Sculpture archive.

55. Letter, Barr to Nelson Rockefeller, April 8, 1947. Painting and Sculpture archive.

56. Letter, Nelson Rockefeller to Soby, April 24, 1947. "Jock Whitney and I have been discussing with Mr. Roland Redmond, President of the Metropolitan Museum, the possibility of working out an agreement between the two institutions which would be mutually advantageous in carrying out their respective purposes and objectives. Mr. Redmond made a first draft which Mr. Whitney and I went over informally with him and as a result of that informal conversation, a second draft has been prepared, a copy of which is attached. This was presented to the Executive Committee yesterday afternoon and is now being studied by Alfred Barr and Jim Husted [counsel for The Museum of Modern Art]. . . ." MoMA Archives: James Thrall Soby Papers, III.57.2.

Barr's surprise at reading this document can be judged from the alarmed tone of his letter to Rockefeller of the same date (see n. 57 below), and from his other communications in following days with Soby and other members of the Committee on Museum Collections (see, for example, the letter to Clark cited in n. 58 below).

57. Letter, Barr to Nelson Rockefeller, April 24, 1947: "I have been thinking over the proposed agreement with the Metropolitan and want immediately to raise some questions about handling the agreement within our own institution.

"I have not yet examined the agreement with adequate care but it is clear that it raises certain very fundamental questions of policy concerning our Collection.

"For this reason it seems to me urgently desirable that our Committee on the Museum Collections be consulted not simply as a matter of protocol and courtesy but because the members of the Collections Committee are more interested and knowledgable [sic] about the collection than the other trustees. Furthermore two of them, Mr. Clark and Mr. Lewisohn, have between them collections worth around a million dollars which we might reasonably expect would be bequeathed to the Museum. Another member, Bill Burden, personally superintended and edited the most elaborate study of the contents and policies of the Collections ever made. That was about 1941 when he was Chairman of the Advisory Committee. Jim Soby, another member, knows more all around about the problem both in the personal and technical aspects than anyone else including myself. Mrs. Guggenheim (though she may in a sense be represented by Mr. Moe) has been by far the largest donor of funds, and Mrs. [George W.] Warren has been actively interested in the collection for over 15 years. . . .

"[What I feel should be done now is:] 1) that just as soon as possible after clearing with Mr. Clark, copies of the proposed agreement be sent to members of the Committee on the Museum Collections with covering letters either from you or Mr. Clark, asking them to examine the document as quickly and as carefully as possible.

"2) that a meeting of the Committee be held in the near future at which Mr. Husted be asked to be present and possibly yourself, depending on how you feel about it.

"You may not feel a meeting to be necessary but I am convinced that in that case the Committee members individually should be consulted and made to feel and take real responsibility since so much is at stake.

"Meanwhile I am going to study the agreement and am asking Jim Soby, who happens to be in town today, to examine it too. His opinion will be extremely valuable.

"We have a really delicate problem here with two great private collectors represented on the Collections Committee. As it stands, I believe the agreement with the Metropolitan might well lose us one or both of those collections. If the agreement is altered with the sympathetic study of these two collectors, we will take an important step in maintaining their interest and increasing the probability of their bequest." Painting and Sculpture archive.

58. Letter, Barr to Clark, April 26, 1947. The text reads in part:

"A line to tell you that I have been studying the proposed agreement with the Metropolitan very carefully, have got Jim Soby to study it too, and have gone over it line by line with Jim Husted.

"I won't write you in detail the many questions and misgivings I have about it but I have asked Nelson to be sure to send copies to all members of our Committee on the Museum Collections and to ask you to call a meeting for thorough discussion if you have no objections.

"My principal concern is with the date 1910 which according to Jock and Nelson was proposed by the Metropolitan as a date to prevent us for asking for their paintings by Manet and Monet. Actually this is a date which has been mentioned by Francis Taylor on several occasions in the past few years and if allowed to stand, would mean that we would lose the "backfield" of our Collection plus those pictures of the Post-Impressionist generation which we might acquire in the future—*unless* the donors were to specify that pictures cannot be passed on to the Metropolitan for a stated number of years.

"I have several solutions to this and other problems about which, it you would like, I would be glad to talk with you." Painting and Sculpture archive.

59. Letter, Soby to Nelson Rockefeller, April 27, 1947. The full text is as follows:

"Thank you for sending me the proposed agreement with the Metropolitan Museum. I have had time to go over it only casually, and I would like very much to study it carefully and to send you in a

day or so any detailed suggestions which may occur to me. Meanwhile, however, there is one point, of extreme importance, which I'd like to mention at once.

"This has to do with the date—1910—set as a dividing line between the Metropolitan's field and ours. I know that Francis Taylor has always had this date in mind. Indeed he mentioned it to me several years ago, when I was the Museum's Director of Painting and Sculpture, during informal conversations on this subject. I looked as astonished as I could; this in fact was not very difficult, because I was actually very astonished indeed.

"If we agree to let the Metropolitan take over the work of deceased artists "whose work was substantially completed before 1910," we will give them late nineteenth and early twentieth century works which are of the greatest importance for our own purposes—as historical background for more recent paintings and sculpture. We will give them the period whose drawing power for the public is far greater than any other: the period of the great Post Impressionists, Cezanne, Seurat, Van Gogh and Gauguin. The public's interest in these men is nowhere near spent. Indeed, Wildenstein told me that only last week their Cezanne exhibition has been packed to the doors every single day.

"Under this arrangement we would also give the Metropolitan some of the very finest modern art. The cases are endless and I will give only one. Vuillard, one of the outstanding artists of our period, has become an important influence on a small but growing group of young painters in Paris. He is dead, and he did perhaps his finest work in the 1890s. But he is a live force today. And influence aside, his pictures are so remarkable in sheer quality that it would be a painful sacrifice to turn his *Mother and Sister of the Artist* over to the Metropolitan.

"I am worried, too, about the effect of such an arrangement on the important collectors who might be interested in leaving their collections to our Museum. On the other hand, I agree profoundly in working out some agreement with the Metropolitan, and your efforts in this direction have been the greatest possible encouragement to those of us who have worked on the Museum Collections. Can't we persuade the Metropolitan to accept 1880 as the dividing date? I do very much hope so." Painting and Sculpture archive.

60. Alfred H. Barr, Jr., "Highly Simplified Analysis of Metropolitan Proposal," April 27, 1947. MoMA Archives: Soby Papers, III.52.7.

61. Letter, Husted to Barr, May 17, 1947. Painting and Sculpture archive.

62. On May 16, 1947, Barr and Husted received copies of notes made by Susan Cable from her conversation on May 15 with Clark regarding the date of division. Clark's views were terse; he said only: "Our interest is in the modern field. That modern field might be considered to cover 60 years, but where there is any question of a derivation of ancestry, we might want to reach further back than 60 years, but in no case would we go back more than 100 years." Painting and Sculpture archive.

The dialogue between Clark and Barr on these matters seems in retrospect somewhat ironic. Every bit as much as Barr could have wanted—and perhaps *more* than he would have wanted—Clark seems always to have seen The Museum of Modern Art as a place that should always stay up-to-date and progressive. Yet Clark's own tastes as a collector made him unsympathetic with a great many contemporary acquisitions Barr made; eventually, in 1951, Barr's purchase of Alberto Giacometti's *Chariot* sealed for Clark the feeling that his "archaic views on the subject of what constitutes a work of art" were so removed from current collecting policies that he should resign from the Committee on Museum Collections; see letter, Clark to Barr, January 9, 1951 (MoMA Archives: Soby Papers, III.51.3). Barr's fervent hope was that Clark might leave to the Modern his exceptional Post-Impressionist masterpieces by Cézanne, Seurat, van Gogh and others. However, perhaps in part because he saw the Modern as essentially devoted to contemporary art (as well as for other reasons), Clark eventually divided his collection between the Metropolitan and the Yale University Art Gallery.

A similar disparity marked the courting of Sam Lewisohn: Barr struggled to persuade the collector of the justice of the Museum's commitment to the contemporary avant-garde, while he coveted much earlier and more traditional works from Lewisohn's collection. Lewisohn seems particularly to have been put off by the Museum's acquisitions, in the late 1940s, of paintings by New York School artists such as Adolph Gottlieb and Theodoros Stamos. (On the matter of what Lewisohn deemed the Modern's "esoteric" collecting in American art, and his reaction to Gottlieb and Stamos, see Barr's letter to Burden of May 22, 1947, in the Painting and Sculpture archive.) Ironically, when Lewisohn joined the board of the Metropolitan in 1949, he apparently felt rejuvenated by the more traditional context, and became a progressive force on that board until his death in 1951; see Lynes, *Good Old Modern,* p. 313.

63. A memorandum from Husted to Soby of June 3, 1947, states that both museums had agreed "to omit any date from the definitions of classic art and modern art and to leave this question to be agreed upon by the parties." MoMA Archives: Soby Papers, III.52.7.

64. An extensive file memorandum in the Painting and Sculpture archive details the discussions of this June 9 meeting. The group met at 3 P.M. and had before them a document for discussion dated June 5, 1947.

The text of the 1947 agreement did not mention an accord that had been struck verbally between Barr and the Metropolitan, whereby Picasso's 1905–06 *Portrait of Gertrude Stein,* which had been bequeathed to the Metropolitan by Stein on her death in July 1946, would be put on extended loan to the Modern during the ten-year period covered by the agreement. News of this loan agreement did, however, reach Alice B. Toklas, Stein's companion, and she wrote Barr in protest: "In spite of Gertrude Stein's liking for you . . . and her respect for your work she was never interested in The Museum of Modern Art. She made a deliberate choice between the two museums and she chose the Metropolitan" (October 2, 1947). Barr responded in a letter of October 17, mentioning his attempt to borrow the portrait from Stein for the 1939 Picasso show (she was willing, but complications associated with the outbreak of war in Europe prevented the loan), and his great disappointment at learning that the picture had been bequeathed to the Metropolitan. He enclosed a copy of the 1947 agreement between the two museums, and tried to summarize its import:

"Very Briefly: the agreement binds us to offer to the Met. at a reasonable price the best works from our collection when we feel that they are no longer part of the modern movement. With the money we will add new works to our collection. This permits us to keep our collection modern. At the same time the Met. no longer has to worry about a field which it has always considered an awkward problem, namely, the previous 50 years of the kind of progressive art which Miss Stein has championed.

"Acting upon this friendly agreement, the Met. has now bought from us a number of paintings which you will find listed. However, none of these paintings need be delivered for a period of ten years. For instance, the two Picassos which we have sold we will probably keep in our galleries until 1957 along with the dozen other Picassos we now own and those we may but or inherit in the future. At the same time the Met. no longer h[as] to *lend* us the only 20th c. painting of international importance it has acquired, namely, the portrait of Gertrude Stein by Picasso.

". . . Within 10 years we would then return the Gertrude Stein to the Met. permanently along with many of the best older works in our collection."

Toklas apparently was not mollified. Roland Redmond of the Metropolitan wrote to her on December 10, 1947, assuring her that, "As soon as the Metropolitan Museum is prepared to exhibit the work of the earlier modern artists, we will place on exhibit permanently the magnificant portrait which Miss Stein left to the Metropolitan by her will."

The portrait arrived at The Museum of Modern Art in late 1947; the label for its display is dated January 22, 1948. Barr wrote again to Toklas on February 7: "I thought you would like to have a copy of the release announcing the exhibition of the Picasso portrait of Gertrude Stein. We have hung the painting in the place of maximum honor opposite the entrance of the Museum." On February 24, Barr also wrote to Thornton Wilder, who was soon to see Toklas, explaining her distress and asking Wilder to convey "a few reassuring words on this point." On March 3, Wilder responded to Barr: "Yes just back from seeing Alice. Yes she is unhappy about it. For same reason. Gertrude had a prejudice against your museum. I never heard why. I think that Alice will be somewhat reconciled when she sees that it is a ten year loan and realizes that it will be side by side with the other fine Picassos." A letter from Toklas to Barr, also

dated March 3, thanked him "for sending the two photographs of the portrait in its present surroundings."

The Stein portrait remained at the Modern through the next year, with the exception of a brief period from September 14 to October 17, 1948, when it was loaned to the San Francisco Museum of Art. On December 12, 1949, Taylor of the Metropolitan wrote Barr: "We have had many requests to have the picture shown here at the Museum. I wonder, if you could let us have it at your earliest convenience as we would like to show it during the winter and spring of 1950 in connection with the paintings galleries which we have repainted and rehung. I also gather from communications which have been received that Miss Alice B. Toklas would welcome such an arrangement." On December 14, Barr gave instructions to return the painting to the Metropolitan, writing at the same time to Taylor: "We shall miss it very badly. . . . If after the winter-spring of 1950 . . . you could let us have it again we should greatly appreciate it." Apparently the picture never returned to the Modern. The loss of this additional benefit of the 1947 agreement may well have been a contributing factor in the Modern's growing disenchantment with the agreement after 1950. All correspondence, MoMA Archives: Barr Papers [AAA: 2176].

65. Letter, Barr to Nelson Rockefeller, June 11, 1947. MoMA Archives: Soby Papers, III.52.7.

66. Letter, Barr to Clark, June 18, 1947. Painting and Sculpture archive.

67. On June 18, 1947, Barr wrote to Jock Whitney to recount a meeting between Barr, Clark, and Redmond that morning, hours before Redmond was to bring the inter-museum agreement before the Metropolitan's board. The trio revised some wording with regard to apparent limitations placed on the Whitney and the Metropolitan, but the principal anxiety Redmond raised was that surrounding delay in delivery of artworks from The Museum of Modern Art to the Metropolitan: "Mr. Redmond then raised one very important problem. He said he feared that certain members of his Board might object to our retaining title and possession of the works we were selling to the Metropolitan for as long a period as ten years. Did I think we would be willing to transfer certain pictures within a short period (whereupon the Metropolitan would assume title).

"I replied that it was conceivable that we might be willing to pass on one or two of our Cézannes, but that I could not give him any real assurance, knowing that our Trustees much preferred to keep title and possessions for at least the decade of the installment payments.

"We discussed this at some length, going into the problem of what might already be considered classic. Mr. Redmond mentioned Gauguin, certain pictures by Van Gogh, Toulouse-Lautrec, even certain Matisses and early Picassos. I replied that I thought we would want to keep paintings by such artists for at least a decade and in some cases a good deal longer. I said I thought the Metropolitan was getting a very good bargain, considering the double possibilities of monetary inflation and the natural rise in value of such artists as Matisse and Picasso, and that from a purely financial point of view I would prefer to have our resources in these pictures rather than in money during the next decade. Furthermore that the Metropolitan was actually receiving, as a gift, works of art valued at about $65,000 (the Rainey Rogers' Daumier [*The Refugees* (n.d.)] and Mrs. Rockefeller's American Folk Art).

"Our discussion was frank and very amiable, but I gathered from it that we might well be faced with a great deal of pressure from the Metropolitan to deliver some of their purchases sooner than I, for one, had anticipated. From his arguments, it was clear that an arbiter would be much impressed by the fact that, as Mr. Redmond put it, Gauguin and Matisse were already exhibited in "classic" museums such as Boston." (*The Refugees* ultimately was replaced by the Daumier *Laundress* originally in the Bliss collection; see n. 9 above.)

Sending Clark a copy of his letter to Whitney on the same day, Barr told him that, immediately upon Clark's leaving the morning meeting, Redmond had produced a draft of a press release describing the three-museum agreement. Barr added, "He seemed rather nervous about his meeting with his Board this afternoon; but what he said made me nervous about the pressure we are likely to be under to deliver some of our pictures sooner than we wanted." All correspondence, Painting and Sculpture archive.

68. Redmond wrote to Barr on June 19, 1947, to report that there were "a number of points which gave the [Metropolitan's] Board considerable concern," and that approval in principle was contingent on clarifications, the principal among which would address "the question of when the objects of art to be purchased by the Metropolitan, listed in Schedule B, should actually be delivered to the Metropolitan Museum." He went on: "The discussion of the Board made it clear that the date of delivery of the objects of art to be purchased by the Metropolitan was the feature of the agreement which caused the greatest concern. As you know, the present draft provides that delivery shall not be made until such objects become 'classic art,' and the definition of the latter term is far from precise. It was pointed out by some of the Trustees, that the Metropolitan might pay the entire purchase price and acquire title to the objects but would not have the use of them until they ceased to be significant in the contemporary movement in art. Therefore, the Board felt that it might be subject to criticism if the paintings and sculpture should remain indefinitely in the possession of The Museum of Modern Art." Painting and Sculpture archive.

69. Letter, Barr to Nelson Rockefeller, June 20, 1947. Painting and Sculpture archive.

70. Letter, Soby to Barr, June 23, 1947. Painting and Sculpture archive.

71. Amended version of Redmond's press release of June 18, revised June 23. Painting and Sculpture archive.

72. Letter, Barr to Nelson Rockefeller, June 26, 1947. Painting and Sculpture archive.

73. Letter, Barr to Soby, July 1, 1947. "A little breakfast at the Knickerbocker Club at 8:15. Clark, Nelson, Husted, [Edward W.] Root, Redmond. Conclusion: Problem of time of delivery to be solved by setting a specific date on each picture. Trial balloon to include most important pictures which I list below. When you are relaxing, please put down a number after each title indicating the minimum period of years during which we should keep the picture, all things considered.

"Meeting amiable. Metropolitan inclined to humor us providing they have something definite by way of terminal date for delivery." Painting and Sculpture archive.

74. Letter, Soby to Barr, July 4, 1947. Soby here classifies twenty-seven works into three categories ("R for works whose impact is still strongly revolutionary —Q for works whose main virtue may be quality —M for works with some of both, medium") and lists not only a delivery date for each, but also figures indicating how long they would have been in the Museum by that time, and how much time would have elapsed since their creation. At the end of the letter he notes "One thing I should mention, though. I've tried to give the Met. a few things conspicuously early—the Picasso *Woman in White,* for example." Painting and Sculpture archive. (Soby's categorized list, with annotations by Barr, is reproduced as App. 4b, p. 55.)

The Cézanne still lifes were a special case. They had been bequeathed by Miss Bliss, but in her will it had been stipulated expressly that, should the Museum decide it no longer wanted them, they were to be given to the Metropolitan; see n. 9 above.

75. Memorandum, Soby to Barr, July 10, 1947. Soby describes the major change in the revised agreement as the elimination of any definitions of "modern" and "classic"—a change that he feels "virtually gives full power of decision to the depositing party. This seems to me an enormous advantage from our point of view. . . . Most successful meeting I think. Everyone most pleased both with principle of agreement and with the details of date, pictures involved, etc., etc. When I say we in all this I mean you of course, since you did all the work; it was simply easier to say we since I was doing the gabbing at the moment." Painting and Sculpture archive.

76. Memorandum, Barr to Nelson Rockefeller, July 10, 1947. "I am answering your question about Mrs. Guggenheim. Let me say that I talked with her again on Monday afternoon and went with her over the tentative lists of dates of delivery of pictures which we are selling to the Metropolitan. She seemed very much relieved to find that on the list very few important works would be delivered within fifteen years, and such pictures as her *Sleeping Gypsy* have a delivery date of twenty-five years from now. She repeated what she had said before, that she could not imagine the Museum without these important works as the foundation stones of the collection, although of course she is aware, if not entirely reconciled, to the idea that eventually they ought to pass to the Metropolitan. She seemed at the end of the conversation to be really satisfied with the plan as it now stands. If the Metropolitan should start haggling over

the dates, I doubt that we could lower the period of the terminal date of the big Rousseau to less than twenty five years without causing Mrs. Guggenheim some disquiet. I prefer to keep it at twenty-five." Painting and Sculpture archive.

77. Letter, Barr to Redmond, July 11, 1947. "I telephoned you this morning to see whether we could find a time next week for a discussion of the terminal dates of delivery of works of art in Schedule B. . . .

"Mr. Rockefeller has asked me to arrange this meeting. . . . I have in mind asking Mr. Moe, a wise counselor and one who, I think, can explain the point of view of our older Trustees better than I can. . . .

"Meanwhile before we meet I would like to explain how we fixed the terminal dates which are listed in the enclosed pages.

"I think we can all agree that excellent representation of the leading modern masters should eventually be included in the Metropolitan's collection after they have served an appropriate period here. My own feeling is that we should not keep paintings longer than 50 or 60 years after they were painted and perhaps considerably less. Our problem is to put this procedure in motion with due regard to the status quo. Passing by the American masters of the late 19th century who are superbly represented in the Metropolitan, let us consider the European painters who are still important as pioneers of 20th century movements.

"Cézanne is fairly well represented in both the Metropolitan and in our Museum. Of our five pictures, two or three might be passed on to you within 15 years or less, to help round out your group. We would like to keep a couple of the Cézannes which seem most closely to anticipate cubism and abstract art for as much as fifteen years longer, namely, 30 years from now. At that time we should be ready, I think, to pass along to you our principal cubist pictures, perhaps retaining a few as connecting links. When the Metropolitan becomes the center of study of cubist painting, we will no longer need even two Cézannes so that they, too, can go to you.

"Van Gogh and Gauguin were the principal forerunners of Expressionism, the other great movement of the first quarter of our century—a movement which includes Matisse, Rouault and Nolde on our list. If we had five Van Goghs, I should think that we should pass on to you one of them in the near future, two or three more in 15 years, keeping one or two until we are ready, and you are ready, to have the Expressionist generation fully represented at the Metropolitan, perhaps 25 years from now. At least one Van Gogh is essential to our survey of the history and principles of modern painting. . . ."

Barr then goes on to discuss further the cases of van Gogh and Gauguin, and the dearth of each in both collections; he hopes for gifts in the future "which would make it possible for us then to pass one or more to you without gravely weakening the educational structure of our collection. . . .

"Aside from these educational and circumstantial factors there are others which we touched on in recent conversation, namely, the feelings of some of our trustees whose activities as collectors and patrons of modern art have been deeply involved with the work of Cézanne, Van Gogh, Gauguin and Rousseau. For them—and with good reason—these artists are the pillars of modern painting and in a sense the principal glory of our collection. As one of them said to me the other day, 'I just can't imagine the Museum without Miss Bliss' Cezannes and the Rousseau *Sleeping Gypsy.*' I think we can understand this sentiment, at least we must not overlook it."

Attached to this letter is a memorandum Barr had drafted on July 9, 1947, titled simply "Summary" and listing the periods during which he wanted to keep at the Museum all the major works which were up for sale: the Cézannes for fifteen years, except for two smaller late oils and watercolors "which are less 'important' but valuable to us as sources for cubism and abstract art" (see App. 6, p. 58). For the generation of the 1880s—van Gogh, Gauguin et al.: "We keep 25 years to serve as background to expressionism and fantastic art." Rousseau should also stay twenty-five years "for influence on cubists and surrealists." Barr also wants to keep Pickett, Kane and other great 'primitivists' for 25 years. For Matisse, Rouault, and Nolde—"the expressionist generation"—he wanted to keep the best works for twenty-five years.

His notes on Picasso are: "Picasso *Coiffure* (1906) early work, fairly traditional; keep 20 years as part of Picasso group.

"*Woman in White,* important as our only example of Picasso's revolutionary post-cubist neo-classicism—keep 30 years unless we acquire others." Painting and Sculpture archive.

78. Letter, Redmond to Barr, July 16, 1947. "As suggested in our interview the other afternoon, I have drafted a proposed footnote to be added to Schedule B. I have assumed that there would be a column headed 'Final date by which delivery is to be made to the Metropolitan Museum,' and that in this column various dates will appear after each object. At the foot of the schedule there might be a note reading as follows:

"'Note: The parties have fixed the final dates by which the above objects of art are to be delivered to the Metropolitan Museum in the light of existing conditions and the present needs of Modern Museum. Should these conditions change or should Modern Museum acquire other examples of the work of said artists so that the said objects of art are no longer required to maintain the educational character of its collections, Modern Museum will deliver said objects of art as promptly as possible to Metropolitan Museum.'

"I believe such a footnote will soften the blow of the extreme length of time which the Modern Museum proposes to retain these objects of art. Even so, I am very doubtful as to the reaction of my Board to such long delays in the delivery of a number of important objects. I quite appreciate the point of view which you and Mr. Moe expressed but it is difficult to justify the present expenditure of large sums of money for objects of art which the Metropolitan will not be able to include in its collections until a generation hence." Painting and Sculpture archive.

79. See "Notes on discussions concerning the inter-Museum agreement, held on July 22 and 23, with Redmond, Whitney, Barr, and Moe added on the 23d," July 22, 1947. The notes read in part:

"Mr. Redmond said that he did not think he could persuade his board to accept the schedule of delivery dates, even with the changes proposed by Mr. Moe and Mr. Barr in a previous meeting on July 14. He suggested that we should reconsider the whole schedule with a view to selecting works which the Museum of Modern Art would be willing to deliver within ten years. Adding up the value of the paintings previously proposed for ten-year delivery, the total came to approximately $160,000, which with the 20% discount amounted to less than $130,000. Mr. Redmond suggested that we might try to increase this amount by adding certain other works so that the total would come to around $250,000. He suggested that the Metropolitan should agree to make payments of whatever total was agreed upon over a period of five years, delivery to be made within ten years. (Question of when title should be passed on was not discussed).

"No commitments were made on either side, but it was apparent that some such radical revision of Schedule B would answer the Metropolitan's desire for delivery within ten years of purchase, and our need to keep certain pictures for a much longer period.

"Mr. Redmond also proposed that at the end of five years or any time before that, a new schedule might be drawn up with additional works, as conditions change or as our collection increased." MoMA Archives: Soby Papers, III.52.7.

80. Letter, Barr to Nelson Rockefeller, July 29, 1947. "I explained [to Sam Lewisohn] that we now had a new plan involving cutting Schedule B so that we could keep all the pictures we wanted to more than ten years, selling to the Metropolitan only those we felt free to deliver at the end of ten, thereby reducing our income from over 500,000 in ten years to 200,000 or less payable in five years.

"Sam said that he was delighted with the new plan and felt relieved at the changes—not only because we were keeping certain pictures longer, but because he had felt we were biting off more than we should at one time.

"Now we are all clear in the Lewisohn direction." MoMA Archives: Soby Papers, III.52.7.

81. Letter, Redmond to Barr, August 6, 1947. Barr says of his discussions with Francis Taylor and others, "They were rather inclined to suggest the omission of the Davies, Du Bois, Hart, Kuhn and Speicher pictures. This would leave the list exclusively foreign art and might be helpful in our relations with the Whitney Museum." MoMA Archives: Soby Papers, III.52.7.

Much later, in a letter of August 15, 1949, Barr wrote to the Metropolitan's curator Robert B. Hale, saying of the 1947 reluctance to purchase these works: "I gathered that the Metropolitan at that time was looking to the Whitney Museum for advice on its American paintings and therefore did not want to

consider our American pictures until after the Whitney-Metropolitan merger had been finally enacted." Painting and Sculpture archive.

Barr was unhappy about this change. Writing to Redmond on August 13, 1947, he called it "an unfortunate precedent to set (though it might be to our advantage financially). It would give the impression that the Metropolitan is not interested in American art, even in works of outstanding excellence. You will recall that you asked to have Picasso included for fear his omission would be publicly interpreted as lack of interest on your part. Aren't you running a similar risk by omitting the Americans?" MoMA Archives: Soby Papers, III.52.7.

82. Letter, Horace H.F. Jayne (Vice-Director, The Metropolitan Museum of Art) to Barr, August 26, 1947. "Mr. Redmond tells me that Mr. Rockefeller now wishes to have the selection of objects of American Folk Art belonging to his mother included among the items to be purchased under the proposed agreement. In view of this fact Mr. Redmond suggested that we go over the list—Schedule C—again and determine which pieces we feel to be essential additions, since obviously the change of status from gift to purchase requires stricter discrimination." Painting and Sculpture archive.

Barr wrote to Soby on September 1, 1947: "Nelson wants to build up our purchase funds by selling, not giving, our Folk art to the Met. . . ." MoMA Archives: Soby Papers, III.52.7.

83. A telegram was sent to Barr in Vermont on September 10, 1947, with the message "IF YOU HAVE COMMENTS ON AGREEMENT OR RELEASE RENE WANTS YOU TO PHONE BEFORE EXECUTIVE COMMITTEE MEETING THURSDAY 3 PM." Painting and Sculpture archive.

A memorandum of the same day records "Comments of Alfred Barr on list of works to be sold to the Metropolitan Museum": "Recommends holding Cézanne *Bather* for the present. Believes Jim Soby agrees strongly with this. This means deducting $60,000 market value from the sales list.

"Recommends selling Maillol *Ile de France* and Picasso *Woman in White.*

"Believes we should keep Cézanne. Important for the Collection as a better security than $48,000 in the bank.

"Greatly regrets omission of American pictures; believes will make bad public impression. Suggests either that Metropolitan not interested in American painting, or our American pictures are bad." Painting and Sculpture archive.

84. "Amended Agreement Between The Metropolitan Museum of Art and The Museum of Modern Art," September 15, 1947. MoMA Archives: Barr Papers, Box 2.34.

85. Letter, Redmond to Barr, February 19, 1948. Painting and Sculpture archive.

86. Letter, Barr to Redmond, February 25, 1948. Painting and Sculpture archive.

87. On the Institute's name change and its disagreements with The Museum of Modern Art, see Serge Guilbaut, "The Frightening Power of the Brush: The Boston Institute of Contemporary Art and Modern Art," in *Dissent: The Issue of Modern Art in Boston* (Boston: The Institute of Contemporary Art, 1985), pp. 52–93.

88. Taylor's article contained a memorable metaphor of the contemporary artist "reduced to the status of a flat-chested pelican, strutting upon the intellectual wastelands and beaches, content to take whatever nourishment he can from his own too meager breast"; see "Modern Art and the Dignity of Man," *Atlantic Monthly,* no. 182 (December 1948), p. 32. See also "A Life Round Table on Modern Art," Life 25, no. 15 (November 11, 1948), pp. 56–79.

89. MoMA Archives: Soby Papers, III.52.7.

90. See Tomkins, *Merchants and Masterpieces,* pp. 307–08.

91. Ibid., pp. 307–09. In a press release issued October 1, 1948, the Whitney's board stated that it had become "increasingly apparent that there were serious divergences in the attitude toward contemporary art of the two institutions, especially with respect to the showing of advanced trends in the art of today. This disagreement in fundamental principles raised grave doubts . . . whether the Museum's liberal tradition could be preserved after the coalition." Painting and Sculpture archive.

The Metropolitan issued its own press release on the same day, stressing all that the larger museum had tried to do to accommodate the Whitney, and professing to lament the dissolution of their planned coalition. This release, dated October 1, 1948, cites the original board approval of a plan for coalition in January 1943, and the initial plan for the addition of a new building to the Metropolitan. It continues:

"While no formal agreement was ever executed because it was impossible to estimate building costs, many other steps were taken in the last five years in line with the proposed coalition. The plans for the reconstruction of the Metropolitan Museum were revised so as to provide for the location of a Whitney Wing on the Southerly side of the Metropolitan Museum. These plans also contemplated moving the American wing from its present site so that it could be directly connected with the Whitney Wing, thereby bringing the Metropolitan's collections of American decorative arts in close proximity to the space assigned to the exhibition of American paintings and sculpture. Mrs. Juliana Force, the Director of the Whitney Museum, was appointed an adviser in American art to the Trustees of the Metropolitan Museum and, on her recommendation, more than $40,000.00 was spent by the Metropolitan Museum in purchasing works of art by contemporary American artists. The Metropolitan Museum subordinated its exhibitions of American art to the Whitney Mseum and thereafter did not regularly exhibit contemporary American art. The expectation that the coalition would finally be achieved played an important part in the agreement between the Metropolitan Museum, the Museum of Modern Art and the Whitney Museum which was executed in September, 1947. The Trustees of the Metropolitan Museum have consistently indicated their willingness to carry out the proposed coalition and greatly regret the decision of the Trustees of the Whitney Museum to abandon this plan which would have made available to the public a comprehensive exhibition of American art by combining the artistic resources of both museums."

At the end of this release, the Metropolitan figuratively fired a warning shot across the bow of the Whitney, in a declaration of competitive policy that would have raised concerns at The Museum of Modern Art as well: "As a result of the abandonment of the plan of coalition, the Trustees of the Metropolitan Museum have decided to take an active part in the collection and exhibition of contemporary American art." Painting and Sculpture archive.

92. In the minutes of the meeting of the Coordination Committee of The Museum of Modern Art on June 13, 1949, happiness was expressed at the prospect of a Whitney building next to the Modern's, and it was suggested that the latter be built with its floor levels exactly even with those of the Modern. At this meeting the idea of a partial merger of trustees and staff was raised; but the failure of the proposed Whitney–Metropolitan merger was held as cautionary in suggesting that the friendship might be better preserved with less formal linkages. At subsequent meetings of November 30 and December 6, 1949, further evidence is given of the strong bond between the two programs; John Hay Whitney, had, for example, agreed to underwrite The Museum of Modern Art's sponsorship of the Whitney Museum's traveling exhibitions (which up till then had been under the aegis of the American Federation of Arts). MoMA Archives: Minutes of the Coordination Committee, Box I.2.

93. James N. Rosenberg, "Open Letter to Roland L. Redmond," no. 1, *The New York Times,* January 6, 1949. MoMA Archives: Soby Papers, III.51.9. See also "Rosenberg vs. the Met," *Newsweek,* January 31, 1949; and "Storm Center," *The New Yorker,* March 12, 1949.

94. See the minutes of the meeting of the Board of Trustees of The Museum of Modern Art, October 19, 1950, approving the loan to the Metropolitan of the works on the list of purchases. It is explained to the trustees that "The Metropolitan requested this loan, which would include important works by Cezanne, Maillol, Picasso, et al, to prove to the public that it was not neglecting modern European painting and sculpture as it had been publicly charged during the year." MoMA Archives: Board of Trustee Minutes, V.10.

The idea of this exhibition came from Nelson Rockefeller, who served on the boards of both museums. His proposal of such a show to the Metropolitan, without the prior assent of Barr or the Museum Committee on the Collections, Barr thought ill-advised, because it might seem to slight the other trustees on the committee. In an internal memorandum to d'Harnoncourt of June 22, 1950, he wrote: "I want to resume briefly some of the questions you and Nelson have raised recently about the Metropolitan.

"1) I think it would be of real advantage to the

Metropolitan to be able to show briefly the whole group of things bought from the Museum. . . . I gather that Nelson feels this might pave the way to further concord. I think he is right. . . .

"From our point of view also, I think it is wise to help the Metropolitan make clear to the public in general . . . that it is assuming responsibility for building up its future collections of modern art in collaboration with us. . . .

"Taylor, and probably Redmond also realize that the public is more interested in the 20th century than in any other period except perhaps the late 19th. Furthermore Rousseau has really been active in soliciting gifts and loans of modern European pictures even though they are poor in quality and the resulting exhibition is half-baked, fragmentary and does a real disservice to the prestige and understanding of modern painting.

"2) There is another side to the question which frankly disturbs me. This is purely internal. I gathered from what you said that Nelson actually felt he had promised this exhibition to the Metropolitan. If this is really true, he would have been acting without the knowledge of anyone on the Collections Committee or myself. I don't need to tell you that the Collections Committee includes a number of people who are quite jealous of their prerogatives in relation to the Collection. I know this from personal experience. We may also look back to the original Metropolitan negotiations which were at first carried on by Nelson and Jock, but which were then radically revised, I think greatly to our advantage, when the members of the Committee on the Museum Collections were brought in. The Metropolitan's present request incidentally again involves a delicate area, namely the late 19th century, which is closest to the hearts of our older Trustees. At the same time it seems enviable territory to the Metropolitan from the point of view of popular interest.

"I don't anticipate any serious objections from the Committee, but I do think it is extremely important not to commit the Committee on the Museum Collections to such a loan without giving the matter regular consideration.

"I realize that there are occasions in which you and Nelson and Jock may want to carry on discussions with the Metropolitan's opposite numbers without me. I do not in the least object to this, but I do want to be in on any decisions, and any serious discussions of policy, involving the Museum Collections." Painting and Sculpture archive.

95. O'Keeffe apparently held a grudge against the Modern for its failure to underwrite a catalogue of Stieglitz's work for a show held in 1947. In a memorandum to d'Harnoncourt of June 22, 1950, Barr noted that, "because of various resentments and her feeling that we were too unstable and 'fly-by-night,' O'Keeffe decided to give New York's share of the [Stieglitz] Bequest to the Metropolitan although the Metropolitan had an unrivaled record of hostility toward modern art." Interestingly, Barr, at the request of Frances Taylor, helped the Metropolitan choose which portion of the donation it would take (the other half went largely to The Art Institute of Chicago), and obtained from O'Keeffe the stipulation that works from the gift should be made available to The Museum of Modern Art for display when they were not being shown at the Metropolitan. Painting and Sculpture archive.

96. Carlyle Burrows, "Art in Review: Some Questions on the Collecting of Modern Art at the Metropolitan," *Herald Tribune,* July 10, 1949.

97. Barr wrote D'Harnoncourt on June 22, 1950, that "Taylor, and probably Redmond, also realize that the public is more interested in the 20th century than in any other period except perhaps the late 19th. Furthermore, Rousseau has really been active in soliciting gifts and loans of modern European pictures. . . ." Painting and Sculpture archive.

98. For an extended discussion of the perceived link between American art and U.S. Government propaganda during the Cold War, see Michael Kimmelman, "Revisiting the Revisionists: The Modern, Its Critics, and the Cold War," in *Studies in Modern Art 4. The Museum of Modern Art at Mid-Century: At Home and Abroad* (1994), pp. 38–55.

99. Letter, Barr to Nelson Rockefeller, July 20, 1950. MoMA Archives: Soby Papers, III.51.7. The minutes for the meetings of the Coordination Committee of the Museum on July 11, July 18, October 10, December 12, and December 19, 1950, show that it was discussing precautions to be taken to protect the institution's holdings in case of bombing attack; see MoMA Archives: Minutes of the Coordination Committee, Box 1.4–5.

100. According to Messer, "By 1951 the Metropolitan was making subtle overtures to Adele Levy, who had been a Trustee of The Museum of Modern Art since 1940, and was one among some half dozen School-of-Paris-oriented collectors that the Museum hoped might leave their pictures to the collection.

"The Metropolitan's flirtation with a member of this private preserve featured an aspect considered a pressing concern for both museums and collectors in the early 1950's—the necessity of safeguarding their art works in case of atomic attack.

"The Metropolitan had been allocated storage space at West Point by the government that it was supposed to distribute among the other New York museums. It confined The Museum of Modern Art to 1,000 cubic feet, urging it to take less if it could. At the same time it offered space to Mrs. Levy. She said she wanted to consult first with her 'own' museum" ("MoMA: Museum in Search of an Image," p. 276).

101. Francis Henry Taylor, in *Babel's Tower: The Dilemma of the Modern Museum* (New York: Columbia University Press, 1945); cited in James N. Rosenberg, "Open Letter to Roland L. Redmond," no. 7, *The New York Times,* January 12, 1949.

102. Robert Beverly Hale, "A Report on American Painting Today—1950," *The Metropolitan Museum of Art Bulletin* 9, no. 6 (February 1951), p. 167.

103. Tomkins, *Merchants and Masterpieces,* p. 309.

104. See Clark's letter to Barr of January 9, 1951, cited in n. 62 above. Upon Goodyear's resignation, Barr excerpted a letter sent to him by Goodyear on April 29, 1952, in which he resigned and stated his objections to the Rothko; see Barr's memorandum to Soby and d'Harnoncourt of May 13, 1952. MoMA Archives: Soby Papers, III.51.3.

105. Letter, Husted to Nelson Rockefeller, July 5, 1951. MoMA Archives: René d'Harnoncourt Papers.

106. See Barr's letter to d'Harnoncourt of March 31, 1952. MoMA Archives: D'Harnoncourt Papers. A later article, "An Important Change in Policy," in *The Bulletin of The Museum of Modern Art* 20, nos. 3–4 (Summer 1953), makes explicit the close relationship between the masterworks idea and the cancellation of the agreement: "In the course of putting this new policy into effect The Museum of Modern Art terminated the agreement of 1947 with the Metropolitan Museum of Art" (p. 3).

107. Letter, J. Kenneth Loughry (Treasurer, The Metropolitan Museum of Art) to Charles T. Keppel (Treasurer, The Museum of Modern Art), September 28, 1951. Painting and Sculpture archive.

108. Minutes of the meeting of the Board of Trustees of The Museum of Modern Art, March 13, 1952. MoMA Archives: Board of Trustee Minutes, V.3.

109. Ibid. After describing his conversations with Redmond, Whitney stated, "It was recognized in the agreement that it would be unwise to bind institutions indefinitely to a particular course of conduct or to the expenditure of funds for specific purposes. For these reasons, the agreement was for a ten year period, terminating on October 1, 1957. Under the terms of the agreement the Metropolitan Museum agreed to purchase twenty-six paintings, drawings, sculpture and the collection of American Folk art, for the sum of $191,000 payable in four annual installments, and the final installment was paid on October 1, 1951.

"The Chairman said that there has seemed to some of the Trustees, since the agreement has served its purpose and the Museum's relationship with the Metropolitan Museum is on a friendly basis, that there would be little value in continuing a binding agreement for the remaining five-year period. Mr Redmond has consulted his Executive Committee in regard to this matter, and they have agreed to terminate the agreement provided that delivery is made immediately of some, if not all, of the works they have purchased. [It was stipulated that some works could remain, and that d'Harnoncourt and Theodore Rousseau were to discuss this question further.]

". . . Mr. Alfred H. Barr, Jr. said that an obligation to deliver these works at this time would deprive the Museum of eight paintings and sculptures on view continuously and he expressed the hope that the Museum could exhibit the objects until we find some substitutions. . . .

"After discussion and upon motion made by Mr. Husted and seconded by Mr. David Rockefeller, it was voted unanimously to authorize the proper officers of the Museum to negotiate the termination of the present agreement between the Metropolitan Museum of Art and the Museum of Modern Art on such terms as they deem wise, in the common inter-

est of all concerned and with the well-being and welfare of the community in mind."

110. Memorandum, Barr to d'Harnoncourt, March 20, 1952. MoMA Archives: D'Harnoncourt Papers.

111. Minutes of the meeting of the Board of Trustees of The Museum of Modern Art, June 12, 1952. "The Chairman reported that the termination of the agreement with the Metropolitan Museum had been agreed to by the Board of the Metropolitan and that the negotiations had been conducted on a high and friendly level. The question of when the pictures the Metropolitan had bought would be delivered, has been determined to the satisfaction of both parties. Under the circumstances and in light of developments, Mr. Alfred H. Barr, Jr. has negotiated for the repurchase of two paintings by Matisse, 'The Gourds' and 'Interior with a Violin Case,' which were sold to the Metropolitan under the terms of the agreement. He would have liked to have bought back also the Rouault, 'Portrait of Lebasque,' but the Metropolitan would not consent to its sale. Prior to concluding the negotiations, Messrs. Whitney, Clark, Moe and d'Harnoncourt were consulted and approved the conditions." MoMA Archives: Board of Trustee Minutes, V.13.

112. In a letter to Rousseau of October 14, 1952, Barr reviewed the negotiations between the Metropolitan and the Modern regarding the return of the two Matisses:

"On May 31st I wrote you suggesting that we follow the terms of the original agreement, which require us to pay you the market value in case we failed to make delivery. This market value represented the appraisal as of 1947 ('unless redetermined' at 'intervals of not less than one year'). You paid us 20% less than this value so that if we now paid the full value it would represent 25% more than what you paid. In the case of the two Matisses this would come to $14,500, as René has already pointed out in his letter of July 24th. This represented a more or less legalistic approach.

"On May 25th, while I was in Europe, René called me to say that the presidents of our two institutions had agreed that you should keep the Rouault which had been in question and that we would repurchase the two Matisses at a current appraised market value. He asked me to suggest an appraiser and I proposed [Justin K.] Thannhauser, in the belief that he knew the market and would be completely fair-minded as well as realistic. (Actually I believe that Thannhauser has done a great deal more business with you than he has with us, if it came to any question of unconscious prejudices.)

"I believe that you approved Mr. Thannhauser as appraiser and that he gave the following valuations:

"*Gourds*—$5,000

"*Interior with a Violin Case*—$10,000

"Later on, in your letter of June 19th, you suggested that we add 25% to these valuations, a proposal which was based on your belief that original 'market value' was the price you actually paid, though actually you paid 20% less as I have indicated above. Since you were not involved in the original negotiations this misunderstanding was quite natural—but your proposal would have raised the price almost $4,000 above Mr. Thannhauser's appraisal.

"This does not seem to us quite fair in view of the fact that we accepted 20% less than the mutually agreed upon market value in 1947, whereas you are now suggesting that we pay 25% more than a valuation proposed by a mutually agreed upon commercial appraiser in 1952.

"In support of this you quote Paul Rosenberg's valuations of $8,000 and $15,000 respectively. I have just returned from Paris where, as you know, prices are quite a lot higher than they are here. I happened to see at Galerie Maeght a Matisse the same size as ours and even the same year, 1919, an interior with a figure standing by a window, of good quality and coming from one of the greatest twentieth century collections, that of Alphonse Kahn. The *asking* price of this picture was $12,000 and that was at the most"expensive" gallery in Paris. I suppose that Maeght would have lowered this price considerably to us as a museum purchaser. This would seem to me to confirm Thannhauser's rather than Rosenberg's valuation. And we both know that Mr. Thannhauser is definitely inclined toward high rather than low prices.

"However, in deference to your feeling that Thannhauser undervalued the paintings, I now propose that we compromise on $16,000.

"Won't you let me know how you feel about this? We are having a meeting of our Committee on the Museum Collections on the 21st of October. We should like to clear up the matter at that time."

Rousseau replied on October 21: "I have discussed the question of the two Matisse paintings and am glad to be able to say that the Metropolitan Museum of Art will accept your suggestion that we compromise at $16,000." Three days later, Barr reported to Nelson Rockefeller that the matter had been resolved, adding, "I hope that this is the last obstacle which stands in the way of concluding our institutional divorce." All correspondence, Painting and Sculpture archive.

113. See Barr's memorandum to d'Harnoncourt of March 20, 1952, in which he evaluated the works sold to the Metropolitan through the 1947 agreement, and discussed the new committee. MoMA Archives: D'Harnoncourt Papers.

Barr further urged d'Harnoncourt in a memorandum of March 31, 1952, that the committee should be set up soon, and proposed that its membership should include "Clark, Goodyear, Mrs. Guggenheim, Whitney, Soby (ex officio as chairman of the other committee) and Nelson if he would like to. . . . In any case, as I understand it, I should not take the initiative or lead the discussion." See also the letter from Whitney to Soby of March 3, 1953, announcing that the time had come to form the committee, and naming its members as Goodyear, Rockefeller, Clark, Guggenheim, Soby, and Mrs. David Levy. All correspondence, Painting and Sculpture archive.

114. See n. 98 above.

115. Minutes of the meeting of the Board of Trustees of The Museum of Modern Art, December 11, 1952. MoMA Archives: Board of Trustee Minutes, V.14.

116. Cited in "An Important Change in Policy," *The Bulletin of The Museum of Modern Art* (Summer 1953), p. 3.

117. Minutes of the meeting of The Board of Trustees of The Museum of Modern Art, December 11, 1952. MoMA Archives: Board of Trustee Minutes, V.14.

118. When the trustees received the first report of the committee on masterworks, it came with a preamble: "Inasmuch as two Trustees had recently asked the Committee to make selections from their collections, it was decided to commence with a choice of one work of art from recent important gifts and lists of future bequests. It was not felt urgent to make immediate selections from the Museum Collections, though many works acquired through the Lillie P. Bliss Bequest and funds provided by Mrs. Guggenheim and Mrs.John D. Rockefeller, Jr., would certainly be included"; see the minutes of the meeting of the Board of Trustees, June 10, 1954. MoMA Archives: Board of Trustee Minutes, V.15.

It is clear that, among trustee pictures, Barr was especially keen to secure several owned by Clark. In a memorandum to d'Harnoncourt of December 14, 1953, Barr affirmed that he thought the Seurat *Parade* was "the most important single canvas in any of our Trustee's collections," and that the van Gogh *Night Café* and the Cézanne *Card Players* "were almost in the same class." He added, parenthetically: "Perhaps I've never told you that the *Parade* was the first picture I tried to secure for the Museum. That was in the fall of 1929. The price was, as I recall, $125,000.00. I think we were able to raise $30,000.00 but what with the crash, no more. Clark, a trustee at that time, bought the picture shortly afterwards." Painting and Sculpture archive.

119. Minutes of the meeting of the Board of Trustees of The Museum of Modern Art, June 10, 1954. MoMA Archives: Board of Trustee Minutes, V.15. The idea was presented here by Soby.

120. Minutes of the meeting of the Coordination Committee of The Museum of Modern Art, June 3, 1953. MoMA Archives: Minutes of the Coordination Committee, Box 2.2.

121. See the minutes of the meetings of the Coordination Committee of The Museum of Modern Art on June 3, June 17, and September 29, 1953. MoMA Archives: Minutes of the Coordination Committee, Box 2.2. The stumbling block in these plans for a show of pledged works seems to have been Clark's feeling that the move was a little too transparent and pushy in its acquisitive overtones, and hence that it might offend potential donors. Barr wrote to Burden on December 14, 1953: "I think we are wise to give up the 'pledged' show in view of Stephen Clark's very firm opposition. Had he opposed it simply on the grounds that he did not want to take part, we might still have proceeded, but when he extended his opposition by *advising* us that we might offend peo-

ple generally, I feel we would run a serious risk of estranging him by not accepting his council." MoMA Archives: Soby Papers, III.51.1.

Nonetheless, such an exhibition was held, at the end of the anniversary year (opening May 24, 1955), as a complement to the "25th Anniversary Exhibition" held October 19, 1954–February 6, 1955, and as a "fishing ground" for possible new "masterworks" acquisitions. Barr wrote to Burden on June 17, 1955, that he and d'Harnoncourt both thought "that we ought to ask the members of the Committee to examine the exhibition of paintings now on the second floor very carefully in order to make their choices for the masterworks list. Both the exhibition and the lists are directly connected with the principal function of the Policy Committee, namely the direction and formation of the Masterworks collection, both actual and potential." MoMA Archives: Soby Papers, III.50.12.

122. No minutes were taken at this meeting, but a memorandum prepared by Barr and Soby on April 9, 1953, reconstructs the discussion; see MoMA Archives: Soby Papers, III.51.1.

Apparently, "one of the proposals agreed upon" at the meeting was that members of the committee should be notified whenever an exceptionally important work of art appeared on the market so that the work might be considered for purchase by an individual or directly for the Museum" (letter, Barr to Goodyear, May 6, 1953). Accordingly, Barr sent all committee members a memorandum on May 5, 1953, regarding Rousseau's *Dream,* which Sidney Janis was evidently preparing to sell. All correspondence, Painting and Sculpture archive.

123. The Policy Committee made these designations at a meeting on May 27, 1954; see the minutes of the meeting of the Board of Trustees of The Museum of Modern Art, June 10, 1954. MoMA Archives: Board of Trustee Minutes, V.15.

124. Letter, Barr to Burden, June 17, 1955. MoMA Archives: Soby Papers, III.50.12.

125. Letter, Barr to Mrs. David Levy, April 12, 1957. Interestingly, when Mrs. Levy did make her gifts to the Museum (not including the Manet), she declined to have them designated as Masterworks or otherwise restrict their future "since she did not wish to handicap the Museum by a 'dead hand'"; see letter, Barr to Soby, April 30, 1957. MoMA Archives: Soby Papers, III.50.11.

126. Memorandum, Barr to members of the Policy Committee on the Museum's Permanent Collection of Masterworks, December 27, 1954. Painting and Sculpture archive.

127. Memorandum, Barr to members of the Committee on the Museum Collections, December 27, 1954. Painting and Sculpture archive.

128. Memorandum, Barr to members of the Policy Committee on the Museum's Permanent Collection of Masterworks, March 3, 1955. Painting and Sculpture archive.

Barr discussed the draft of the masterworks policy statement in a letter to Whitney of March 29, 1955, explaining the reservations and amendments that had come from various sources, with special attention to the suggestions of Clark. Another letter, of March 30, 1955, from Barr to Burden further illuminates the reservations of other committee members, especially as regards questions of eventual changes in the policy and possible deaccessioning of masterworks. All correspondence, Painting and Sculpture archive.

129. The minutes of the meeting of the Board of Trustees of The Museum of Modern Art on May 2, 1956, include the following "PREAMBLE AND RESOLUTION TO ESTABLISH THE MUSEUM'S PERMANENT COLLECTION OF MASTERWORKS":

"In its early years the Museum of Modern Art, primarily devoted to loan exhibitions, planned its Collections with the stated policy of eventually passing on the works of art to other institutions or otherwise disposing of them as they matured or no longer seemed useful.

"However, the Trustees have recently determined, as a radically new departure, to establish a collection of works of art, limited in number and of the highest quality, which shall remain permanently in the Museum's possession. This new policy, proposed by the Chairman of the Board, was approved after lengthy discussion by the Trustees at their meeting of December 11, 1952, and publicly announced on the following February 15. Nevertheless, it still remains to pass a formal motion officially establishing the collection.

"After discussion, it was, on motion made and seconded, unanimously resolved that:

"1. The Trustees of the Museum of Modern Art herewith confirm the establishment of a Permanent Collection of Masterworks of Modern Art.

"2. The Permanent Collection of Masterworks shall comprise works of art selected from the Museum's general Collection together with such additions as may be approved by from time to time by the Board of Trustees.

"3. In general, the Permanent Collection of Masterworks shall not include works of art executed prior to the mid-nineteenth century.

"4. The Collection of Masterworks shall have the same degree of permanence as the collections of the other great museums of this country. No work of art accepted as a gift for the Permanent Collection of Masterworks shall be eliminated from it except in accordance with the conditions, if any, originally stipulated by the donor.

"5. No works of art shall be eliminated from the Permanent Collection of Masterworks, and no material change shall be made in the policies governing the Permanent Collection of Masterworks, unless approved by three quarters of the Trustees of the Museum then in office." MoMA Archives: Board of Trustee Minutes, V.17.

130. Letter, Barr to Nate Springold, December 14, 1956. Painting and Sculpture archive.

131. Letter, Barr to Nelson Rockefeller, December 21, 1956. Painting and Sculpture archive.

132. The eleven works were Brancusi's *Bird in Space* (?1928), Cézanne's *Still Life with Apples,* van Gogh's *Starry Night,* Kane's *Self-Portrait* (1929), Lehmbruck's *Kneeling Youth* (sic) and also his *Standing Woman* (1910), Matisse's *Piano Lesson,* three paintings by Picasso—*Les Demoiselles d'Avignon, The Three Musicians* (1921), and *Night Fishing at Antibes* (1939)—and Rousseau's *Sleeping Gypsy.*

133. No official minutes of the meeting of November 30, 1956, were kept. Notes made by Barr were formalized in a document titled "Meeting of the Policy Committee for the Permanent Collection of Masterworks Held on Friday, November 30, 1956, at 10:00 A.M. at Mr. Burden's Residence." In this same document the proposed amendment is reported as follows:

"*Whereas* heretofore it has been the Museum's policy eventually to pass along to other museums, or otherwise dispose of, all works of art in its collection unless included in the Permanent Collection of Masterworks;

"*And whereas* it appears that this policy by discouraging donors would result in the loss to the Museum Collections of highly desirable works of art;

"*Be it resolved* that the Museum be empowered to accept for permanent possession certain works of art of acknowledged excellence even though they should not immediately qualify for its Masterworks Collection, and that the donors be assured of the permanent status of suich works in the Museum's Collections." Painting and Sculpture archive.

In Barr's report of a subsequent meeting ("Meeting of the Policy Committee for the Museum's Collection of Masterworks Held on Thursday, January 24, 1957, at 11:00 A.M. in the Sixth Floor Committee Room"), a further problem was noted in the practice of ranking potential gifts from donors (especially non-trustee donors) according to "A" lists (nominated for "masterwork" status) and "B" lists (held to be desirable); though the idea was expressed that this distinction should be abolished lest potential donors not take seriously the desire for "B-list" works, the committee eventually reaffirmed the wish to keep the masterwork designation rather exclusive, in order to maintain its appeal as an elite category. Painting and Sculpture archive.

134. Letter, Barr to Jonathan Marshall (Editor, *ARTS Magazine*), January 23, 1957. MoMA Archives: Soby Papers, III.50.11.

135. In the Department of Painting and Sculpture, the Museum has long had an explicit injunction against selling the works of living *American* artists; more recently, it has followed the policy of never selling the work of any living artist, except to "trade up" to what is considered a better, more important work—and this, if at all possible, with the artist's consent.

136. MoMA press release no. 20a, "Museum of Modern Art Opens Large Exhibition of its Own Painting and Sculpture," June 15, 1945. Department of Publication Information, The Museum of Modern Art.

Nothing Sacred. William Wellman. 1937. Carole Lombard, Walter Connolly, and Fredric March

Nothing Sacred: "Jock Whitney Snares Antiques for Museum"[1]

The Founding of The Museum of Modern Art Film Library

Mary Lea Bandy

"First catch your hare!," Iris Barry liked to say, borrowing from a classic approach to haute cuisine.[2] Barry, The Museum of Modern Art's first film curator, was referring to the challenge, however preposterous it might have seemed in the mid-1930s, of archiving films. It was not only a matter of determining the condition of existing prints and negatives, a difficult enough task in itself. As Richard Griffith, Barry's successor, would note in his informative "Report on the Film Library, 1941–1956," it was also nearly impossible to locate the "very important films made between the invention of motion picture projection in 1896 and about the year 1918. . . . [The] films of this period, which saw the invention and elaboration of motion picture narrative by such pioneers as D. W. Griffith, Georges Méliès, Mack Sennett, Edwin S. Porter, and Thomas H. Ince, seemed to have disappeared utterly. These films were for the most part the mislaid property of defunct or forgotten corporations and men. Not even their owners cared what became of them, and often did not remember where they were."[3]

No more easily warned off the case than Philo Vance or Sam Spade,[4] Barry searched locally and globally, saving thousands of motion pictures during her tenure as film curator from 1935 to 1951. The securing of the Museum's Film Library, and Barry's role at its helm, could appear in retrospect to be as eccentric or as fanciful as the plots of the Warner Bros., Metro-Goldwyn-Mayer, and Harold Lloyd releases of the silent and early sound periods that Barry eagerly sought to acquire.[5] Underlying her efforts was a fundamental commitment to the overall mission of the Museum, and in particular to the structuring of a methodology for film education, that would carry the Film Library through six decades of achievement and occasional setbacks, and which remains remarkably cogent today.

The original plan for a museum representing all the arts of the twentieth century took into account the notion that objects produced in their final form by machines, and in multiple editions, should be included selectively and representatively as works of art. Collections of design objects, photographs, and films were envisioned, to be assembled by curators whose intelligence and knowledge of modernist art would enable them to recognize works of quality and achievement. Adherence to the highest standards of taste and discrimination was required, with

Safety Last. Fred Newmeyer and Sam Taylor. 1923. Harold Lloyd

Philip Johnson setting the example as head of the Department of Architecture in the early 1930s.[6]

It was perhaps inevitable that, from time to time, reaction to such a rigorous premise would result in shifts in the Museum's curatorial policy. In the previous issue of Studies in Modern Art, *The Museum of Modern Art at Mid-Century: At Home and Abroad*, essays on exhibitions mounted in the 1950s by the departments of Photography and Architecture and Design examined attempts to broaden support for, or to democratize, their collections.[7] If the "Family of Man" photography exhibition and the Good Design program departed from the traditional curatorial postures established at the founding of the originating departments' respective collections—which had derived from a purist, even elitist approach to modernism—these projects were consistent with the Museum's intent at mid-term, so to speak, to attract a larger public.

By contrast, the Film Library embraced issues of popular taste and broad audience appeal right from its start in the 1930s. Essential to the Film Library's development was the staff's perception of, and relationship to, the most popular art—and one of the major industries—of the twentieth century: the movies. The Film Library faced the challenge of articulating a pastime as art (it still does), and throughout its history the department[8] has felt it necessary to point out its awareness that film is at once art and entertainment. As early as 1933, for example, Barry wrote brief reviews of current films for members in the Museum *Bulletin*, including this comment on *She Done Him Wrong*, directed by Lowell Sherman: "The Hollywood product at its vital best—perfect pace, brilliant execution, robust approach to and attack upon a simple subject, and a perfect vehicle for that original screen personality, Mae West."[9]

Her approval of West's Diamond Lil, who invited a rather younger Cary Grant to come up and see her sometime, stirred up "something of a hornet's nest. Friends of Mrs. John D. Rockefeller, Jr.,[10] indignantly called her on the phone. How could the Museum endorse that vulgar film with that awful Mae West? . . . Mrs. Rockefeller made inquiries. . . . [Barry] explained that in writing these reviews she thought she was performing one of the Museum's most important functions, that of distinguishing the original from the academic in contemporary art," and that the film's adaptation from West's stage play was "wholly recreated in terms of the screen by Lowell Sherman and the author-star. Mrs. Rockefeller saw the point and from then on was an enthusiastic supporter of efforts to have the Museum include motion pictures in its program."[11]

At the time of the Museum's founding in 1929, there were no film programs in U.S. cultural institutions, no film festivals, repertory movie theaters, or graduate schools of cinema studies. The new medium of television, then in its experimental phase, had not yet spawned TNT or AMC or Blockbuster Video stores. There were a few film societies and undergraduate courses, and what we nostalgically recall (or attempt to restore) in cities and towns across the country: motion-picture palaces, stunning in their Art Deco, Moorish, Egyptian, Mayan, Chinese, and mix-and-match décors—the flagships among some twenty-three thousand theaters that in the late 1920s screened the newest "talking pictures" to over one hundred million people each week.[12] By the mid-1930s, when the Museum was experimenting with selected screenings, the Depression had registered a decline in movie-theater attendance to a weekly average of seventy to eighty million ticket-buyers. While much of the country was still traversed on dirt roads, local theaters went deeper into debt to install the newest projection and sound systems. By the 1950s, when the Eisenhower Administration undertook to pave the nation with interstates (our first superhighways), and televisions were being purchased by millions of American consumers, the motion-picture industry itself had to change tactics to keep, if not broaden, its public. Experiments in wide-screen formats such as CinemaScope and VistaVision, as well as the drive-in movie theater, were pushed forward. The traditional studio system—its strict controls of creativity, style, and production—collapsed, with location shooting, international co-productions, and the rise of the independent producer changing the industry. Studio control of film distribution was shattered by Federal antitrust legislation, and studio libraries, known as "backlogs," and photo archives began to be sold (to television companies), dispersed, or discarded.[13]

She Done Him Wrong. Lowell Sherman. 1933. Cary Grant and Mae West

The instability of the industry in the 1950s would affect the Museum's Film Library. The Library had not altered its original curatorial approach, nor did it intend to, but "by the time of Miss Barry's retirement as Director and Curator in 1951, the Film Library was having to run very fast to stay in the same place."[14] As this article will discuss, the Library was burdened by its rapid expansion during the late 1930s and the 1940s, and had much to do to take care of the collection, which by 1950 included some nineteen million feet of film. The principles underlying its founding, and the agreements established with the industry and filmmakers in the mid-1930s, had made it possible to be in this curatorial pickle.

Three Who Dared

Three members of the Museum family, each expert, knowledgeable, and daring, had

worked together to give shape and form to the Film Library, and by the mid-1950s none was any longer at the helm. In guiding the Library's birth and adolescence, Barry and the Museum's Founding Director, Alfred H. Barr, Jr., proved to be masterful in their dual roles as sophisticated showmen and serious educators; they were supported by a Trustee who was something of a showman himself, John Hay Whitney. Surviving correspondence reveals the sympathy, intelligence, and shared hunting instincts of this trio, each of whom respected the others' talents and ability to seize the right moment.

Alfred Barr had traveled extensively in Europe and the Soviet Union, and had met the Russian director Sergei Eisenstein in 1928, when Eisenstein was editing the film *October*.[15] Barr was concerned that the Museum's film program be international in scope, and he was keen to bridge the gap between the avant-garde film artist and the public. As early as 1929, in his report to the Founding Trustees of The Museum of Modern Art, Barr had expressed his commitment to establishing departments of architecture, photography, and film.[16] However, "in its first crowded years, which also coincided exactly with the first years of the depression, the new Museum could spare neither time, money, nor personnel to develop this plan."[17] In June 1932, Barr revisited the subject:

That part of the American public which could appreciate good films and support them has never been given a chance to crystallize. People who are well acquainted with modern painting or literature or the theatre are amazingly ignorant of modern films. The work of and even the names of such masters as [Abel] Gance, [Mauritz] Stiller, [René]Clair, [E. A.] Dupont, [Vsevolod] Pudovkin, [Jacques] Feyder, [Charles] Chaplin (as a director), Eisenstein, and other great directors are, one can hazard, practically unknown to the Museum's Board of Trustees, most of whom are interested and very well informed in other modern arts. But many of those who have made the effort to study and to see the best films are convinced that the foremost living directors are as great artists as the leading painters, architects, novelists and playwrights. It may be said without exaggeration that the only great art peculiar to the twentieth century is practically unknown to the American public most capable of appreciating it.[18]

The exception to Barr's premise was the young venture-capitalist, polo player, and thoroughbred breeder John Hay Whitney, nicknamed "Jock." A Museum Trustee, Whitney recently had begun to acquire late–nineteenth-century paintings, by Degas, Whistler, and Renoir.[19] By the early 1930s, he also had become a keen investor in an array of businesses, and was well on his way to becoming one of the leading backers of the legitimate theater, sponsoring *The Gay Divorce*, *Dark Victory*, *On Borrowed Time*, and *Life with Father* before the end of the decade (with a few misses among the hits). In 1933, his foresight and shrewdness, stimulated by his eagerness to become involved in the film industry, led Whitney to gamble on what would prove to be a major investment in the development of motion pictures: Technicolor. His enthusiasm for the movies no doubt was a principal factor in the decision, arrived at with his sister, Joan Whitney Payson, and his cousin Cornelius Vanderbilt ("Sonny") Whitney, to invest in a production company to make films in Technicolor. Jock Whitney also liked to take risks, where no one else saw the opportunity as he did.

Whitney frequently went to Hollywood. Early in 1933, he was taken to see a screen test by his friend Merian C. Cooper, who had succeeded David O. Selznick as head of production at RKO Radio Pictures. (During Selznick's tenure Cooper had produced and codirected *King Kong,* released in March of that year—the phenomenal success of which rescued RKO, just then put into receivership by the Irving Trust Company. Sonny Whitney had invested in *King Kong.*) Cooper and Whitney met Herbert T. Kalmus, a chemical engineer who in the 1910s had pioneered the development of Technicolor, a two-color process that resulted in release prints dyed bluish green and red. In the early 1930s, short films but few features were produced in Technicolor. Kalmus continued to improve the system until in 1932 he had perfected a three-color process, with release prints dyed yellow, cyan, and magenta. Kalmus screened for the two men a test of Mary Pickford as Alice in Wonderland (for a proposed project with Walt Disney that did not go into production) that had been shot using the improved process. By this time, Technicolor, Inc., "had completed the building of its first three-component camera and had one unit of its plant equipped to handle a moderate amount of three-color printing. The difference between this three-component process and the previous two-component process was truly extraordinary. Not only was the accuracy of tone and color reproduction greatly improved, but definition was markedly better."[20]

In 1933, Disney was one of the few filmmakers seriously interested in Technicolor. Disney realized the potential of color in animated films, designing scenes and characters imaginatively without worrying about a resemblance to "real" colors. He first released a three-color Technicolor short, *Flowers and Trees,* in 1932,

Steamboat Willie. Walt Disney. 1928. Mickey Mouse

continued his Silly Symphony series with the highly successful *Three Little Pigs* in 1933, and introduced Mickey Mouse in color in 1935.[21] (Disney had pioneered the use of sound in animated films, releasing the first sound cartoon, *Steamboat Willie,* in 1928.)

Whitney, too, readily grasped Technicolor's potential. His response was expressed in a cable to his cousin Sonny on April 1, 1933: "HAVE VERY INTERESTING PROPOSITION POSSIBLE BIG MONEY MAKER AT LOW RISK WITH ATTENDANT GREAT ARTISTIC SUCCESS OR HAVE I GONE TO HOLLYWOOD?"[22] Kalmus later reported that "after thorough investigation of the Technicolor situation by Mr. Whitney and his associates, and as a result of many conferences, a contract was signed between Technicolor and Pioneer Pictures, Inc., on May 18, 1933, which provided for the production of eight pictures, superfeature in character and especially featuring color."[23]

With characteristic confidence and swiftness, Whitney thus plunged into the motion-picture business, and as President of Pioneer Pictures he hired Cooper as its principal producer. Of the screen tests made at that time, Pioneer donated to the Museum those of John Barrymore as Hamlet (1933)—unique color footage of the actor in one of his most famed roles—and Katharine Hepburn as Joan of Arc (1934). *Becky Sharp* (1935, direction begun by Lowell Sherman, completed by Rouben Mamoulian) would be the company's first full-length Technicolor production. Although the film seems static, its cinematographic rhythms limited by the difficulties of manipulating three cameras in unison, Mamoulian composed scenes of richly saturated color to enhance dramatic effects, notably in a sequence of blue-uniformed officers racing across the screen, red capes swooping behind them.[24]

In October 1935, Whitney and Selznick formed Selznick International Pictures, with Whitney as Chairman and East Coast manager, and Selznick as President in charge of production. Whitney immediately asked his partner to produce motion pictures in Technicolor, and he pressed for a comedy. In 1937, after some resistance and two Technicolor dramatic features—*The Garden of Allah* (1936, Richard Boleslawski) and *A Star Is Born* (1937, William Wellman)—Selznick produced *Nothing Sacred,* directed by Wellman in 1937 and starring Carole Lombard and Fredric March.[25] Ben Hecht, coauthor with Charles MacArthur of the 1928 Broadway hit *The Front Page,* scripted for *Nothing Sacred* another scornful exposé of the newspaper business, centered on a particularly nasty publicity stunt, to satisfy Whitney's demand for comedy—but with an edge: Selznick cabled Whitney, "YOU WANTED COMEDY–BOY YOU'RE GOING TO GET IT, AND BE IT ON YOUR OWN HEAD, AFTER THIS ONE I AM EITHER THE NEW MACK SENNETT OR I RETURN TO DR. ELIOT."[26] The culmination of the Whitney-Selznick partnership, the most successful of their Technicolor films and of Hollywood productions to date, was *Gone with the Wind* (1939, Victor Fleming, with Sam Wood and George Cukor, uncredited).

Whitney had invested in Technicolor to enable him to produce and distribute films in color; in turn, he produced color films to promote the Technicolor process, thereby protecting the family's investment (the Whitneys were, collectively, the major holder of Technicolor common stock). He was also a collector of paintings by artists preoccupied with renderings of texture and space—of structure, form, and light—in color. In the 1940s and 1950s, he would expand his collection of Post-

Impressionist and Fauvist painting, acquiring work by Cézanne, van Gogh, Seurat, Matisse, Derain, and Vlaminck, among others. I believe it was not only the unique combination of the collector's and the investor's instincts but also his appreciation of color experiments and his eye for the new in art that intrigued Whitney about making Technicolor films and made him eager to push filmmaking in a new direction. He took calculated risks, and he was willing to fail. Whitney may or may not have believed that in the future almost all films would be shot in color, but his support and enthusiasm for Technicolor made him an important contributor to the development of the motion picture.

Such seemingly coincidental activities of collecting art and producing motion pictures also made Whitney a sympathetic backer of the Museum's newest curatorial effort. He agreed to serve as the first Chairman of the Film Library Trustee Committee—an entirely appropriate choice, as he was the only Trustee then actively involved in the industry. As such, he fully understood, and moved comfortably in, the worlds of high art and entertainment.[27]

The third member of the trio was, of course, Iris Barry. Barry's tenure at the Museum began in 1932 and ended with her retirement in 1951.[28] Born in Great Britain, she had belonged to the circle of vanguard poets, writers, and young filmmakers such as Alfred Hitchcock that gathered in London in the 1920s. She "had been taken up by the contentious, dynamic artist-writer Wyndham Lewis"[29] and later married the poet and critic Alan Porter. Barry, too, wrote poetry, as well as several books and reviews of books and plays; most notably, she served from 1925 to 1930 as a film critic for the London weekly *The Spectator* and as motion-picture editor for the *Daily Mail.* Also in 1925, she became a founding member of the London Film Society, and her first volume on the cinema, *Let's Go to the Movies,* was published and well received.[30] In crisp and witty style, Barry took on the motion-picture world, its practitioners and its audience; she described the star system, and film comedy, and distinguished the accomplished from the banal. Her defense of cinematography as art presaged her efforts a decade later to establish a collection of film art:

Wyndham. Lewis. *Iris Barry Seated.* 1921. Pencil, ink, and watercolor, 12½ x 13¼" (31.7 x 33.7 cm). Reprinted from *Wyndham Lewis: The Early Decades* (New York: Washburn Gallery, 1985)

It is true that each scene, or each second of time, can be aesthetically beautiful in itself in the same way as a painting can: but all the scenes can also be beautiful in relation to each other, and in the passage from scene to scene, from moment to moment, detail by detail . . . is a fugitive and unanalysable beauty, similar to that of the ballet, but still richer because less stereotyped, and more spiritual. I wonder sometimes why the Montmartre cubists go on cubing when the cinema exists.[31]

Clear-eyed and unsentimental, Barry analyzed the great early talents whose films she would later acquire—Griffith, Chaplin, Lloyd, Douglas Fairbanks, Mary Pickford, Lillian Gish, and Buster Keaton—cited Hitchcock as a "promising recruit for the future," and worked her way around the European and American studios discerning how good films got made:

Warner Bros. are the sole owners of pictures of Rin Tin Tin*, the dog. The money that Warner Bros. make out of their* Rin Tin Tin *pictures is almost enough to float a battleship.* Rin Tin Tin *makes it possible for Warner Bros. to give us films like [Ernst Lubitsch's]* The Marriage Circle. . . . *We all learn to write in our copybooks, "The dog is the friend*

of man." In this case the copybooks are right.[32]

After her marriage with Porter broke up and she lost her job at the *Daily Mail* (she was, as she put it, "severed rather forcefully"[33]), Barry found her way to the United States. She initiated the forming of the New York Film Society in 1930, and in Fall 1932 she was hired (as a volunteer) by Philip Johnson to be the Museum's librarian. Alfred Barr was then on an extended leave in Europe,[34] and that same fall, in Rome, he spent several weeks preparing "a carefully graded list of films which I thought worthy of inclusion in a film collection,"[35] using as his guide Paul Rotha's *The Film Till Now*, a study of international film history published in 1930.[36] Barry was introduced to Barr shortly after he returned to New York, in 1933. She had come to the right place at the right time. Like Hedda Hopper, Barry knew the importance of wearing just the right hat (she liked broad brims), and she was soon recognized for her sharp intellect and enthusiasm, her extensive knowledge of film, and her firm critical eye. Barr could have found no one more expertly qualified to assemble an international film collection in New York.

Although it is evident that Barr intended the Museum to build such a collection from the start, there were aspects to consider in its establishment, starting with financing, and including searching for prints and negatives, clearing rights, and determining technical and preservation needs. In the years 1929–32, the Museum had concentrated on exhibiting modern painting while it considered principles and policies of organizing a permanent collection. From 1932 to 1935, the debate extended to film. A committee was formed in 1933, with Edward M.M. Warburg as chairman and Mrs. Rockefeller and Whitney as principal members. At their urging, Barry prepared a series of ten film programs, "The Motion Picture, 1914–1934," which were presented in 1934 at the Wadsworth Athenaeum in Hartford, Connecticut. An inquiry was made to the presidents of several hundred colleges and museums, offering to circulate the series "should the Museum decide to found a film collection. . . . The response was so emphatically positive that from here on events moved rapidly. In April 1935, John E. Abbott and Iris Barry presented to the Trustees a report outlining the scope of the projected new department, the purpose of which was stated to be 'to trace, catalog, assemble, preserve, exhibit and circulate to museums and colleagues single films or programs of all types of films, so that the film may be studied and enjoyed as any other one of the arts is studied and enjoyed.' In May, the Museum of Modern Art Film Library was established as a separate corporation, all the stock being held by the Museum, with John Hay Whitney as president . . . and Iris Barry curator. On June 25, 1935, the founding of the Film Library was made known publicly. On July 10, its first acquisitions were announced, including Edwin S. Porter's celebrated *The Great Train Robbery* (1903). Thus swiftly, in less than four months after the final decision was made, the first Film Library in the world was created."[37] The Rockefeller Foundation committed a major grant of $100,000 to found the Film Library, and Whitney provided continuous and generous support, underwriting the initial research, making contacts within the industry, acquiring films, and much more in his two decades as Chairman.

Barry emphasized that the work of the Film Library would be first and foremost "to create a consciousness of history and tradition within the new art of the motion picture."[38] What was radical in her concept was stated in the legal document

***The Great Train Robbery*. Edwin S. Porter. 1933. Justus D. Barnes**

Signing of the document establishing the Film Library Corporation, The Museum of Modern Art, New York, July 1935; left to right, John Abbott, Iris Barry, Jock Whitney (seated), Conger Goodyear, and Nelson A. Rockefeller representing the Board of Trustees

signed by Whitney and Museum President A. Conger Goodyear establishing the Film Library Corporation in July 1935, "for the purpose of assembling a collection of motion picture films suitable for illustrating the important steps historically and artistically in the development of motion pictures from their inception and making the said collection available at reasonable rates to colleges, schools, museums, and other educational institutions."[39]

At the time of Barry's appointment as Curator of the Film Library, she was married to John E. Abbott, who had been employed in a Wall Street firm and who soon joined Barry at the Museum as Director of the Film Library.[40] Their immediate goal was to build the Film Library into an inclusive, yet selective, archive. In their April 1935 report they stated their intent to search out "all kinds of films . . . narrative, documentary, spectacular, Western, slapstick, comedy-drama, musical, animated cartoon, abstract, scientific, educational, dramatic and news-reel."[41] If Alfred Barr had stressed the need to make European and Soviet films better known, Barry and Abbott knew they had to pursue a two-pronged approach: Both Hollywood and Europe would have to be visited as soon as possible.

Hooray for Hollywood

Hollywood in the mid-1930s, as the world capital of film production, was chockablock with émigrés and visitors from foreign film studios as well as the West End and Broadway. As earlier styles and movements establishing modern painting, sculpture, and graphic arts had evolved in Europe's principal cities and in sunny Provence, so film production had flourished in the same locales in its first decades, from London, Berlin, and Moscow to Nice. Major developments in film, however, quickly progressed not only in New York but also in the previously unchartered territories, artistically speaking, of northern New Jersey, Florida (briefly), and Burbank. From the end of World War I, when film production was severely hampered throughout

Sunrise. F. W. Murnau. 1927. George O'Brien and Janet Gaynor

Europe, "Hollywood"—meaning a sizable portion of Southern California—saw the rise of sprawling studio complexes and a network of supporting trades. Hollywood imported leading foreign talent, directors, actors, writers, and art directors such as Chaplin and Garbo, Lubitsch, and Victor Sjöström, who would have a major impact on every aspect of film art. F. W. Murnau, to cite but one example, renowned as the director of *Nosferatu* (1922) and *Der Letzte Mann* (*The Last Laugh,* 1924), was invited by the Fox Film Corporation to abandon Germany's UFA Studios for Hollywood, where he directed *Sunrise* (1927), a masterpiece of the late silent period, with a music and effects soundtrack. Murnau brought with him European expressionism, and the exquisite lyricism of the film's rhythms, atmosphere, poetic performances, and pessimistic outlook profoundly touched John Ford and other young directors.[42]

Filmmakers had been lured to Hollywood in the 1910s and 1920s because they were highly successful, or at least were seen to hold promise as future stars. In the 1930s, others less fortunate arrived, having been forced to flee, or wisely choosing to leave, an increasingly fascistic Europe. (Some, like Billy Wilder, would stay and become major artists; others, like Jean Renoir and Douglas Sirk, would do significant work and return to their native countries some years after World War II.) Barry knew the recent, and earlier, work of a wide range of filmmakers and realized the importance of enlisting their cooperation to acquire their films.

Of critical importance as well was how to locate and save the earliest films, whether made in New York and New Jersey or on the West Coast or abroad. It was clear that a core purpose of the Film Library was to conserve the work of the pio-

neers who had developed the narrative form: The films of Méliès, Porter, Griffith, Sennett, and Ince, previously noted, and those of Thomas Edison and European masters were essential to an analysis of an evolving art form that swiftly had become the world's most popular entertainment. Lillian Gish, the innovative and exquisite leading actress in Griffith's films who is properly considered the First Lady of the Screen, often spoke of film's great power as the "universal language"; she meant that silent films, which were screened throughout the world in the 1910s and 1920s, could be enjoyed and understood by all peoples whether or not they could read or write. Expressive acting and camerawork, simple but "true" stories, exciting action, "slapstick" comedy, powerful drama, and tender emotions enabled millions of viewers to experience and to appreciate great art firsthand, and in quantity, thanks to a highly competitive global distribution network.

By the mid-1930s, however, the pioneering producers and directors had been forgotten in the rush to turn out new films every week. The entire era of the silent film, which had come to a close so recently in the late 1920s in America, was considered the distant past. In later years, Barry reflected:

It was, I think, the advent of the talkies and—by that time—their prevalence which had slowly made us realise what we lacked or had lost. True enough, we had seen, heard and rejoiced in Public Enemy *[and] the first husky words of Garbo in* Anna Christie. *Yet something, not only of technique, seemed missing. Should we never again experience the same pleasure that* Intolerance, Moana *or* Greed *had given with their combination of eloquent silence, visual excitement and that hallucinatory "real" music from "real" orchestras in the movie theatres which buoyed them up and drifted us with them into bliss? . . . But the silent films and the orchestras had vanished forever and when could one hope to see even the best of the early talkies again? How could movies be taken seriously if they were to remain so ephemeral, so lacking in pride of ancestry or of tradition?*[43]

Le Voyage dans la lune (A Trip to the Moon). Georges Méliès. 1902

Lady Windermere's Fan. Ernst Lubitsch. 1925

Barry and Abbott set their tasks, and in Summer 1935 they went to Hollywood to meet industry leaders, establish good relations, and convince producers to donate prints to the new Film Library. Jock Whitney persuaded Mary Pickford to host a reception (for which he was sent an itemized bill) at Pickfair, the famous home of Pickford and Douglas Fairbanks. Barry and Abbott were to be introduced to Hollywood's nobility by Pickford, who was then waiting for a divorce decree to end her marriage to Fairbanks. On August 24, after a garden reception and candlelit dinner on the terrace, Barry screened scenes from several movies, arguing convincingly that films should be deposited in a museum.

Assuring her audience that the Museum would not be commercially competitive, Barry pointed out that in 1935, film already had a brief (some forty years) but important history, and that "unless something is done to restore and preserve outstanding films of the past, the motion picture from 1894 onwards will be as irrevocably lost as the Commedia dell'Arte or the dancing of Nijinsky."[44] She illustrated her point by showing a selection of films from 1896 to the then-present: *The May Irwin–John Rice Kiss* (1896, The Edison Company); *The Great Train Robbery* (1903, Edwin Porter; Edison), an early Western with tinted gunsmoke; an excerpt of another tinted film, the historical drama *The Coming of Columbus* (1912, Colin Campbell; Selig); *The New York Hat* (1912, D. W. Griffith; Biograph), starring Pickford and Lionel Barrymore; the New Year's Eve sequence in which Chaplin stages a ballet with dancing rolls of bread in *The Gold Rush* (1925, Chaplin; United Artists); and a reel from *All Quiet on the Western Front* (1930, Lewis Milestone; Universal), concluding with a stunning new Technicolor short of 1935, *Pluto's Judgement Day*, starring Pluto, Mickey Mouse, and a bevy of hellcats, no doubt loaned for the occasion by Walt Disney himself.[45]

The guest list was reported by *The Los Angeles Times* to have included Harry

Reception at Pickfair, Hollywood, California, August 24, 1935; left to right, Mrs. Samuel Goldwyn, John Abbott, Samuel Goldwyn, Mary Pickford, Jesse Lasky, Harold Lloyd, and Iris Barry

Cohn, Merian Cooper, Sam Goldwyn, Harry Warner, Jesse Lasky, Walter Wanger, Walt Disney, Harold Lloyd, Ernst Lubitsch, Mervyn LeRoy, and Will H. Hays, among others.[46] Barry recalled in 1941:

That evening, pioneers of the industry like Mack Sennett met newcomers like Walt Disney for the first time, old acquaintances were renewed and new ones made. . . . This glimpse of the birth and growth of an art which was peculiarly their own both surprised and moved this unique audience. . . . There was a tiny, shocked gasp at the first appearance of Louis Wolheim in the program's brief excerpt from All Quiet on the Western Front*: he had been dead so very short a time. Was fame so brief? Of course there ought to be a museum of the film! At the close of the program, Will H. Hays and Mary Pickford endorsed the Film Library's undertaking in enthusiastic speeches. Samuel Goldwyn and Harold Lloyd as well as Miss Pickford promised their films. A major obstacle had been overcome in gaining the attention and understanding of the industry as a whole. It remained to work out a basis on which films owned by large corporations rather than by individual producers could be made available to the Film Library.*[47]

Although no films were acquired during the Hollywood stay ("We never did get to see Louis B. Mayer"[48]), the Film Library, with help from Jock Whitney, secured donations from Harold Lloyd and Warner Bros in October 1935.[49] Samuel Goldwyn, Twentieth Century–Fox, Paramount, M-G-M, and Walt Disney would follow, with verbal promises from Columbia, RKO, Universal, Mary Pickford, Walter Wanger, and Leon Schlesinger Productions for Méliès's films. Chaplin and Griffith both said no. (With the persuasive charm of Lillian Gish, Griffith would

Potemkin. Sergei M. Eisenstein. 1925

acquiesce two years later; see pp. 93–95 below.) Before securing prints, however, it required extensive negotiations with the financial and business chiefs of the major producer-distributor companies, headquartered in New York. In October 1935 agreements were negotiated with Warner Bros., Universal, Twentieth Century–Fox, and Paramount, and subsequently with M-G-M, RKO, and others, that the Film Library might make prints, at its own expense, from negatives held by the companies, and in some cases even could make negatives, for preservation, and for use "both within and without the Museum's walls for strictly educational and non-commercial purposes only."[50]

The importance of this agreement cannot be overstated. "This was a signal triumph," Barry later remarked, "for not only could the institution obtain and use prints of the films it wanted but the propriety of its undertaking had thus been recognized."[51] In a broader sense, by successfully securing donations and acquisitions from the pioneers and practitioners of the American motion picture, and making them available to schools, Barry could be said to have launched film studies in the United States. It was a brilliant step, ensuring that the study of film history could be independent of commercial exploitation. For the first time, Hollywood producers would allow their films to be seen without charging a fee. We can only imagine how difficult it was to sell this concept, and to keep it alive through the years. (In a changed Hollywood, even Whitney ultimately became discouraged: He quit the movie business in 1954, and in November 1955 he retired as Chairman of the Film Library Trustee Committee.)

The pace of acquisitions from 1935 through the early 1950s was rapid, nonetheless. After their Hollywood foray, Barry and Abbott searched for films throughout Europe in 1936, meeting colleagues in London, Paris, Berlin, Warsaw, Moscow, and Stockholm who were building collections and willingly would exchange films. Their first stop was London, where old friends were visited and many films acquired—early works such as *Rescued By Rover* (1905, Cecil Hepworth) and Len Lye's animation

shorts, including *Kaleidoscope* (1935). Nonfiction films included a recent poetic masterpiece, *Night Mail* (1936, Harry Watt and Basil Wright, with verse by W. H. Auden), on the overnight postal service by train from London to Glasgow, produced by the GPO Film Unit, a documentary group under the auspices of the General Post Office; and *Housing Problems* (1935, Arthur Elton and Edgar Anstey), from the British Gas, Light & Coke Co. Next was Paris, where in addition to a print of Fernand Léger's *Ballet mécanique* (1924), Barry acquired films by Louis Lumière, Ferdinand Zecca, and Emile Cohl, as well as avant-garde works by Marcel Duchamp, Eugène Deslaw, Germaine Dulac, Jean Epstein, Louis Delluc, and Alberto Cavalcanti.

Barry and Abbott went on to Berlin, during the summer Olympics when foreign visitors were welcome, and they were able to make contact with staff at the Reichsfilmarchiv. "It was a relief to find that, contrary to rumor, the rather markedly non-Aryan films of Germany's great silent period 1919–28 had not been destroyed, so that the Film Library was able to obtain virtually everything it desired"—including Robert Wiene's *Das Kabinet des Dr. Caligari* (*The Cabinet of Dr. Caligari*, 1919)—"without anyone's seeming aware that most of the men who had made [the films] were in exile. (We had talked to [Alexander] Korda and to [Erich] Pommer in London, to [G. W.] Pabst in Paris.)"[52] A print of Eisenstein's *Potemkin* (1925) was made from an original negative purchased by Joseph Goebbels from the Soviet Union in 1933 as a model for Nazi propagandists. In Moscow, a young American, Jay Leyda, introduced Abbot and Barry to Eisenstein, and Barry acquired a selection of Soviet films, by Lev Kuleshov, Yakov Protazanov, and others; Leyda would soon follow them back to New York to be Barry's assistant, bringing with him Eisenstein's drawings and film material.[53]

Iris Barry in Berlin, summer of 1936

By December 1937, the Film Library had secured the right to choose films from five existing collections of films produced between 1898 and 1917: Edison, Biograph, Kleine, Triangle, and Vitagraph (through Warner Bros.). Barry and her colleagues had discovered hundreds of prints and negatives "by tracing and investigating old vaults and by receiving the cooperation of contemporary producers through personal conversations in New York, Chicago, Hollywood, London, Paris, Berlin, Moscow, Leningrad and Stockholm."[54] All of the major Hollywood producers were cooperating, with one exception: Chaplin was reluctant to donate features or to allow many of his films to be shown by the Film Library. This seemed something of a sore point with Barry, who made note of his resistance in her reports and articles through the years:

And where, especially, are the Charlie Chaplins? True, there are a few here . . . early and delicious, but so few. . . . [Chaplin] has paid the Museum protracted visits, has enjoyed seeing its films as well as its paintings . . . and has promised it his films, ultimately: for the present, the Film Library can do nothing but wait, sad though expectant.[55]

According to Barry, during her summer 1935 visit to Hollywood, D. W. Griffith had "said amiably but firmly that he, for one, was not interested in the preservation of his own films and that nothing could convince him that films have anything to do with art. It is pleasant to record that he has latterly become a warm supporter of the Film Library's undertakings."[56] Subsequently, "more than 2,000,000 feet of the product of the Edison Company, headed by the father of

motion pictures, was acquired from his heirs; a like amount of the productions of the American Biograph and Mutoscope Company [sic], for which D. W. Griffith did his crucial early work, was salvaged from the mouldering Biograph studio. Most of the mature work of Griffith, and some of that of Ince, was rescued from forgotten storage vaults, while individual films were tracked down in such unlikely places as cellars, attics, hat closets, and even garbage cans."[57] Over the next decade, "to the immense Biograph, Edison, and Griffith collections were added the almost equally large collections of Douglas Fairbanks, Sr., and William S. Hart, consisting of almost the entire output of these distinguished film-makers. Players such as Gloria Swanson, Colleen Moore, Douglas Fairbanks, Jr., Richard Barthelmess and Irene Castle presented considerable numbers of their films, while single pictures came from individuals all over the world."[58]

Let's Go to the Movies

Nineteen thirty-five to 1939 was a period of reaching out to a worldwide community, a time to build relationships with a variety of film organizations, museums, and schools. The Film Library expanded its efforts to circulate organized series, beginning in 1935 with two programs that initiated a structure for the study of film in broad chronological strokes, in the process unwittingly establishing a rigid pattern that would have to be broken periodically in the decades that followed. The first series, "A Short Survey of the Film in America, 1895–1932," grouped new acquisitions into six categories: The Development of Narrative, The Rise of the American Film, D. W. Griffith, The German Influence, The Talkies, and The End of the Silent Era. Barry chose to focus on pioneers of the East Coast and Hollywood for the second series, "Some Memorable American Films, 1896-1934," in which she introduced genre categories: The "Western" Film, "Comedies," Documentary Films, Mystery and Violence, and Screen Personalities. In 1937, two European programs were organized: "The Film in Germany" comprised Legend and Fantasy, The Moving Camera, and Pabst and Realism, and "The Film in France" offered From Lumière to René Clair and The Advance Guard. Nineteen thirty-eight saw the addition of "The Swedish Film," "Post-War American Films," and "The Work of D. W. Griffith, 1907–24."

In 1936–37, the Film Library was in correspondence with 1,520 universities, colleges, preparatory schools, museums, film societies, high schools, hospitals, the Works Progress Administration projects, Jewish centers, drama groups, and prisons, of which more than one hundred organizations rented film series. It was estimated that 288,904 people had attended screenings by June 1937.[59] Extensive staff work was required to meet demands. Scores for musical accompaniment for silent films were newly arranged by composer and collector Theodore Huff. The scores and program notes written by Film Library staff were distributed with the film series. A key staff member was William L. Jamison, formerly with The Edison Company, who researched, traced, and secured films and photographs, made photographic enlargements of film frames, and reshot faded stills. Three fellowships sponsored by the Rockefeller Foundation brought additional staff: Paul Rotha, from London for documentary work, for five months; and two researchers who stayed on, Jay Leyda, from Moscow and Eisenstein's studio, to write a summary of the film history of Russia and the Soviet Union; and Richard Griffith, a student from Haverford College, to assist Barry.

In 1937, the Academy of Motion Picture Arts and Sciences (AMPAS) voted to present a Special Award for Distinctive Achievement to The Museum of Modern Art Film Library "for its significant work in collecting films dating from 1895 to the present, and for the first time making available to the public the means of studying the historical and aesthetic development of the motion picture as one of the major arts."[60] The award was announced on March 10, 1938, at the Academy's annual ceremonial dinner in Los Angeles, at which Special Awards were also given to Mack Sennett, "that master of fun, discoverer of stars," for his comic technique; to Edgar Bergen, for his comedy creation, Charlie McCarthy; and to W. Howard Greene, for color photography on *A Star Is Born*. Also presented that year was the first Irving G. Thalberg Memorial Award, to Darryl F. Zanuck. Thalberg, who had died suddenly in September 1936, had been a member of the Film Library Advisory Committee, and had assisted in the acquisition of a dozen M-G-M features of 1919–30.[61]

AMPAS had been formed in 1927, in part to smooth over the chaos created by competing technologies and standards, and the distribution of motion pictures in sound; to ease labor disputes; and to keep censorship of content under industry, rather than governmental, control.[62] (Lubitsch noted at the Pickfair event in 1935, after seeing the *Irwin–Rice Kiss* of 1896, that "current restrictions would bar it today."[63]) The Academy immediately began to promote the "sciences" of sound recording, engineering, photographic techniques, and color processes, as well as the "arts" of directing, acting, screenwriting, and cinematography. In March 1936, it presented a Special Award to D. W. Griffith for distinguished achievement and for "his invaluable initiative and lasting contributions to the progress of the motion picture arts."[64] According to Frank Capra, then Academy President and worried about a boycott of the ceremonial dinner due to labor fights over the setting up of guilds within the industry, "our top caper to hype the attendance was to persuade the giant of all filmmakers, D. W. Griffith, to come out of his retired oblivion and accept from the Academy a special statuette for his legendary pioneering in films."[65] The Academy's recognition of the careers of the pioneers, and of the Museum, was further validation by the industry of the Film Library's work, and a long and cordial relationship with the Academy was underway.[66]

Iris Barry, ca. 1940. Photograph by George Platt Lynes

In Winter 1937–38, Barry and Abbott were invited by Columbia University's Department of Fine Arts to teach a course on "The History, Aesthetic, and Technique of the Motion Picture." Classes were held at the East 46 Street screening room, comprising a one-hour lecture, a ninety-minute screening, and a half-hour discussion:

[A] small class of students undertook an examination of the physical, intellectual and psychological bases of the motion picture. An introduction to the practical elements involved in production . . . was paralleled by a study of diverse theories of composition and of the functions of the various executants. The financial structure of the industry and the aesthetic peculiarities of the medium came under survey. . . .

This course was necessarily experimental in nature, for before it the methods and instruments of instruction in the subject were as unmarshalled as those for the study of Greek drama in the 15th century. Since many colleges and universities are establishing permanent cinema divisions, doubtless many among them will look to the findings of this course.[67]

I Am a Fugitive from a Chain Gang. Mervyn LeRoy. 1932

So successful was the first course that Barry and Abbott offered it again in 1938–39 and 1939–40, shifting from the screening room to the new Museum and the Columbia campus. Actors, writers, and directors traveling back and forth from Europe and New York to Hollywood—Hitchcock, Selznick, King Vidor, James Cagney—shared their experiences with the classes. An active member of the Film Library Advisory Committee was Erwin Panofsky, Professor of Fine Arts at the Institute for Advanced Study at Princeton University; the renowned scholar of the Van Eycks and Dürer lectured on Sarah Bernhardt and Buster Keaton, *The Great Train Robbery*, Garbo, and Mickey Mouse.[68]

This was a particularly hectic period for Barry. In 1938, she traveled to Paris for a meeting to establish the International Federation of Film Archives, jointly sponsored by the Museum, the Cinémathèque Française, the British Film Institute, and the Reichsfilmarchiv. The Federation, known as FIAF, was founded as a nonpolitical membership organization that would strive to collect and save films from every film-producing country, creating a network for the exchange of materials, research, and programs.[69] That same year, at the invitation of the French Government, the Museum mounted an exhibition of American art at the Musée du Jeu de Paume.[70] The "Brief History of the American Film" prepared by the Film Library was the most widely attended exhibit, and, along with the architecture and photography sections, was "the most enthusiastically received of all the [exhibits in this] comprehensive show. In films and in architecture the United States was seen at its most original, most exuberant, most enjoyable, most understandable."[71]

Back in New York, Barry and colleagues prepared for the opening of the new Museum building on West 53 Street, in 1939, with a 490-seat theater for daily screen-

ings. Barry inaugurated the film program with three series: "A Cycle of 70 Films, 1895–1935," "Georges Méliès: Magician and Film Pioneer," and "The Non-Fiction Film: From Uninterpreted Fact to Documentary." Whitney was quite occupied then, too, with the December premieres of *Gone with the Wind*, first in Atlanta, then in New York and Los Angeles. (The Museum's Film Study Center conserves the forty-pound, 260-page *Gone with the Wind World* Premiere Campaign Scrapbook that thoroughly covers the many activities of the 1939 siege of Atlanta.[72])

The Film Library wished to demonstrate, in its first regular programs, the origins of the medium and developments in all its subsequent forms, from fantasy to nonfiction. Cycles presented at the Museum in 1940 advanced themes from the various circulating series prepared in 1935–39, and were intended to be a continually expanding series of films immediately available to educational and cultural institutions. These included: "Ten Programs: French, German and Russian Films," "A Short History of Animation: The Cartoon, 1879-1933," "Three French Film Pioneers: Zecca, Cohl and Durand," "Abstract Films," "Great Actresses of the Past: Bernhardt, Rejane, Fiske and Duse," "The March of Time," "The Films of Douglas Fairbanks," and "Forty Years of American Film Comedy: Part I."

After assisting Paul Rotha, who had come to New York in 1936–37 to lecture and do research on the documentary film, Richard Griffith continued as Barry's assistant, authoring the program notes for "The Non-Fiction Film." Noting that "the first movies were entirely factual," Griffith traced the evolution of the newsreel and instructional and travel films to the documentary film, using as one example Robert Flaherty's *Moana* (1926), which interweaves dramatic interpretation with observation of traditions, rituals, seascape.[73] Films were screened on such subjects as housing, labor, malnutrition, the Mississippi River basin, the coming world war, and people in faraway lands; narrative films using documentary technique, including LeRoy's *I Am a Fugitive from a Chain Gang*, were also shown.

Barry was vitally concerned with placing D. W. Griffith within the museum context in the early days of the Film Library's exhibition program, having finally persuaded the director in December 1937, with invaluable assistance from Lillian Gish, to donate his papers, which included production records, letters, ledgers, scrapbooks, scripts, and music scores as well as negatives and prints of his features. In 1939 the Film Library acquired some 400 Griffith films, mostly one reel in length,[74] made for the American Mutoscope and Biograph Company in 1908–13, a portion of a large collection found in a warehouse. Barry conceived a project to study the prints firsthand, then to show the films and publish a monograph on Griffith's career,[75] even if the filmmaker distrusted such an appraisal. With "D. W. Griffith, American Film Master" planned as a companion exhibit to a major presentation of the life and work of Frank Lloyd Wright, the Museum intended to honor "the two greatest living Americans at one time."[76] Barry hoped to restore Griffith's fading fame "and also to overcome the long-lived intellectual prejudice . . . that because Griffith worked for vast audiences and made (and lost) a great deal of money, his achievement could not be classed with 'real' art. The experiment "was not an unqualified success":

Outside the then tiny circle of film scholars the book provoked little cerebration and comment, and it did not sell; overstocks remained on the Museum's shelves for years. In 1940 Griffith and his era seemed fantastically remote and irrelevant to most people who

Intolerance. D. W. Griffith. 1916

thought of themselves as cultivated. His spotty knowledge of history, his literary eccentricities, his "petit bourgeois" morality quite overshadowed for them the beauty, power and humanity of his formal structure and pictorial composition.[77]

The opening of the retrospective was intended as a celebratory event. On November 12, 1940, Jock Whitney hosted a black-tie dinner at his Fifth Avenue home. Neither Griffith nor the Gish sisters attended. Whitney sent a telegram to Griffith, then in Las Vegas, congratulating him on "AN EXCITING SUCCESS AND AN IMPORTANT EVENT IN THE HISTORY OF MOVIE MAKING. WE ONLY WISH YOU COULD HAVE BEEN WITH US TO ENJOY PERSONALLY THE TRIUMPH YOU SO OBVIOUSLY DESERVE."[78]

The ensuing retrospective provided, in a coherent chronological pattern, a lucid presentation of Griffith's development of the basic principles of the narrative form in his early work at Biograph (1908–13), and his major achievements in feature-length films in the 1910s and 1920s. Barry traced his background as a son of southern culture and poverty, his childhood fascination with nineteenth-century "magic lantern" slide shows, his acting career, and his early attempts to sell his stories to Biograph. His first script, *Old Isaacs, the Pawnbroker*, was filmed by Biograph in March 1908, and by June he had begun his sixteen-year association with cameraman G. W. ("Billy") Bitzer; together, they would make virtually all of Biograph's films from mid-1908 through 1909, and many thereafter until 1913. Bitzer continued to work with Griffith, photographing his features into the 1920s. For her program at the Museum, Barry sought Bitzer's assistance, and he renovated the original Biograph printer, which allowed the Library to make conventional release prints from the surviving non-standard negatives. William Jamison, who had been a key researcher and restorer for the Film Library since the mid-1930s, arranged for Pathé to make these prints.

Barry summarized Griffith's development of film language and his successes and failures through two decades of directing, both as an independent and for the film production companies Mutual, Triangle, First National, United Artists (of

which he was a founder, with Chaplin, Pickford, and Fairbanks), Paramount, and Art Cinema. At Biograph, Griffith wanted to "liberate the motion picture from stage forms and conventions and to compose his films out of brief shots taken at varying distances from the action"; in *The Lonely Villa* (June 1909) he "employed cross-cutting to heighten suspense throughout the parallel scenes where the burglars are breaking in upon the mother and children while the father is rushing home to the rescue."[79] "Breathless excitement and suspense" were created by using the camera flexibly, moving it everywhere, by employing a variety of set-ups and camera angles, and by editing in brief, terse sequences. Griffith brought the camera "closer and closer to the actors in scenes where it was important to indicate emotional interplay or where small gestures or expressions were of special interest. This had two results: it identified the audience more closely with the action while it also made the acting much quieter and more intimate."[80] In this short period, Griffith and the Biograph team of cameramen and actors saw to it that "the confines of the stage, so oppressive in earlier films, were being broken, movement in any direction on the screen was employed freely and the motion picture began finally to be a fluid, eloquent and utterly novel form of expression."[81] In 1913, Griffith began directing longer films, with *The Battle of Elderbush Gulch* in two reels and *Judith of Bethulia* in four reels, and then feature-length productions, most notably *The Birth of a Nation* (1915) and *Intolerance* (1916), two epic films dramatizing historical events which, pretty literally, took the world by storm. Gance, Eisenstein, Fritz Lang, Cecil B. DeMille, and others would feel their impact. Griffith "had conferred both magnitude and complexity as well as expressiveness on the motion pictures and in Europe and America alike, all the most ambitious films of the 1920s reflected his influence and followed his example."[82]

Gloria Swanson and Iris Barry at The Museum of Modern Art, New York, 1941

What the Griffith project established was the curatorial apparatus for the medium of film: Barry demonstrated how and why he was a pioneer through the study and showing of works that had become unavailable in their original form. She had closely studied each film, and had had extensive conversations with Griffith; she had even visited Griffith's home town, Louisville, Kentucky, to deepen her understanding of his character and his approach to filmmaking. Bitzer and Jamison had assisted in preserving and screening the films. Beaumont Newhall, the Museum's curator of photography, had interviewed Bitzer and included in the catalogue Bitzer's recounting of innovative camera devices. The essence of curatorial work, which is the analysis and conservation of the object itself and its placement historically and critically through exhibition and publication, could have no finer paradigm than the Griffith project.[83]

Barry's efforts were not broadly understood at the time. Yet she was doing exactly what Alfred Barr had done in opening the Museum in 1929 with an exhibition[84] of modern, if not contemporary, masters: She was placing a pioneer of modern art in context. That Griffith seemed rearguard at that time, or since, was not the issue; Barry wanted the public to realize that because film's entire history falls within the period generally labeled "modern," from the late nineteenth century on, the "modern versus contemporary" debate becomes irrelevant. Griffith's development of narrative in cinema was demonstrably as worthy of study as the Cubism of Picasso, the Fauvism of Matisse.

The Battle of San Pietro. John Huston. 1945

The Film of Fact

By 1940, the Film Library had acquired some 1,600 titles, and the staff looked forward to having a "breathing space," to concentrate on organizing and preserving the film collection. Such work came to a halt during World War II, immediately after Pearl Harbor, Richard Griffith noted in his 1956 report, "when all of the Film Library's funds and energies were devoted to supplying a host of government agencies with films for strategic, informational, or morale purposes."[85] Footage from propagandistic "Nazi pictures" acquired by Barry from her trip to Berlin in 1936, and from other sources in subsequent years, was supplied to the U.S. Army Signal Corps, U.S. Navy, Coast Guard, Office of Strategic Services, Office of War Information, and British Ministry of Information "for use in documentary and counter-propaganda films."[86]

On the eve of the war in 1940, Nelson A. Rockefeller (who had succeeded Goodyear as Museum President the preceding year) established the Office of the Coordinator of Inter-American Affairs (CIAA) in Washington, D.C., and asked Whitney to head its Motion Picture Division; the Museum and its Film Library were called into service in the CIAA's efforts to promote a strong relationship between the two Americas, in hopes of dissuading Latin America from befriending Axis powers. By mid-1941, Barry proudly noted that the Film Library housed "a project under the Office of the Coordinator of Cultural and Commercial Relations Between the American Republics for the provision of educational and documentary films in Spanish and Portuguese to the twenty sister nations of the hemisphere. With the growing recognition of the film as a major social and cultural force in our time the

Film Library's horizon becomes unlimited."[87]

Barry, "who had never been political, plunged into war work. When the U.S. Government called together all the Hollywood greats, whom she had worshipped for so long, the studio producers and directors who had volunteered for war work bade Iris lecture them on documentary."[88] Richard Griffith left the Film Library to serve as editor and researcher for Frank Capra on the Why We Fight film series, produced in 1942–45 by the Army Signal Corps, which combined combat footage with fiction film sequences and animation. Capra had studied Leni Riefenstahl's *Triumph of the Will* (1938), a print of which had been acquired by the Film Library in 1938 from the German Embassy, and incorporated some of its footage into the films he directed for the series.

The Film Library prepared an excerpt of *Triumph of the Will* in 1942, and screened it with other German propaganda films in an extraordinary cycle blandly titled "The Documentary Film, 1922–1945." The major Museum film series organized after the war's end, it was presented in the first six months of 1946. Barry included British and American "wartime documentaries" such as *The Memphis Belle* (1944, William Wyler), *The Battle of San Pietro* (1945, John Huston), the entire Why We Fight series, and a selection of Army-Navy Screen Magazine newsreels, which featured Snafu and other cartoon figures drawn by Theodor Geisel, better known as Dr. Seuss.

Barry's selection of these documentaries was based on her involvement through five years of research and screenings for filmmakers. She and her staff had located rare or obscure films during the war, and much Film Library material had been incorporated into British and U.S. Government productions. According to Griffith, "Barry was more continuously in touch with all aspects of war-time filmmaking than any other individual, and thus [had] a wider knowledge of the subject than even those of us who were engaged in actual film production."[89] Her excitement is evident in her catalogue essay, as she cites the progress of the "film of fact" through its wartime phase, of which the "total sum is a vast, impressive panorama of contemporary history. . . . The documentary film has had a turbulent existence, full of set-backs, punctuated by bold if hardly extravagant claims, and marked throughout by the devotion and missionary spirit of its chief exponents. Finally, during the war years, it earned full recognition and demonstrated its usefulness to a degree hitherto undreamed. A Nazi general declared, early in the conflict, that the side with the best cameras, rather than the side with the best armaments, would win."[90]

"The Documentary Film" was intended particularly to show the range of wartime productions to "a vast segment of the public that has heard these films spoken about without being able to see them . . . it includes much that has previously been seen only by the fighting men or shown only abroad."[91] Although Hollywood talent was involved in numerous films, credit belonged to "those cameramen of the allied fighting services to whose valor and skill we owe the picture," and who "remain among the unnamed masters of the art."[92] Most importantly, to Barry, the film of fact no longer needed an apology; it had mastered all the complexities of the medium:

To enlarge the world of experience for the individual was the proper function of the film, so the pioneers and commentators of the art believed fifty years ago: this function is ful-

filled now that—just as literature includes much besides fiction—the motion picture at last conspicuously includes the film of fact. [93]

Concurrent with the war effort, in 1942–45, the Rockefeller Foundation funded the Motion Picture Project, a joint program of the Film Library and the Library of Congress. Barry and a team of experts selected fiction and nonfiction films released in those years; the Film Library acquired and stored the films for the Library of Congress, which handled copyright and other arrangements. Poet Archibald MacLeish had been appointed Librarian of Congress in October 1939, and he oversaw the creation and expansion of the Library's Motion Picture division before resigning in December 1944 to become Assistant Secretary of State. The Library of Congress had a splendid collection of film materials before 1912, when "paper prints" (contact prints made on photographic paper instead of film stock) were accepted in lieu of films, as visual records of the objects to be copyrighted; since then, it had returned films submitted for copyright because it could not store nitrate stock. The immediate goal of the Motion Picture Project was to reestablish the national collection. By May 1943, Barry had drafted a list of 104 titles of films made in 1942, and by the end of April 1945, the Film Library had acquired for the Library of Congress a group of features, newsreels, documentaries, and short subjects.

The criteria for selection had been suggested by Barry in 1942, to include the "most characteristic and most original of films produced" in America: 1) "films which adequately and excitingly as well as accurately recreate historical events or famous characters from American history," 2) films based on current events, fiction as well as documentary and newsreel, 3) films that capture a particular phase of American life, 4) films of outstanding technical or artistic originality, 5) exceptional films of great performances, 6) especially lively or imaginative films not fitting the above categories, such as Mickey Mouse cartoons or Buck Rogers serials, 7) films of scientific interest, 8) films that are phenomenally popular, and 9) films that are outstanding examples of bad taste, ostentation, triviality, or untruth to life.[94]

The Library of Congress polished the "Basis of Selection of Films" to draw upon copyrighted films that would provide future generations with the "most truthful and revealing information . . . as to the life and interests of the men and women of the period." Included were newsreels, documentaries, films with documentary significance including "entertainment films," films of artistic or technological advances, films such as animated cartoons "which have had a currency so great as to provide elements of the common imaginative life of the period," and outstanding films of scientific or geographic interest.[95]

There were, of course, disagreements over Barry's choices.[96] As with any project that is based on selectivity, the Film Library's collecting and exhibition programming would be critiqued over the years, as curatorial interests and preferences were evaluated within and without the Museum. If in later decades it required the *Cahiers du Cinéma* critics François Truffaut, Claude Chabrol, and Jean-Luc Godard, as well as the journal's American contributor, the brilliantly perceptive Andrew Sarris, to prod Americans to acknowledge and appreciate the fine art of Hitchcock and Ford and Nicholas Ray, Barry had already assembled a good deal of evidence that she knew fully well what had been accomplished. She was much admired, contrary to her inevitable detractors, not only for the breadth of her knowledge of film

history, but for her freedom from snobbery:

[At] a time when it was fashionable to admire a foreign film like Ekk's Road to Life, *she preferred (and rightly) William Wellman's* Wild Boys of the Road*—and added it to the Museum's collection. She felt (and rightly) that John Ford's* The Informer *was too self-consciously 'artistic'; she preferred his 'programmers,' like* The Lost Patrol, The Prisoner of Shark Island, *and* Stagecoach. *She loved the early Disneys, the Astaire-Rogers musicals, the Jimmy Cagney gangsters, and anything with Garbo. She championed 'difficult' films like Lang's* You Only Live Once *and (somewhat later) Nicholas Ray's* They Live by Night.[97]

The Treasurer's Report

From 1946 until her retirement, Barry served as both Curator and Director of the Film Library. Richard Griffith returned to the Museum in 1949, and was named Curator following Barry's departure in 1951. Griffith observed that, not unlike the heady days of 1935, "steering a course through the twin currents of economic and technological change toward the Film Library's educational and cultural goals is at once an adventure, a gamble, and a challenge."[98] Throughout the 1950s it would be necessary to re-evaluate programs, and Griffith and his colleagues undertook to revise historical surveys and broaden exhibitions. Griffith organized the series "Through the Looking Glass," to reveal the art of the cinema in films about filmmakers and the medium itself. Programs included new acquisitions of European films, ranging from *Rashomon* (1950, Akira Kurosawa) to *Pather Panchali* (1955, Satyajit Ray), and experimental work, such as the influential *Meshes of the Afternoon* (1943) by the American filmmaker Maya Deren and her husband, Czech filmmaker Alexander Hammid. Although Griffith added films by Len Lye, Oskar Fischinger, Norman McLaren, James Broughton, and others in these years, he was criticized for not acquiring a broader range of avant-garde work.

Richard Griffith speaking at a conference of film teachers at the Worcester Art Museum, Worcester, Massachusetts, November 3, 1956

In 1953, Upton Sinclair donated some fifty hours of footage shot by Eisenstein in Mexico in 1930–32 for his unfinished film *Que Viva Mexico!* (1932), as well as two films made from this material, *Thunder Over Mexico* (1933, edited by Harry Chandlee) and *Time in the Sun* (1939, edited by Marie Seton with Paul Burnford). Leyda compiled and annotated Eisenstein's footage into a two-part study film, and the three compilation films were put into distribution by the Film Library's circulating division, which continued to grow under the capable leadership of Margareta Akermark.[99] As television acquired studio backlogs and competitive film distributors expanded, Griffith and Akermark acquired Hollywood films on social issues as well as documentaries and films about the arts. Of primary importance, cataloguing and preservation had to be acknowledged and supported as the Film Library's key responsibilities, to protect the collection and keep pace with current acquisitions.

As Griffith and Barry knew all too well, most of the feature films made in the United States, whether donated or deposited at the Museum, the Library of Congress, George Eastman House, UCLA, or any other archive, are protected by the copyrights registered at the Library. This protection has distinguished the Film Library from the Museum's holdings of other visual arts, in that the Museum does not own the bulk of the film collection. From Barry's earliest acquisitions to the present, film curators have continued to acquire original productions in the form of

print and "pre-print" materials (original and duplicate negatives, fine-grain masters, soundtracks, and other materials), which may be donated or deposited on long-term loan. The department may make "preservation master" materials and prints, which it owns. All "intellectual rights," or rights to the subject rather than physical content of the films, belong to the rightsholder. Curators must negotiate permission, usually at the time of acquisition, to present a film for study or exhibition, and the department insists on the right to preserve film materials.[100]

From its inception, the Film Library recognized the need to preserve films; film is inherently fragile, and thus susceptible to deterioration and to damage through repeated use. Films were printed on nitrate-based stock until the early 1950s, when the invention of triacetate made it possible to consider more permanent preservation. By the mid-1950s, it was evident that a major effort would have to be undertaken to protect the collection, and fund-raising would have to be expanded. It then cost approximately $400 to make a print of a feature-length film; on this basis, it was estimated that more than $100,000 would be required to copy the priceless Biograph Studio collection of over 400 short films.[101] In 1955, Griffith launched the Film Preservation Fund, and a goal was set to raise $50,000. Once again, the Rockefeller Foundation made a grant, of $25,000, to be matched. The Museum contributed $5,000, and a new Committee for the Film Library Collection pledged to raise $18,000. The first Thursday Evening Film Series for the benefit of the Film Preservation Fund, held in October–December 1955, raised an additional $2,000; the program of six evenings began its first screening with a film donated by David Selznick—appropriately enough, Robert Benchley's *The Treasurer's Report* (1928)—and a print loaned by Selznick of his 1932 production of *A Bill of Divorcement*, starring John Barrymore and Katharine Hepburn.[102]

Iris Barry had overseen the Film Library's acquisition of a "remarkable proportion of the masterpieces of the motion picture, together with an immense amount of material . . . of incalculable importance to historians of the twentieth century,"[103] and Griffith had inherited its care and keeping. Both knew that film decomposition could "be retarded by storage at proper temperature and relative humidity,"[104] but the means were not then available to fully safeguard the collection. It would be exactly four decades before the Film Preservation Center could be built to house the Museum's collection of more than 13,000 titles spanning 102 years of cinema history.[105] The new Center's buildings, planned over the past decade, have been designed to provide state-of-the-art systems to retard the deterioration of all types of nitrate and acetate film stock, video materials, photographs, posters, and papers. Security, temperature and humidity controls, fire-safety systems, and a barcode inventory retrieval system will be linked to the Museum by computer, providing daily access to curators, conservators, and cataloguers for acquisition, research, loan and inventory details, exhibition programming, and other collection management matters.[106]

Barry and Griffith knew the danger if the Film Library was not saved. In establishing the Film Preservation Fund, a warning bell was rung; in Griffith's words: "These have been and are exciting, changeful years, full of promise and menace."[107]

Notes

The author acknowledges Steven Higgins, John Johnson, Richard Koszarski, Patrick Loughney, Ronald Magliozzi, and Peter Williamson, whose critical insights and corrections were most gratefully received.

The designation *Film archive* refers to uncatalogued source material in the Department of Film and Video, The Museum of Modern Art, New York.

1. *Variety*, October 9, 1935 (clipping). Film archive.
2. Iris Barry, "Film Library, 1935–1941," *The Bulletin of The Museum of Modern Art* 8, no. 5 (June–July 1941), p. 8.
3. Richard Griffith, "A Report on the Film Library, 1941–1956," *The Museum of Modern Art Bulletin* 24, no. 1 (Fall 1956), p. 5.
4. Notable sleuths in top-tier pulp fiction and popular Hollywood films of this period. As the urbane Philo Vance, created by S. S. Van Dine, William Powell and, later, Warren William unmasked the culprit in fourteen pictures, including Powell's hit, *The Kennel Murder Case* (1933, Michael Curtiz), remade as *Calling Philo Vance* (1940, William Clemens)—the only Vance film in the Museum collection. The Museum is more fortunate to have film elements of the third and final version of Dashiell Hammett's classic, *The Maltese Falcon* (1941, John Huston), starring Humphrey Bogart as tough-guy Sam Spade.
5. Among the first acquisitions of Hollywood features were *Lady Windermere's Fan* (1925, Ernst Lubitsch) and *Little Caesar* (1931, Mervyn LeRoy), from Warner Bros.; *Sherlock Jr.* (1924, Buster Keaton) and *The Wind* (1928, Victor Sjöström), starring Lillian Gish, donated by M-G-M; and *Safety Last* (1923, Fred Newmeyer and Sam Taylor), from Harold Lloyd. For other films acquired from this period, see n. 42.
6. Between 1932 and 1934 Johnson mounted eight exhibitions of architecture and design, including the ground-breaking "Machine Art" show of 1934.
7. See John Szarkowski, "The Family of Man" (pp. 12–37), and Terry Riley and Edward Eigen, "Between the Museum and the Marketplace: Selling Good Design" (pp. 150–79), in *Studies in Modern Art 4. The Museum of Modern Art at Mid-Century: At Home and Abroad* (1994).
8. The Film Library was redesignated the Department of Film in 1966 and, in 1993, the Department of Film and Video.
9. Iris Barry, "Film Comments," *The Bulletin of The Museum of Modern Art* 1, no. 1 (June 1933), n. p.
10. Abby Aldrich Rockefeller was a founding trustee of the Museum.
11. Richard Griffith (attributed), "The Film Collection of The Museum of Modern Art," typescript, n.d., pp. 3–4. Film archive.
12. The author's favorite childhood movie theater, by the southern shore of Lake Michigan in Wilmette, Illinois, was decorated in "Spanish patio" style and known as the Teatro del Lago.
13. Ownership of film libraries, production units, and distribution networks has shifted frequently since the 1950s, reconsolidated through mergers and acquisitions by individual investors and corporations. For example, Turner Entertainment Co., which owns the film libraries of M-G-M (titles produced from 1924 to June 1986), Warner Bros. (1918–50), and RKO (1930–57), donated to the Museum its holdings of original "pre-print" materials, in the form of fine-grain masters, of the Warner Bros. and RKO features and shorts.
14. Griffith, "A Report on the Film Library, 1941–1956," p. 7.
15. The film had been commissioned in 1927 to commemorate the tenth anniversary of the Revolution of 1917; also known as *Ten Days That Shook the World,* it was based in part on the book of the same title by John Reed (1919), and was released in 1928. The Museum acquired a print in 1940.
16. See "The 1929 multidepartmental plan for the Museum of Modern Art: its origins, development, and partial realization," prepared by Alfred H. Barr, Jr., for A. Conger Goodyear, August 1941. The Museum of Modern Art Archives: Alfred H. Barr Papers, 1.9A.
17. Richard Griffith (attributed), untitled typescript, n.d., p. 1. Film archive.
18. Alfred Barr (attributed), "Notes on Departmental Expansion of the Museum," typescript, June 24, 1932, pp. 5–6. Film archive.
19. John Rewald, in *The John Hay Whitney Collection* (Washington, D.C.: National Gallery of Art, 1983), pp. 11–14, recounts Whitney's collecting in the late 1920s: *The False Start* (1864) and *Before the Races* (1881–85) by Degas, *Wapping on Thames* (1860–64) by Whistler, and *The Ball at the Moulin de la Galette* (1876) by Renoir.
20. H[erbert] T. Kalmus, in an untitled essay in the *Journal of the Society of Motion Picture Engineers* (December 1938); cited in *"Becky Sharp"* entry (F3.0258) in *The American Film Institute Catalog of Motion Pictures Produced in the United States, Feature Films, 1931–1940* (Berkeley: University of California Press, 1993), p. 128.
21. Walt Disney donated animated shorts to the Film Library, including *Steamboat Willie* (1928), the first released animated cartoon featuring Mickey Mouse; *Plane Crazy* (1928), an earlier Mickey Mouse cartoon; *Skeleton Dance* (1929), the first Silly Symphony; and in Technicolor, *Flowers and Trees* and *Three Little Pigs.*
22. E[ly] J[acques] Kahn, Jr., *Jock: The Life and Times of John Hay Whitney* (New York: Doubleday, 1981), p. 105.
23. Kalmus, cited in *The American Film Institute Catalog,* p. 128.
24. During a visit to the Museum in 1986, Mamoulian noted the difficulties of shooting in Technicolor at that time: If he couldn't move the cameras, he could move the actors instead. The film has been restored to its dazzling original colors by the UCLA Film and Television Archive.
25. The David O. Selznick Collection, comprising original negatives of most of his feature productions, was donated to the Museum by ABC Pictures International in 1978. In addition to *A Bill of Divorcement* (1932, George Cukor), *Rebecca* (1940, Alfred Hitchcock), and *Notorious* (1946, Hitchcock), the collection includes four films key to the early history of Technicolor—*The Garden of Allah, Nothing Sacred, The Adventures of Tom Sawyer* (1938, Norman Taurog), and *Duel in the Sun* (1946, King Vidor)—in their original form of three-color separation negatives on black-and-white nitrate stock. Preservation of the Selznick Collection was a priority for the department in the 1980s, and the Museum was fortunate to receive generous grants from Celeste Bartos and Mrs. John Hay Whitney and Greentree Foundation to protect key titles.
26. Cable, Selznick to Whitney, June 12, 1937; reprinted in *Memo From: David O. Selznick,* ed. Rudy Behlmer (New York: Grove Press, 1972), p. 116. "Dr. Eliot" was Charles William Eliot, editor of the Harvard Classics series.
27. For several years prior to 1939, Selznick International and the Film Library shared a screening room at 125 East 46 Street in New York.
28. Upon her retirement, Barry moved to the Provençal village of Fayence, where she lived until her death in 1969; see also "The Changing Stream" by James Thrall Soby," p. 213 of the present volume.
29. John Houseman, "A One-woman Blitz," in Margareta Akermark, ed. *Remembering Iris Barry* (New York: The Museum of Modern Art, 1980), p. 10.
30. Iris Barry, *Let's Go to the Movies* (New York: Payson & Clarke, 1926).
31. Ibid., p. 43.
32. Ibid., pp. 206–07.
33. Alistair Cooke, "To Recall Her Pluck," in Akermark, ed. *Remembering Iris Barry,* p. 11.
34. According to Russell Lynes, "By the late spring of 1932 Alfred Barr had worked himself into a frenzy of fatigue. In the thirty months since the Museum had opened in the Heckscher Building [in November 1929] it had held sixteen exhibitions and had organized and published sixteen illustrated catalogues with texts either written by Barr or prefaced by his comments." Barr requested three months' vacation; he was granted a year's leave, which he spent traveling and studying in Europe. See Lynes, *Good Old Modern: An Intimate Portrait of The Museum of Modern Art* (New York: Atheneum, 1973), pp. 102–03.
35. Quoted in Griffith, "The Film Collection of The Museum of Modern Art," p. 2. The author has yet to locate a copy of Barr's list.
36. Paul Rotha, *The Film Till Now* (London: Jonathan Cape, 1930).
37. Griffith (attributed), untitled typescript, pp. 1–2.
38. [Iris Barry], "Work and Progress," *The Museum of Modern Art Film Library* (January 1937), p. 1. Film archive.
39. A five-page Memorandum of Agreement

dated July 2, 1935, stipulated that The Museum of Modern Art Film Library Corporation, so named on June 27 of that year, would be operated for educational purposes and not for profit. The entire capital stock of 200 shares would be held by the three appointed trustees—Whitney, Warburg, and Gerald Donovan—who would cooperate with the Museum on all matters relating to the Film Library. A. Conger Goodyear signed the memorandum on behalf of the Museum. Film archive.

40. John E. ("Dick") Abbott was Director of the Museum's Film Library from 1935 to 1946, and a member of its Board of Trustees from 1939 to 1946.

41. John E. Abbott and Iris Barry, "An Outline of a Project for Founding the Film Library of The Museum of Modern Art," typescript, April 17, 1935, p. 3. Film archive.

42. Of Murnau's films, the Museum acquired *Der Letzte Mann* and *Sunrise* in the 1930s; the Museum also has material on *Nosferatu*. In the 1970s, Twentieth Century–Fox donated 313 features made between 1916 and 1950. The Fox Collection includes the largest extant holdings of the silent films of John Ford—*Just Pals* (1920), *The Iron Horse* (1924), and *Three Bad Men* (1926) among them—as well as Ford's sound films *Judge Priest* (1934), *How Green Was My Valley* (1941), and *My Darling Clementine* (1946), and films by Frank Borzage, Raoul Walsh, and others. Sjöström is represented by *The Scarlet Letter* (1926) and *The Wind* (1928), and Garbo by *Flesh and the Devil* (1927, Clarence Brown), *Woman of Affairs* (1928, Brown), *The Kiss* (1929, Jacques Feyder), *Camille* (1937, George Cukor), and *Ninotchka* (1939, Lubitsch). Lubitsch is well represented by *Lady Windermere's Fan*, *The Marriage Circle* (1924), *The Love Parade* (1929), *The Smiling Lieutenant* (1931), and *Trouble in Pradise* (1932); see also n. 52.

43. Iris Barry, "The Film Library and How It Grew," typescript, n.d., p. 1. Film archive. By the late 1930s, the Film Library had acquired a print of each film cited by Barry in this passage: *The Public Enemy* (1931, William Wellman) from Warner Bros. in 1935; *Anna Christie* (1930, Clarence Brown) and *Greed* (1925, Erich von Stroheim) from M-G-M in 1936; *Moana* (1926, Robert Flaherty) from the Harvard University Film Foundation in 1936; and *Intolerance* (1916, D.W. Griffith) from Griffith in 1937.

44. Quoted in *The Museum of Modern Art, New York* (New York: Harry N. Abrams in association with The Museum of Modern Art), p. 527.

45. "A Special Program Given at Pickfair on Saturday, August 24th, 1935, To Make Known the Work of the Newly Established Museum of Modern Art Film Library." Film archive.

46. *The Los Angeles Times*, September 1, 1935 (clipping). Film archive. Will Hays was President of the Motion Picture Producers and Distributors of America, the predecessor of the Motion Picture Association of America, now headed by Jack Valenti. Hays served as the first Chairman of the Museum's Film Library Advisory Committee, which included David H. Stevens of the Rockefeller Foundation; Stanton Griffis, a director of Paramount; Irving Thalberg of M-G-M; and Erwin Panofsky of Princeton University.

47. Barry, "Film Library, 1935–1941," pp. 5–6.

48. Barry, "The Film Library and How It Grew," p. 8.

49. Whitney went to Hollywood and "snared antiques": a gift of nine Warner Bros. features and selected Vitagraph and Vitaphone films of 1924–33, including the Warner hits *The Public Enemy*, *The Jazz Singer* (1927, Alan Crosland), and *I Am a Fugitive from a Chain Gang* (1932, Mervyn LeRoy), and eleven Harold Lloyd films of 1915–29, among them *Grandma's Boy* (1922, Fred Newmeyer) and *The Freshman* (1925, Sam Taylor and Fred Newmeyer). Reported in *Variety*, October 9, 1935, and *Motion Picture Herald*, October 12, 1935; see also n. 5 above.

50. "[T]he form of agreement was worked out, largely by Austin Keough (vice-president and general counsel of Paramount Pictures) and J. Robert Rubin of M-G-M, which most of the major companies signed shortly thereafter" (Griffith, "A Report on the Film Library, 1941–1956," p. 4). Copies of the agreements made with the individual studios are housed in the Film archive.

51. Barry, "Film Library, 1935–1941," p. 7.

52. Ibid., p. 9; and Barry, "The Film Library and How It Grew," p. 11. Twenty-eight German silent and sound films were listed in "The Report of The Museum of Modern Art Film Library as of November 6, 1936," including *Der Golem* (1920, Paul Wegener), *Die Nibelungen* (1924, Fritz Lang), *Metropolis* (1926, Lang), *Faust* (1926, F. W. Murnau), and *Der Letzte Mann;* see pp. 8–9.

53. Leyda subsequently had a distinguished career as a teacher and a scholar; at his death in 1988 he was the Pinewood Professor of Cinema Studies at New York University. His publications include translations of three volumes of Eisenstein's theoretical writings, histories of the Russian and Soviet cinema (*Kino* [London: Allen and Unwin, 1960]) and Chinese cinema (*Dianying* [Cambridge, Mass.: MIT Press, 1972]), and studies and anthologies of the writings of Herman Melville and Emily Dickinson.

54. John E. Abbott, "Report on the Work and Progress of the Film Library, December 9, 1937,: typescript, p. 4. Film archive.

55. Barry, "Film Library, 1935–1941," p. 13. A group of Chaplin shorts of the 1910s was acquired in the 1930s, including *The Pawnshop* (1916); features and other shorts were slowly added, most recently, a print of *A Woman of Paris* (1923), the gift of Lady Chaplin on the occasion of the one-hundredth anniversary of the filmmaker's birth in 1889.

56. Ibid., p. 6. The D. W. Griffith Collection was formally acquired December 29, 1937, the gift of D. W. Griffith. It included nineteen films directed and produced by Griffith between 1913 and 1930, as well as extensive production records.

57. Griffith, "A Report on the Film Library, 1941–1956," p. 5. The Edison Collection was acquired May 18, 1940, the gift of R. L. Giffen, a former employee of the Edison Company. It included some 400 negatives from the period 1895–1916, as well as script and assembly-sheet files. The Biograph Collection was acquired in 1939, the gift of the Actinograph Corporation through the Empire Trust Company. It comprised some 1,000 films of the years 1896–1916, a Biograph printer necessary to restore the nonstandard negatives, and production logs.

58. Ibid., p. 6. The Douglas Fairbanks Collection was acquired in 1939, the gift of Douglas Fairbanks. Records indicate it consisted of 2,519,000 feet of film produced by and starring Fairbanks, including original negatives, prints, and outtakes. Douglas Fairbanks, Jr., later added to the collection with gifts of prints of films in which he appeared.

59. Abbott, "Report on the Work and Progress of the Film Library, December 9, 1937," p. 15.

60. The citation is housed in the Film archive.

61. John E. Abbott, "Report of The Museum of Modern Art Film Library as of November 6, 1936," typescript, pp. 3, 4. Film archive. In addition to *Sherlock, Jr.*, *Greed*, *The Wind*, *Flesh and the Devil*, and *Anna Christie*, the M-G-M titles included *The Navigator* (1924, Donald Crisp and Buster Keaton), *The Big Parade* (1925, King Vidor), and *The Student Prince* (1927, Ernst Lubitsch).

62. For a fuller understanding of the Academy's role, see Robert Osborne's introductory chapter, "The Beginning. . . ," in *60 Years of the Oscar: The Official History of the Academy Awards* (New York: Abbeville Press, 1989), pp. 7–17.

63. *The Los Angeles Times*, September 1, 1935. (clipping). Film archive.

64. Osborne, *60 Years of the Oscar*, p. 43.

65. Ibid., p. 15.

66. At the 1979 Academy Awards, Mrs. John D. (Blanchette) Rockefeller 3rd, President, and Richard E. Oldenburg, Director of the Museum, received from Gregory Peck an "Academy Honorary Award to The Museum of Modern Art Department of Film for the contribution it has made to the public's perception of movies as an art form." The Oscar is on display at the Museum in the gallery adjacent to The Roy and Niuta Titus Theater I.

67. *The Museum of Modern Art Film Library Bulletin, 1938–1939*, pp. 4–5. See also *Film Library Bulletin, 1940* and *Film Library Bulletin, 1941*, in the Film archive.

68. Panofsky presented his lecture and screened eleven short films on February 1, 1938, ending with the Walt Disney animated shorts *Plane Crazy* and *The Skeleton Dance*. He posited that the art of the movies was unlike the traditional evolution of an art, in which an artistic urge led to a development of technique; rather, at the beginning of film history, a technical invention that registered and produced movement in turn enabled the invention of a true art. A transcript of the lecture is housed in the Film archive.

69. The FIAF organizers, who apparently met at the Hôtel Crillon, were Barry, representing the

Museum; Henri Langlois and Franju for the Cinémathèque Française; and Olwen Vaughan for the British Film Institute. They were joined by Frank Hensel from the Reichsfilmarchiv, and it was agreed there could be four founding institutional members. The first annual FIAF meeting was held in 1939 in New York , as was the FIAF Congress of 1985, marking the Department of Film's fiftieth anniversary. The 1995 FIAF Congress in Los Angeles was attended by representatives of more than one hundred film archives from sixty countries. Department staff have continued to be active as officers and members of the executive committee and commissions on preservation and documentation.

70. The exhibition, "Trois Siècles d'Art aux Etats-Unis," was shown at the Jeu de Paume from May 21 to July 13, 1938. Selected by Barr, Goodyear, and members of the curatorial staff, it included works drawn from all departments within the Museum, as well as examples of American folk art.

71. Barry, "Film Library, 1935–1941," p. 11.

72. The scrapbook was donated in 1982 by the family of the late William F. Rogers, who had been M-G-M General Sales Manager during the film's 1939 release. At the time of the premiere, the full-length portrait of Scarlett O'Hara was donated to the High Museum of Art in Atlanta, the gift of David Selznick. See Ron Magliozzi, "Crazy with the Wind: The *Gone with the Wind* World Premiere Campaign Scrapbook," *MoMA Magazine* (New York), no. 18 (Fall/Winter 1994), pp. 32–34.

73. Richard Griffith, *A Note on Documentary Film* (New York: The Museum of Modern Art, 1940), pamphlet accompanying "The Non-Fiction Film" series.

74. A typical reel of a Biograph short, projected at a speed of 16 frames per second, or "silent speed," could run to approximately 16 minutes.

75. Barry's monograph is titled *D. W. Griffith, American Film Master* (New York: The Museum of Modern Art, 1940, rev. 1965).

76. Iris Barry, untitled typescript, n.d. Film archive. The Griffith retrospective and "Frank Lloyd Wright, American Architect" were shown concurrently under the broader title "Two Great Americans," November 13, 1940–January 5, 1941.

77. Richard Griffith, Foreword to Iris Barry, *D. W. Griffith, American Film Master,* rev. ed. (New York: The Museum of Modern Art, 1965), p. 5.

78. Cable, Whitney to Griffith, November 13, 1940. Film archive.

79. Barry, *D. W. Griffith, American Film Master* (1965), p. 16.

80. Ibid., p. 17.

81. Ibid.

82. Ibid., p. 25.

83. Eileen Bowser, who retired as curator in 1993, added significantly to the catalogue, publishing an annotated list in *D. W. Griffith, American Film Master* (1965), pp. 39–88. Film Conservator Peter Williamson has overseen and carried out the restoration of Biograph shorts and Griffith features, including *Birth of a Nation, Intolerance, Broken Blossoms* (1919), *Way Down East* (1920), and *Orphans of the Storm* (1921). More than $500,000 has been spent on preservation of the Griffith and Biograph films to date, with funds from the National Endowment for the Arts and the New York State Council on the Arts, matched by generous support from the Celeste Bartos Fund for Film Preservation.

Celeste Bartos, Chairman of the Committee on Film since 1971, generously established a major endowment to support the film collection. In 1979, Lillian Gish created the Lillian Gish Trust, which was received by the Museum in the year following her death in 1993, specifically for the storage and preservation of the films of Gish and her sister, Dorothy; Griffith; and the Biograph Company.

84. *Cézanne, Gauguin, Seurat, and van Gogh,* a loan exhibition selected by Barr, inaugurated the Museum, then located in the Heckscher Building at Fifth Avenue and Fifty-seventh Street in New York, November 7–December 7, 1929.

85. Griffith, "A Report on the Film Library, 1941–1956," p. 6.

86. Iris Barry, *The Documentary Film, 1922–1945* (New York: The Museum of Modern Art, n.d.), p. 15.

87. Barry, "Film Library, 1935–1941," p. 13.

88. Ivor Montagu, "Birmingham Sparrow," in Akermark, ed., *Remembering Iris Barry,* p. 6.

89. Richard Griffith, "The Use of Films by the U.S. Armed Services," in Paul Rotha, *Documentary Film,* 3rd ed. (London: Faber and Faber, 1952), p. 344.

90. Iris Barry, "The Documentary Film: Prospect and Retrospect," in Barry, *The Documentary Film, 1922–1945,* p. 2.

91. Ibid., p. 3.

92. Ibid., p. 4.

93. Ibid.

94. Barry, "Basis for Selection for Motion Pictures for the Library of Congress: Recommendations," p. 2; attached to memorandum, Barry to Abbott, June 25, 1942. Film archive.

95. Press release no. 139, Office of the Secretary, Library of Congress, Washington, D.C., [1942]. Film archive.

96. The Museum and the Library of Congress are collaborating on a major retrospective of the latter's collections, including films selected by the Film Library, to be presented at the Museum in 1996–97. A forthcoming catalogue will examine in detail the cooperation and relationship of the Museum and the Library of Congress in this period.

97. Arthur Knight, "It Has All Been Very Interesting," in Akermark, ed., *Remembering Iris Barry,* p. 9.

98. Griffith, "A Report on the Film Library, 1941–1956," p. 14.

99. Akermark became Circulation Director of the Film Library in 1943. She was named Associate Director in 1974, serving until her retirement in 1978.

100. The initial agreements with the major studios had included the right to exhibit the films for educational purposes.

101. Restoration of a Biograph short costs between $3,000 and $4,000 at current laboratory rates; a feature can cost between $15,000 and $120,000 (the cost of restoring Griffith's *Intolerance*).

102. See memorandum, Griffith to Burden, July 26, 1954; and letter, Griffith to Whitney, August 1955. Film archive. Subsequent benefits, many co-chaired by James G. Niven, Vice-Chairman of the Committee on Film, have greatly enhanced the Film Preservation Fund. The most recent benefit, "An Evening with Clint Eastwood" in October 1993, raised $770,000 to support construction of the Film Preservation Center. This event was chaired by Gerald M. Levin, Chairman, Time Warner, Inc.

103. Griffith, "A Report on the Film Library, 1941–1956," p. 5.

104. Ibid.

105. The film collection currently spans the years 1893 (*Blacksmith Scene,* Thomas Edison) to 1995 (*The Bridges of Madison County,* Clint Eastwood). Donations of major collections from producers and distributors, as well as exchanges with other archives, have enriched the collection internationally. American filmmakers such as Eastwood, Martin Scorsese, Stanley Kubrick, John Cassavetes, Stan Brakhage, Francis Ford Coppola, and Oliver Stone have generously donated prints of their work. Among the key collections at the Museum are Scorsese's extensive holdings of international titles, including important post–World War II American films; and the Andy Warhol collection of his films made in the 1960s, acquired with the cooperation and support of The Andy Warhol Foundation for the Visual Arts.

106. Located in northeastern Pennsylvania, the Film Preservation Center was designed by Davis Brody Associates, with the engineering firms of Jaros, Baum Bolles and Ove Arup Partners; mobile shelving was manufactured by Automated Storage and Retrieval Systems of America and customized shelving for nitrate films supplied by Modern Office Systems, Inc. Film Committee Chairman Celeste Bartos has taken the leadership role as the principal supporter of the Center, which is currently nearing completion. The Center has also received major contributions from the Sony Corporation, the National Endowment for the Arts, the Museum's Board of Trustees, led by Agnes Gund and David Rockefeller, and the Lillian Gish Trust, as well as donations from Columbia Pictures, Twentieth Century–Fox, and others.

107. Griffith, "A Report on the Film Library, 1941–1956," p. 4.

1. Alfred H. Barr, Jr., in front of Picasso's *Guernica,* The Museum of Modern Art, New York, 1962

Alfred H. Barr, Jr., as a Writer of Allegory: Art History in a Literary Context

James Leggio

The writings of critics and historians of modern art are often presented as detached and objective, concerned only with sober analysis and logical argument. When examined closely, however, the word-by-word texture of their language can seem quite otherwise. Even during the decades of so-called formalist analysis, modes of writing that can fairly be called "poetic" or even "allegorical" in their purposeful deployment of metaphor played an important part in how artworks were discussed and understood. In this regard, the writings of Alfred H. Barr, Jr., make surprisingly significant use of metaphorical language. And to understand this extra dimension of their meaning, I believe, they need now to be read within not only an art-historical but a literary context—read, that is, from within the culture of modernist literature. The purpose of the present essay, therefore, is to explore the poetic, metaphorical side of Alfred Barr's critical writing, identifying several characteristic uses of figurative language and their effect on his way of presenting the history of art, a way, I will argue, that sometimes opens out toward the allegorical. Figurative language offers the critic precisely that power, the ability to suggest an allegory—in this instance, letting the writer step outside the confines of a single, narrowly defined discipline and gather into narrative form the scattered hints of a broadly humanistic view of an era. Used this way, such language can suggest—lightly and delicately, without polemics—how historic changes in thinking cross the boundaries between disciplines and alter how we all can speak of the world we hold in common.

The Uses of Metaphor

The reason for bringing out this intriguing feature of Barr's writings is obvious enough: Barr played a central role in shaping the definition of modern art that was widely accepted by mid-century. Founding Director of The Museum of Modern Art and, from 1947 to 1967, Director of the Museum Collections, he pursued an active, multifaceted career in which the writing of books and articles was only a part; yet while building the collection, organizing exhibitions, and, for many years, dealing with myriad administrative duties, he nonetheless became a major voice in the developing criticism of this century's art. In the thirties and forties Barr had transformed

Left:
2. Pablo Picasso. *Night Fishing at Antibes*. 1939. Oil on canvas, 6' 9" x 11' 4" (205.7 x 345.4 cm). The Museum of Modern Art, New York. Mrs. Simon Guggenheim Fund

Right:
3. Henri Matisse. *Le Bonheur de vivre*. 1905–06. Oil on canvas, 68½" x 7' 9¾" (174 x 238.1 cm). The Barnes Foundation, Merion, Pennsylvania

the exhibition catalogue, notably with *Cubism and Abstract Art* (1936), while his books on Picasso set the standard for monographs on twentieth-century artists. Among the most widely read and influential of all the proselytizers for modern art then writing in English, he could be compared perhaps only with Roger Fry, earlier in the century, or with Herbert Read. After two decades of eminence, Barr reached the zenith of his career as an author in 1951, with the publication of his most ambitious monograph, *Matisse: His Art and His Public*. And throughout the 1950s the influence of his accumulated writings broadened, as his best-selling *What Is Modern Painting?*, first issued in 1943, went through three new editions and two translations.[1]

Barr's publications on modern art proved effective for many reasons, including their painstaking research and rigorous method. But what we notice at once about his writing is its cool clarity. Barr's prose often seems the quintessence of objectivity—almost scientific in its dispassionate pursuit of the origin of the species of modern art, and high-mindedly academic in its commitment to limpid, meticulous exposition. When art historians speak of his writing, what they praise most often is its rigor—its "detachment and objectivity,"[2] even its "willed selflessness, in which the demands of historical truth and internal coherence override the author's private persona."[3] But the verbal texture of Barr's writing is not quite as austere as we sometimes think. A more personal note is often struck, frequently through witty wordplay. For example, at one point in *Matisse: His Art and His Public,* Barr quotes the artist on the "terror of microbes"; shortly after, in his account of Matisse's brief association with the Neo-Impressionists, Barr reminds us that they are "commonly called 'pointillists' because they painted in little points or spots," and then on the next page he mischievously has the "spots" still in mind, telling us that "when Matisse returned to Paris from Toulouse he had not yet recovered from his first attack of pointillism"[4]—as if Neo-Impressionism were a contagious childhood disease, like the measles, that made young artists break out in spots. Or, in discussing Picasso's *Night Fishing at Antibes* (fig. 2), Barr describes the fishermen at work: "One of them, in a striped jersey, with a four-tined spear pierces a sole (most Picassoid of fishes!) lying on the bottom";[5] we cannot help but smile at learning that even in nature, some creatures do indeed have both eyes on one side of the face—an alien configuration captured perfectly by the word "Picassoid."

Barr's delight in words led him to a lively appreciation of poetry, and of the value of poetic figures in writing about art. He often goes out of his way to remark on the value of figurative language when talking about artworks. He points out, for instance, that the works in the 1936 exhibition "Fantastic Art, Dada, Surrealism" reflect "the deep-seated and persistent interest which human beings have in the fantastic, the irrational, the spontaneous, the marvelous, the enigmatic," and notes that "these qualities have always been present in the metaphors and similes of poetry."[6] Or he proposes poetic language as a model, explicating the "similes and metonymies"[7] of Joan Miró's *The Hunter (Catalan Landscape)* (1923–24). Again using a figure of speech as a model, he describes the piper and the two overlapping figures at the lower center and right of Matisse's *Le Bonheur de vivre* (fig. 3): "The pair of lovers . . . together form a shape which approximately repeats that of the piping girl. This repetition, emphasized by the fact that the lovers appear to have only one head, is a remarkably ingenious pictorial simile, comparable indeed to a poetic simile which might liken the lovers to the double pipes animated by a single breath."[8] What Barr is describing here is not so much a visual simile as a visual "conceit," a special kind of comparison—remote, surprising, yet powerful—that T. S. Eliot and others admired in seventeenth-century Metaphysical poetry, as in John Donne's likening of a pair of separated lovers to the two legs of a drawing compass,[9] which is parallel to Barr's likening of Matisse's two lovers to the two pipes animated by a single breath. Barr himself came close to defining the conceit when he said that "a cubist picture is not only a *design* but a precisely controlled and far-fetched metaphor."[10] A connection with Donne would be no accident: in his introduction to a catalogue of Abstract Expressionist artists, *The New American Painting*, published in 1959, Barr tries to find a poetic figure for the autonomous creativity of artists working to free themselves from influences or schools; in that instance, seeking to portray the independence of those diverse artists from one another, their "uncompromising individualism," he writes: "For them, John Donne to the contrary, each man is an island."[11]

In understanding Alfred Barr as at times a poetic writer, we let his figurative language play out its own role to the fullest extent. By so doing, we can see more clearly why in certain noteworthy passages in his books and articles, the prose becomes almost wholly figurative in character. In such passages, which occasionally find the author at the limit of what he can say by conventional means, poetic devices can go further, and sketch out a novel thought by effectively relating it to what is more securely known. Indeed, some of an artist's concerns can be discussed perhaps more sympathetically in figurative language than in mundane prose, because an artist, too, like a poet, is often trying to render concrete an emerging new insight not yet ready or able to be framed in strictly analytical terms. When Wallace Stevens came to the Museum in 1951 to speak on "The Relations Between Poetry and Painting," he saw the two as closely allied, both arising from "the typical function of the imagination which always makes use of the familiar to produce the unfamiliar."[12] In this, he would have agreed with Aristotle, who held that metaphors were in fact not mere ornaments, tacked on to a text, but were instead constitutive of new meaning: "The greatest thing by far is to be a master of metaphor. It is the one thing that cannot be learned from others; and it is also a sign of genius, since a good metaphor implies an intuitive perception of the similarity in dissimilars. . . .

Ordinary words convey only what we know already; it is from metaphor that we can best get hold of something new."[13]

Using what he called a "precisely controlled and far-fetched metaphor" to get hold of something new, concerning the passage of time, Barr in 1933 presented the evolving nature of the Museum's collection in these terms: "The Permanent Collection may be thought of graphically as a *torpedo moving through time*, its nose the ever advancing present, its tail the ever receding past of fifty to a hundred years ago . . . with a propeller representing 'Background' collections. . . ."[14] This striking image, as notable for its military character as for its resemblance to a Metaphysical conceit, is high on immediate illustrative value—a picture of the collection's passage or "voyage" through time. It helps Barr represent the collection's movement into the future in a vivid, economical way. Without recourse to such an image or poetic figure, the "story" part of history, the overall direction of its "plot," would be exceedingly difficult to convey.

The need for a metaphorical model is felt not only when he talks about the evolution of the collection; Barr uses figurative language also to describe the course of art history itself. The metaphor of time as a river, for example, permeates an important summarizing statement in *Cubism and Abstract Art:*

At the risk of grave oversimplification the impulse towards abstract art during the past fifty years may be divided historically into two main currents. . . . The first and more important current finds its sources in the art and theories of Cézanne and Seurat, passes through the widening stream of Cubism and finds its delta in the various geometric and Constructivist movements. . . . The second—and, until recently, secondary—current has its principal source in the art and theories of Gauguin and his circle, flows through the Fauvisme *of Matisse to . . . the pre-War paintings of Kandinsky. After running under ground for a few years, it reappears vigorously among the masters of abstract art associated with Surrealism.*[15]

The metaphor was familiar in contemporaneous fiction, such as Thomas Wolfe's *Of Time and the River* (1935). Another version would manifest itself in Clement Greenberg's notion of the "mainstream," the "aquatic metaphor" that is, as Robert Storr has pointed out, "Greenberg's signature trope."[16] Though common enough in history writing, this particular figure carries considerable dangers with it, implying as it does a sense of historical teleology, as every tributary joins the river's set course toward one foreknown end. For Greenberg, it implies as well a hierarchy, the mainstream being the one central current, with everything else left marginal to drift off in aimless eddies.

For Barr, however, what the metaphor pictures is not one central, dominant mainstream, but rather two contrary, competing currents; first one is stronger and then the other. It is a dramatist's view of historical process, as a dialectic between two opposing forces. Fifteen years later, in his 1951 Matisse book, Barr rewrites the "two currents" passage largely in terms of the relation between two great artworks, and between two great personages, Picasso and Matisse:

Whatever the similarities and differences between the two paintings [Le Bonheur de vivre *and* Les Demoiselles d'Avignon], *they represent moments of climactic achieve-*

ment in the careers of the two artists and they are both landmarks in the history of modern painting. Both are signposts pointing in the same general direction, toward abstraction, but by very different routes: Matisse, with the brilliant, singing color and organic, curving, fluid forms of the Joy of Life, *opens the way to Kandinsky and, after him, to Miró and the more recent masters of color-cloud-and-flowing-line abstraction; Picasso's austere, stiff, angular structure leads on to cubism—in fact the* Demoiselles *has justly been called the first cubist picture—and beyond cubism to Malevich, Mondrian and "geometric" abstraction.*[17]

Here, the two artists do not simply exemplify the two ways of the imagination, they embody them. And in general, Barr often elaborates ideas about history through this sort of dualistic (almost, one might say, Manichaean) arrangement. Much of his language displays the same basic pattern: It searches out the drama of opposing forces; and it wants to personify those forces in major artists. This subtly pervasive scheme, which is perhaps the principal consequence of how Barr uses poetic devices, especially personification, takes on great significance. Such configurations keep making themselves felt as he leads us through the history of objects: They throw events into highly suggestive patterns of significance, and thereby play a part in the readability of his prose. We can see this in those arresting passages where Barr's pleasure in lan-

4. Frederick Kiesler. *Galaxy*. 1948–51. Wood and rope, 12 x 14 x 14' (365.8 x 426.7 x 426.7 cm). The Museum of Modern Art, New York. Gift of Mrs. Nelson A. Rockefeller

guage leads him more openly to adopt a poet's voice—passages where, instead of tracing continuous lines of temporal succession like those in the passage above, as we expect of a historian, he chooses instead a different, more elliptical, more daring kind of storytelling, one in which the impulse toward narrative metaphor takes over, producing a story about modern times that is rich in ramifications and allusive in structure.

A possible ending of this story can be foreseen in a piece Barr wrote in 1952. That year, Dorothy C. Miller organized the exhibition "Fifteen Americans" at the Museum. Along with work by artists such as William Baziotes, Jackson Pollock, Mark Rothko, and Clyfford Still, the show included Frederick Kiesler's environmental sculpture *Galaxy* (fig. 4). Heralding the exhibition in the April issue of *Harper's Bazaar*, Barr wrote about the sculpture, rather than about any work of those leading painters. What he gives us is not a sober historical analysis but a prose poem, "Kiesler's *Galaxy.*" Based on metaphors of shipwreck and debris, it offers a return to an earlier, simpler life, and to ideas about mythic storytelling:

Galaxy *is architecture for star-gazers; its plan is a cross with arms raised in amazement; its major axis slopes abruptly toward a vanishing point like Borromini's false perspective in the Palazzo Spada; its four caryatids are a dolphin's spine, a hippocampus, a lobster claw and an ichthyosaur caressed by a boomerang; its lintels are driftwood and a comb-finned gar.*

Galaxy *is a four-poster in which Sinbad, Jonah, Crusoe and Ahab may sit eternally, back to back, telling each other their stories, slowly, with low voices and credulous ears.*

Galaxy *is a pergola built of jetsam where refugees from the compass and the ruler may dry their nets in peace.*

Galaxy *is a drifting raft where common sense, watched by the skeletons of the four winds, will die of thirst.*

Galaxy *is a conspiracy for discrediting Cadillacs.*

Galaxy *is the tomb of know-how, the supreme anti-technological gazebo.*[18]

The text may look like an anomaly, but if so it is an instructive one. Serious art historians generally refrain from publicly indulging their poetic fancy to this extent, even in a squib for the popular press; elaborate poetizing risks professional dis-approbation. Yet even more striking that the language itself is its content, its *narrative* content, for with his poetic images what Barr conjures up is a dramatic story of shipwreck—like Jonah, Crusoe, and Ahab "telling each other their stories" of disaster at sea—and of castaways marooned on a remote desert island. His images imply a calamitous turn in some unspecified plot: Modern inventions, and all they stand for, have somehow run aground. The story that Barr seems to be telling is about what happens next—about how to keep the imagination alive amid the ruins of a lost world.

What could have led the man who for many Americans had defined modern art in the thirties and forties apparently to change his mind by 1952, and speak of a favorite contemporary artwork in terms of driftwood and wreckage—of "refugees" and a structure "built of jetsam"? Why would he speak of modernism's rationalist enterprise as a lost lifeboat, "a drifting raft where common sense . . . will die of thirst," and where navigators and their astral instruments have been replaced

by fortune-tellers and astrologers—"star-gazers"? We might well ask. For it should be noted that the verbal images here are pervasively anti-modern—seeking to overturn the logic of the modern Machine Age. The drift of the imagery undercuts our era's preoccupation with the latest technological advances; *Galaxy* thus participates in "a conspiracy for discrediting Cadillacs," rendering absurd the most ostentatious of streamlined luxury machines. Moreover, it is "the tomb of know-how, the supreme anti-technological gazebo." In preferring quaint gazebos and pergolas to, say, the light shells and rectilinear volumes of International Style architecture, *Galaxy* rejects a coolly logical "machine for living"[19] for the remains of marvelous beasts; the shapes of the gar and the ichthyosaur are hewn from wood to construct a castaway's dwelling, like Robinson Crusoe's, built of hospitable debris. A product of rude carpentry, and not industrial metal and glass, it gives shelter to the survivors of a ship lost at sea, a foundered vessel, which—like Crusoe's or Captain Ahab's—is very often an emblem of a wayward civilized world, a ship of fools. In these many ways, "Kiesler's *Galaxy*" seeks refuge from the mechanical advances we have come to understand as defining the twentieth century. By the end of this essay, I hope to suggest some of the reasons why.

Part of the answer lies precisely in the kind of literary narrative Barr suggests—a story told with metaphors. Through its extravagantly figurative language, "Kiesler's *Galaxy*" evokes a number of well-known stories that are also based on metaphors, including myths and other symbolic tales, some of them dating to antiquity. Such a story can be offered to the reader as an allusive, poetic counterpart to the austere art history narrative we might have expected. It suggests, in other words, something that can be called an allegory. The word *allegory* is meant in the sense of a thematically rich narrative whose plot conforms to the structure of a familiar model; related literary forms include the parable, the fable, and the prophecy. Barr once wrote that Picasso "originally conceived [the *Demoiselles*] as a kind of *memento mori* allegory."[20] And he described the enigmatic etching *Minotauromachy* (1935) as "a kind of private allegory"[21]—the sort of symbolic story we tell ourselves in order to make sense of experience. It will be possible, ultimately, to see a personal notion of allegory at work in Barr's prose.

Inscribed in the metaphors of Barr's great exhibition catalogues, of his popular-audience books such as *What Is Modern Painting?* and *Masters of Modern Art* (1954), and of his magazine pieces such as "Kiesler's *Galaxy*" (1952) and "Will This Art Endure?" (1957), there are traces of this nascent, symbolic story. They may hint at the shape the twentieth century sometimes assumed in his imagination. To a remarkable extent, Barr's metaphors construct an allegory on the compelling political drama of the century's middle years. He tells a fable of art's participation in certain world events that haunted his thinking in the forties and fifties.

With this larger use of metaphor in mind, we can now look in Barr's published writings for the kinds of figurative language that specifically set up a narrative framework—poetic figures that suggest a story about the contending forces and figures surrounding modern art. As Panofsky tells us, "Allegories . . . may be defined as combinations of personifications and/or symbols"; he goes on to observe, "A story may convey . . . an allegorical idea . . . conceived as the 'prefiguration' of another story."[22] Two particular poetic devices can therefore be especially useful in writing an allegory. The first is what I have been calling personification, in which an idea or a

quality or even an inanimate object is identified with a person. The second is the notion of "typology," in which one individual prefigures another. In pursuing Barr's use of these two devices, we will see him building up metaphorical structures, framing the conflicted history of the mid-twentieth century in figurative terms. After considering these devices, we then can turn to the larger allegory they make possible.

Personification in the Machine Age

In fiction, and in real life, individuals often come to stand for abstract qualities. The characters in the medieval morality play *Everyman*, for example, with names like Friendship and Good Deeds, make the drama a straightforward allegory of everyone's journey through life and preparation for death. At the same time, an object can take on a personal, human existence, and this, too, is personification. When Samuel Taylor Coleridge writes of "The one red leaf, the last of its clan / That dances as often as dance it can," he gives the leaf the human characteristic of belonging to a family, or "clan," and the human ability to dance. John Ruskin cited these lines from Coleridge as an example of the "pathetic fallacy," or the kind of personification that ascribes human feelings to the inanimate.[23]

When Alfred Barr speaks of Picasso's creating a mutant "race"[24] of tripod sculptures, he employs the same trope Ruskin pointed to in Coleridge's leaf, the last of its "clan." Personification is a versatile device in Barr's published writings, but above all, it is a principal means of talking about the new visual forms of the modern era, whether in abstract art or in the industrial aesthetic of the Machine Age. For example, personification makes a conspicuous contribution to how we understand the passage quoted earlier from *Cubism and Abstract Art*. Of the two great currents Barr discerned in abstract art—the geometric and the non-geometric (or biomorphic, including shapes that Barr described as resembling, for instance, "a liver or an amoeba"[25])—it is not surprising that the biomorphic would be endowed with human characteristics. But it is indeed surprising that geometric forms as well take on lives of their own. We are told that "a square is as much an 'object' or a 'figure' as the image of a face,"[26] and that "the Surrealists . . . would, as conscientious Freudians, maintain that even squares and circles have symbolic significance."[27] This is not unrelated to the way in which Vasily Kandinsky saw the triangle as emblematic of the soul and its aspirations. In such modes of thought, "the cylinder, the sphere, the cone"[28] become little characters, like the "figures" in El Lissitzky's story *About Two Squares* (1920). And so when, in summarizing at the end of the "currents" passage, Barr brings together his "two main traditions of abstract art," he arranges them in a *tableau vivant:* "The shape of the square confronts the silhouette of the amoeba."[29]

Apparently, the intent of Barr's distinction between geometric and biomorphic abstraction is thus to make them *both* biomorphic. He quotes Picasso's statement, "Nor is there any 'figurative' and 'non-figurative' art. Everything appears to us in the guise of a 'figure.' Even in metaphysics ideas are expressed by means of symbolic figures. . . . A person, an object, a circle are all 'figures.'"[30] Barr's reasons for endorsing the personalization of geometry are stated forthrightly: Geometric perfection is beautiful, but it can be boring. In *Cubism and Abstract Art,* he quotes Plato on "the beauty of shapes . . . made . . . by the lathe, ruler and square. . . . These are not beautiful for any particular reason or purpose, as other things are, but are always by their very nature beautiful."[31] But three years before, he had written: "By 1915 some

painters had achieved such purity of design that they were working with ruler and compass. By 1920 several of these purists had (literally) painted square canvases in pure white or black, thrown them (figuratively) out the window and turned to something really interesting such as photography or architecture."[32] Perhaps they are the ones Barr has in mind when in "Kiesler's *Galaxy*" he speaks of "refugees from the compass and the ruler," who shun the perfect forms made by mechanical-drawing instruments. He addresses this problem with geometric abstraction again in *What Is Modern Painting?* Defining in his conclusion three key terms—"Truth, Freedom, Perfection"—he notes that of all modern artists perhaps Mondrian comes the closest to perfection; yet "artistic perfection . . . can be, but should not be, 'too' perfect," because "complete perfection in art would probably be as boring as a perfect circle, a perfect Apollo, or the popular, harp-and-cloud idea of Heaven."[33] But it is not only sheer geometric perfection that makes it possible to speak of God as a circle, or the Trinity as a triangle, or indeed for Walt Whitman to speak of God as a square—his "square deific" and "square entirely divine"—as Meyer Schapiro tells us: "The capacity of these geometric shapes to serve as metaphors of the divine arises from their living, often momentous, qualities for the sensitive eye."[34] The stability of the square, the floating self-enclosure of the circle, the upward indication of the triangle can give them distinct personalities. Hence the urge to personify, to endow with life, the little square and not just the squirming amoeba.

Throughout Barr's writings, there is a related insistence on the lives of other sorts of inanimate things. The grandfather clock in the center of Matisse's *Red Studio* (fig. 5) is not simply a timepiece: It is "a one-eyed monitor"[35] who stands guard over the scattered paintings and sculpture, keeping them from harm. Artworks themselves have living bodies, as when Cubist pictures are said to have a "skeleton"[36]—unlike "boneless" Impressionist works,[37] but like an International Style building with its "skeleton enclosed by . . . a thin light shell."[38] Barr quotes Picasso as saying of a painting's genesis that "a picture is not thought out and settled beforehand. . . . A picture lives a life like a living creature, undergoing the changes imposed on us by our life from day to day. This is natural enough, as the picture lives only through the man who is looking at it."[39] When the work later becomes part of a museum collection, Barr himself writes, that life continues:

5. Henri Matisse. *The Red Studio*. 1911. Oil on canvas, 71¼" x 7' 2¼" (181 x 219.1 cm). The Museum of Modern Art, New York. Mrs. Simon Guggenheim Fund

You may feel that the works of art in our care should be allowed to live their own lives undisturbed by research or other educational activity. Yet I believe that works of art, like human beings, thrive on the attention paid them.

Consider, for instance, a newly acquired painting. It enters the museum collection on a wave of excitement. . . . Other museums want to borrow it, and painters want to copy it. Thus for a time it leads a gala life. . . . But . . . a little later the new painting takes its normal place in gallery 34 B and the honeymoon is over.

Whether the work of art subsequently lives or dies depends partly on its intrinsic qualities, partly on the attention we are able to give it by our continued interest.[40]

Promised gifts are, in a sense, betrothed to the museum; when they enter the collection, it is as if the museum has married them, and thereafter always needs to remain on guard against taking them for granted. They must be loved and honored. Only if paintings live and breathe and conduct lives involved with our own does it

make sense for Barr, as he does in his preface to *Italian Masters*, to wish a group of them safe passage on the dangerous journey back to their home in the fascist Italy of 1940: "Welcome, then, to these great works of art—and after we have enjoyed them may they return safely to the land which gave them life."[41] And only if paintings can feel pain does it make sense to "rescue"[42] them from their Nazi captors, to "ransom" them, as was Matisse's *Blue Window* (1913) when it was purchased "privately . . . out of the cellar of Göring's *Luftministerium*"[43] by The Museum of Modern Art, its escape to a new life in a free country assured—just as many European refugees seeking asylum in the United States were indeed helped by the Museum at that time.[44] (These were the fortunate ones; Barr, continuing his metaphor, mentions "the handsome group of impressionist and post-impressionist paintings in the Neue Staatsgalerie [in Munich], some of which survived the Nazi purge.")[45] The suppression of avant-garde art, particularly in the Soviet Union and in Nazi Germany, but also closer to home, was much on Barr's mind at the time of *Cubism and Abstract Art* in 1936. In his closing remark in the introduction to the catalogue, there is a paradoxical sense that those artists, by giving life to harmless geometric forms, have put themselves at risk: "This essay and exhibition might well be dedicated to those painters of squares and circles . . . who have suffered at the hands of philistines with political power."[46]

•

To a remarkable extent, Alfred Barr presents us with an animated universe, where objects of contemplation live lives closely intertwined with the lives of men and women. This impulse toward personification is not an isolated rhetorical device, useful for explaining how lively visual forms interact; it is instead a view of the nature of modern life and what is needed to live it. With the coming of the Machine Age and with the development of abstract art, especially the geometric varieties, human beings were confronted to an unprecedented degree with alien forms that bore no resemblance to what had been understood as living, handmade forms—as forms that are seen to be alive not only because they depict living things but because they show the touch of the living maker's hand. Barr pointed out, "Malyevitch, Lissitsky, and Mondriaan have used technicians' tools, the compass and the square, to achieve 'abstract' geometrical paintings of a machine-like precision."[47] In everyday living, too, one could now encounter stark, undisguised geometric shapes, in anonymous, mass-produced objects of daily life. During the first century after the Industrial Revolution, some industrialized design therefore continued to appear "inhuman" to writers such as John Ruskin and William Morris. But Barr did not want people to turn away from these developments and retreat into a medieval-craft notion of handwork, as Morris had.[48] Instead, he wanted them to learn to live productively in a new, modern world. And if people were to deal with these new, "dehumanized" forms, they needed to understand how such forms did in fact relate to what was human—to understand not only how such things worked within a mechanical system, but also how they served human needs and ends. Personification facilitated that human connection.

This was especially necessary with chromium and steel. So much could the modern era be defined as the Machine Age that in 1926, Barr had intended to write a thesis with the title "The Machine in Modern Art,"[49] and his fascination with the living machinery of the modern world remained strongly in evidence, whether in

his advocacy of the influential "Machine Art" exhibition of 1934, organized by Philip Johnson, which inaugurated the Museum's design collection; or in his writings about the humanoid machines envisioned by Francis Picabia and Fernand Léger; or in his frequent praise of the modern artist's role as a kind of "engineer." Barr wanted people to see that machines can be beautiful, in the same way as geometric abstract art, because "Machines are, visually speaking, a practical application of geometry."[50] When Barr wrote of "Léger's love of the beauty of machinery," he was talking about *Three Women* (fig. 6), with its three lounging figures "drawn, modeled and, as it were, polished as if they were an assembly of crank shafts, cylinders, castings and instrument boards." He lavished this description on them not just for the fact that "the *Three Women* may be compared to the beauty of a superb motor running smoothly, powerfully," but also for a larger reason: "Léger has been attacked by several varieties of 'humanists' for 'dehumanizing' art by mechanizing its figures; but has he not at the same time helped to humanize the machine by rendering it esthetically assimilable?"[51] And that was the point, to humanize the machine and fold it into the story of our aesthetic, and our organic, life. Thus it was that Barr could write in his foreword to the catalogue for "Machine Art": "If . . . we are to 'end the divorce' between our industry and our culture we must assimilate the machine aesthetically as well as economically. Not only must we bind Frankenstein—but we must make him beautiful."[52] Much of the personification evident throughout Barr's writing has that aim, to make the modern Machine Age more fit for human habitation. The process of working out a relationship with new mechanical inventions is an overall plot line for his nascent allegory of the modern era.

6. Fernand Léger. *Three Women*. 1921. Oil on canvas, 6' ¼" x 8' 3" (183.5 x 251.5 cm). The Museum of Modern Art, New York. Mrs. Simon Guggenheim Fund

•

Barr's playful allusion to *Frankenstein* reminds us that there is a difference between personification as applied to abstract shapes and as applied to mechanical devices: With machines, we are no longer in the realm of imaginative projection or of mere descriptive analogies, but rather in a realm of the increasingly literal. In a sense that Marshall McLuhan would popularize, beginning with his book *The Mechanical Bride* (1951), certain machines were *already* partly human, both through their intimate involvement with human beings when in use, as with prosthetic extensions of the body, and through their quasi-autonomous functioning, as with an airplane's "automatic pilot." Usurping the proper role of the artist, and of the God of Genesis, Mary Shelley's Dr. Frankenstein had undertaken to invent a lifelike representation of the human form. The fictional character is thus understood as a danger signal, a forecast of that technological hubris which would afflict the future—as Barr recognized in writing about the Futurists, whose devotion to modern machinery and the concept of speed was allied to a worship of modern warfare and its supposed therapeutic effects, and was later linked with fascism. When Filippo Tommaso Marinetti said that "a roaring motor-car, which runs like a machine gun, is more beautiful than the *Winged Victory of Samothrace*," he demonstrated the negative inversion of an attempt like Barr's to associate the beauty of the mechanical with the beauty of the organic: ending the "divorce" could result in dehumanization perhaps as easily as it could in humanization. Frankenstein might remain unbound. New inventions could produce a world like the one depicted in Karel Capek's robot drama, *R.U.R.* (1923), for which Frederick Kiesler had designed sets. The robot in human form, and the human-devouring dynamo called Moloch, at the heart of Fritz Lang's *Metropolis*

(1927), a film Barr admired,[53] come immediately to mind as the malign adversaries of Barr's efforts at humanization. In a different vein, so does the industrial age as presented in Charles Chaplin's *Modern Times* (1936). They all convey the enormity of what in the wake of the mechanized combat of 1914–18, with its tanks, machine guns, and biplanes, was sometimes seen as the machine's war against the human.

In light of this, it is significant that when Barr in *Cubism and Abstract Art* quoted Marinetti's famous sentence about the racing automobile and the *Winged Victory*, he carefully omitted the words about the machine gun.[54] Perhaps Barr's reasons for leaving out the machine gun were like those given by Arthur Drexler, Director of the Museum's Department of Architecture and Design from 1956 to 1986, in explaining the exclusion of arms from the design collection: "Some things are inherently uncollectible . . . because their functions are antisocial. Deadly weapons are among the most fascinating and well-designed artifacts of our time, but their beauty can be cherished only by those for whom aesthetic pleasure is divorced from the value of life—a mode of perception the arts are not meant to encourage."[55]

Messianic Time

At the beginning of the twentieth century, one of Barr's favorite writers, Henry Adams, had established the larger metaphorical terms in which the Machine Age might be understood. Adams visited the Gallery of Machines at the Paris World's Fair of 1900 and was struck with a kind of fearful wonder at the immense electrical generator on display there. In "The Dynamo and the Virgin," the chapter of his autobiography that presents the generator as the very embodiment of the modern age, he would write, "Before the end, one began to pray to it."[56] He was not thinking simply of the old Enlightenment analogy of the machine as a model of the universe, the cosmos conceived as a vast clockworks mechanism, its rotating and revolving parts the work of some divine clockmaker. More than that, for Adams the generator's unprecedented, almost terrifying power made manifest the fact that the world had entered a wholly novel era, a kind of mechanical millennium. Machines had utterly transformed life; the dynamo's all-pervasive, energizing presence was what now animated the modern world, even as the cult of the Virgin Mary and all it symbolized had animated the Middle Ages and raised the great cathedrals. Thus to Adams, the opposition between a figure (or "type") from theology and a great invention from technology defined the nature of the modern; an old symbol was losing its hold and a new one, made of metal, was taking its place as the faith of the emerging era. In the twentieth century, he suggested, industrial technology would become a new kind of Messianic religion—one whose advent could be cause for alarm.

For, as Adams saw, the epoch-making impact of machines on modern life is often ambiguous, having the potential for great harm as well as great benefit. To some in the nineteenth century, it had still seemed that the dawning Machine Age might turn out to be a golden one; in the burgeoning Industrial Revolution, mechanical inventions were expected to free workers from tedious labor and radically improve daily life. As one Victorian writer put it, "Are not our inventors absolutely ushering in the very dawn of the millennium?"[57] But to many in the twentieth century, especially after World War I, the prospects for global improvement did not look so rosy. Technology might indeed change the world, but not always for the better. As Barr himself wrote in 1934, "Today man is lost in the . . . wilderness of . . . indus-

trial civilization. On every hand machines literally multiply our difficulties and point our doom."[58] Or, as Adams had written much earlier, "The engines [man] will have invented will be beyond his strength to control. Some day science may have the existence of mankind in its power, and the human race commit suicide by blowing up the world."[59]

In dealing with these portentous aspects of the Machine Age, Barr, like Adams, had recourse to millennial metaphors—another feature of his language that we should examine. Sometimes, Barr looked back to Christian "types" and allegories—back, so to speak, from the Dynamo to the Virgin—in constructing a narrative about modern art. His prose goes out of its way to allow for a reading of events in terms of a New Testament time scheme. As in a biblical allegory, the plot points toward a final conflict between two great, symbolic, contending forces. For Barr, as for Henry Adams, it is a conflict between a mechanical invention and a theological "type." That is to say, on the one hand Barr's use of personification defines our potential adversary, in machine form. And on the other, it creates a hero—the sort of millennial figure developed in the New Testament through the device of typology. With these special uses of literary language, Barr sometimes articulates a new, modern sense of Messianic time.

We can see how this happens by further exploring Barr's uses of personification, this time its extension into biblical typology. In this regard, all Christian narrative is potentially allegorical; the Incarnation is simply the theological version of personification, understood in this case as a person's embodying divine attributes. Typological allegory along these lines is familiar to students of medieval and Renaissance art, and it is well to remember that Barr had studied medieval art with the eminent Charles Rufus Morey at Princeton and had specialized in the Italian Renaissance as a graduate student. He would have been intimately acquainted with typology also through the work of his father, the Reverend Alfred H. Barr, Sr., who, as a distinguished member of the Presbyterian clergy, wrote two books on homiletics, the art of presenting such thematic analogies to a popular audience in sermons. Through the notion of typology, it is understood that one biblical individual or event can prefigure or recapitulate another. Adam falls by eating the fruit of a tree, and is saved by Christ, the Second Adam, who mounts another "tree." Jonah—mentioned in "Kiesler's *Galaxy*," in connection with storytelling—is swallowed by a whale; emerging after three days, he prefigures Christ, who will be swallowed by the earth, to emerge after three days. In each case, the earlier figure or event, the one that prefigures, is technically called the *type*, while the second, culminating figure or event, the one that fulfills the promise of the first, is called the *antitype*. The type turns out to have been a prophetic allegory of the antitype.We could, in a less technical and more familiar vocabulary, call the first, preparatory figure the prototype, and the second, climactic figure the archetype.

The type/antitype scheme extends to future time, indeed, to the end of time, through the projection of a third figure. For example, Eve, through whom humankind falls, is the type, and Mary, through whom humankind will be redeemed, is the antitype—and she in turn prefigures the Woman Clothed with the Sun, in Revelations, the apocalyptic figure who helps bring the whole cosmic pattern of redemption to its ultimate, eschatological conclusion. When Meyer Schapiro interprets Vincent van Gogh's *Starry Night* (1889), he gives it a specifically typolog-

ical reading, and sees "in the coiling nebula and in the strangely luminous crescent—an anomalous complex of moon and sun and earth-shadow, locked in an eclipse—a possible unconscious reminiscence of the apocalyptic theme of the woman in pain of birth, girded with the sun and moon and crowned with stars, whose newborn child is threatened by the dragon (Revelations 12, 1 ff.)."[60]

This anticipated third occurrence is highly illuminating, and in a unique way. As in fairy tales, the third is a charm. In particular, the third—the apocalyptic—occurrence can provide a key to the operative symbolism, by showing the "shaping ends" that organize events. A typological plot works "in anticipation of a terminal structuring moment of revelation."[61] In other words, to the writer it is a means of showing the true, final significance of present events. Indeed, in Romantic and modern versions of this scheme, the apocalyptic crisis becomes not a global or cosmic catastrophe, but rather a revelatory moment of almost preternatural understanding, like William Wordsworth's vision on Mount Snowdon, or James Joyce's "epiphanies."[62] In Christian and Christian-derived allegories of this sort, based on ideas of Messianic expectation, it is in some sense always the end of the world: The conflated time scheme makes the end (and the beginning) always present in the here and now.

The example of Joyce is important in understanding Barr, for such allegory is not confined to the Middle Ages or the Renaissance; it has been a leading feature of much modern literature. T. S. Eliot's review of Joyce's *Ulysses* (1922), titled "*Ulysses,* Order, and Myth,"[63] appeared in *The Dial* in 1923, at a time when the young Alfred Barr was avidly reading that same magazine, in which hard-to-find reproductions of modern artworks often appeared.[64] Commenting on the structure of *Ulysses*, with its episode-by-episode recasting of Homer (Odysseus is the type, Leopold Bloom the satirical antitype, and his heavenly city of the "New Bloomusalem" a millennial culmination), Eliot said that "Mr. Joyce's parallel use of the *Odyssey* has a great importance. It has the importance of a scientific discovery." Comparing it to the discoveries of Einstein, he wrote that "in manipulating a continuous parallel between contemporaneity and antiquity, Mr. Joyce is pursuing a method which others must pursue after him." What makes this method so important is that it enables the writer to impose a kind of rough plot-outline on the bewildering diversity and fragmentation of modern life. As Eliot says: "It is simply a way of controlling, of ordering, of giving a shape and a significance to the immense panorama of futility and anarchy which is contemporary history."

Instead of presenting time as a string of merely serial happenings, the use of allegorical types offers a way of making a leap of significance across a large span of time; it becomes possible to see a specific part of the past as not only reflected, but fulfilled—consummated—in the present. As Walter Benjamin wrote in this regard, a historian who conceives history this way "stops telling the sequence of events like the beads of a rosary. Instead, he grasps the constellation which his own era has formed with a definite earlier one. Thus he establishes a conception of the present as the 'time of the now' which is shot through with chips of Messianic time."[65]

Such concepts of Messianic time are invoked on those occasions when, for example, Barr quotes with approval Fernande Olivier's characterization of Matisse as "the type of the great master."[66] And indeed, in his discussions of "great masters," metaphors from typology permeate Barr's writing. For Barr, too, most especially during the 1940s, the present is shot through with chips of Messianic time. This is per-

haps most evident in the formula of artistic influence, centered on a dominating figure, that Michael Baxandall has called the "prophet–savior–apostles" form.[67] We do sometimes think of, say, Cézanne, Picasso, and Juan Gris in the respective roles of the John the Baptist, the Messiah, and the Beloved Disciple of Cubism. The formula is simply a variant of the typological precursor, or prefiguration, pattern, wherein the major artist is foretold by a prophet who, like the Baptist, is a type of the savior that is to come.

This verbal formula has been applied to artists before, of course. In this respect Barr follows a venerable line of allegorists going back to John Ruskin and *Modern Painters*. Like others of his generation, born around the turn of the century, Barr still at times referred to Ruskin's way of mixing visual analysis with moral sermonizing. Reviewing an exasperating book by Dr. Albert C. Barnes in 1926, Barr finally threw his hands up and said that "Mr. Barnes will yet drive us to re-reading Ruskin."[68] It has been pointed out that Barr was reacting on that occasion against the almost hedonistic formalism of Barnes's focus on plastic means and values, as derived from Roger Fry and Clive Bell.[69] A similar reaction would be articulated by Edmund Wilson in 1931: "Such a critic as Clive Bell writes about painting so exclusively and cloyingly from the point of view of the varying degrees of pleasure to be derived from the pictures of different painters that we would willingly have Ruskin and all his sermonizing back."[70] What Wilson—as well as Barr, I think—invokes is the popular critic's "prophetic" mode; when Ruskin wanted to introduce to a general Victorian audience the work of "the greatest living artist,"[71] J. M. W. Turner, he had found it natural to rely on a familiar language of biblical allegory:

> *Turner—glorious in conception—unfathomable in knowledge—solitary in power— . . . [is] sent as a prophet of God to reveal to men the mysteries of His universe, standing, like the great angel of the Apocalypse, clothed with a cloud, and with a rainbow upon his head, and with the sun and stars given unto his hand.*[72]

Of its very nature, this is where the typology leads. And, perhaps somewhat unexpectedly, such allegorical themes of the artist-prophet and the apocalypse find expression, as we shall see, in Barr's own writings, particularly with respect to Picasso.

Though the verbal formula is an old one, it has rarely been used with such consistency and purposefulness as Barr's: He employs this language to identify those he considers the most important modern artists. Perhaps, recalling the "two currents" passage from *Cubism and Abstract Art* and Barr's recasting of it in his Matisse book, quoted earlier, it may seem as if Picasso and Matisse will become two rival Messiahs. Elaborating their potential conflict, Barr often gives his typology this special ecclesiastical twist, emphasizing divisive issues of heresy. At his art school the mature Matisse is said to have not just students but "disciples" (after having himself been dubbed by the critics in his younger days an "apostle of ugliness"); more than forward-looking, his works are "prophetic"; as a radical artist, his views are considered "heresy" by the establishment, and it threatens to "excommunicate" him from the Salons.[73] When his followers André Derain and Georges Braque alter their styles in 1907 under the influence of Picasso, these are not mere changes of manner, they are "conversions" as if to a new cult.[74] Following new models, in his L'Estaque landscapes Braque paints "in a more pious discipleship of Cézanne" than does his new friend

Picasso.[75] And when Picasso in 1915 begins to make realistic drawings, he does not just depart from his Cubist style for a time: He commits "apostasy."[76] Yet there are also "heretic" Cubists, such as Robert Delaunay.[77] In fact, in 1912 Delaunay's "heresy [runs] riot"; he feels he is "rebelling against intricate cubist scholasticism."[78] (This despite the fact that in *Les Demoiselles d'Avignon*, "obviously Picasso was interested in other than homiletic problems."[79]) Cubism threatens to become a new orthodoxy.

This dramatic metaphor of heresy versus orthodoxy, of conflict between two rival masters, a true and a false Messiah, complicates the whole idea of the great, individual artist-savior who forever alters how art can be made. Ultimately, we will have to address the problem of rival Messiahs more fully, especially with Picasso, for it is he who is finally treated in true Messianic terms. He transforms the nature of art, bringing about a change that can be deemed "epoch-making"—one of Barr's favorite terms. Picasso paints the *Demoiselles*, which Barr calls "one of the few pictures in the history of modern art which can be called 'epoch-making.'"[80] It is the first step in "the radical, epoch-making development of cubism,"[81] and, as he quotes Jacques Lipchitz: "Cubism . . . was not a school, an aesthetic, or merely a discipline—it was a new view of the universe."[82]

•

From such metaphorical conceptions, a poetic view of modern times begins to emerge. It is the story of a recurring type: the tale of the great, almost Messianic individual artist who, accomplishing an epoch-making breakthrough, seems to embody the revolutionary new age he initiates. It is conceived also as a fable of the Machine Age and of the sometimes inhuman products of modern creativity—the negative as well as the positive outcomes of mechanical inventiveness. A tragic view of history emerges, in which lofty aspirations often lead to disaster. And it becomes possible to plot out a specific allegory: It is an ambiguous story of the creative artist as a counterpart to the scientist and the inventor—one who produces a device that makes it possible to fly, but also to crash back to earth. Unexpectedly, the modern era takes shape as an allegory of Icarus.

The Allegory of Flight

Modern artists are not only painters or sculptors; they are also what Barr calls them at the opening of *What Is Modern Painting?*:

> *The greatest modern artists are pioneers just as are modern scientists, inventors and explorers. This makes modern art both more difficult and more exciting than the art we are already used to. Galileo, Columbus, the Wright brothers suffered neglect, disbelief, even ridicule.*[83]

This is one of Barr's master metaphors, and the one I shall pursue through the rest of this essay: Modern artists are scientists and inventors, like the Wright brothers, or perhaps like Leonardo with his anatomical diagrams, his siege-weapon designs, and his suggestive sketches of machines for flight.[84] In the twentieth century, the term *scientist* encompasses "atom scientists" (Niels Bohr and Albert Einstein, among others), a group Barr mentions on the first page of his text, as well as artists who use a "scientific system," as Georges Seurat did, so that people "looked on his paintings as complicated laboratory demonstrations."[85] Modern artists are scientific also in the hands-on,

practical sense of being mechanical draftsmen and technicians; Mondrian's paintings, for instance, are "put together and adjusted to a hair's breadth, with the conscience and precision of an engineer."[86] Barr quotes with approval Antoine Pevsner's remark that "we shape our work as the engineer his bridge, the mathematician his formula of a planetary orbit."[87]

It is in this context that Barr on numerous occasions calls Picasso's *Demoiselles* an "experimental" painting—"an imposing laboratory experiment," conducted in "the alchemical laboratory of Picasso's mind."[88] Cubism resembles a scientific experiment: it breaks objects down, like a chemical analysis, into their constituent elements. And like a diagnostic X-ray, it shows views into bodies, penetrating through surface contours; it dissects the object, revealing the very structure of matter. Indeed, the notion of Picasso the advanced research scientist leads Barr to mention under the heading of Cubism "some relationship to Einstein's theory of relativity," and "interesting analogies between cubism and the space-time continuum of modern physics."[89] It is not, of course, that Barr takes fourth-dimensional interpretations of Cubism very seriously. On the contrary, after speaking of the "cubist vestiges" and the "general flatness" of Matisse's *Piano Lesson* (1916), he jokes that "only the metronome (*pace* Einstein!) seems solidly three-dimensional."[90] It is not the fourth dimension Barr is seeking, I believe, but the special nature of the creative mind—its ability to see things in a different way, to reconfigure the familiar elements of the world through the imagination, and from them invent something new. Einstein was renowned for the way he arrived at revolutionary scientific theories largely intuitively—by visualizing objects in space, in his remarkable "thought experiments" (there is the well-known example of picturing the movement of articles within a falling elevator), rather than relying on the more customary computations. In such experiments, it has been observed, Einstein was "working at the very limits of physical imagination."[91] Artists, too, envision the objects of the world radically altered for the purposes of "research." An artist like Picasso and a scientist like Einstein are brothers under the skin; to make their respective breakthroughs, both conduct experiments in visual intuition.

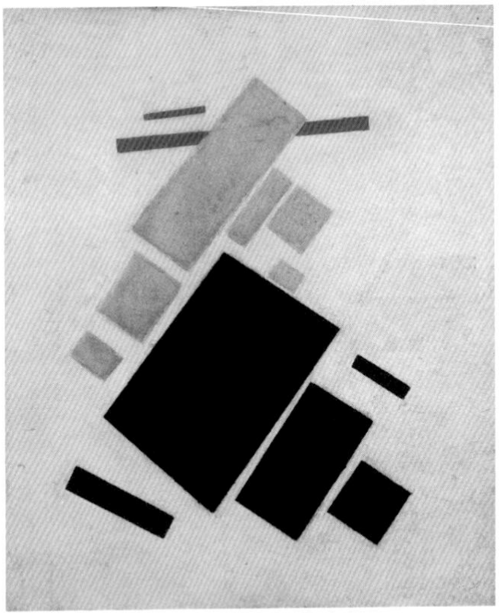

7. Kazimir Malevich. ***Suprematist Composition: Airplane Flying***. 1915 (dated 1914). Oil on canvas, 22⅞ x 19" (58.1 x 48.3 cm). The Museum of Modern Art, New York. Purchase

I shall later return to Einstein as the type of the advanced scientist, but first let us consider more closely the other prototype Barr cites for the modern artist: the inventor. Barr's mentioning the Wright brothers should remind us that throughout the early years of the century, there was a natural association between the invention of flying machines and the upward aspirations of modern artists.[92] Kazimir Malevich's *Suprematist Composition: Airplane Flying* (fig. 7), though abstract, looks at the new visual facts revealed by aviation; as Barr wrote, Malevich "drew inspiration for some of his compositions from airplane views of cities with their interesting patterns of rectangles and curves."[93] But from this aerial perspective Malevich glimpsed not a terrestrial but a non-objective world, and he sought to convey a sense of flight through the dynamics of abstract forms floating in empty space; inventing Suprematism, he seemed to reenact the invention of the airplane, what he termed the "great yearning for space . . . for flight . . . which, seeking an outward shape, brought about the birth of the airplane."[94] Working along different lines, Marinetti would inaugurate "aeropainting" and "aerosculpture"; Carlo Carrà, too, pursued such goals with his collage *Manifesto for Intervention* (1914), a view from the air of a demonstration. And Constantin Brancusi sought "the essence of flight";[95] his *Bird*

in Space (1928) allowed pure, clean, polished metallic forms to soar free of gravity. As William Carlos Williams wrote: "The *Bird in Space* gives an undoubted sense of flight, of the surrounding air, which is difficult for a sculptor to depict with the weight of his materials always before him. Most do not succeed but find their pieces anchored heavily at their feet, even the best of them—the wind in the clothes of the *Nike of Samothrace* [is a case] in point."[96]

Henri Rousseau featured aircraft in a number of paintings, basing his depictions on images that appeared in the popular press; above magical landscapes, he placed craft notable for their accuracy and precise detail. The dirigible in *The Quay of Ivry* and *View of the Bridge of Sèvres* (both 1908) is painted with such clear features that it can be identified as the *Patrie*—recognizable by the ailerons, with which it was the first lighter-than-air craft to be equipped—the first dirigible to be ordered by the French army.[97] *View of the Bridge at Sèvres* shows in addition Wilbur Wright's 1907 aircraft, identifiable by its lack of landing gear, as does *The Fishermen and the Biplane* (fig. 8). Robert Delaunay painted *Homage to Blériot* (c. 1914) to honor the French flyer Louis Blériot, and the celestial *Astra (The Cardiff Team)* (1912–13).[98] When Le Corbusier, in *Towards a New Architecture* (1923), sought a model for all that rational, elegantly functioning modern design could be, he chose the airplane, devoting a twenty-two-page chapter with sixteen photographs to the subject, and writing: "The airplane is indubitably one of the products of the most intense selection in the range of modern industry. . . . The airplane mobilized invention, intelligence and daring: *imagination* and *cold reason.* It is the same spirit that built the Parthenon"; for him, the ascent of the flying machine figured forth a certain kind of creative imagination: "The man who is intelligent, cold and calm has grown wings on himself."[99] The aeronautical ascent continued into the century: In 1927, when Barr was a young man beginning his career, Charles Lindbergh flew *The Spirit of Saint Louis* solo across the Atlantic.

8. Henri Rousseau. *The Fishermen and the Biplane*. 1908. Oil on canvas, 18⅛ x 21⅝" (46 x 55 cm). Musée National de l'Orangerie, Paris. Collection Jean Walter et Paul Guillaume

In the same spirit of the romance of engineering, Arshile Gorky painted his Cubist-derived WPA mural *Aviation: Evolution of Forms Under Aerodynamic Limitations* (see fig. 9), a work that Barr championed. Gorky wrote of his designs that "the engine becomes in one place like the wings of a dragon and in another the wheels, propeller and motor take on the demonic speed of a meteor cleaving the atmosphere."[100] In recommending Gorky's project, Barr as a member of the jury praised its unconventional methods and meanings; superior to a competing proposal, "the Gorky project is better anyway from almost every point of view except a purely conventional or academic [one]. I think the public would be much more interested in it than in the conventional allegories of [the other] project."[101]

Barr would seek ways to link the practices of painters with the technological feats of aviators. When Matisse painted the Barnes Foundation mural, he did much of his preliminary work at full scale, rather than enlarging a small model, in order to preserve, he said, a direct "physical encounter between the artist and some fifty-two meters of surface." Citing this, Barr then quotes Matisse's figurative explanation for going beyond an earthbound, small-scale study: "A man with his searchlight who follows an airplane in the immensity of the sky does not traverse space in the same way as an aviator."[102]

Among these many affinities between modern artists and aeronautical engineers, perhaps the most significant ones connect the invention of the flying machine

with the rise of Cubism. It is now well known, for example, that in the years they were inventing Cubism together, Picasso sometimes called Braque "Wilbourg," for Wilbur (Wright),[103] since the creative collaboration of the two inventor brothers was much like the collaboration of the two "brothers in Cubism."

Generally, Barr seeks to transmute the technical triumph of Cubism into something more human. In his commentary on Roger de La Fresnaye's *The Conquest of the Air* (fig. 10), Barr discusses Wilbur Wright's record flight of 1908, but, as in "Kiesler's *Galaxy*," he betrays some reservations about purely technical progress. He prefers instead to dwell on the gentler notion of conquest La Fresnaye depicts:

La Fresnaye does not insist upon technological triumphs—though the abstract parallels in the right foreground possibly refer to a biplane. Instead the air is gently conquered by a sailboat, the French tricolor and, in the distant empyrean, a balloon. Perhaps the chief conquest takes place in the minds of the men at the table who, with cubist indifference to gravity, float high above the roofs of the village.[104]

A puff of wind propels a sailboat, the tricolor flutters in the breeze, and a balloon levitates into the heavens. Through these airy means the painting depicts the ability of the inventive mind to master the most elusive of elements.

Part of the attraction of flight for artists was the excitement of seeing the world from a new point of view, from above.[105] Ascending to the heavens and covering great distances quickly, at high speeds, the power of flight made it truly seem that humankind had conquered time and space. So much did the Cubist revolution seem a matter of learning how to fly—"with cubist indifference to gravity"—that at the end of her book on Picasso, published in 1938, Gertrude Stein would say:

When I was in America I for the first time travelled pretty much all the time in an airplane and when I looked at the earth I saw all the lines of cubism made at a time when not any painter had ever gone up in an airplane. I saw there on the earth the mingling lines of Picasso, coming and going, developing and destroying themselves . . . as everything destroys itself in the twentieth century . . . Picasso . . . has that strange quality of an earth that one has never seen and of things destroyed as they have never been destroyed.[106]

Left:
9. Arshile Gorky. *Activities on the Field.* Panel for the left side of the north wall of the mural *Aviation: Evolution of Forms Under Aerodynamic Limitations,* 1936–37, commissioned for the Administration Building, Newark Airport, New Jersey. From a model (now lost) created for the exhibition "New Horizons in American Art," The Museum of Modern Art, New York, 1936

Right:
10. Roger de La Fresnaye. *The Conquest of the Air.* 1913. Oil on canvas, 7' 8⅞" x 6' 5" (235.9 x 195.6 cm). The Museum of Modern Art, New York. Mrs. Simon Guggenheim Fund

Her association of an aerial view with the idea of Cubist decomposition or deformation of objects was more than a fanciful comparison. In 1943, a war-related show at The Museum of Modern Art, "Airways to Peace: An Exhibition of Geography for the Future," organized by Monroe Wheeler, examined the many meanings of aviation, from Leonardo to the current hostilities. It had a special section on aviation's implications for mapping, "How Man Has Drawn His World." The catalogue answered the question "How much does Mercator distort?" by aligning a globe with a Mercator-projection map, and thus showing how the flat projection deformed the earth by pulling the continents seriously out of shape. Therefore, the catalogue urged, "man must re-draw his world."[107] Alfred Barr in his 1939 Picasso catalogue had allowed a recent portrait (fig. 11) to pass without comment, but in his second Picasso book, in 1946, three years after "Airways to Peace," he unexpectedly uses a particular geographical figure, describing the same portrait as a kind of navigational map of the head:

The heads of this period are popularly called "double-faced." Actually in this magnificently painted Portrait *Picasso has kept the usual number of features: he has merely drawn the face in profile with the mouth and one eye in front view and both ears and both nostrils visible, liberties which he has taken since cubism. After all, Mercator in his commonly used flat projection of the map of the world distorts the physiognomy of his spheroid more than Picasso does when he creates on a flat canvas his projection of a woman's head.*[108]

11. Pablo Picasso. *Portrait (Seated Woman).* 1938. Oil on canvas, 28 ¾ x 23 ⅝" (73 x 60 cm). Collection William and Donna Acquavella

His use of Mercator to describe Cubist "distortion" confirms how closely Barr observed the "Airways" show. Its attendant theme, the technology of aviation in war and peace, will come to the fore elsewhere in his writings.

The dawn of flight was a high point of the twentieth century's romance with the machine. The flying machine personified a dream humans had had for millennia, allowing them to soar like birds, like angels—or, perhaps, like Icarus. At the end of *A Portrait of the Artist as a Young Man* (1916), Joyce's improbably named Stephen Dedalus goes off to the continent—in 1903, the year of the first Wright brothers flight—to seek the "fabulous artificer," his namesake; he crashes back to earth shortly after, we learn at the beginning of *Ulysses*, and returns to Dublin and to his dying mother in a fall that shows he has failed to live up to his name, and is not the father, Daedalus, but the son, Icarus.[109] The myth of Icarus figured in T. S. Eliot's fascination with the way Joyce manipulated a parallel between the mythic and the modern; it tells something of what Eliot, and presumably his young reader, Alfred Barr, could understand the myth of the modern to be. If flight was modernist technical experiment par excellence, it was also a premonition of possible disaster. The plane's test flight provided a metaphor for progress—trying out an advanced way of getting from here to there, say from New York to Paris—and its pulsing machinery was thus an engine that drove the experimental "plot" of modern history forward into future time. Yet the test could fail, and thereby become a metaphor also for aspiration's collapse—for rise and fall, as with the Roman Empire, or the myth of Icarus.

This sense of failed aspiration makes itself felt, in an ironic way, even with Picasso and "Wilbur" Braque. As Picasso continued to think about flight, in 1912, the year of Wilbur Wright's death, he incorporated into some works the painted representation of a brochure with the printed slogan *"Notre avenir est dans l'air"* ("Our

future is in the air").[110] Though apparently a hopeful statement of the glorious future, the booklet in fact urged France to develop a military air corps, with the kinds of airborne munitions that within two years would buzz in the skies over Flanders.

•

The "downside" of modern inventiveness was evident in the mechanical weapons of World War I, such as the tank and the machine gun, and was symbolized by the sudden collapse of aviation's hopes into the grim reality of aerial combat and Zeppelin raids on London. The liabilities would be revealed on a much larger scale in the second war. Gertrude Stein was right: After the conquest of the air, things would be destroyed as they had never been destroyed before. And she was not being whimsical in seeing this somehow reflected in artists' work. It was becoming common to speak of modern art, with its "deformations" and its often "dehumanized" forms, as not only highly creative but also highly destructive. Picasso had called a painting a "sum of destructions,"[111] laying waste the familiar world in order to create a new one. Picking up his tone, Barr would find the *Demoiselles* "a purely formal figure composition," but one "which as it develops becomes more and more dehumanized."[112] The deformation or dissection, the visual violation, of the abstracted human form in the *Demoiselles*, and as seen in even more radical form in the attack of a late 1930s picture such as *Weeping Woman* (fig. 12), with its "taste for paroxysm,"[113] was among the prime characteristics that made Picasso's work modern. The *Weeping Woman* studies are a series of almost clinical experiments in evoking the utmost expressions from the specimen subjects. This quasi-scientific attitude toward the analysis of forms seemed to arouse the last vestiges of the Romantic fear of scientific research, a fear that Wordsworth, for one, had articulated long before:

> *Our meddling intellect*
> *Mis-shapes the beauteous forms of things: —*
> *We murder to dissect.*[114]

12. Pablo Picasso. *Weeping Woman*. 1937. Oil on canvas, 23⅝ x 19¼" (60 x 49 cm). The Trustees of the Tate Gallery, London

Thinking of Cubism's analytical impulses, struggling to take the world apart and reveal its inner stresses, Barr could speak of the *Demoiselles* as "a laboratory or, better, a battlefield."[115] He would point out that Cubism is "a process of breaking up" an object systematically "until a fragment of the visual world is completely conquered."[116] The military metaphor comes to play a central role, growing by the time of World War II into something that could be read as an allegory of the modern period. If Meyer Schapiro saw *Starry Night* as an apocalyptic revelation of the Woman Clothed with the Sun, Barr saw its visionary stars as "bursting bombshells."[117] A little later, Barr's view of the *Demoiselles,* too, became more militarized: Beyond "epoch-making," by the 1950s he could call the picture "the first detonation of a great historic movement"[118]—as if it were like the first atomic bomb, which recently had inaugurated the Nuclear Age.

But we are getting ahead of our story. To return to the interwar period: Aviation temporarily regained its luster after World War I, and went on to the great era of expansion that fostered the extraordinary careers of Lindbergh and Amelia Earhart, two almost superhuman beings who were to the popular imagination "like gods from outer space," as Gore Vidal has remarked, and who came to embody "the gospel of flight."[119] Yet the progress of aviation would still be marred by the occasional spec-

13. Pablo Picasso. *Guernica*. 1937. Oil on canvas, 11' 5½" x 25' 5¾" (349.3 x 776.6 cm). Museo Nacional Centro de Arte Reina Sofía, Madrid. On permanent loan from the Museo del Prado, Madrid

tacular failure: not only Earhart's mysterious disappearance over the Pacific in 1937, but also, in the same year, and more ominously, the crash of the *Hindenburg*, the dirigible whose fiery descent has sometimes been retold in fiction as premonitory of the disaster of its Nazi owners.[120] An even more serious downward turn came in April of that same year. When German bombers flying for General Francisco Franco in the Spanish Civil War devastated the Basque town of Guernica, it was, Barr carefully noted, "the first 'total' air raid."[121] An epoch-making change in the nature of warfare, this was the first calculated mass attack on a defenseless population, behind the lines, and it prefigured the fate of many other cities, in England, Germany, and Japan, during the coming world war—through its systematic execution, its use of experimental incendiary weapons, and its deliberate targeting of civilians, who were strafed by machine-gun fire as they fled the attack. *Guernica* (fig. 13) becomes an allegory of that atrocious event—and an allegory as well of artists' fighting back, for in painting it, Picasso "took an artist's revenge," bringing to bear "the special weapons of modern art."[122] Barr quotes Picasso: "No, painting is not done to decorate apartments. It is an instrument of war."[123] If advances in scientific techniques could be put to political purposes in war, then advances in artistic techniques could be put to political purposes, too—in propaganda. This was never more evident than at the 1937 Paris World's Fair, for which *Guernica* was commissioned; at the same fair, Leni Riefenstahl's film *Triumph of the Will* (1935) was awarded a gold medal.[124]

•

Consider for a moment the ramifications of juxtaposing these two famous works. The contrast between them represents a conflict between two opposed allegories of flight—and between two opposed ideas of a Messiah. *Triumph of the Will,* the record of the 1934 Nazi Party congress, opens with the notorious sequence of Adolf Hitler's arrival, his private airplane descending noiselessly from the billowing clouds above Nuremberg, as if its passenger were a god borne gently to earth.[125] This is the sequence, "the sea of clouds at the start of the film, the spires and gables of Nuremberg looming through," that Riefenstahl particularly evokes in her autobiography.[126] The words flashed on the screen to introduce this sequence make its Messianic pretensions explicit: "Twenty years after the outbreak of the World War, sixteen years after Germany's Passion, nineteen months after the beginning of the German Rebirth, Adolph Hitler again flew to Nuremberg to review the assembly of

his faithful followers."[127] The airplane—gliding high above the earth in an ethereal, otherworldly realm, then descending to the human world—is the vehicle of a debased theology. That is, its flight comprises in effect an allegory of the Party line, comparable (though much more aesthetically sophisticated) to the infamous painting by Otto Hoyer of Hitler delivering a speech early in his career, a picture flagrantly titled *In the Beginning Was the Word* (1937). Barr clearly understood, and attacked, these Messianic pretensions, specifically identifying the Hoyer painting as among the most blatant of "Aryan allegories."[128] The idea of Hitler as a "savior" self-consciously exploits the aspect of Christian tradition that looks for a "savage Messiah" and recalls the militant words in chapter 10 of Matthew: "I came not to send peace, but a sword." But if to the Nazis the Führer descending appeared like the Messiah, to everyone else he looked more like the Anti-Christ. To a large extent, the massive, geometrically organized crowd scenes that fill the rest of *Triumph of the Will*, including endless ranks and files of troops marching with obediently mechanical precision, manifested the worst of the dehumanizing tendencies so long feared in the developing Machine Age.

The co-opting of the role of artist to promote the goals of the state was implicit in totalitarian thinking, in its various forms among the Soviets, the Italians, and the Germans. As an extreme example, Josef Goebbels in 1933 said that politics is "the highest and most comprehensive art there is, and we who shape modern German policy feel ourselves to be artists."[129] And Hitler considered himself not only a painter, and capable of being "as great an architect as Michelangelo,"[130] but also, in his selection of works for the annual National Socialist exhibitions in Munich, a curator and a connoisseur, a judge of physical beauty. Barr had seen the danger firsthand when, on leave from the Museum, he happened to be in Germany as the Nazis came to power in 1933 and witnessed their growing mastery of propaganda.[131] In reaction Barr would write, "We detest the policy of the totalitarian state that rigidly controls all thought and creative expression in order to make them serve its own ends."[132]

This monstrous expropriation of art was allied to a general aesthetics of the racially "pure" and "perfect"; as Susan Sontag has observed, "Fascist art displays a utopian aesthetics—that of physical perfection."[133] When Hitler campaigned against modern art, especially through the exhibition "Degenerate Art" (*"Entartete Kunst"*), which opened in July 1937,[134] he was propounding a reactionary notion of ideal physical beauty, supposedly to be achieved in actuality, through eugenics. What he specifically found "degenerate" was the apparent deformation of the figure in advanced art—primarily by the German Expressionists but also, as Barr noted, by Picasso, "the painter of *Guernica* and the chief of all *entarteten Kunstbolschewisten*" and "the most renowned and formidable master of 'degenerate' art."[135] Such artists were accused of violating the beauty of utopian and racial perfection. National Socialist propaganda pretended that the world could be a work of art if only the ugliness represented by its enemies were stamped out. Barr icily condemned such gross abuses of art, pointing out that the Führer's "personal hatred of modern art" arose from the fact that "Hitler himself was a disappointed, mediocre, academic painter."[136]

When in Barr's writing Picasso comes to play the role of hero in an allegorical tale about modern art, he does so by taking up a position directly opposite to that of Hitler, the Anti-Christ as failed artist. Not only does Picasso make "a public statement intended to arouse public feeling against the horrors of war and implicitly, at

least, against Franco and his German bombers," and thereby create "the most famous of all anti-Axis propaganda pictures."[137] But also, by becoming the painter of that work, Picasso embodies in general *the idea of modern art,* which the Nazis had set out to eliminate. For *Guernica* is a further instance of the deformation, or violation, of the female form as seen since the *Demoiselles* and as seen in *Weeping Woman*—one of the very attributes that had first defined Picasso's work as "modern," and the feature of modern art that the Nazis found most repellent.

As the foremost master of the kind of challenging, sometimes distressing figural art the Nazis despised, Picasso carries its standard in an allegorical tale about the fate of modernism. Barr quotes him as saying in 1937, while painting *Guernica* and after being accused of harboring fascist or reactionary sympathies, "My whole life as an artist has been nothing more than a struggle against reaction and the death of art."[138] Defending art, in *Guernica,* he takes a rebarbative style the fascists hate and throws it in their faces, in the name of their victims. This modern Slaughter of the Innocents owes its effect to what Barr calls its "modern techniques," "the special weapons of modern art"[139]—to how its aggressive deformations and distortions of the female figure, so closely associated with this particular artist, here function as an act of defiance *against* aggression. Like the *Minotauromachy* etching, *Guernica* is to this extent what Barr termed "a kind of private allegory"—in this instance a psychomachy, a struggle between the forces of life and death, acted out within the artist's creative psyche. That inner drama is a microcosm of the struggle going on in the world at large.

This is perhaps why Matisse, for example, did not undertake similar subjects: they were too remote from his intrinsic sensibility. Barr points out that Matisse's *Woman in Blue* (1937) "was finished a few days before Picasso began his *Guernica.* No one of course thought of comparing them. But even Matisse's major works of the 1930s . . . can scarcely compete with the black and white fury of *Guernica.*"[140] Matisse was exempt from mortal combat on grounds of being incorrigibly life-affirming. Barr intimates as much; after quoting Clement Greenberg's assertion that "Matisse is the greatest living painter," Barr goes on to say:

Greenberg's enthusiasm may be balanced by a remark made by another young American painter and writer, Robert Motherwell: "Matisse may be the greatest living painter but I prefer Picasso: he deals with love and death." To which one might reply, on the same level, yes, but Matisse deals with love and life.[141]

The Typology of Armageddon

Themes of the potential destructiveness of modern inventions, whether technical or aesthetic, and of the artist as ambiguous Messiah permeate *Guernica* and Barr's discussions of it. They indicate some reasons why this particular picture plays a central role in a story about modern times that is clearly taking on tragic, even apocalyptic, overtones. Perhaps we can define that sense of looming catastrophe, of art's implication in the disasters of the mid-twentieth century, by continuing with our specific allegory, which sees the flight of Icarus as a symbol of modernism's aspirations and failures.

The allegory of flight makes a journey of three stops across Barr's writings. The first stop is Cubism, with its liberating inventiveness evident, like the Wright brothers', in its disregard of gravity and its view from the air. The second stop is *Guernica*

and the calamitous turn that ingenuity took in the conflict surrounding it. The third and last stop is in certain works of the postwar period, with their ominous new permutation of the relations among science, politics, and the creative arts, seen especially in another work Barr favored, the sculpture *Spectre of Kitty Hawk* by Theodore Roszak (see fig. 21). In this story, each inspired modern experiment tends to go somehow awry, yielding the most surprising and devastating consequences. In the artistic realm, the advances typified by Picasso evoke the ferocious retaliation of "Degenerate Art." In the technological realm, the Wrights' homemade contraption unexpectedly gives rise to the attack aircraft. We can retrace how modern inventions went wrong by following the imaginative movement from *Guernica* to *Kitty Hawk*.

•

Guernica came to the United States in 1939, to be exhibited for the benefit of the Spanish Refugee Relief Campaign, at the Valentine Gallery in New York in May and at the Stendahl Galleries in Los Angeles in August. It then came to The Museum of Modern Art, in November, to be shown, like the newly acquired *Demoiselles*, in the Picasso retrospective exhibition of that year. It remained for more than forty years, decades during which it became arguably the best-known of all modern paintings. In Barr's 1946 book on Picasso, *Guernica* is a main structural principle—mentioned first in the introduction, touched upon in the pages on the *Demoiselles*, foreshadowed in the passages about *Minotauromachy* and *Dream and Lie of Franco* (1937), discussed at length late in the book, and then recalled one last time at the end, in the page on the "postscript" painting *The Charnel House* of 1944–45 (fig. 14).[142] It also became the centerpiece of *What Is Modern Painting?*, where Barr discusses it at greater length than any other work, and under the explicit section-heading "Allegory and Prophecy." The painting forms the center of the allegory of flight: The airplane, which had embodied aspiration, became in aerial bombardment an instrument of the defeat of modernism's hopeful visions of the future—the way that totalitarian governments, as Barr had seen in Nazi Germany and Stalinist Russia, crushed the aspirations of advanced artists along with the freedom of everyone. If the warplane is emblematic of technical ingenuity gone desperately wrong, it suggests also a wider indictment of the uses to which modern science could be put. This we see at the end of the Picasso book, when, after referring to *Guernica* in his discussion of *The Charnel House*, Barr relates the latter painting to "Buchenwald, Dachau and Belsen."[143] Those appalling names should remind us that not only artists thought of themselves as inventors and scientists—so did the Nazis, whose vicious "scientific" theories of eugenics were used to rationalize their policy of racial experiment.

14. Pablo Picasso. ***The Charnel House***. 1944–45. Oil and charcoal on canvas, 6' 6⅝" x 8' 2½" (199.8 x 250.1 cm). The Museum of Modern Art, New York. Mrs. Sam A. Lewisohn Bequest (by exchange) and Mrs. Marya Bernard Fund in memory of her husband, Dr. Bernard Bernard, and anonymous funds

The biological sciences were perverted by the Nazi regime in tandem with the aeronautical sciences. Indeed, in presenting themselves to the world, the Nazis sometimes made the technical advancement signaled by the airplane function as a code for their experimental ideas of biological and societal "advancement" and "triumph." We see this in their use of striking aerial imagery in propaganda, even before the war. In *Triumph of the Will*, the divine descent of Hitler's airplane through the enveloping clouds is a sequence as visually arresting as it is disturbing. There was a specific reason, other than sheer megalomania, why Hitler was portrayed as a god come down to earth: The Nazi regime liked to think of itself as inaugurating the "third age" of sacred history, which is to bring on a cleansing apocalypse, as in the eschatological writings of Joachim of Flora.[144] The Age of the Father and the Age of the Son are followed by the pentecostal

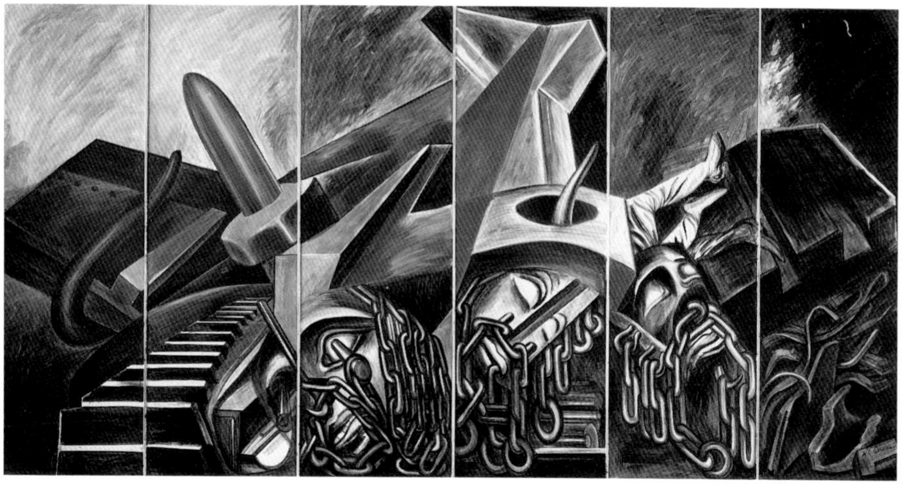

15. José Clemente Orozco. *Dive Bomber and Tank.* 1940. Fresco, 9 x 18' (275 x 550 cm), on six panels, 9 x 3' (275 x 91.4 cm) each. The Museum of Modern Art, New York. Commissioned through the Abby Aldrich Rockefeller Fund

Age of the Holy Spirit (symbolized by the flight of the dove). In this third age, there is no law: mere terrestrial law is crumbling, while the Redeemed—also called the Perfect—need no laws.[145] A third age of the triumphant Perfect, who are above earthly law, was implicit in the term "Third Reich."

This imagery of heavenly descent—to be made credible by the hard evidence of aeronautical triumph—is one of the reasons why the Nazis cultivated Charles Lindbergh in his prewar trips to Germany and awarded him a medal. In retrospect, however, Lindbergh's Nazi contact tarnished his silver wings and made him seem not the demigod he had been to the public, but rather an Icarus fallen to earth. In 1936, Lindbergh visited Berlin, met with Air Marshal Hermann Göring, and inspected aircraft factories. As he later wrote: "I knew theoretically what modern bombs could do to cities," but "in Nazi Germany, for the first time, war became real to me . . . and I realized how destructive my profession of aviation might become. . . . Now I began to think about the vulnerability of men to aircraft carrying high-explosive bombs."[146]

The kind of aerial bombardment he began to think about has been a powerful image in literature at least since H. G. Wells's science-fiction story *The War in the Air* (1908), which told of the destruction of New York by aerial bombing.[147] Wells returned to this theme in *The Shape of Things to Come* (1933), which envisioned a twenty-five-year global war (imagined as beginning in 1940), punctuated by periodic air raids; the film version, *Things to Come*, released in 1936, would seem unnervingly prophetic only a few years later. When that vision did become a reality, during the London Blitz, T. S. Eliot chose to see German bombers in theologically charged terms:

The dove descending breaks the air
With flame of incandescent terror
Of which the tongues declare
The one discharge from sin and error.
The only hope, or else despair
  Lies in the choice of pyre or pyre —
  To be redeemed from fire by fire.[148]

Incendiary bombs spew what Eliot earlier in the poem had called "pentecostal fire," and the planes' flaming forward guns "discharge" the "tongues" of sacred fire that hovered above the apostles' heads at Pentecost. It is apocalyptic imagery displaced into modern technology, purging the world in a second, fiery deluge, a baptism of fire, and giving the details of aerial destruction a sense of divine participation in them. This is comparable in some ways to the strange light-form in *Guernica,* at the top, left of center: is it only a modern electric bulb, juxtaposed to the kerosene lamp of the watcher in the window? Or is it a bomb bursting, with rays of shrapnel? Or is it the eye of God, who sees but remains as remote and aloof as the bull? A great, unnaturally blazing sun (related to the Woman Clothed with the Sun, in Revelations, and the typological culmination of the *fiat lux* from the Creation) has often been a feature of apocalyptic scenes. The nocturnal "sun" in *Guernica* may perhaps be read as one of these.[149] To describe it, Barr composes a metaphor: "And over all shines the radiant eye of day with the electric bulb of night for a pupil."[150] This doubling of human inventiveness (Edison's light bulb) with God's own radiance makes it hard to tell whether the calamity we witness is merely manmade or participates in some way in a larger story—the working out of a divine "plot" that requires us to pass through the refiner's fire.

Many artists focused on aerial bombardment as the essence of barbaric, modern warfare. For example, during the Blitz, Henry Moore made drawings of people sheltering in the Underground during air raids. In their wanton devastation, such attacks on cities and noncombatants struck at the fabric of civilization. This was seen also in attacks on museums and works of art: not only the fascist bombing of the Prado,[151] for instance, but the combat that ruined the frescoes of the Camposanto in Pisa in 1944,[152] or the U.S. air raid that destroyed Mantegna's great fresco cycle in the Ovetari Chapel in Padua. And in Milan, the refectory housing Leonardo's *Last Supper* was largely destroyed, though the fresco, behind sandbags, was spared.[153] Within The Museum of Modern Art, the response of artists to the new circumstances of aerial attack was conveyed through *Guernica*'s continuing exhibition, as well as through the commissioning of José Clemente Orozco to paint, on the Museum's premises, the multiple-panel *Dive Bomber and Tank* (fig. 15). Barr records that Orozco painted the work "in the Museum before the eyes of the public during the last days of June, 1940 while the world was still reeling from the fall of France," and calls it a "sinister grey allegory."[154] Referring to "the shock of the mechanical warfare that had just crushed western Europe," he says that Orozco "makes us feel the essential horror of modern war—the human being mangled in the crunch and grind of grappling monsters 'that tear each other in their slime.'"[155] This was the Machine Age with a vengeance.

In 1943, Monroe Wheeler's "Airways to Peace" exhibition tried to shift the focus somewhat, from the importance of air power for the war then in progress to its importance for the peace to come. Nonetheless, a sharp awareness of the Frankenstein aspect of many modern inventions, their potential for great destructiveness as well as great good, underlay this exhibition. The United States had been brought into the war by the aerial attack on Pearl Harbor. Now, though looking ahead to peacetime, the exhibition still began on an allegorical note, with a large photomontage depicting a surreal combination of an airplane and the Fall of Icarus (fig. 16), while inside, a sequence of photographs in the section "The Progress of Flight" traced an evolution from Icarus (here termed, only half in jest, "the first air

Left:
16. Photomontage in the exhibition "Airways to Peace: An Exhibition of Geography for the Future," The Museum of Modern Art, New York, 1943. From *The Bulletin of The Museum of Modern Art* 11, no. 1 (1943), p. 2

Right:
17. Photograph in the exhibition "Power in the Pacific," The Museum of Modern Art, New York, 1945. From Edward J. Steichen, ed., *Power in the Pacific* (New York: U.S. Camera Publishing Corporation, 1945), p. 137

casualty"),[156] through Leonardo's birdlike "ornithopter," to Lindbergh.

Other wartime exhibitions at the Museum sometimes deciphered the meaning of the hostilities explicitly with the tools of biblical exegesis, seeing the heroic casualties as martyred "types." The exhibition "Power in the Pacific," organized by Edward Steichen in 1945, included a dramatic photograph of a badly wounded Navy flyer being dragged out of his plane's cockpit by fellow servicemen (fig. 17). The spontaneous, momentary poses of the figures look something like a Deposition, and the picture was in fact captioned (in Old English lettering): "—took him down and wrapped his body in clean linens."[157]

•

In these allegories of flight, it is not just the town of Guernica or even the target cities of World War II that are implicated. Commenting on *Guernica* at both the beginning and end of his 1946 Picasso book, Barr speaks of specific grief but also of a larger suffering. At the outset he says:

> Guernica *was damned and praised as propaganda. We see now that it was not so much propaganda as prophecy. Like all great prophecy the language of* Guernica *was allegorical. . . . Now when humanity may be forging its own doom on a scale which dwarfs the puny bombs of Guernica, Picasso might be moved to paint an apocalypse.*[158]

On the last page of his text Barr writes:

> Guernica *was a modern Laocoon, a Calvary, a doom picture. Its symbols transcend the fate of the little Basque city to prophesy Rotterdam and London, Kharkov and Berlin, Milan and Nagasaki—our dark age.*[159]

The last phrases are the telling ones. It took courage to write those words in 1946 and mention in the same breath the fascist atrocity at Guernica and the American atomic bombing of Japan.[160] John Hersey's moving account based on the testimony of survivors, *Hiroshima* (1946), had been published in *The New Yorker* while the Picasso book was being prepared, but even so, this was still a time when the narrator of an American newsreel, in his commentary on aerial footage of Hiroshima, could joke that the city looked "like Ebbets Field after a doubleheader."[161] In certain quarters, compassion was in short supply, and taking a critical attitude toward the

morality of the act was not encouraged. Yet some remained disturbed by the possibility that, like the German use of experimental ordnance at Guernica, the American bombing of Japan had been pursued as an experiment, a rare opportunity to test the effects of a powerful new weapon on an actual city under controlled conditions.

In the postwar edition of *What Is Modern Painting?* Barr expanded his litany of bombed-out cities and again cast Picasso in the role of apocalyptic prophet:

Picasso employed these modern techniques [in Guernica*] not merely to express his mastery of form or some personal and private emotion but to proclaim publicly through his art his horror and fury over the barbarous catastrophe which had destroyed his fellow countrymen in Guernica—and which was soon to blast his fellow men in Warsaw, Rotterdam, London, Coventry, Chungking, Sebastopol, Pearl Harbor and then, in retribution, Hamburg, Milan, Tokyo, Berlin, Dresden, Hiroshima.*[162]

There is a disturbing moral crux in these lines. Of course they condemn Axis aggression, especially against civilians; yet they seem uneasy with the eye-for-an-eye morality of the Allied "retribution" that took a toll on noncombatants every bit as horrible as the acts that provoked it. In either case, the innocent are made to suffer, and in immense numbers. (Even the U.S. Secretary of War, Henry L. Stimson, had worried about the morality of saturation-bombing Japanese cities; he told President Harry S. Truman that he "did not want to have the United States get the reputation of outdoing Hitler in atrocities."[163]) By describing Hiroshima as the climax of a series of "barbarous catastrophes" that have befallen humankind, Barr seems to question the moral basis of the assertion that the atomic bombing was "necessary," or somehow justified, as a "humane" way to end the war quickly, the official argument made at the time. For even if the bombing could be understood as in a strange sense necessary, that would render the U.S. action not guiltless, but rather something disquietingly ambiguous.

Perhaps the word for it is "tragic," for again, a literary model seems most apposite. A tragedy, in the classical or Elizabethan sense, is a high moral allegory carried to an abolute conclusion; its catastrophic ending can be explicitly a type of the apocalypse, as when characters rhetorically ask at the end of *King Lear,* "Is this the promised end?" / "Or image of that horror?" In the present case, the closest analogue might be the Elizabethan "revenge" tragedy, of which *Hamlet* is the most highly developed example. That drama (like World War I) is set in motion by the murder of a royal person, which the play's hero must put right by taking revenge. But it is virtually inevitable that in the bloodbath of retribution in the final scene, many of the good and the innocent will be destroyed along with the evil. The demand for primal justice, the moral imperative to take an eye for an eye, sets off a chain reaction of lethal reprisals and retaliations, until the stage is littered with corpses. It is this unexpected link between moral motives and cataclysmic consequences—an honorable intent somehow triggering an avalanche—that makes the fateful ending fit to be called "tragic." Perhaps this particular sense of fate (Barr spoke of "doom")—of a predictably deadly outcome for the innocent that one could thus "prophesy"—lies behind the action-and-reaction mechanism by which wars, including so-called just ones, escalate to their disastrous conclusion.

A few years after World War II, during the Korean conflict, Americans would be disturbed when Picasso painted *Massacre in Korea* (1951), a work purportedly showing atrocities committed by U.S. troops (although the robotic soldiers' nation-

ality is not obvious). And in the sixties, Picasso would again become the instrument of criticism of America's conduct of foreign wars, as *Guernica* was reproduced on many antiwar posters condemning the bombing of Vietnam; the incendiary weapons of Guernica were equated with the napalm attacks in Southeast Asia.[164] Some who reproduced the painting may have remembered that at the very beginning of the post–World War II era, Barr had seen *Guernica* as a way to recall his victorious fellow citizens to a sense of their common humanity.

•

Among physicists, it was not uncommon to speak figuratively about the development of nuclear weapons in a manner comparable to Barr's, and to use literary models, as he did, to suggest what history had come to. The metaphors used by physicists tend to confirm the aptness of Barr's comparison of scientists with modern artists. Most notably, the cautionary type for the modern artist—the ambiguous model for the twentieth century, as Leonardo was for the Renaissance, of the artist-scientist or artist-inventor who seeks beauty but also invents weapons of war—might indeed be one of the "atom scientists" Barr alluded to in *What Is Modern Painting?*, Einstein foremost among them, with his love of the elegant calculations of theoretical physics. Though Einstein was a pacifist, it was nonetheless his 1939 letter to President Franklin D. Roosevelt that brought to the government's attention the possibility of building weapons of unprecedented power, based on his formulations about energy and matter. Shortly after the war, Einstein was quoted as saying, "Let my hand be burned for writing that letter," and he put the consequences of scientific research in these terms:

Penetrating research and keen scientific work have often had tragic implications for mankind, producing, on the one hand, inventions which liberated man from exhausting physical labor, making his life easier and richer; but on the other hand, introducing a grave restlessness into his life, making him a slave to his technological environment, and—most catastrophic of all—creating the means of his own mass destruction. This, indeed, is a tragedy of overwhelming poignancy![165]

But perhaps an even better example of the artist-inventor would be not the grandfatherly Einstein but the more conflicted and unsettling figure of J. Robert Oppenheimer, who, as head of the Los Alamos laboratory during the wartime

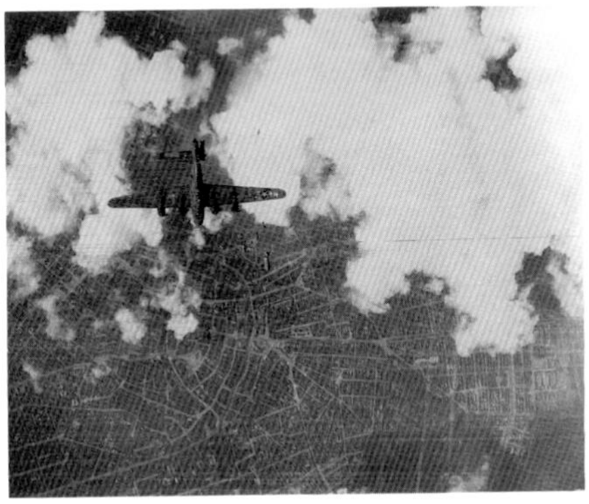

18. Unknown photographer (automatic camera). *Accident, B-17 Raid over Berlin*. 1944–45. Five gelatin-silver prints, 18 x 22⅝" (45.7 x 55 cm) each. The Museum of Modern Art, New York

Manhattan Project, was in practical terms the true father of the atomic bomb, his masterpiece.[166] The long-awaited Trinity test was an event whose unearthly nature he implicitly recognized in advance in the code name he gave it. In a letter to General Leslie Groves, his military commander on the Project, Oppenheimer later tried to explain his choice of the name Trinity. He gave a poet's reasons:

I did suggest it. . . . Why I chose the name is not clear, but I know what thoughts were in my mind. There is a poem of John Donne, written just before his death, which I know and love. From it a quotation:

. . . As West and East
In all flatt Maps—and I am one—are one,
So death doth touch the Resurrection.

This still does not make Trinity; but in another, better known devotional poem Donne opens, "Batter my heart, three person'd God."[167]

Donne's poetry of resurrection is framed within the traditional typology of apocalypse. Recall that when Joachim of Flora in his eschatological writings divided the history of the earth into three periods, with the third—the Age of the Holy Spirit—ushering in the Final Days, he did so on the tripartite model of the Trinity. It was from within such a trinitarian tradition that Kandinsky spoke of our time as an era of "the revelation of the spirit, Father–Son–Spirit" and of "receiving the 'third' revelation, the revelation of the spirit," connecting it to his apocalyptic works, such as *Composition 6* (1913).[168]

And so, on the day of the Trinity test, when Oppenheimer witnessed what could be called "the first detonation of a great historic movement," for him the world was shown the image of its final end. When the brilliant fireball illuminated the pre-dawn sky like a new sun and slowly rose in a mushroom cloud, he later recounted,

A few people laughed, a few people cried, most people were silent. I remembered the line from the Hindu scripture, the Bhagavad-Gita: *Vishnu is trying to persuade the Prince that he should do his duty and to impress him he takes on his multi-arm form and says, "Now I am become Death, the destroyer of worlds."*[169]

Precisely in his role as a leading scientist of the age, Oppenheimer suddenly saw himself as a personification of death, and a bringer of global cataclysm.[170] A few moments

after the blast, as if in confirmation, his friend Ken Bainbridge came up to him, took his hand, and said, "Oppie, now we're all sons of bitches."

After Hiroshima and Nagasaki, Oppenheimer would learn in detail—as Lindbergh had—just how destructive his once otherworldly and idealistic profession could be. There are perhaps no more compelling exemplars of the ambitions and failures of the modern inventor—of symbolic, allegorical disasters akin to those of the fire-bringing Prometheus and the winged Icarus.

•

Following World War II, the potential for mass destruction that marked the onset of the Nuclear Age continues to be mentioned in Alfred Barr's writings, even in remote or ironic contexts. In what he termed "our dark age," he finds opportunities to remind us of the ever-present possibility that the Cold War could become a nuclear war. Discussing John Marin's 1922 overhead view of New York (fig. 19), with its yellow starburst at the bottom center, Barr says, "*Lower Manhattan* looks like an explosion—ominous simile—but the radiant nucleus . . . was inspired by the gold leaf on the dome of the old World Building."[171] About one of Adolph Gottlieb's Burst paintings (fig. 20), he says: "*Blast!* Does the red disc suggest apocalyptic doom glowing over the world's charred ruins? Is this a succinct 1957 version of *Guernica*? Don't jump to conclusions—the disc may be the rising sun."[172] Since the rising sun is the national emblem of Japan, Barr's remark about "charred ruins" takes on strange, but perhaps unintended, overtones.[173]

Artists, too, continued to see in the advent of the Nuclear Age a historical turning point as "epoch-making" as those inaugurating the modern age itself. But some of them were not always as soberly compassionate as Barr. During a symposium at The Museum of Modern Art in 1951 titled "What Abstract Art Means to Me," Willem de Kooning struck a visionary note:

Today, some people think that the light of the atom bomb will change the concept of painting once and for all. The eyes that actually saw the light melted out of sheer ecstasy. For one instant, everybody was the same color. It made angels out of everybody. A truly Christian light, painful but forgiving.[174]

Barr would later quote other things de Kooning said at the symposium—his remark "I do not think of inside or outside, or of art in general, as a situation of comfort"[175] would appear in the next edition of *What Is Modern Painting?*—but not the comment about the bomb, with its uncertain and perhaps insensitive mixture of Messianic themes from T. S. Eliot and William Blake, and its apparent attempt to ascribe to heat radiation the qualities of the Beatific Vision.

In 1954, in *Masters of Modern Art,* Barr would quote at length Theodore Roszak about the welded sculpture *Spectre of Kitty Hawk* (fig. 21), and thus return to the nuclear issue by means of the Wright brothers (Orville having died in 1948) and the myth of Icarus. He quotes Roszak as saying:

In the same way that the forms of a sculpture try to reconcile the ambiguities that are within it and that produce it . . . the subject metaphorically tries to relate at once several things in remote periods of history. The Spectre *is the pterodactyl, an early denizen of the air both savage and destructive. Present day aircraft has come to resemble this beast of prey, hence the re-incarnation of the pterodactyl at Kitty Hawk. . . . I think it is inter-*

19. John Marin. *Lower Manhattan (Composition Derived from Top of Woolworth).* 1922. Watercolor on paper, 21⅝ x 28⅞" (55.4 x 73.1 cm). The Museum of Modern Art, New York. Acquired through the Lillie P. Bliss Bequest

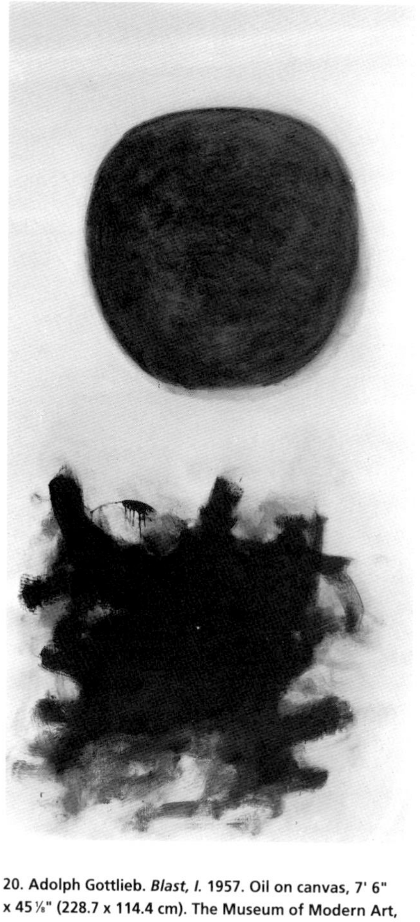

20. Adolph Gottlieb. *Blast, I.* 1957. Oil on canvas, 7' 6" x 45⅛" (228.7 x 114.4 cm). The Museum of Modern Art, New York. Philip Johnson Fund

esting and relevant that Orville Wright in the last days of his life mused about his brain-child with apprehension and misgivings. He died a disillusioned man, and the Myth of Icarus completes another circle, tangent to pragmatic America.[176]

In his concern with relating "several things in remote periods of history" to each other, and relating the myth of Icarus to "pragmatic America," Roszak takes up the allegorical themes and typological configurations that Barr had been pursuing for some time. When he sees the "re-incarnation" of a prehistoric type in the warplane, its antitype, there seems little doubt that his modern "beast of prey" includes the *Enola Gay*, in its flight over Hiroshima.

Three years later, in 1957, Barr and several museum directors were each invited to select and write briefly about a postwar American artwork that they thought would "endure"; it was natural that Barr's thoughts again turned to Roszak's *Spectre of Kitty Hawk,* and he wrote the following commentary. His text in "Will This Art Endure?" is a culminating statement of the allegory of flight:

A million years after the last pterodactyl flapped to the cretaceous earth, forty-three years after the Wrights first flew their contraption over the Carolina sands, one year after the bomb fell on Hiroshima, a sculptor set to work. Thoughts of these disparate events haunted his mind along with the recollection that Daedalus' ingenuity had led to his own son's fatal crash and that even Orville Wright, before he died, had suffered some misgivings. Imagining the convulsed forms of the giant flying reptile, he welded and hammered this image in steel, then braised it with bronze and brass. I think it will endure.[177]

21. Theodore Roszak. ***Spectre of Kitty Hawk.*** **1946–47. Welded and hammered steel brazed with bronze and brass, 40½ x 18 x 15" (102.2 x 45.7 x 38.1 cm). The Museum of Modern Art, New York. Purchase**

Welded metal sculpture had developed in part from the work of Julio González, and Barr in *Masters of Modern Art* quoted with approval González's statement that "the age of iron began many centuries ago by producing very beautiful objects, unfortunately, for a large part, arms. Today, it provides as well, bridges and railroads. It is time this metal ceased to be a murderer. . . . Today the door is wide open for this material to be, at last, forged and hammered by the peaceful hands of an artist."[178] We note that the "ingenious" artist-inventor Daedalus, Joyce's "fabulous artificer," through misguided creativity becomes implicated in the death of his own son, associated here by Roszak to the deaths of aerial-bombing victims. The idea of excessive inventiveness or ingenuity causing the death of a blood relative, and the notion of metal as a "murderer," may remind us that in the story of Cain and Abel, the murderous brother's offspring go on to develop metallurgy (Cain's name being related to the word for "smith"),[179] the technological advance that later makes possible the forging of iron knives and swords as more efficient instruments of death. In the Old Testament, metalworkers are therefore often associated with destructiveness, with the fiery furnace, in contrast to the helpful constructiveness of, say, carpenters.

The remote past and the Messianic present are conflated in Barr's specific choices of words. The Fall of Icarus is spoken of not in the language of classical mythology, in which flying too close to the sun can be said to melt the wax of wings, but instead in the language of mechanical technology: It is only pilots, not feather-winged legends, who can "crash." The unbirdlike clatter of that fall extends the sense of improvised, wired-together construction first suggested by the word "contraption" (with its overtones of the crackpot inventor). Yet the final word, "endure,"

refers back in ironic contrast to the opening mention of another flying species—one that has, on the contrary, been dead for aeons. It thus places recent events in a framework of vast geological time, through the extinct flying reptile, the pterodactyl, recalled also from Alberto Giacometti's *The Palace at 4 A.M.* (fig. 22) and from the ichthyosaur in "Kiesler's *Galaxy*." Barr's carefully gauged equivocation, "I *think* it will endure," puts everything in the particular state of historical suspense characteristic of the Cold War and its nuclear standoff; at the time it was, after all, a commonplace that if there ever were an all-out atomic war, the next war after that would be fought with clubs. In a world bombed back to the Stone Age, the *Enola Gay* would give way to the pterodactyl.

As Roszak had himself said in a 1952 symposium at the Museum: "The forms that I find necessary to assert, are meant to be blunt reminders of primordial strife and struggle, reminiscent of those brute forces that not only produced life, but threaten to destroy it"; they expressed his "all-consuming rage against those forces that are blind to the primacy of life-giving values."[180] Roszak was explaining his own abrupt change, around 1945, from clean, pure, Machine Age forms to the harsher, rougher appearance of works like *Kitty Hawk*. "The work that I am now doing constitutes an almost complete reversal of ideas and feelings from my former work. . . . Instead of sharp and confident edges, its lines and shapes are now gnarled and knotted, even hesitant. Instead of serving up slick chromium, its surfaces are scorched and coarsely pitted." He was marking the imaginative changeover from the "smooth" aesthetics of a Machine Age to the "rough" aesthetics of a Nuclear (or Stone) Age, and reflecting on an epoch-making transformation. (It is a change to which Kiesler, too, was reacting, in making not a shiny, ultra-modern stage set like his design for *R.U.R.,* but instead what Barr had described as "the supreme anti-technological gazebo," made of "jetsam.") Not the gleaming futuristic invention, but the pitted refuse it produces, like bomb debris.

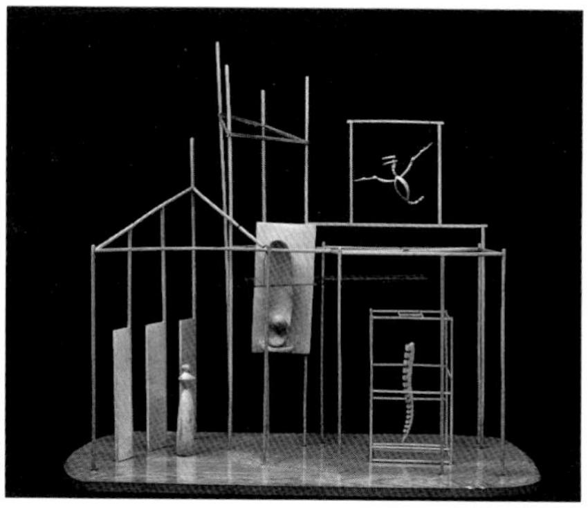

22. Alberto Giacometti. *The Palace at 4 A.M.* 1932–33. Construction in wood, glass, wire, and string, 25 x 28¼ x 15¾" (63.5 x 71.8 x 40 cm). The Museum of Modern Art, New York. Purchase

A similar sense of a failed "experimental" age, soon to be replaced by another, underlies the allegory of Icarus that Barr had constructed with Roszak's work as a late episode. It was an allegory of the utopian aspirations of the early modernists, who perhaps put too much confidence in notions of social and artistic progress and perfection, and eventually saw some of their ideas fall victim to a totalitarian element, which twisted to its own ends the longing to bring about the millennium and make a "perfect" world. The discussion of "perfection" that closes *What Is Modern Painting?* is therefore restrained, chastened by the knowledge of what had actually been brought to pass during the middle years of the century by a ruthless pursuit of so-called progress and perfection in the social, political, and technological realms. It carefully keeps its distance from thinking that tries to achieve what Barr calls the "'too' perfect." The hubris of some inventive modern minds (even those of humane disposition), in believing they had the power to bring about a more perfect world, had been shown to be akin to the hubris of the tragic hero, who tries to achieve good but ultimately brings about terrible suffering as well. In its essentials, this is the vision of Shakespearean tragedy that A. C. Bradley had offered at the beginning of the century: "We remain confronted with the inexplicable fact, or the no less inexplicable appearance, of a world travailing for perfection, but bringing to birth, along with glorious good, an evil which it is able to overcome only by self-torture. And this fact or appearance is tragedy."[181]

Postscript

The 1960s would write a postscript to this allegorical tale. In that decade, the Nuclear Age would touch the life of the Museum in a very personal way. At several critical junctures in its history, the institution's aspirations have seemed to be plagued by coincidental disaster in the larger world. In October 1929, ten days before the Museum opened its doors to the public, the stock market crashed. In 1939, the Museum unveiled its new, permanent building—and World War II broke out while the inaugural exhibition was still on the walls. In the autumn of 1962, the Museum was nearing the end of the most ambitious fund-raising drive in its history, to finance its largest expansion to date and create space to show much more of the collection; then, as Barr chillingly records in his "Chronicle of the Collection," the Cuban missile crisis erupted:

October 22: The Cuban crisis broke; two days later twenty-eight of the Museum's best paintings were sent to prepared vaults over a hundred miles from the city. Soon seventy-four others, almost as valuable, followed—and then still more, including drawings and prints. Other works were substituted on the gallery walls. The crisis was terrible but short.[182]

As the nation feared a nuclear exchange with the Soviet Union, there was a strange irony at work: Having given safe haven to *Guernica* and honored it as a "prophecy" of the Nuclear Age, the Museum would now see that prophecy nearly fulfilled, and be forced to send its own collection to fallout shelters.

•

There were, however, other ways of looking at these ominous events. By the sixties, the Nuclear Age had been with us a long time, long enough for apocalyptic anxiety to become available as an object of parody. The tragic model gave way to the comic. This was the decade that saw *Dr. Strangelove, or How I Learned to Stop Worrying and Love the Bomb* (1964).[183] It saw a Manhattan Project alumnus, Edward Teller—the leading proponent of the newer, more powerful hydrogen bomb—in the grotesquely hilarious caricature created by Peter Sellers in the movie's title role. His comic-book performance satirizes another noted scientist, too; his accent and origins recall the German-born rocket scientist Dr. Wernher von Braun. In the burgeoning Pop culture of the late fifties and early sixties, this was what antiwar art could look like. And at the same time, a vast, serious, high modernist allegory on the scale of *Guernica* could increasingly seem to some viewers not only ponderous and overdone but also, for those very reasons, like a gigantic cartoon. Although Henry Moore said in 1961 that *Guernica* "was like a cartoon, just laid in in black and grey,"[184] apparently he meant it was like the cartoon, or full-size preliminary drawing, for a fresco. Others, though, meant cartoon in the other sense. In a 1967 panel discussion, Ad Reinhardt, speaking of the mother and dead child at the left of the painting, said to Leon Golub, "They're like cartoons. . . . They have no effectiveness at all."[185] Reinhardt had in fact turned *Guernica* into a literal comic strip twenty years earlier, when he made his cartoon-collage *How to Look at a Mural* (see figs. 23, 24), published in the magazine *P.M.* in January 1947; there he had pointed out that "the mural is an allegory," then proceeded to label and identify somewhat antically each element, such as "a sun (source of life), a radiant eye of the dark night, an electric-artificial-light-bulb (man's fateful discovery), all-seeing-

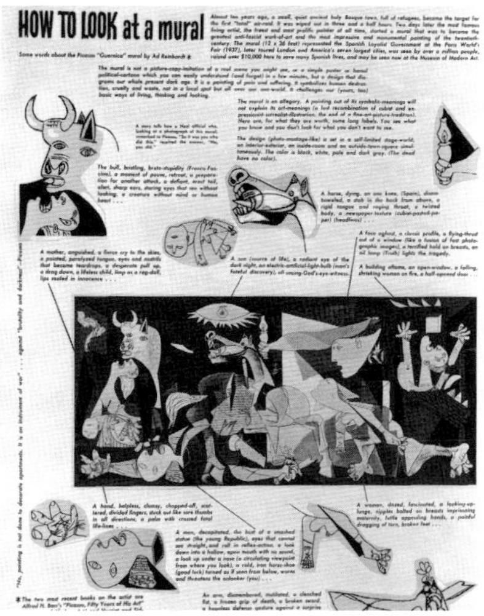

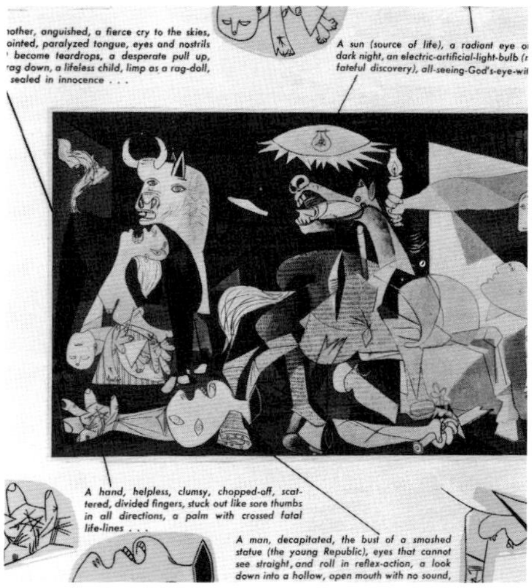

Left:
23. Ad Reinhardt. *How to Look at a Mural.* Cartoon collage, published in *P.M.*, January 5, 1947

Right:
24. Ad Reinhardt. *How to Look at a Mural* (detail)

God's-eye-witness." In 1971, Darby Bannard would assert that because of Picasso's problems with working on the large scale of *Guernica*, "the unfortunate effect is that of vulgar cartooning. The bright lamp at the top of the picture, for example, gives off a jagged body of light just like a 'kaboom' in a war comic."[186] By this time, Thomas B. Hess wrote in the same year, "*Guernica* was sneered at."[187] And Peter Saul felt free to parody it since, he said, it was already "Pop Art, before Pop."[188] What Barr had called its "special weapons of modern art" seemed as obsolete as the biplane.

When Barr revised and expanded *What Is Modern Painting?* again, in the sixties, he took into account the changed sensibility of the times. He had long before said that of Picasso's "three extraordinary allegories" (*Minotauromachy, Dream and Lie of Franco*, and *Guernica*), the second was a "nightmare comic strip."[189] In the sixties, he added a section on Pop and Op art that included a work by Roy Lichtenstein. Noting its war subject and commenting that "*'Flatten—Sand Fleas!'* was originally an exclamatory 'comic' book incident of U.S. Marines landing on a beach," he invited the reader to make a surprising comparison: "In character and quality of violence compare it with . . . Picasso's *Guernica*."[190] But to what end he did not say. Perhaps in encouraging the comparison he was to some extent overturning what had been a long-standing bias in conservative taste against a specific kind of art. When U.N. Secretary-General Dag Hammarskjöld spoke at the Museum's twenty-fifth anniversary exhibition, in 1954, the diplomat had observed with relief that the works in the collection were not "modern" in a particular pejorative sense of the word: "Nor is [the art] modern in the sense of the comic strips."[191] Yet not everyone saw comics as without interest, and not everyone thought they were completely incompatible with works of grandiose solemnity elsewhere in the Museum, even *Guernica*.

•

In a freewheeling new era, it was rarely possible to speak of apocalyptic themes in the same elevated language of allegory and prophecy that Barr had been using since the forties. Even when addressing similar subjects, young poets studiously avoided Barr's quasi-religious tone. Frank O'Hara wrote of Reuben Nakian's sculpture, "When tragedy is implied, as in . . . *Hiroshima,* it is the tragedy of physical, not metaphysical death," and he praised the work for "natural reticence."[192] Lawrence

25. Roy Lichtenstein. *"Whaam!"* 1963. Magna on canvas; two panels, overall 68" x 13' 4" (172.7 x 406.4 cm). The Trustees of The Tate Gallery, London

Ferlinghetti went so far as to make light of *Guernica* in his "Special Clearance Sale of Famous Masterpieces."[193] The tone altered for artists as well. To pick an absurd example of how drastically attitudes changed in postwar America: Already in 1957, when Larry Rivers appeared on the TV quiz show "The $64,000 Challenge," following weeks of intense study, he entered the isolation booth only to be asked, after a drumroll, "Mr. Rivers, for four thousand dollars, what's the name of the Spanish painter who painted *Guernica* and whose last name begins with the letter P?"[194] This was not to be an age of heroic prophecy.

In this new time of the increasingly Pop, Barr therefore had to recast his old themes into different terms if he was, for instance, to talk about Lichtenstein. He also recast his allegorical rhetoric in order to talk about a Neo-Dada kinetic work of Jean Tinguely, in 1960 (fig. 26), a piece made of old motors, washing-machine parts, baby-carriage wheels, metal tubing, and various other bits of detritus, and designed, when activated, to demolish itself. Indeed, in his remarks delivered in the Museum's Sculpture Garden before *Homage to New York* was set in motion, Barr used Tinguely's self-destroying contraption as an opportunity to reconsider, even parody, his own apocalyptic metaphors. For openers, the angst evident in some Abstract Expressionism (by then well into its second generation) is deflated into amiable absurdity, as Barr points out that the artist "has devised machines . . . which at the drop of a coin scribble a moustache on the automatist Muse of Abstract Expressionism." Belying the title Tinguely gives one of these machines, with that scribbling gesture his works do not pay "homage" to New York, but instead mock the New York School. Then Barr looks on with eager anticipation as—through an animated mechanical device that personifies it—the Machine Age is at last to be overthrown (in a garden, appropriately enough)[195] and reduced to a pile of spare parts. *Homage to New York* is:

. . . (wipe that smile off your face) an apocalyptic far-out breakthrough which, it is said, clinks and clanks, tingles and tangles, whirrs and buzzes, grinds and creaks, whistles and pops itself into a katabolic Götterdämmerung of junk and scrap.[196]

A far-out breakthrough that parodies those in art as well as science, it is, in a sense they had not anticipated, a "self-consuming artifact" (a model later proposed for

what would come to be understood as postmodernist critical analysis).[197] The willful disorder of the collapsed "junk and scrap" here, like the "jetsam" of "Kiesler's *Galaxy*," comes almost as a relief to certain sorts of neat, orderly, but now exhausted modernists, "refugees from the compass and the ruler." And like *Galaxy*, this is a "tomb of know-how." Barr therefore fittingly calls on the great tinkerers of the past and present—his confraternity of artist-scientists and artist-inventors—to witness this final experiment:

Oh great brotherhood of Jules Verne, Paul Klee, Sandy Calder, Leonardo da Vinci, Rube Goldberg, Marcel Duchamp, Piranesi, Man Ray, Picabia, Filippo Morghen, are you with it?
TINGVELY EX MACHINA
MORITVRI TE SALVTAMVS

Hilariously, he sends the sputtering machine off to its ritual death with the words proclaimed by Roman gladiators to the Emperor at the Colosseum: "We who are about to die salute you."

It is the fate of literary apocalypses, being only figures of speech, however illuminating, to find themselves disconfirmed by continuing events; the world will not stop, and it outruns our images of its end. In Barr's high-flown rhetoric of the forties, the allegory of the modern inventor seemed headed for a tragic ending, with no *deus ex machina* in sight. Abstract Expressionism, too, in its grave lyricism and its "tragic and timeless" themes,[198] could partake of that lofty, pessimistic view. Yet Barr came somewhat belatedly to Abstract Expressionism, and by the time he wrote about these crisis-ridden artists in the introduction to *The New American Painting* of 1959, perhaps he was weary of such concerns and ready to move on to other developments; a year earlier, he had supported the acquisition of four works by Jasper Johns. As

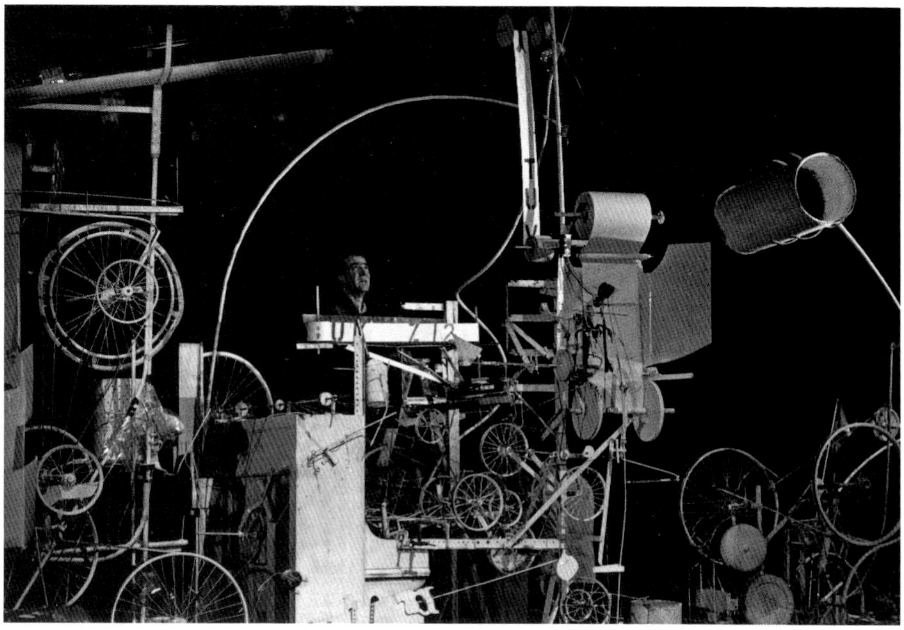

26. Jean Tinguely. ***Homage to New York***, in the Abby Aldrich Rockefeller Sculpture Garden, The Museum of Modern Art, New York, March 17, 1960

Barr had pointed out, "After the war, painters in general turned away from destruction and horror,"[199] and ultimately so did he, turning away not only from the war itself, but from the Messianic view of history that it had helped foster.[200] The events he wrote about in the late forties continued to affect some of his central metaphors for more than a decade, notably those of "Will This Art Endure?" in 1957, but the residual sense of crisis eventually did pass, in his writing no less than in the national mood.[201] By 1962, Frank O'Hara could view the change of mood flippantly, saying that "abstract expressionism is the art of serious men," while "in a capitalist country fun is everything."[202] Perhaps what was needed to endure the day-to-day life of a new era was not only a grand sense of the tragic and timeless, but also the thing that some Abstract Expressionists so conspicuously lacked: a self-deprecatory sense of humor. In daring to write a mock rhapsody on *Homage to New York,* a work destined to "pop" itself into oblivion, Barr at the beginning of his fourth decade at the Museum remained open-eyed, and young enough to poke a little fun at his own apocalyptic ruminations.

Notes

1. The following books by Alfred H. Barr, Jr., all published by The Museum of Modern Art, will be cited in abbreviated form: *Cubism and Abstract Art* (1936, rpt. 1966, 1974, 1986); *Picasso: Forty Years of His Art* (1939, rev. c. 1939–40, 1941); *Italian Masters* (1940); *What Is Modern Painting?* (1943; rev. c. 1952, 1956, 1959, 1963, 1966; rpt. 1968, 1975, 1980, 1988); *Picasso: Fifty Years of His Art* (1946, rpt. 1966, 1974); *Matisse: His Art and His Public* (1951, rpt. 1966, 1974); *Masters of Modern Art,* ed. (1954); and *Painting and Sculpture in The Museum of Modern Art, 1929–1967* (1977), which includes his "Chronicle of the Collection of Painting and Sculpture." Whenever possible, briefer writings, such as catalogue prefaces and magazine articles, will be cited from *Defining Modern Art: Selected Writings of Alfred H. Barr, Jr.,* ed. Irving Sandler and Amy Newman (New York: Abrams, 1986), instead of from their scattered original sources. Writings not included there will be cited in full.

A short list of sources for the study of Alfred Barr's life and work would begin with Margaret Scolari Barr, "'Our Campaigns': Alfred H. Barr, Jr., and The Museum of Modern Art—A Biographical Chronicle of the Years 1930–1944," and Rona Roob, "Alfred H. Barr, Jr.: A Chronicle of the Years 1902–1929," both in the special issue titled "Alfred Barr at MoMA" of *The New Criterion,* Summer 1977, with an Introduction by Hilton Kramer. The Chronology by Jane Fluegel in *Defining Modern Art* should also be consulted. The only biography of Barr, by Alice Goldfarb Marquis (*Alfred H. Barr, Jr.: Missionary for the Modern* [Chicago and New York: Contemporary Books, 1989]), is inadequate and unreliable; its shortcomings are reviewed in Brian Wallis, "The Man Who Made the Modern Modern," *Art in America* 77 (December 1989), pp. 39–43; and Helen M. Franc, "Alfred Barr at the Modern," *Art Journal* 49 (Fall 1990), pp. 325–29. More useful are A. Conger Goodyear, *The Museum of Modern Art: The First Ten Years* (New York: [privately printed], 1943); Russell Lynes, *Good Old Modern: An Intimate Portrait of the Museum of Modern Art* (New York: Atheneum, 1973); *Alfred H. Barr, Jr.: A Memorial Tribute* (New York: The Museum of Modern Art, 1981); Sam Hunter, Introduction to *The Museum of Modern Art, New York: The History and the Collection* (New York: Abrams in association with The Museum of Modern Art, 1984); and Sybil Kantor, "Alfred H. Barr, Jr., and the Establishment of the Culture of Modernism in America" (Ph.D. dissertation, City University of New York, 1993).

Specifically on Barr's writings, see Irving Sandler, Introduction to *Defining Modern Art,* and John Elderfield, "Matisse: Myth vs. Man," *Art in America* 75 (April 1987), pp. 13–21. Meyer Schapiro's brief remarks in *Alfred H. Barr, Jr.: A Memorial Tribute* are also of considerable interest. There are illuminating discussions of Barr's *Cubism and Abstract Art* in Robert Rosenblum's Foreword to the Belknap Press reprint of that volume (Cambridge, Mass.: Harvard University Press, 1986); Benjamin H. D. Buchloh, "From Faktura to Factography," in Annette Michelson, Rosalind Krauss, Douglas Crimp, and Joan Copjec, eds., *October: The First Decade, 1976–1986* (Cambridge, Mass., and London: MIT Press, 1987); Susan Noyes Platt, "Modernism, Formalism, and Politics: The 'Cubism and Abstract Art' Exhibition of 1936 at the Museum of Modern Art," *Art Journal* 47 (Winter 1988); and W. J. T. Mitchell, "*Ut Pictura Theoria:* Abstract Painting and Language," in his *Picture Theory* (New York and Chicago: University of Chicago Press, 1994), pp. 230–39. "Alfred H. Barr, Jr.: A Bibliography of Published Writings," compiled by Rona Roob and printed in *Defining Modern Art,* is indispensable; copies of the works it lists are available in the Museum Archives.

2. Elderfield, "Matisse: Myth vs. Man," p. 13.

3. Rosenblum, Foreword to *Cubism and Abstract Art,* p. 3.

4. *Matisse: His Art and His Public,* pp. 35, 47, 48.

5. *Masters of Modern Art,* p. 93. Barr is apparently referring to the fact that a flatfish such as the sole begins life with one eye on each side of its face's ridge, and it swims in a vertical position; as the fish matures, it begins to swim in a horizontal position, and the eye on what has become the lower side migrates across the ridge, joining the other eye on the upper side.

6. "A Brief Guide to the Exhibition of Fantastic Art, Dada, Surrealism" (1936), in *Defining Modern Art,* p. 93.

7. *Masters of Modern Art,* p. 142.

8. *Matisse: His Art and His Public,* p. 89.

9. "If they be two, they are two so / As stiff twin compasses are two; / Thy soul, the fixed foot, makes no show / To move, but doth, if th'other do. . . . / Such wilt thou be to me, who must / Like th'other foot, obliquely run; / Thy firmness draws my circle just, / And makes me end where I begun." John Donne, "A Valediction Forbidding Mourning," in J. William Hebel and Hoyt H. Hudson, eds., *Poetry of the English Renaissance, 1509–1660* (New York: Crofts, 1929, rpt. 1947), pp. 474–75. Eliot's influential essay "The Metaphysical Poets," with its talk of the conceit as an antidote to "a dissociation of sensibility," and its reference to these same lines in Donne, was published in the *Times Literary Supplement* in October 1921, while Barr was a student at Princeton. (The essay is reprinted in *Selected Prose of T. S. Eliot,* ed. Frank Kermode [New York: Harcourt Brace, 1975], pp. 59–67.) Later discussions of how the Metaphysical poets used this kind of figure include K. K. Ruthven, *The Conceit* (London: Methuen, 1969).

10. *Picasso: Fifty Years of His Art,* p. 74.

11. "The New American Painting, as Shown in Eight European Countries, 1958–1959: Introduction" (1959), in *Defining Modern Art,* p. 231. Barr is of course referring to the well-known passage from Donne's *Devotions:* "No man is an island, entire of itself; every man is a piece of the continent, a part of the main. . . . any man's death diminishes me, because I am involved in mankind; and therefore never send to know for whom the bell tolls; it tolls for thee" (Donne, Meditation XVII, in *Devotions, upon Emergent Occasions—Together with "Death's Duel"* [Ann Arbor: University of Michigan Press, 1959, rpt. 1969], pp. 108–09).

12. Wallace Stevens, "The Relations Between Poetry and Painting" (lecture delivered at The Museum of Modern Art, New York, January 15, 1951), in Stevens, *The Necessary Angel: Essays on Reality and the Imagination* (New York: Knopf, 1951; rpt. New York: Random House, n.d.), p. 165.

13. *Poetics,* 1458b; *Rhetoric,* 1410b. On figurative meaning, see, for example, Carl R. Hausman, "Figurative Language in Art History," in Salim Kemal and Ivan Gaskell, eds., *The Language of Art History* (New York and Cambridge: Cambridge University Press, 1991). On related aspects of writing about art, see W. J. T. Mitchell, *Iconology: Image, Text, Ideology* (Chicago and London: University of Chicago Press, 1986); David Carrier, *Artwriting* (Amherst: University of Massachusetts Press, 1987); and Carrier, *Principles of Art History Writing* (University Park: Pennsylvania State University Press, 1991). A literary approach is taken in Murray Krieger, *Ekphrasis: The Illusion of the Natural Sign* (Baltimore and London: Johns Hopkins University Press, 1992); and James A. W. Heffernan, *Museum of Words: The Poetics of Ekphrasis from Homer to Ashbery* (Chicago and London: University of Chicago Press, 1993).

14. Excerpted in "Chronicle of the Collection of Painting and Sculpture," in *Painting and Sculpture in The Museum of Modern Art, 1929–1967,* p. 622. The italics are Barr's.

15. *Cubism and Abstract Art,* p. 19.

16. Robert Storr, "No Joy in Mudville," in Kirk Varnedoe and Adam Gopnik, eds., *Modern Art and Popular Culture: Readings in High and Low* (New York: Abrams in association with The Museum of Modern Art, 1990), p. 170.

17. *Matisse: His Art and His Public,* p. 86. Although one might want to go less far in associating Picasso's work of that time with geometric abstraction, Barr does nonetheless take the trouble to point out that Picasso did "play with ruler and compass" in a notebook of these years (*Picasso: Fifty Years of His Art,* p. 67).

18. "Kiesler's *Galaxy,*" *Harper's Bazaar,* no. 2885 (April 1952), pp. 142–43. *Galaxy* originally formed part of Kiesler's stage set for Darius Milhaud and Jean Cocteau's *Le Pauvre Matelot,* performed at the Juilliard School of Music, New York, in 1948.

19. Barr cites Le Corbusier's "slogan"—"the house as a *machine à habiter*"—in his preface to Henry-Russell Hitchcock and Philip Johnson, *The International Style: Architecture Since 1922* (New York: Norton, 1932), reprinted as *The International Style* (New York: Norton, 1966), pp. 13–14; and in his Foreword to *Machine Art* (New York: The Museum of Modern Art, 1934), n.p.

20. He added: ". . . though probably with no very fervid moral intent" (*Picasso: Fifty Years of His Art,* p. 57).
21. Ibid., p. 193.
22. Erwin Panofsky, "Introductory," in *Studies in Iconology: Humanistic Themes in the Art of the Renaissance* (London: Oxford University Press, 1939; rpt. New York: Harper & Row, 1972), p. 6.
23. *Modern Painters,* vol. 3 (1856); in *The Works of John Ruskin (Library Edition),* ed. E. T. Cook and Alexander Wedderburn, 39 vols. (London: George Allen, 1903–12), vol. 5, p. 205. The poem is Coleridge's "Christabel," ll. 49–50.
24. *Picasso: Fifty Years of His Art,* p. 156.
25. Ibid., p. 133.
26. *Cubism and Abstract Art,* p. 11.
27. Ibid., p. 15.
28. Cézanne's remark is quoted in *Cubism and Abstract Art,* p. 30.
29. Ibid., p. 19.
30. "Statement by Picasso: 1935," in *Picasso: Fifty Years of His Art,* p. 273.
31. *Philebus,* 51c; quoted in *Cubism and Abstract Art,* p. 14. Not only these mechanically drawn shapes were beautiful; so were the devices for making them: Barr and Johnson included a number of mechanical-drawing instruments in *Machine Art* (cat. nos. 344–348).
32. Letter to the editor, *The New Republic* (1933), quoted in *Defining Modern Art,* p. 25.
33. *What Is Modern Painting?,* p. 48. Similarly, in his eulogy at the memorial service for Mondrian in 1944, Barr had referred to the artist's single-minded pursuit of artistic purity as making him a painter of "quiet and complete fanaticism" (quoted in "Memorial Service," *Knickerbocker Weekly,* February 14, 1944, p. 23).
34. Meyer Schapiro, "On the Humanity of Abstract Painting" (1960), in his *Modern Art: Nineteenth and Twentieth Centuries—Selected Essays* (New York: Braziller, 1979), p. 230.
35. *Masters of Modern Art,* p. 49.
36. *Picasso: Fifty Years of His Art,* p. 73.
37. *Cubism and Abstract Art,* p. 20.
38. Foreword to *Modern Architecture: International Exhibition* (1932), in *Defining Modern Art,* p. 79.
39. "Statement by Picasso: 1935," in *Picasso: Fifty Years of His Art,* p. 272.
40. "Research and Publication in Art Museums" (1946), in *Defining Modern Art,* p. 209.
41. *Italian Masters,* p. 7.
42. *Matisse: His Art and His Public,* p. 166.
43. Ibid., p. 224.
44. These efforts are described in Margaret Scolari Barr, "Our Campaigns," p. 60; and in Varian Fry, *Surrender on Demand* (New York: Random House, 1945).
45. *Matisse: His Art and His Public,* p. 109.
46. *Cubism and Abstract Art,* p. 18.
47. Foreword to *Machine Art,* n.p.
48. Philip Johnson criticized Morris along these lines in his text for *Machine Art,* and the "Short List of Books" in *Machine Art* includes not only volumes on the Bauhaus and Van de Velde and the like, but also Lewis F. Day's *Of William Morris and His Work* (1899).
49. See *Defining Modern Art,* p. 8.
50. Foreword to *Machine Art,* n.p.
51. *Masters of Modern Art,* pp. 84–85. Similarly, Hart Crane wrote that "unless poetry can absorb the machine, i.e., *acclimatize* it as naturally and casually as trees, cattle, galleons, castles . . . [it] has failed of its full contemporary function" (Crane, "Modern Poetry," in *Collected Poems of Hart Crane,* ed. Waldo Frank [New York: Liveright, 1946], p. 177).
52. Foreword to *Machine Art,* n.p. It can be noted that James Whale's film *Frankenstein,* with Boris Karloff, had been released in 1931, three years before *Machine Art.* On relations between modern art and horror films, see David J. Skal, *The Monster Show: A Cultural History of Horror* (New York and London: Norton, 1993), especially the chapters "'You Will Become Caligari': Monsters, Mountebanks, and Modernism" and "1931: The American Abyss"; the latter touches on predecessors of the visual style of the *Frankenstein* film in, for example, Bauhaus design.
53. See, for example, "Nationalism in German Films" (1934), in *Defining Modern Art,* p. 161.
54. *Cubism and Abstract Art,* p. 54. The phrase "which runs like a machine gun" is restored when Marinetti's statement, from the "Manifesto of Futurism," reappears, in Barr's contribution to *Twentieth-Century Italian Art* (reprinted in *Defining Modern Art,* p. 179) and in *Masters of Modern Art,* p. 100.
55. Arthur Drexler, "Architecture and Design," in *The Museum of Modern Art, New York: The History and the Collection,* p. 388.
56. Henry Adams, "The Dynamo and the Virgin (1900)," in *The Education of Henry Adams: An Autobiography* (1918; Boston: Houghton Mifflin, 1971), p. 380. Barr's reading of Adams's *Mont-Saint-Michel and Chartres* is noted in Roob, "Alfred H. Barr, Jr.: A Chronicle of the Years 1902–1929," p. 2.
57. Quoted in Leo Marx, *The Machine in the Garden: Technology and the Pastoral Ideal in America* (London and New York: Oxford University Press, 1968), p. 198. Marx discusses Adams's dichotomy of the Dynamo and the Virgin at some length, pp. 345–50.
58. Foreword to *Machine Art,* n.p.
59. Quoted in Marx, *The Machine in the Garden,* p. 350.
60. Meyer Schapiro, *Van Gogh* (New York: Abrams, 1950, rpt. 1983), p. 45. For a related discussion of Franz Marc's reference to the Woman Clothed with the Sun, in his cataclysmic *Tyrol* (1914), see Robert Rosenblum, *Modern Painting and the Northern Romantic Tradition: Friedrich to Rothko* (New York: Harper & Row, 1975), p. 145.

The central figure can also reappear at the third stage, as with the Second Coming of Christ, instead of being replaced by a new figure. It is the third *occurrence* of the typological configuration that is important.
61. Peter Brooks, *Reading for the Plot: Design and Intention in Narrative* (New York: Knopf, 1984; rpt. Cambridge, Mass., and London: Harvard University Press, 1992), p. 313. Brooks is here discussing "endgames" in fiction such as Samuel Beckett's, and is concerned with those final moments of revelation that are postponed indefinitely and in fact never come.
62. See M. H. Abrams, *Natural Supernaturalism: Tradition and Revolution in Romantic Literature* (New York: Norton, 1971).
63. Reprinted in *Selected Prose of T. S. Eliot,* p. 177.
64. In "Boston Is Modern Art Pauper" (1926), in *Defining Modern Art,* pp. 52–53, Barr especially praises facsimiles and photographs, of paintings, drawings, and watercolors, published in *The Dial* in 1923, the same year as Eliot's review.
65. Walter Benjamin, "Theses on the Philosophy of History" (1940), in *Illuminations,* ed. Hannah Arendt (New York: Schocken, 1969), p. 263. On this aspect of Benjamin's thought, see the sections headed "Messianic Time Versus Historical Time" and "Allegory" in Richard Wolin, *Walter Benjamin: An Aesthetic of Redemption* (2nd ed., Berkeley, Los Angeles, and London: University of California Press, 1994).
66. "Matisse, Picasso, and the Crisis of 1907" (1951), in *Defining Modern Art,* p. 196.
67. Michael Baxandall, *Giotto and the Orators: Humanist Observers of Painting in Italy and the Discovery of Pictorial Composition, 1350–1450* (Oxford and New York: Oxford University Press, 1971), pp. 71 ff., 117. For a somewhat different approach, see the section "The Typology of Artists' Lives" in George Kubler, *The Shape of Time: Remarks on the History of Things* (New Haven, Conn., and London: Yale University Press, 1962), pp. 86–92.
68. "Plastic Values" (review of Albert C. Barnes, *The Art in Painting*), *The Saturday Review of Literature,* July 24, 1926, p. 948.
69. See Sandler, Introduction to *Defining Modern Art,* p. 12.
70. Edmund Wilson, "T. S. Eliot," in his *Axel's Castle: A Study of the Imaginative Literature of 1870–1930* (New York: Scribners, 1931, rpt. 1969), p. 123.
71. *Modern Painters,* vol. 1 (1843); in *The Works of John Ruskin (Library Edition),* vol. 3, p. 3.
72. Ibid., p. 254. In quoting this passage, George P. Landow notes that some contemporaneous reviewers found it blasphemous, and Ruskin deleted it from the third edition of *Modern Painters;* see Landow, *The Aesthetic and Critical Theories of John Ruskin* (Princeton, N.J.: Princeton University Press, 1971), p. 434. Landow's chapter "Ruskin and Allegory" is of great interest.
73. *Matisse: His Art and His Public,* pp. 11, 49, 51, 53, 81, 115.
74. "Matisse, Picasso, and the Crisis of 1907" (1951), in *Defining Modern Art,* p. 198. The next year, in his essay "The American Action Painters," Harold Rosenberg would write that "based on the phenomenon of conversion the new movement is, with the majority of painters, essentially a religious move-

ment. In every case, however, the conversion has been experienced in secular terms. The result has been the creation of private myths" (Rosenberg, "The American Action Painters," *Art News* 51 [December 1952]; reprinted in David Shapiro and Cecile Shapiro, eds., *Abstract Expressionism: A Critical Record* [Cambridge and New York: Cambridge University Press, 1990], p. 80).

75. *Picasso: Fifty Years of His Art,* p. 63.

76. Ibid., p. 94

77. *Cubism and Abstract Art,* pp. 17, 73.

78. *Masters of Modern Art,* p. 76.

79. Ibid., p. 68. Elsewhere, a conflict among Constructivist factions will be a "schism" (*Cubism and Abstract Art,* p. 17), and later, Russian artists will witness "recurrent heresies and pathetic repentences" ("Is Modern Art Communistic?" [1952], in *Defining Modern Art,* p. 217). André Breton of course becomes known as "the surrealist pontiff," like a schismatic pope in residence at Avignon (*Masters of Modern Art,* p. 141). Ultimately, Barr fears that a movement such as Abstract Expressionism may harden into "an orthodoxy of abstraction" ("The New American Painting, as Shown in Eight European Countries, 1958–1959" [1959], in *Defining Modern Art,* p. 234), or even a "dogma" (*Masters of Modern Art,* p. 174).

80. "Chronicle of the Collection of Painting and Sculpture," in *Painting and Sculpture in The Museum of Modern Art, 1929–1967,* p. 626.

81. "Matisse, Picasso, and the Crisis of 1907" (1951), in *Defining Modern Art,* p. 201.

82. Quoted in *Masters of Modern Art,* p. 78.

83. *What Is Modern Painting?,* p. 5.

84. Among recent general studies, see Giancarlo Maiorino, *Leonardo da Vinci: The Daedalian Mythmaker* (University Park: Pennsylvania State University Press, 1992), especially the chapters "The Art of War and the Inventor's Rhetoric of Power" and "The Daedalian *Artifex:* Myth, Technology, and Doom"; and A. Richard Turner, *Inventing Leonardo* (New York: Knopf, 1993), especially the chapter "Leonardo the Harbinger of Modernity."

85. *What Is Modern Painting?,* p. 27.

86. Ibid., p. 29.

87. Quoted in *Masters of Modern Art,* p. 126.

88. *What Is Modern Painting?,* p. 28; *Art in Our Time* (New York: The Museum of Modern Art, 1939), cat. no. 157; *Masters of Modern Art,* p. 68. Picasso himself is said to have scoffed at the notion of artistic "research"; see the statement in *Picasso: Fifty Years of His Art,* pp. 270–71.

89. *What Is Modern Painting?,* p. 31.

90. *Masters of Modern Art,* p. 53. His other comments on *Piano Lesson* are in *Matisse: His Art and His Public,* p. 174.

91. Simon Blackburn, "What If . . . ? The Uses and Abuses of Thought Experiments" (review of Roy A. Sorenson, *Thought Experiments*), *Times Literary Supplement,* June 18, 1993, p. 10.

92. See the comprehensive study by Robert Wohl, *A Passion for Wings: Aviation and the Western Imagination, 1908–1918* (New Haven, Conn., and London: Yale University Press, 1994).

93. *Cubism and Abstract Art,* p. 124. One might also mention here Gustav Klucis's design for the cover of *The Daily Life of Airplane Pilots* (1928).

94. Kazimir Malevich, *The Non-Objective World,* trans. Howard Dearstyne (Munich: Bauhaus Books, 1927), p. 96.

95. Brancusi, quoted in Sidney Geist, *Brancusi: A Study of the Sculpture* (New York: Hacker, 1983), p. 38.

96. William Carlos Williams, "Brancusi" (1955), in *A Recognizable Image: William Carlos Williams on Art and Artists,* ed. Bram Dijkstra (New York: New Directions, 1978), p. 249.

97. See Carolyn Lanchner, William Rubin, et al., *Henri Rousseau* (New York: The Museum of Modern Art, 1985), pp. 194–99, where the three paintings mentioned here are reproduced with commentary on Rousseau's interest in aviation.

98. *Homage to Blériot* is in the Kunstmuseum Basel; *Astra (The Cardiff Team)* is in the Musée d'Art Moderne de la Ville de Paris. For a brief discussion of the airplane imagery of *Astra (The Cardiff Team),* under the rubric of advertising, see Kirk Varnedoe and Adam Gopnik, *High and Low: Modern Art and Popular Culture* (New York: The Museum of Modern Art, 1990), pp. 247–48.

99. Le Corbusier, *Vers une Architecture* (1923); English ed., *Towards a New Architecture* (London: John Rodker, 1931; rpt. New York: Dover, 1986), pp. 109, 127. Another passage in the chapter titled "Airplanes" (pp. 105–27) suggests the origin of Le Corbusier's famous phrase about the house as a "machine for living," in a move from the organic to the inventively mechanical: "The lesson of the airplane is not primarily in the forms it has created, and above all we must learn to see an airplane not as a bird or a dragon-fly, but as a machine for flying; the lesson of the airplane lies in the logic which governed the enunciation of the problem. . . . The problem of the house has not yet been stated" (p. 110). Just as the "problem" of designing an airplane was how to conceive it not as a bird but as a "machine for flying," so the problem of designing a house was how to conceive it not as a nest but as a "machine for living."

100. Most of Gorky's statement about the airport murals is reprinted in Ethel K. Schwabacher, *Arshile Gorky: Memorial Exhibition* (New York: Whitney Museum of American Art, 1951), pp. 24–26; and in Schwabacher, *Arshile Gorky* (New York: Published for the Whitney Museum of American Art by the Macmillan Company, 1957), pp. 70, 73–74. It is reprinted in full in Ruth Bowman, *Murals Without Walls: Arshile Gorky's Aviation Murals Rediscovered* (Newark, N.J.: The Newark Museum, 1978), pp. 13, 15–16, which also reprints Frederick Kiesler's 1936 *Art Front* article on the murals (pp. 30–33).

101. Letter to Mrs. Audrey McMahon, December 3, 1935; printed in Schwabacher, *Arshile Gorky* (1957), p. 70. In a subsequent letter, to Olive M. Layford of the Federal Art Project, October 14, 1936, Barr writes: "I think they [Gorky's murals] would form magnificent decorations of great appropriateness to an airport, for an airport should be one of the most modern architectural projects. Any conservative or banal or reactionary decorations would be extremely inappropriate. It is dangerous to ride in an old-fashioned airplane. It is inappropriate to wait and buy one's ticket surrounded by old-fashioned murals" (ibid., pp. 76–78).

102. *Matisse: His Art and His Public,* p. 242.

103. See William Rubin, *Picasso and Braque: Pioneering Cubism* (New York: The Museum of Modern Art, 1989), pp. 32–34. See also Kirk Varnedoe, "Overview: The Flight of the Mind," in his *A Fine Disregard: What Makes Modern Art Modern* (New York: Abrams, 1990), pp. 270–73.

104. *Masters of Modern Art,* p. 74. The two figures in the painting are generally considered to be the artist and his brother Henri, who was the director of the Nieuport airplane factory. See the catalogue entry in *Painting and Sculpture in The Museum of Modern Art, 1929–1967,* p. 557.

105. See the discussion of the overhead view in Varnedoe, "Overview: The Flight of the Mind." See also the discussion of La Fresnaye's *The Conquest of the Air* in Robert Rosenblum, *Cubism and Twentieth-Century Art* (1960; rev. New York: Abrams, 1976), p. 180.

106. Gertrude Stein, *Picasso* (London: Batesford, 1938; rpt. New York: Dover, 1984), p. 50.

107. Catalogue, including transcription of the wall-panel texts by Wendell L. Willkie, in *The Bulletin of The Museum of Modern Art* 11, no. 1 (1943). The passages just cited are on pp. 4–6. The exhibition took place July 2–October 31, 1943. President Roosevelt was among the lenders.

108. *Picasso: Fifty Years of His Art,* p. 215. In *Forty Years of His Art,* the portrait appeared on p. 187 (cat. no. 349).

109. Late in the novel, as Richard Ellmann tells us, Stephen "throws off sonhood and becomes his own father. . . . At this stage he remembers his dream of having flown . . . and it seems that he is now Daedalus *père,* successful airman, rather than Icarus *fils*" (Ellmann, *Ulysses on the Liffey* [London and New York: Oxford University Press, 1972], p. 88). Joyce's flight pattern would become highly significant to a young World War II pilot, Joseph Beuys, who, having been shot down over the Crimea in 1943 and fallen to earth as a *Luftwaffe* Icarus, would later undertake an elaborate *Ulysses* project; see Bernice Rose, "Joseph Beuys and the Language of Drawing," in Ann Temkin and Bernice Rose, *Thinking Is Form: The Drawings of Joseph Beuys* (Philadelphia: Philadelphia Museum of Art; New York: The Museum of Modern Art, 1993), pp. 95–96.

Other contemporary reminders of the myth of Icarus for Barr during the period under discussion would include the *Icarus* plate (designed during the war) that comes at the end of the "Aeroplane" section of Matisse's *Jazz* (1947), and which has sometimes been interpreted as a parachuting airman falling amid bursts of anti-aircraft fire. And earlier there is W. H. Auden's well-known poem "Musée des Beaux-Arts" (1938).

On various allegories of flight depicted in

Western art, based not only on Icarus but on such Christian subjects as the Fall of the Rebel Angels and on the failed flight of Simon Magus, see Peter Greenaway, *Flying Out of This World* (Chicago and London: University of Chicago Press, 1994). See also several books by the Joyce scholar Clive Hart, including *The Prehistory of Flight* (Berkeley, Los Angeles, and London: University of California Press, 1985) and *Images of Flight* (Berkeley, Los Angeles, and London: University of California Press, 1988).

110. See Varnedoe, "Overview: The Flight of the Mind," pp. 270–71; *The Scallop Shell ("Notre Avenir est dans l'air")* is reproduced on p. 272.

111. In his statement to Christian Zervos, reprinted in *Picasso: Fifty Years of His Art,* p. 272.

112. *Picasso: Fifty Years of His Art,* p. 57.

113. Paul Haesaerts's phrase is quoted in *Picasso: Fifty Years of His Art,* p. 206.

114. William Wordsworth, "The Tables Turned," from *Lyrical Ballads* (1798).

115. *Picasso: Fifty Years of His Art,* p. 56.

116. *What Is Modern Painting?,* p. 29.

117. *Masters of Modern Art,* p. 29.

118. Ibid., p. 9.

119. Gore Vidal, interview in *Amelia Earhart* (1993), a documentary film by Nancy Porter for the PBS television series *The American Experience.*

120. Perhaps there is something of this in the choice of image for Emmett Williams's *Brandenburg Gate and the "Hindenburg"* (1981); reproduced in Kynaston McShine, ed., *BerlinArt, 1961–1987* (New York: The Museum of Modern Art; Munich: Prestel, 1987), p. 156; the volume reproduces as its frontispiece Helmut Middendorf's *Airplane Dream* (1982), a work that "expresses an urban angst particular to our own time, and especially meaningful to Berlin" (p. 18). One could perhaps mention also Anselm Kiefer's large lead sculpture of an airplane, *Poppies and Memories* (1989).

121. *What Is Modern Painting?,* p. 39. In this connection, it should be noted that military history was one of Barr's special interests. At the memorial service for Barr in 1981, Philip Johnson pointed this out: "How many of you know that he knew the strategy, the tactics, the logistics of three-quarters of the great battles of the whole world? Not just the simple, ordinary battles we all have read about in the schoolbook—he knew the technical language. And I remember the time he had to give up that interest because of his fantastic amount of work here. I gave him General Fuller's three-volume work on the great battles of the world, and he almost cried because he would never have time to read that book all the way through" (*Alfred H. Barr, Jr.: A Memorial Tribute,* n.p.).

122. *What Is Modern Painting?,* pp. 39, 40.

123. *Picasso: Fifty Years of His Art,* p. 250.

124. Leni Riefenstahl makes much of this award in the section "The Paris World's Fair" of her autobiography, *A Memoir* (New York: St. Martin's Press, 1992), pp. 208–09; the certificate of the award is reproduced between pp. 338 and 339.

125. The presence of *Triumph of the Will* in the Museum's Film Library collection is specifically pointed out in *Masters of Modern Art,* p. 199, while the section of Barr's book headed "The Film of Fact and Opinion," p. 212, includes a still from Riefenstahl's *Olympia* (1938). In *A Memoir,* p. 218, Riefenstahl recounts the following conversation she says she had with the director Josef von Sternberg on New Year's Eve, 1938, at Saint-Moritz:

"*. . . the film you made of him [Hitler],* Triumph of the Will, *is first class.*"

"*Where did you see it?" I asked in surprise.*

"*In New York, at the Museum of Modern Art.*"

"*Do you really like it?*"

"*My dear girl," said Sternberg, "it will make film history—it's revolutionary. . . .*"

126. Riefenstahl, *A Memoir,* p. 164.

127. As translated in the subtitled print now circulated in the United States on videotape by Film Preserve Ltd. The thousand years of the millennium are also evident in Hitler's idea of his "Thousand-Year Reich."

128. "Is Modern Art Communistic?" (1952), in *Defining Modern Art,* p. 219.

129. Quoted in Susan Sontag, "Fascinating Fascism" (1975), in her *Under the Sign of Saturn* (New York: Farrar, Straus & Giroux, 1980; rpt. New York: Doubleday, 1991), p. 92.

130. Quoted in Igor Golomstock, *Totalitarian Art* (New York: HarperCollins, 1990), p. xiii.

131. See "Nationalism in German Films" (1934) and "Art in the Third Reich—Preview, 1933" (1945), in *Defining Modern Art,* pp. 158–75.

132. "It Can Happen Here," *The Art Digest* 23 (August 1, 1949), p. 23.

133. Sontag, "Fascinating Fascism," p. 92.

134. See Stephanie Barron et al., *"Degenerate Art": The Fate of the Avant-Garde in Nazi Germany* (Los Angeles: Los Angeles County Museum of Art; New York: Abrams, 1991).

135. *Matisse: His Art and His Public,* p. 257; *Picasso: Fifty Years of His Art,* p. 226; see also "Is Modern Art Communistic?" (1952), p. 218.

136. "It Can Happen Here" (1949), p. 23.

137. *Picasso: Fifty Years of His Art,* pp. 202, 226.

138. Ibid., p. 202.

139. *What Is Modern Painting?,* p. 41.

140. *Matisse: His Art and His Public,* p. 263.

141. Ibid., p. 266.

142. See *Picasso: Fifty Years of His Art,* pp. 12, 57, 193, 196, 200–07, 226, 250.

143. Ibid., p. 250. Barnett Newman, too, saw certain art of the time as "prophetic." In an unpublished essay of 1945, he wrote: "The surrealists' work was in the nature of prophecy. For the horror they created and the shock they built up were not merely the dreams of crazy men; they were prophetic tableaux of what the world was to see as reality. They showed us the horror of war; and if men had not laughed at the surrealists, if they had understood them, the war might never have been. No painting exists [that is better surrealism] than the photographs of German atrocities. The heaps of skulls are the reality of Tchelitchew's vision. The mass of bone piles are the reality of Picasso's bone compositions, of his sculpture" (Newman, "Surrealism and the War," in *Barnett Newman: Selected Writings and Interviews,* ed. John P. O'Neill and Mollie McNickle [New York: Knopf, 1990], p. 95).

144. See Frank Kermode, *The Sense of an Ending: Studies in the Theory of Fiction* (London, Oxford, and New York: Oxford University Press, 1967), pp. 12–13.

145. Riefenstahl's *Olympia* (documenting the 1936 Berlin Olympics, with Hitler in attendance), though less obviously political than *Triumph of the Will,* nonetheless conveys a similar message; both are intended to illustrate ideas of physical perfection. *Olympia* draws attention to the fact that the games' original "patrons" were the Greek gods. The film's worship of athletes' perfect bodies is prefaced by an opening sequence in which the camera wanders through classical Greek ruins before finding its way, across a map of Europe, to the second Mount Olympus of Berlin.

146. Charles A. Lindbergh, *Autobiography of Values* (New York: Harcourt Brace, 1976, rpt. 1992), p. 147.

147. Some of Jules Verne's tales, notably *Robur-le-conquérant* (1886) and *Le Maître du monde* (1904), also predict a malevolent future for aviation.

148. T. S. Eliot, "Little Gidding," in *Four Quartets* (1943; rpt. New York: Harcourt Brace, n.d.), ll. 200–06.

149. See Robert Rosenblum's discussion of sun imagery in the chapter "The Pastoral and the Apocalyptic" in *Modern Painting and the Northern Romantic Tradition.*

150. *Picasso: Forty Years of His Art,* p. 174. Compare the variations in *Fifty Years of His Art,* p. 200, and in Barr's Introduction to Juan Larria, *Guernica/Pablo Picasso* (New York: Curt Valentin, 1947), p. 11, where the sentence is simplified to read, "And over all shines the radiant eye of night with an electric bulb for a pupil."

151. Picasso's comments on "the barbarous bombardment of the Prado Museum by rebel airplanes" appear in *Picasso: Fifty Years of His Art,* p. 264.

152. The underdrawings of the ruined frescoes are now displayed in the Museo delle Sinopie del Camposanto Monumentale.

153. By coincidence, *Guernica,* the painting inspired by an air raid, when shown in Milan after the war, would be examined by the same conservator who had just inspected *The Last Supper* for damage after the removal of its wartime covering; recounted in Douglas Cooper, "Picasso's *Guernica* Installed in the Prado," *The Burlington Magazine* 124 (May 1982); reprinted in Ellen C. Oppler, ed., *Picasso's "Guernica"* (New York and London: Norton, 1988), p. 322.

154. *Masters of Modern Art,* p. 155. See also *Painting and Sculpture in The Museum of Modern Art, 1929–1967,* p. 634.

155. *What Is Modern Painting?,* p. 8.

156. *The Bulletin of The Museum of Modern Art,* 11, no. 1 (1943), p. 11.

157. In the accompanying booklet, the photograph appears on a dramatic two-page spread with a

caption in Old English type reading: "—took Him down and wrapped Him in clean linens"; see Edward J. Steichen, ed., *Power in the Pacific* (New York: Published for The Museum of Modern Art by Wm. E. Rudge's Sons, 1945), pp. 26–27. In the book-length version of *Power in the Pacific* (New York: U.S. Camera Publishing Corporation, 1945), the photograph appears on p. 137 with somewhat less ornate type and slightly different wording: "—took him down and wrapped his body in clean linens."

158. *Picasso: Fifty Years of His Art,* p. 12.

159. Ibid., p. 250.

160. Picasso was quoted to the effect that accounts of the Allied bombing of Nazi Europe put him in mind of *Guernica;* see Oppler, ed., *Picasso's "Guernica,"* p. 102.

161. Included in *The Atomic Café* (1982), a compilation documentary about the Cold War, directed by Kevin Rafferty, Jane Loader, and Pierce Rafferty.

162. *What Is Modern Painting?,* p. 41.

163. Quoted in Conrad C. Crane, *Bombs, Cities, and Civilians: American Airpower Strategy in World War II* (Lawrence: University Press of Kansas, 1993), p. 37. J. Robert Oppenheimer recounted another statement of Stimson's about the bombing of cities: "He didn't say that the air strikes shouldn't be carried on, but he did think there was something wrong with a country where no one questioned that" (ibid.).

164. See the many documents gathered in Oppler, ed., *Picasso's "Guernica,"* pp. 236–46.

165. Albert Einstein, message to the Peace Congress of Intellectuals, in Wroclav, released to the press August 29, 1948; in Einstein, *Out of My Later Years* (New York: Philosophical Library, 1950, rev. 1956; rpt. New York: Wing Books, 1993), p. 152.

166. Oppenheimer was a lender to The Museum of Modern Art in 1939; see *Art in Our Time,* p. 8.

167. *Robert Oppenheimer: Letters and Recollections,* ed. Alice Kimball Smith and Charles Weiner (Cambridge, Mass: Harvard University Press, 1980), p. 290. The first poem cited is Donne's "Hymn to God My God in My Sickness."

168. See "Reminiscences/Three Pictures" (1913), in *Kandinsky: Complete Writings on Art,* ed. Kenneth C. Lindsay and Peter Vergo (New York: Da Capo Press, 1994), pp. 376–77, 379.

169. This and the following quotation are from Richard Rhodes, *The Making of the Atomic Bomb* (New York: Simon & Schuster, 1986, rpt. 1988), pp. 675, 676. On the moral issues considered in the scientific development of the weapon and in the military decision to use it, see also Gregg Herken, *The Winning Weapon: The Atomic Bomb in the Cold War, 1945–1950* (New York: Knopf, 1981; rpt. Princeton, N.J.: Princeton University Press, 1988); Michael S. Sherry, *The Rise of American Air Power: The Creation of Armageddon* (New Haven, Conn., and London: Yale University Press, 1987); and Crane, *Bombs, Cities, and Civilians.*

170. In a farewell speech to his Manhattan Project colleagues at Los Alamos later that year, Oppenheimer saw their triumph in inventing the atomic bomb as an epoch-making change in the course of history, comparable, in a negative way, to the Renaissance: "But the real impact of the creation of the atomic bomb, and atomic weapons—to understand that one has to look further back, look, I think, to the times when physical science was growing in the days of the renaissance, and when the threat that science offered was felt so deeply throughout the Christian world. . . . This quantitative change has all the character of a change in quality, of a change in the nature of the world" (speech to the Association of Los Alamos Scientists, November 2, 1945; in *Robert Oppenheimer: Letters and Recollections,* pp. 316, 318).

171. *Masters of Modern Art,* p. 114.

172. *What Is Modern Painting?,* p. 44.

173. Similarly, in 1951, Barr refers to a contorted figure's "swastika" pose (*Matisse: His Art and His Public,* p. 51), at a time when the word could hardly have been free of recent associations.

174. Reprinted in Herschel B. Chipp, ed., *Theories of Modern Art: A Source Book by Artists and Critics* (Berkeley, Los Angeles, and London: University of California Press, 1968), p. 560.

175. The statement is quoted in the discussion of de Kooning's *Woman I* in the postwar edition of *What Is Modern Painting?,* p. 44. It also appears in Barr's "The New American Painting, as Shown in Eight European Countries, 1958–1959: Introduction" (1959), in *Defining Modern Art,* p. 230.

176. *Masters of Modern Art,* p. 176.

177. "Will This Art Endure?," *The New York Times Magazine,* December 1, 1957, sect. 6, p. 48. Earlier in the decade, William Faulkner had famously employed the word "endure" in his Nobel Prize address, delivered in December 1950. Speaking of a time "when the last ding-dong of doom has clanged and faded from the last worthless rock hanging tideless in the last red and dying evening," Faulkner had avowed: "I decline to accept the end of man. . . . I believe that man will not merely endure: he will prevail."

178. *Masters of Modern Art,* p. 90.

179. See Northrop Frye's chapter "The Furnace" in his *Words with Power: Being a Second Study of the Bible and Literature* (San Diego, New York, and London: Harcourt Brace, 1990, rpt. 1992), pp. 294–98.

180. Theodore Roszak, statement in the symposium "The New Sculpture," The Museum of Modern Art, New York, 1952; in Andrew Carnduff Ritchie, *Sculpture of the Twentieth Century* (New York: The Museum of Modern Art, 1952); excerpts printed in Chipp, ed., *Theories of Modern Art,* p. 568.

181. A. C. Bradley, "The Substance of Shakespearean Tragedy," in his *Shakespearean Tragedy* (New York and London: Macmillan, 1905); reprinted in Lawrence Sargent Hall, ed., *A Grammar of Literary Criticism* (New York: Macmillan, 1965), p. 79.

182. "Chronicle of the Collection of Painting and Sculpture," in *Painting and Sculpture in The Museum of Modern Art, 1929–1967,* p. 641; the stock-market crash of 1929 and the outbreak of war in 1939 are recounted on pp. 620, 626.

An episode in world affairs, related to the allegory of flight, occurred in 1960. President Eisenhower had spent several years trying to bring about a thaw in the Cold War; but the hope for a nuclear arms agreement from the 1960 Paris summit meeting was lost when the Soviets unexpectedly shot down Francis Gary Powers's U-2 spy plane, as it photographed missile sites in Russian territory, and in the ensuing controversy Khrushchev was forced to respond with belligerence. Again, the Fall of Icarus was the figure of dashed ambitions.

183. In a 1965 interview, Frank O'Hara says of the influence of W. H. Auden's *The Orators:* "I don't believe for one minute . . . that the airmen business in it has failed to influence Terry Southern, who immediately dreamed up *Strangelove.* You know, the sheer flippancy and sarcasm and *accurate* satire is very important" (O'Hara, *Standing Still and Walking in New York* [San Francisco: Grey Fox Press, 1983], p. 25). Loosely based on the novel *Red Alert* (c. 1958) by Peter George, Stanley Kubrick's film *Dr. Strangelove,* with a script by Southern and Kubrick, was released in 1964, less than two years after the Cuban crisis.

Dr. Strangelove is part of a whole genre built around the idea of apocalyptic bombardment, from Nevil Shute's *On the Beach* (published 1957, filmed 1959) and George's *Red Alert* to Eugene Burdick's *Fail-Safe* (published 1962, filmed 1964) and Kurt Vonnegut's *Slaughterhouse-Five* (published 1969, filmed 1972).

184. In Oppler, ed., *Picasso's "Guernica,"* p. 202.

185. Ibid., p. 237. Reinhardt then goes on to discuss Jasper Johns's Flags; it would be interesting to know whether he was prompted by the association that "The Star-Spangled Banner" makes the flag, too, like *Guernica,* an emblem of bombardment, of "bombs bursting in air."

186. In Oppler, ed., *Picasso's "Guernica,"* p. 304.

187. Thomas B. Hess, *Barnett Newman* (New York: The Museum of Modern Art, 1971), p. 68.

188. Quoted in Jean Lipman and Richard Marshall, *Art About Art* (New York: Whitney Museum of American Art, 1978), p. 122. It is disconcerting to note that in 1975, Susan Sontag saw Nazi art, too, as coming to be treated like "a form of Pop Art" ("Fascinating Fascism," p. 94).

189. *Picasso: Fifty Years of His Art,* p. 193.

190. *What Is Modern Painting?,* p. 45. A different Lichtenstein painting is reproduced in the present text (fig. 25). Lichtenstein's large, mural-like pictures on military-industrial themes, *Preparedness* (1968; Solomon R. Guggenheim Museum, New York) and *Peace Through Chemistry* (1970; private collection), painted during the Vietnam war, pursue related questions of the proper application of modern technical inventions.

191. "Chronicle of the Collection of Painting and Sculpture," in *Painting and Sculpture in The Museum of Modern Art, 1929–1967,* p. 638.

192. Frank O'Hara, "Reuben Nakian," in his *Art Chronicles, 1954–1966* (New York: Braziller, 1975), pp. 87–88 (Nakian's *Hiroshima* [1965–66] is in the Museum's collection). O'Hara would, however,

speak of "universal destruction" and "a future which may be nonexistent" in talking about the apocalyptic aspect he saw in the "lyrical desperation" of some of Pollock's paintings (p. 26).

193. In his *Starting from San Francisco* (1961); see Oppler, ed., *Picasso's "Guernica,"* p. 306.

194. Larry Rivers with Arnold Weinstein, *What Did I Do? The Unauthorized Autobiography of Larry Rivers* (New York: HarperCollins, 1992), p. 323. Instead of being called before the House Un-American Activities Committee, as he feared would happen, Rivers was soon interrogated by the district attorney investigating "fixed" quiz shows.

195. On the bucolic versus the mechanical, see Marx, *The Machine in the Garden.*

196. "Tinguely ex machina," statement delivered in the Sculpture Garden of The Museum of Modern Art, March 17, 1960; printed in *Homage to New York: A Self-Constructing and Self-Destroying Work of Art Conceived and Built by Jean Tinguely* (New York: The Museum of Modern Art, [1960]).

It should be noted that Barr delivered his statement in the Sculpture Garden *before* Tinguely's self-destroying work was activated. Helen Franc recalls that after the work was actually turned on, Barr was horrified when in the course of its destruction it broke into flames. Only two years before, in May 1958, there had been a serious fire in the Museum's galleries that, in addition to damaging several major paintings, had caused a fatality.

197. See Stanley Fish, *Self-Consuming Artifacts: The Experience of Seventeenth-Century Literature* (Berkeley: University of California Press, 1972).

198. This well-known phrase of Mark Rothko's is quoted as one of the epigraphs to Barr's "The New American Painting, as Shown in Eight European Countries, 1958–1959: Introduction" (1959), in *Defining Modern Art*, p. 230. Barr himself spoke of "timeless human tragedy" with respect to Orozco's *Dive Bomber and Tank;* see *What Is Modern Painting?*, p. 8.

199. *What Is Modern Painting?*, p. 42. He notes also: "In the art of post-war Paris and its outposts on the Riviera, *Sturm und Drang* had practically disappeared. Picasso, who had drawn his frightful *Charnel-house* in 1945, was within a couple of years engaged in painting lively pastoral frolics" (*Matisse: His Art and His Public,* pp. 263–64).

200. On renouncing the portentous sense of foreshadowing provided by types and exploring instead "the prosaics of daily life," see Michael André Bernstein, *Foregone Conclusions: Against Apocalyptic History* (Berkeley, Los Angeles, and London: University of California Press, 1994).

201. But to return, of course, in the crises that marked the later sixties, when *Guernica* was appearing on antiwar posters.

202. O'Hara, "Art Chronicle" (1962), in O'Hara, *Standing Still and Walking in New York,* pp. 128–29.

Visitors observing a child drawing in the Children's Creative Center, U.S. Pavilion, Exposition Universelle et Internationale de Bruxelles, 1958

From Modernist Utopia to Cold War Reality: A Critical Moment in Museum Education

Carol Morgan

The Museum of Modern Art has played a pivotal role in the history of museum education since 1937, when Museum Director Alfred H. Barr, Jr., hired Victor E. D'Amico to head the nascent Educational Project. The Museum was founded at the end of the 1920s, a decade that had witnessed a significant shift in educational practices. After World War I, great numbers of educators, including D'Amico, began to explore ways in which to implement the theories of John Dewey in their classrooms. Advocates of progressive education defined their aim as "the development to the highest possible point of all the powers of the individual—his capacity to adjust himself effectively to the world around him, his potential for improving that world through the release of his powers of creative self-expression."[1] The progressives in education felt an affinity with modernist artists, and were considered by others to be following a parallel track. D'Amico and his programs thus fit neatly into the broader mission of the young Museum of Modern Art, winning national as well as international acclaim, especially during the 1950s.

September 24, 1951, marked the official opening of the Museum's "21" building on West Fifty-third Street. Two floors of the six-storey building, which was designed by Philip Johnson, were devoted to classroom space, with the fourth floor reserved for the offices of the now-formalized Department of Education. The dedication of this considerable amount of space and resources to the department attests to the Museum's commitment to its educational mission. To mark the occasion of the facility's opening, Museum President Nelson A. Rockefeller wrote to D'Amico in praise of the People's Art Center, the new home of the Museum's educational programs:

The school is an accomplishment of major importance and one which is almost entirely due to your vision, ability and leadership. All of us on the Board of Trustees are particularly proud and happy in our association with you . . . and we share with you in the deep satisfaction of your achievements.[2]

During World War II, D'Amico had helped found the Committee on Art

Education (COAE), remaining its leader until shortly before the group disbanded in 1965. By the mid-1950s, the Committee had grown to include over one thousand members, with nearly twice that number attending its annual conferences. (The majority of these were held at the Museum and were open to students as well as COAE members.) Its members included artists, art teachers, school administrators, and educators who taught at secondary schools and universities. The organization provided an effective forum for the discussion of the theories and practices of creative art education at a critical moment in the history of art, and of art education.

While the ideals of progressive education became prevalent in the 1920s, the 1950s represented another turning point for the educational paradigm in the United States. The first wave of children born after World War II were entering schools that were unprepared to cope with their great numbers, and the development of the individual was lost to the need for order. Responding to a social and political climate that dictated a return to learning basic skills, educators returned to information-based practices. This shift had serious implications for the Department of Education at The Museum of Modern Art, as it did for all institutions whose programs were deeply rooted in creative self-expression rather than in teaching students to conform to predetermined standards.

This paper has two goals: first, to describe the programs of Victor D'Amico at The Museum of Modern Art between 1937 and 1960; and second, to look at the decade of the 1950s through the lens of the annual conferences of the Committee on Art Education. The latter will serve as a means of examining the struggle among the proponents of progressive education as it pertained to art and in the face of the social, educational, and artistic forces that would lead to the discipline-based practices of the next generation of educators.

Establishing Education at The Museum of Modern Art

Historians have adapted the theory articulated in Thomas Kuhn's *The Structure of Scientific Revolutions* (1952) to explain the kind of cyclical reforms that take place in various disciplines, including that of art education.[3] These paradigm shifts are influenced by a broad range of factors that emerge at a similar time and from parallel concerns; in the case of art education, these include current educational practice as well as trends in both art and society. For example, the development of the programs of Victor D'Amico was made possible because of the existence of The Museum of Modern Art and the kind of art it exhibited. The creation of the Museum in 1929 was itself influenced by, among other factors, the "rising expectations of an educated upper middle class elite reacting to new pressures of organization, [and] to systems of socially imposed morality ranging from Prohibition . . . to restraints imposed by traditional schooling."[4] It was the era during which creative self-expression became the dominant concern in education. The opening of John Dewey's laboratory school in 1896 had marked the beginning of the child-centered school movement. Not until the 1920s, however, were Dewey's theories put into practice on a broad scale. In their landmark book *The Child-Centered School* (1928), Harold Rugg and Ann Shumaker outlined the principles on which these child-centered schools were based:

Tolerant understanding and creative self-expression . . . the spirit of adventure, of fear-

less original thinking, of hard work and "concentration upon the object of desire that sets the world aside"—these are the essence of the creative spirit, whether expressed in the arts of intellect or of emotion.[5]

The opposition of modern artists to conventional academic training was similar in spirit to the theories of progressive educators such as Rugg and Shumaker, which can be read as a protest against the formal educational practices of the day:

[T]he creative artist is a vision seer. He is essentially interested in wholes; he sees life as a unit, as an entity. He compels himself to go beyond the surface appearances of things, for it is the feeling, the spirit's intention, not outer details, in which he is interested. He strives to catch the flash of inner spirit, some unit glimpse of life. He expresses what he sees, and his criterion of a creative act is that it shall be his own original and completely integrative portrayal of what is in his imagination. . . . This is essentially what modern art since Cézanne has tried to do. . . .[6]

A year after *The Child-Centered School* was published, The Museum of Modern Art was founded. From its beginning, the Museum blazed the trail for the definition and popularization of modern art, and in 1936 it began to address the need for educating a broader public. At the suggestion of Nelson Rockefeller, the Museum employed Artemas C. Packard, Chairman of the Department of Art at Dartmouth College, to investigate how the Museum could most effectively aid in the development of aesthetic values in American life.[7] Rockefeller's motivation was, of course, not entirely altruistic; given that the future of the Museum would necessarily depend on the interest and support of a larger audience, the question remained how to identify and educate that audience. The Packard Report (1938), as it came to be known, clearly described the situation in which the young Museum found itself:

In fact (but not in theory) the art museums at the present time serve the interest of the expert and the connoisseur far more than they serve the interest of the public. . . . It is only too apparent that its [the Museum's] present enviable reputation has been largely built on the care with which it has avoided catering to the "popular" interest. Yet "popular instruction" is one of the major objects for which the institution exists. . . . What we are really confronted with is the need for two quite consciously and deliberately different kinds of enterprise; on the one hand, the search for what is best in Art according to the highest standards of critical discrimination, and, on the other, the provision of facilities for popular instruction in accordance with the public need. *These two objectives will at times seem mutually antagonistic, but in the long run I am convinced they will be found to complement and reinforce one another.*[8]

The Packard Report asked a crucial question: Should The Museum of Modern Art be maintained as a museum for the few or for the many? Packard, himself an art historian sympathetic toward the theories of Progressive education, singled out as being among "the few" those who represented the current "sources of 'authority'" in art judgment, including "the scholar-specialists, the learned historians, the professional writers and lecturers about art."[9] He held these groups largely responsible for "destroying all normal perspective on relative values in art judgment by exalting the

place of an object in its category above its place in normal experience. [Their] activities have tended to confirm in the average citizen his inherited conviction that art is a deep and unintelligible mystery which is too far removed from his ordinary interests to be worth bothering with."[10]

By the late 1930s, the ideals of progressive education had become the basis for the educational model prevalent in private schools, as well as in public schools in upper-middle-class suburbs. In his report, Packard acknowledged "the general shift which is taking place from the theory of education as a process of acquiring knowledge to the theory that education is a means of developing the capacity of the individual to adapt himself adequately to his environment."[11] Packard noted that most institutions of higher learning had not yet adopted progressive educational practices. He cited the role of The Museum of Modern Art in awakening an interest in modern art among scholars, and saw an opportunity for the Museum "to assist the universities in working out a program of art study which will be more consistent with the needs of the student and less unfavorable to a sympathetic interest in contemporary art."[12]

It is no mistake that Packard linked a more student-focused curriculum with an appreciation of modern art. With art-history courses systemically based on the acquisition of a body of knowledge centered on the art of the past, university students were hindered in developing an appreciation for the new forms of modern art. Conversely, modern art seemed to justify the progressives' theories of art education. Dewey believed that "art as an activity and as a product" is important "when and as it influences human experience. [It] provides a form of expression for the uniqueness of personality."[13] Similarly, Packard advocated "the study of Art as *immediate experience* (deriving its validity from its direct impact on the consciousness rather than indirectly through an understanding of its relation to a sequence of stylistic developments called Art History)."[14] In making his recommendations to the Museum, however, he concluded that "the only safe way to preserve the integrity both of the ideals of 'productive scholarship' on the one hand and of intelligent 'popular instruction' on the other is to consider them as different kinds of enterprise, each equally important, but each requiring its own separate organization and specially trained personnel."[15] He also outlined the need for an education department, and enumerated specific suggestions for its activities. But he warned that, if the Museum were unaware of the paradoxical implications of establishing a program of education that was to be independent of, but equal to, its curatorial activities, it might "very easily fall into the error of encouraging the one to the detriment of the other (the unfortunate condition which now generally prevails) and impede the development of a broader understanding which may harmonize their apparent contradictions."[16]

As Packard observed, in reality it was the so-called "few" who maintained and visited American museums in the early twentieth century, even though the founders of these institutions had intended their collections to be made accessible to a broad public. This was especially true of a museum devoted to modern art, which had neither found its way into academic study on a large scale nor cultivated the interest of the general public. Then, as now, the focus of the debate was the conflict between academic and experiential approaches as means of developing the aesthetic values of a diverse audience. Packard recognized the need for a vision of the institution that

would be flexible enough to embrace this paradox. To have advocated a purely experiential method at the expense of an academic one might have run the risk of replicating the attitudes perpetuated by, for example, The Barnes Foundation in Merion, Pennsylvania, whose antiacademic approach undermined a serious interpretation of the application of progressive education principles to art education.[17] To have continued in the vein of favoring the academic while ignoring the needs of the public—and the Museum's self-interest in educating that public—would have greatly limited the future support and growth of the institution.

The Programs of Victor D'Amico

D'Amico was hired by Barr in 1937 to design and implement educational programs that were, in Packard's words, "in accordance with the public need." As an art teacher, D'Amico had devoted the early part of his career to developing the creative potential of young people through programs he directed in settlement houses in Manhattan and the Bronx in the 1920s, and as head of the art department at the progressive Ethical Culture Fieldston Schools in Riverdale, New York, beginning in 1926. (He would remain on the school's faculty until 1948.) His convictions about people and art also had their roots in the theories of Dewey, whom D'Amico had heard lecture at Teachers' College of Columbia University in New York.

Victor D'Amico

In the inaugural year of the Educational Project, D'Amico worked with ten schools, primarily the "progressive" private schools in New York City, designing eight exhibits—for example, "Modern Architecture," "The Modern Poster," and "Materials and How the Artist Changes Them"—for rotation among the schools. Monthly meetings at the Museum included "guest speakers who presented to the teachers of the participating schools recent trends and developments in art education."[18] Four demonstrations were held for students on the techniques of the artist, two of which were given by D'Amico himself. (During this first year of his association with the Museum, D'Amico also completed a book-length text, *The Visual Arts in General Education*, which would be published in 1940 by the Progressive Education Association.)

In 1939, D'Amico established the Young People's Gallery at the Museum "to provide a place for children in an adult museum, to communicate the ideas and activities of the Department [of Education], and to bring new experiments in art education to parents, teachers and the general public."[19] Exhibitions in the Gallery included "works selected and hung by student juries from material assembled . . . from the permanent collection of the Museum and loan exhibitions from private collections and art galleries."[20] The practice of inviting high school students to organize shows of original works of art speaks to the informality and spirit of exploration that dominated the Museum in its formative years. By 1941, the Young People's Gallery had a permanent space on the third floor of the Museum, where demonstrations by artists and roundtable discussions, among other activities, were held.

During World War II, D'Amico began to expand the Museum's educational programs for adults (which were initially targeted toward high-school teachers) with an experimental project called the War Veterans' Art Center. The purpose of the wartime program, active from 1944 to 1948, was to help reorient veterans to civilian life by encouraging them to make art objects. As always, D'Amico drew from his experience with progressive educational theories and practices: "Two major funda-

Left:
High school students planning the exhibition "We Like Modern Art" in the Young People's Gallery, The Museum of Modern Art, New York, 1941

Right:
Installation view, "We Like Modern Art," Young People's Gallery, The Museum of Modern Art, New York, 1941

mentals [are] basic to this objective: the capacity to discover the nature and extent of each veteran's aptitude, and the means of developing it to his best advantage."[21] In 1949, when the need to cater to veterans was met by other organizations, the program was reorganized as the People's Art Center, which offered expanded programs for adults as well as a new range of activities designed specifically for young children and teenagers.

The Fall 1951 issue of *The Museum of Modern Art Bulletin* was devoted to D'Amico's ideas and the offerings of the Center, which had recently opened in its new space in the "21" building. Included was a discussion of D'Amico's tenet that there were two extremes of teaching: the rule-and-imitation approach and the laissez-faire method of providing a child with materials and leaving him completely alone. D'Amico's method of creative teaching was not a compromise between the two extremes but "a totally new concept of education based on knowledge of the child's creative and psychological growth and on mastery of teaching techniques needed for their development."[22] Although the approach to art education taken at the People's Art Center seemed informal to those expecting to find students "making color wheels, or copying perspective charts," D'Amico was among the first art educators in the United States to put developmental theories such as those of the Swiss developmental psychologist Jean Piaget into practice.

Children between the ages of three and five began with the simple exploration of materials. For children ages six to twelve, teachers guided the art experience (as opposed to lesson) in more challenging directions, with greater emphasis on design and craftsmanship. Reproductions of works in the Museum's collections were placed around the studio in order to be the basis of discussions, although the children were not given specific information about them. These classes in art-making as a means of developing art appreciation were in keeping with D'Amico's assumption that the "visual arts, through properly directed experiences, can help to develop the visual, the emotional, and the kinesthetic senses, which must be developed along with the verbal and intellectual powers, if an integration of personality is ever to be realized through education."[23]

D'Amico began working with the parents of children in his classes as a first step toward educating them about the need for effective art education. By 1950, lec-

tures on children's creative development and conferences between parents and teachers led D'Amico to organize the first Parent-Child Class. In the first session, for parents alone, the teacher discussed the aims of the class and pointed out signs in the child's behavior and work.[24] In succeeding classes, parents worked alongside their children, but they were advised "not to do the work for the children nor to make suggestions which might inhibit the children's own ideas and efforts."[25] Classes for teenagers included the study of individual artists, movements, and concepts designed to extend their experience beyond personal expression. Gallery visits for these students were not formal lectures; rather, the instructors orchestrated discussions in order to discover the interests and inclinations of the group. (High school students participating in the classes were also given membership cards that allowed them entry into the Museum's main galleries whenever they were open to the public.) D'Amico believed that the progression from making one's own art to thinking about and understanding the art of others was a natural progression. A course for senior high school students in 1950 had these goals:

1. To discourage and eliminate unconscious prejudices toward modern art acquired at home or at school.

2. To bring a realization of the social causes in rebellions and revolutions in art in this century and a more fundamental enjoyment of these plastic, poetic and psychological interpretations.

3. To produce . . . a greater freedom of personal creativity. . . . The object is not to memorize formulae for producing paintings, but rather to understand what makes for validity in seemingly strange works.[28]

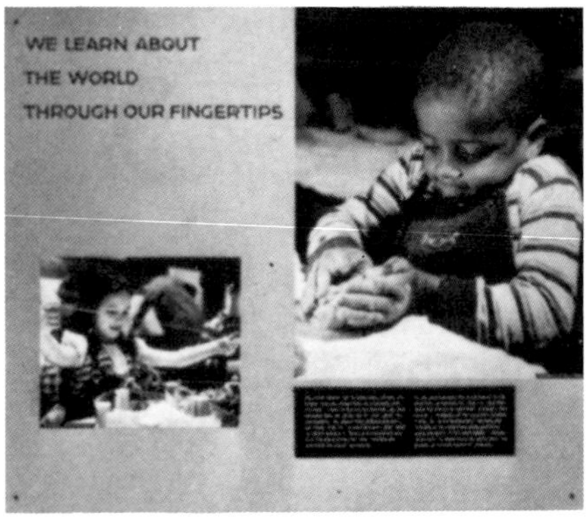

A panel from the educational exhibit "The Human Quality in Creative Experience"

"Design Teaching Model" with mobile cabinet

By 1960, the year the Museum published D'Amico's *Experiments in Creative Art Teaching,* eight hundred children and young people were attending weekly classes at the People's Art Center each semester, and thousands of students had benefited from the materials sent to their schools. The number of schools participating in the Educational Project had expanded to fifty-eight; basic programs continued while many others were added. Materials sent to the schools each month included "over 130 sets of visual materials consisting of exhibitions, slide talks, teaching models, teaching portfolios, films, and libraries of color reproductions and texts."[27] Reproductions of works in the Museum's collections, with captions and text, were mounted on panels for display in the schools. The exhibit "Modern Design in Furniture," for example, included "photographs and labels of explanatory text showing the development of modern furniture design, emphasizing chairs, tables, and storage pieces by such outstanding designers as Eames and Saarinen."[28] Another display, "Design Teaching Model," included "a variety of geometric solids and geometric and organic shapes painted in various colors [with a] platform and background provided for setting up compositions. Units and platform fit into a cabinet 28" high x 37" wide, which [was] mounted on rollers so that it [could] be easily moved about."[29]

The 1950s saw a surge in the numbers of adults attending art education classes. By the end of the decade, thirty different courses—in "painting . . . sculpture, ceramics, drawing and graphic expression, fundamentals of jewelry making, mosaic making, glass as a creative medium, art appreciation, and criticism in painting and in photography"[30]—were attended by five hundred adults annually. As with the War

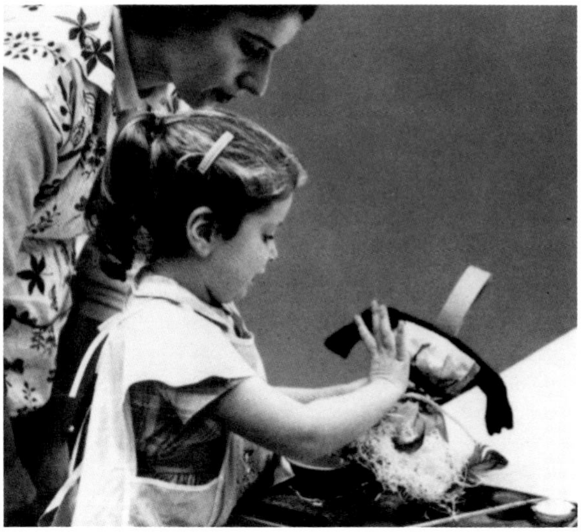

Left:
A child discussing collage construction with her mother in a Parent-Child Class at the People's Art Center, The Museum of Modern Art, New York, ca. 1950

Right:
An adult class at the People's Art Center, The Museum of Modern Art, New York, ca. 1950

Veterans' Art Center, the goal of these classes was to use the practice of making art to "develop more aesthetically-sensitive individuals who [would] derive greater pleasure and understanding from the work of artists of the past and present."[31] In speculating about the growing interest in adult education classes in the years following the war, D'Amico noted:

The majority of adults . . . betray a deadly earnest interest, one almost approaching a spiritual hunger. . . . For the most part the dilettante of yesterday seeking an "artistic patina" or the cultural snob is conspicuously absent. One wonders whether there is not a relationship between the growing power of destructiveness on the part of our scientific genius, and that indescribable urge for creation on the part of the general public.[32]

D'Amico's theory concerning the interrelatedness of destruction and creation was not considered simplistic in its day nor alien to the mainstream of thought within the Museum. Rather, the idea was indicative of a prevalent fear that the scientific community would come to dominate the social and educational agendas of the nation at the expense of the arts and creative art education—as would indeed prove to be the case.

The program for which D'Amico received perhaps the greatest recognition was the Children's Art Carnival, begun in 1942 as an annual holiday event at the Museum. The entrance to the Carnival was through the Contour Gate, a white metal rod curved in the shape of a four-year-old child and a twelve-year-old child standing side-by-side. Once inside, the children entered the Inspirational Area, which D'Amico described as "a semi-darkened room . . . filled with toys either in pools of light or lighted from within, giving a jewel-like effect. The mood intended is one of magic and fantasy, of a friendly forest, cool and quiet, with delightful surprises beckoning the child from every direction. . . . The Inspirational Area provides a new approach to art teaching, for here the child is stimulated to think creatively and is oriented to the fundamentals of design without words or dogma of any kind."[33] Visitors then entered the Studio Workshop, which was painted in warm colors and brightly lit,

Left:
Visitors entering the Children's Art Carnival through the Contour Gate

Right:
A table filled with toys in the Inspirational Area of the Children's Art Carnival

with mobiles hanging from above. Children worked independently at child-size easels and worktables fitted with lazy Susans full of materials to make constructions or collages. According to D'Amico, "A child [was] assisted by a teacher only when he [did] not know how to operate a toy, how to get started on a collage or construction, or when he [did] not seem to be deriving all the satisfaction possible from a given experience."[34]

The Carnival was so successful that it was chosen as the model for the Children's Creative Center pavilions, sponsored by the U.S. Department of Commerce as a feature of the international trade fairs in Milan and Barcelona in 1957 as well as the United States Pavilion at the 1958 Exposition Universelle et Internationale de Bruxelles. (After visiting the Creative Center in Brussels, Prime Minister Indira Gandhi asked that the Museum's circulating version of the Children's Art Carnival be sent on tour throughout India. At the close of the tour in 1963, First Lady Jacqueline Kennedy formally presented the Carnival to the National Children's Museum in New Delhi, a gift from the children of the United States to the children of India.) Children from schools and other organizations visited the pavilions at ninety-minute intervals. D'Amico and his staff also conducted training workshops at the fairs to help teachers learn how to implement some of the techniques in their own classrooms. Adults (other than educators and the press) were relegated to an observation deck, where they watched through portholes (see p. 150), or to the gallery outside the Studio Workshop. In his introductory remarks to television coverage of the Brussels pavilion, comentator Alistair Cooke stated, "One American triumph which will rock no headlines is a play hall that is heaven for the children of all nations and, except you become as a little child, you may no wise enter therein."[35]

Cooke's description lent a punctuation mark to the key words D'Amico used again and again to describe the pillars of his programs: "freedom of personal creativity," "enjoyment," "aesthetic sensitivity," "integration of personality," and "satis-

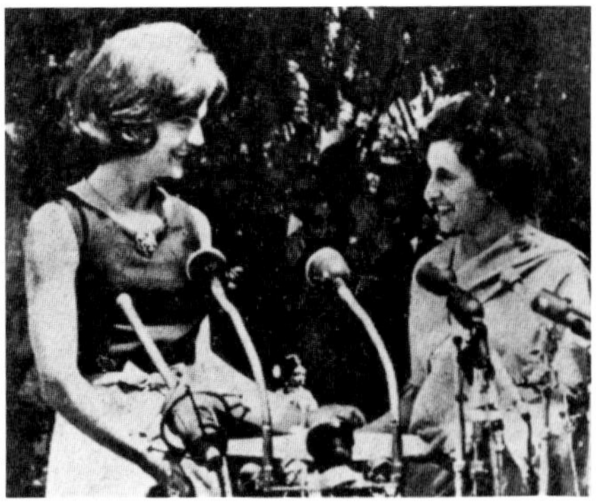

Jacqueline Kennedy and Indira Gandhi during the presentation of the Children's Art Carnival, New Delhi, 1963

faction." Even though the world had forever changed with the launching of *Sputnik I* in 1957, the generation of adults who, like D'Amico, came of age in the first half of what progressives had dubbed "The Century of the Child" would continue to struggle against the realities of the Cold War. Their utopian notions of the primitive, represented by their idolization of the child, would not easily give way to the utilitarian, information-based educational models that re-emerged during this period. D'Amico's programs were identified with modernism and its spirit of discovery. When he was hired in 1937, looking at and teaching about modern art still signified a break from the past and faith in the transformative powers of art. By the late 1950s, when his educational programs reached their zenith, the metaphors of the earlier era had begun to smack of rhetoric, despite the fact that D'Amico and his colleagues firmly believed every word. The Committee on Art Education, founded in 1943, would follow a similar trajectory.

Committee on Art Education

In addition to creating materials and developing techniques for teaching art and art appreciation, the purpose of The Museum of Modern Art's Department of Education was to "study problems in art education . . . and suggest a means of their solution."[36] Although D'Amico was a charismatic and innovative teacher, he was neither a researcher nor a scholar. He needed colleagues who not only shared his progressive views but would also challenge him to think ever more broadly, and he had the astuteness to gather around him some of the best thinkers in the field. As early as 1938, he had established an advisory committee to foster better cooperation with the schools; by 1940 he was planning publications, conferences, and an exchange program to research problems in art education. His ideas for an educational exchange evolved into the first meeting, in January 1943, of the Committee on Art in American Education and Society (later the Committee on Art Education). In a statement that reveals his skepticism of the very research he proposed to undertake, D'Amico defined this group as "a work committee that tackles and solves problems and not one that merely discovers or discusses them."[37] He held steadfastly to this vision throughout his tenure as leader of the organization.

Other professional organizations for art educators already existed when D'Amico founded the Committee, specifically the regional groups that eventually combined to form the National Art Education Association. Then, as now, however, members with an interest in marketing art materials played a significant role at the annual conferences sponsored by these organizations. The desire to create a purer atmosphere for the discussion of the issues of art education clearly influenced D'Amico's decision to form a separate group. When asked why the Committee was created, he replied:

Simply, to form a group which could study art education at its highest level, a group that would be concerned only with the philosophy of teaching. . . . We sought an opportunity to pursue our educational ideals without deference to the commercial interests and without the hawkers of coloring books and other harmful devices selling their cheap wares outside our door. In fact, we wanted no money changers in the temple, and since they could not be driven out of existing organizations, we were determined to set up a new place without them.[38]

D'Amico and the other members of the Committee placed "commercial interests" on a par with the "scientific genius" that they believed threatened not only the arts but the world at large—a reasonable response to mounting Cold War tensions. In 1942, when D'Amico invited selected art educators to attend the inaugural meeting of the Committee, a bulletin accompanying his letter spoke of "the need to develop the creative power of our youth—at a time when youth were being mobilized to destroy" and argued for "courage to defend the creative arts through the crisis, and vision to see their role in the peace to follow."[39] At the meeting, he articulated a theme that would preoccupy him and pervade the group's annual conferences for the next two decades—namely, defending creative art education in the face of economic and national security interests that increasingly dominated the national educational agenda:

We cannot scrap art or the art teacher in the curriculum without scrapping America's creative power, the creative youth of our schools. But we shall be virtually doing that if we remain impassive to the onslaughts on art education, or if we neglect to make art work during this time.[40]

In the mid-1950s, a quarter-century after the founding of The Museum of Modern Art, the art of the day, the national educational paradigm, and the American sociopolitical scene were changing rapidly. The threat of nuclear destruction, the Korean War, and the televised McCarthy hearings dominated the collective American psyche. Nationalist fervor, which had not subsided significantly after World War II, reached epidemic proportions after the Russian space launch in 1957. The following year, Congress enacted the National Defense Education Act to provide loans to college students, with special consideration given to students of mathematics, science, engineering, and foreign languages. Art teachers became art consultants, traveling from school to school, visiting classrooms on a weekly basis at best.

By 1955, the Progressive Education Association—the group espousing Dewey's ideas—had dissolved, and the new educational paradigm placed the scientific community "in a position to provide the model of the disciplines and [show] how they could be used in curriculum reform."[41] D'Amico considered this focus a threat to art education, and continued to argue for a progressive point of view throughout his career:

If we revert to the use of authority in setting up the curriculum, we shall lose all of our gains in the newly found human science of creative education. We shall revert to subject matter as the active part of education and the individual as the inactive part or an empty vessel which is to be filled with knowledge."[42]

In the 1950s, practitioners of creative art education found a lifeline in the Committee on Art Education and in its association with The Museum of Modern Art, which represented the haven of a "purer" space, free of commercial interests. The Museum was a willing sponsor of the new organization because of the link—through its Department of Education—between modern art and creative art education, and because of its commitment to D'Amico's programs:

The Museum of Modern Art . . . was the ideal institution to sponsor such a Committee as ours because our aims and functions were similar. . . . We hoped to follow its example by promoting creative art education in the United States as effectively as the Museum has promoted modern art throughout the world. . . .[43]

From the establishment of the Educational Project in 1937, Alfred Barr had been an unfailing supporter of D'Amico's work, and he would later participate on various panels at the annual meetings of the Committee on Art Education. D'Amico credited Barr, for whom he had the greatest respect, with providing the goals "for my whole professional life."[44] René d'Harnoncourt, who became Director of the Museum in 1948, was an equally staunch supporter of D'Amico. The two had met in 1937 while d'Harnoncourt was on the faculty of Sarah Lawrence College and remained professional allies and close friends until his retirement from the Museum in 1968. In part because both Barr and d'Harnoncourt had been educators before coming to the Museum, D'Amico felt a philosophical kinship with both men: "While [the Committee] enjoyed complete autonomy, the Museum was not just a good neighbor who gave us a room in its house and whose tools we used. The Museum had a genuine interest and an extensive background in education because several of its leaders were outstanding teachers."[45]

By 1953, ten years after the Committee's founding, the core group that formed its governing council had coalesced; it would remain relatively constant for the life of the organization. Whereas during its formative years the focus of its annual conferences had been the articulation of a basic philsophy through the open exchange of ideas, by 1950 that philosophy (which was synonymous with D'Amico's) had been defined and a consensus reached, at least within the governing council. In an effort "to spread the Committee's philosophy and build up a larger and more informed public who are sympathetic to creative education"[46]—and, therefore, to modern art—special sessions for the public were offered for the first time at the annual conference in 1950. The Committee became, in effect, the Museum's "educational underground." Its members "carried the word into primary and secondary schools and into colleges in all parts of the country, and did it with the zeal of converts and the devotion of missionary priests."[47]

The stated purpose of the Committee was "to bring together educators interested in formulating a basic philosophy of art education and promoting creative teaching on the highest possible level."[48] D'Amico's description of the group's philosophical platform echoed that of his own programs at the Museum: the opposition to teaching art either by imitation or by a laissez-faire method; the importance of well-guided creative education for children; the exploration of new techniques while maintaining the basic values of aesthetic education; and the belief that the Committee could assure the survival of creative education by convincing an increasingly hostile world that such practices were an investment toward peace.[49]

From the beginning, a central issue for both D'Amico and the Committee had been the proliferation of school contests and competitions, paint-by-numbers kits, television courses teaching art through copying, and the extravagant claims made by mail-order art-instruction courses, all of which came to symbolize the entrenchment of conformist values in the U.S. educational system. With impassioned conviction D'Amico asserted:

These devices . . . are all based on a method of imitation that is slavish and dictatorial. They deny the right of individual choice and freedom and sow the seed for a dictator type of society. They threaten the creative life of our country because they strike at the heart of creative education. How can anyone who believes himself to be creative, whether he be artist or amateur, or anyone who respects individuality, endure these methods or fail to see the inherent menace?[50]

Such attempts to use the rhetoric of the Cold War for their own purposes reached a peak by mid-decade. In the April 1955 issue of the *COAE Newsletter,* members were encouraged to write to their Congressional representatives to oppose the Universal Military and Compulsory Reserve Resolution. "The 'military' likes conformity," the *Newsletter* stated. "Military control will tend to erode our American principles of respect for individual worth and thought."[51] In 1956, Committee members were similarly encouraged to support several pieces of legislation before Congress that related to President Dwight D. Eisenhower's call for a federal advisory commission on the arts: "We who are so concerned with art couldn't agree more with the framers of these bills who state that 'the growth and flourishing of the arts depend upon freedom, imagination, and individual initiative.'"[52] These were not people who jumped on the bandwagon of Cold War sentiment; rather, they sought to turn conservative rhetoric into support for their progressive views. Those who followed in the wake of the dissolution of progressive art education chided the progressives' naiveté:

The guardians of self-expression attempted to meet the crisis [of the paradigm shift in education] by arguing that it could foster creativity in children which would enable them to become creative adults in fields like science and mathematics . . . an argument which never convinced anyone.[53]

With the exception of five conferences held at various universities,[54] the annual meetings of the Committee were held at The Museum of Modern Art from 1943 through 1963. The format of the meetings from 1950 to 1955—all sponsored by the Museum—varied only slightly each year. Special exhibitions were organized in the Young People's Gallery and in the northwest gallery on the Museum's main floor. These exhibitions, some of which were organized in collaboration with the recently formed United Nations, featured artwork by children from around the world and by students at the People's Art Center. In addition to the general sessions, Committee members could elect to attend three-part seminars that took place over several days. In the early 1950s, seminars for museum educators were introduced as a means to explore both the role of the art museum in education and the planning and design of educational exhibitions. Representatives of most of the major museums participated in the panels of these sessions throughout the decade.[55] (A notable exception was Katherine Kuh of The Art Institute of Chicago, whose exhibitions in the Art Institute's teaching galleries focused on helping visitors understand modern art.[56])

The yearly agenda also included artists' talks, panel discussions, and studio visits. In 1950, d'Harnoncourt chaired the panel "The Relationship Between the Arts in Our Time," which included the art historian Horst W. Janson, the sculptor

Jacques Lipchitz, and the industrial designer and architect George Nelson. Members of the Committee chose from among a dozen artists with whom to participate in informal discussions in the Museum's galleries, including Stuart Davis, Chaim Gross, George Grosz, Ben Shahn, and Max Weber.[57] Robert Iglehart, a long-time member of the COAE executive council, articulated the kinship that members felt with the creative artists of the time:

[The teacher] must be seen as evoking the tenuous order implied by a moving situation; he must not, like the traditional painter, impose a completed sketch (lesson plan) upon the canvas. It is the situation, not the student, which the teacher makes; although we may judge its form, it should invite . . . an active and varied interpretation. We see in the modern painting and in the modern child, immediate reality and value, and are not so interested in what they represent, as in the qualities they embody. The child is not merely to produce a fact on demand, nor the painting [to represent] a cow. We are concerned rather with relationships and meanings with functional and formal power. We understand that the child, in learning, must create the fact as the painter creates the form.[58]

During the 1950s, artists and art educators continued on parallel paths. Jackson Pollock's *One (Number 31, 1950)*, for example, epitomized the belief of the Abstract Expressionists in the transformative power of art as action and experience—their faith in art as a means by which the more "authentic," primal self might find expression. This approach would eventually give way to the more intellectual, emotionally cooler art of the 1960s: Pop art, Minimalism, and Conceptualism. A similar shift occurred in the kinds of artists' discussions that the Committee sponsored. In the earlier years, artists mostly talked in very personal ways about their work. In 1950, for example, Lipchitz spoke about the spiritual in art so movingly that the recording secretary was unable to adequately describe the artist's point of view. In 1951, the painter Ad Reinhardt argued in similarly passionate tones against the assertion, made by another panel member, that a "whole educational program must incorporate the resources of art and the resources of science, to develop the total child in relation to his total environment." "Art is not science," he argued, "nor is it communication, representation, journalism, propoganda, therapy, a hobby, or a livelihood. . . . Art is unique creative activity which has nothing to do with the business of living."[59] In 1954, there was a shift toward a more political approach, with a panel discussion on the topic of "The Artist as a Free Human Being" in the opening session; in 1955, the artist Philip Guston joined psychologists and professors of English, anthropology, and education in a roundtable discussion of "Perception: Reality and Symbolic Reality."

A recurrent seminar topic during the early 1950s was the use of film and television in art education. Iris Barry, Director of The Museum of Modern Art Film Library, chaired the session "What Makes a Good Film?" in 1950. In 1955, Roger Tilton, a lecturer on the history and art of the motion picture at Columbia University and an instructor of design at the Cooper Union for the Advancement of Science and Art, chaired the three-session seminar "Art in Television." Its purpose was to consider the aesthetic aspects of television shows that were broadcast live in contrast to those that were prerecorded.

This was the era during which popular culture increasingly was becoming defined by television. COAE members were interested not only in educating themselves about this phenomenon but also in looking at ways in which they might influence a medium they considered suspect at best. Because the mass media depends on mass acceptance, they believed that television tended "to emphasize the same kind of mass comprehensibility by the broad, untutored audience groups which dictators and would-be dictators insist upon."[60] Clearly, this "mass comprehensibility" would be considered a threat to the principles of creative education, which idealized the individual. From the vantage point of today, when our world-view is dominated by television, this attitude may seem to have been influenced by science fiction. As we have seen, however, tensions and rhetoric ran high in the mid-1950s. The leaders of the Committee were zealous in their beliefs, and in fact were trying to sustain a voice of reason at a moment when their fundamental beliefs and practices were under siege.

(D'Amico himself experimented in 1952 and 1953 with the use of television in teaching art education in the series "Through the Enchanted Gate," which was co-sponsored by the Museum and the National Broadcasting Company. By today's standards the shows appear somewhat stiff and dated; however, along with versions of the Children's Art Carnival sent to Europe and India, they represented the broadest of D'Amico's efforts to spread the word for creative art teaching.)

In the mid-1930s, Nelson Rockefeller had charged Artemas Packard to discover in what way the Museum could most effectively develop aesthetic values in American life. Packard's description of the "charming myth that American taste [was] congenitally inferior to that of any other nation"[61] was widely accepted until after World War II, when New York became the cultural capital of the world. Although the most effective means of teaching aesthetics and art appreciation to greater numbers of people had become a national as well as international question by mid-century, the problem of methods remained at the core of the programs of the People's Art Center, and was the underlying issue of every panel discussion at the annual meetings of the Committee on Art Education.

In his keynote address, "Art Education and the Creative Process," at the March 1954 COAE conference, poet, critic, and Harvard University professor Archibald MacLeish took up the cause of progressive education with the same verve and conviction with which it had been articulated by Dewey and others earlier in the century. MacLeish advocated the experiential, as opposed to art-historical, approach to art education, stating:

[The student] carries them [historical facts] around in the pocket of his memory like coins. He knows, because he has been told, that they are valuable but he does not know why they exist because he does not know how they exist. And not knowing why or how they exist he can only possess them: he cannot make them his. . . . What has been left out of his education is the discovery of the relation between the work of art as it stands there on the page or hangs there on the wall and himself as a living, sentient being. . . . A great work of art is great because it adds to the vision of life of which humanity is capable. . . . [Great works of art] are significant because they are capable of enlarging the area in which we can live; because they are able to carry farther [sic] for us *the experience of being [human]; because they leave us, as the common but truthful saying goes, more alive. . . .*[62]

J. B. Neumann, left, and Charles Sheeler at a reception held during the Committee on Art Education annual conference, The Museum of Modern Art, New York, 1951

Victor D'Amico, left, and Nelson Rockefeller at the 1951 Committee on Art Education reception at The Museum of Modern Art, New York

Many art historians and aestheticians, as well as artists and art educators, share MacLeish's belief that the ultimate importance of art is how it relates to the lives of the people who look at it, read it, or listen to it. But the questions remain: How do we teach it? Can it be taught at all? MacLeish and D'Amico spent their lives trying to answer these questions. MacLeish spoke for both of them when he remarked:

I do not believe that education has any significant relation to the creation of works of art, but I do believe that the creation of works of art has the most immediate relation possible to education. I believe, in other words, that an education which ignores the arts as arts *is a defective education no matter how sedulously it may collect their* works *as objects of appreciation or subjects of scholarship or mementos of culture.*[63]

Discussions in the 1955 COAE seminar "Art History—Creative Teaching" focused on "the role which culture has played in shaping art of the present and past, the nature of art history, and relationships between creative teaching and art history."[64] Margaret Mead spoke on "Relations between Art History and Culture" and editor Milton Fox addressed "The Role of the Work of Art in Creative Teaching." Just as Committee members attended seminars on television in order not simply to understand the medium but also to explore ways in which to influence it, they similarly invited a discussion of the historical approach to art education, in opposition to which most of them had defined themselves as educators. Before 1955, they had asked art historians such as Janson to participate in panels that included the 1950 seminar led by d'Harnoncourt, but they had never before explored possible approaches to teaching art history from a creative-education perspective. (The topic was integrated into various sessions in subsequent years, often under the heading "Research in Art Education.")

D'Amico remained constant in his skepticism about the informational, art-historical approach to museum art education. In a 1963 address to a conference of The International Society for Education Through Art he stated:

My quarrel is not with historians or with art history. . . . My quarrel is *however with a point of view which imposes a subject or a process by authority—by divine right, so to speak. Art history is such a subject and is now being insisted upon because of its approval of authority and not because of its value to the individual and to society.*[65]

Although he never relinquished his conviction that the individual comes to an appreciation of the art of others through making art, late in his career D'Amico wrote:

Art Education which limits the individual to his own expressions is unworthy of the name of education . . . ; the individual expression of any child or adult can be enriched by appreciation of our art heritage and . . . without this he must remain an impoverished, isolated person.[66]

In theory, the Committee on Art Education was a national organization, but its members were primarily from the eastern half of the United States. In order for

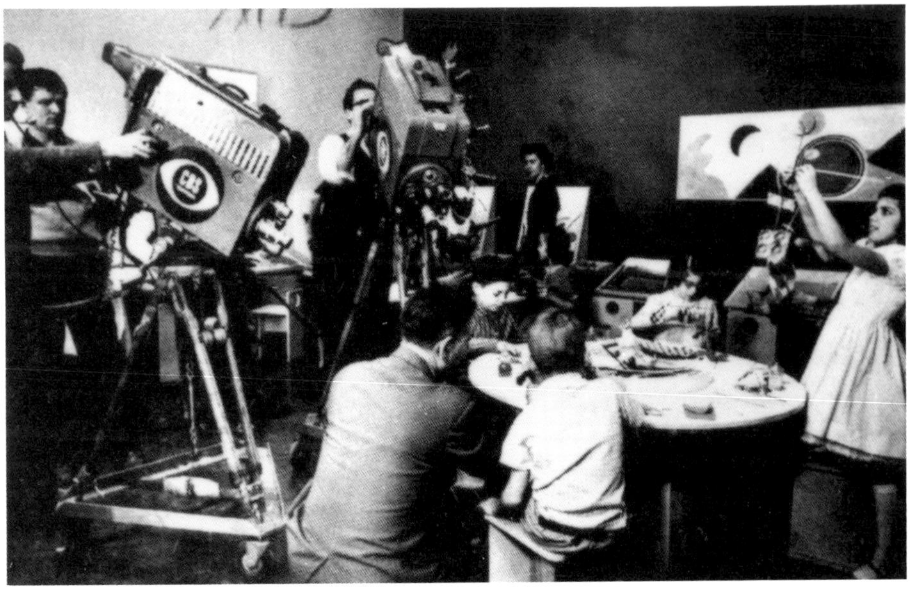

Taping of the NBC television series "Through the Enchanted Gate," featuring art classes led by Victor D'Amico, ca. 1952–53

it to become a truly national organization, it needed to engage a broader membership. Furthermore, if it was to survive the political realities of the 1950s, it would have to expand beyond its original definition, which was deeply rooted in the progressive education movement of the 1920s and 1930s. Because D'Amico was not willing to forsake his commitment to progressive education, his leadership of the Committee inevitably would be challenged from within.

Throughout its two decades, the Committee was structured by D'Amico's philosophies.[67] There was no jockeying for political position: From the beginning it was his organization. One of its strengths had been the general philosophical consensus among its members, but by the mid-1950s, theoretical differences began to emerge that eventually would undermine that solidarity. The most significant rift emerged between D'Amico and Viktor Lowenfeld, who was known internationally for his theories on children and creativity, over the use of psychology in art. D'Amico's programs and the creative-education movement in general depended on understanding child development and adult psychology. As early as 1944, when he opened the War Veterans' Art Center, D'Amico had explored the use of art in psychological therapy. Not a psychologist himself, however, he conducted his experiments from the point of view of an artist and art teacher. His early adherence to the progressive view that creative education was a means of enabling the student to achieve an integrated personality was subsumed by his overarching concern for art and the aesthetic experience.[68] The social and artistic context of the mid-1950s was quite different from the earlier, more pragmatic modernist context in which Packard had written:

[T]he esthetic satisfactions which we find in Art do not and can not exist in vacuo *. . . ; our capacity to respond to esthetic values in Art is a manifestation of our capacity to respond to the whole environment. . . . It may be said that educating people to enjoy art is hardly worth the trouble if it does not lead them to a more vivid realization that all*

human activities seem significant or futile in so far as we succeed or fail in pursuing them as creative enterprises and in the spirit of the artist.[70]

By the mid-1950s, D'Amico had become increasingly focused on the aesthetic and less tolerant of the uses of psychology in art as an end in itself. Other COAE members, including Lowenfeld, appear to have taken the opposite tack, causing a fissure within the organization that was never repaired.[70] In his 1954 book *Your Child and His Art: A Guide for Parents,* Lowenfeld took the position that the child should create art as a means to psychological stability, stating:

It is important [for your child to create] because your child should be happy and free . . . , should develop her thinking and feeling about herself and her environment . . . , should develop into a well balanced human being who uses equally well her thinking, feeling, and perceiving . . . , should be able to put herself into the place of others to discover their needs, too, so that she will grow up to be a cooperative, helpful citizen . . . , an individual who stands on her own feet fearlessly, a happy human being.[71]

In 1955, Charles Cook, Secretary-Treasurer of the Committee and Executive Director of University Settlement in New York City, reported on "The Relation of Art Education to Therapy," the title of a seminar held at the annual COAE conferences for three consecutive years beginning in 1953. (Various psychologists and psychiatrists participated on panels at the conferences as early as 1949, including Antonia Wenkart, Lowenfeld, Rudolph Arnheim, and A. H. Maslow.) Cook aligned himself with D'Amico on the aesthetic-development side of the debate:

The Committee on Art Education's interest in Psychiatry and Psychology has been directed to what can be learned of human development; the implications concerning creativity; the release and development of imagination . . . ; our interest is not in diagnostic techniques for the sake of using the art classroom as a direct treatment center.[72]

Cook believed that the psychologist and the art teacher have in common "the implementation of a broad belief in individual freedom" and that the art teacher had much to learn from the field of psychology. However, he added, "It is not for the art teacher to make the art classrooms into a laboratory any more than it is for the psychologist to teach art."[73]

The annual COAE conference was held outside the Museum for the first time in 1956 at Pennsylvania State University, where Lowenfeld was head of the Department of Art Education. Titled "The Future of Art Education," the conference was attended by about two hundred and fifty people—far fewer than the approximately two thousand participants in the conference meetings and sessions for the general public held at the Museum—and included four sessions on "New Research in Art Education." The reduced participation and change of venue altered the nature of the meeting. Holding the conference outside the Museum in itself might have been enough to make D'Amico uncomfortable, but the focus on psychological research may have made him even more so.[74] At the meeting, he announced that he intended to resign as chairman when his term expired the following year. In the months that followed, the nominating committee urgently

requested that he reconsider his decision. In response, D'Amico expressed "his firm conviction that the present and future of art education [were] being jeopardized by various factors which [were] mainly extraneous to the teaching of art" and "affirmed his belief that the Committee on Art Education should take an unequivocal position in the matter."[75]

By February 1957, the organization had drawn up a new constitution with D'Amico as Chairman; Lowenfeld remained as an Advisory Council member. The organization renamed itself the National Committee on Art Education (NCAE) and became more businesslike, but it never regained the vitality of its formative years. Although the annual meetings were again held at the Museum in 1958 and 1960, D'Amico was preoccupied with the Children's Art Carnival as well as other matters; he would never again turn his full attention to the organization. On the eve of the Committee's twentieth-anniversary conference, in 1962, he wrote a column for the *NCAE Newsletter* in which he tried to look to the future but spoke more readily of the past and his waning energy for the activities of the Committee:

I cannot imagine what my own progress would have been without the Committee. It has been both an inspiration and a discipline. It has pushed my sights far beyond what I could have perceived alone and it has increased my activity and energy manyfold. I feel sure that the Committee has not done less for others.[76]

The final conference of the National Committee on Art Education was held in 1964 at the State University of New York, Buffalo, where Kenneth Winebrenner, the new chairman of the organization, was a professsor of art. Winebrenner's call to arms was an attempt to rally members and to answer the question "Where do we go from here?":

Recognizing many possible advantages in newer teaching techniques—automation in the school, as well as in the home, work and culture—somebody still needs to ask what becomes of the child in the process. . . . Does art, by its very nature, have something to offer education as an antidote to the effects of standardization, conformity, and the new authoritarianism of the machine?[77]

By November of that year, the *NCAE Newsletter* had announced the founding of the Institute for the Study of Art Education, which was to succeed the National Committee on Art Education. In reality, a successor organization was never formed; what remained was a loose coalition of members who had been active throughout the twenty-year history of the Committee.[78]

Coda

Throughout the 1950s, the programs of the People's Art Center became increasingly independent of The Museum of Modern Art. Beginning in 1955, D'Amico taught summer classes for adults in East Hampton on Long Island; soon after, the Museum purchased a nearby property from D'Amico's wife, Mabel, and towed to it a former Navy barge for use as an art studio. In 1960, the Institute of Modern Art was incorporated as a nonprofit organization separate from the Museum but responsible for its school programs; the Institute also sponsored the Museum's summer programs,

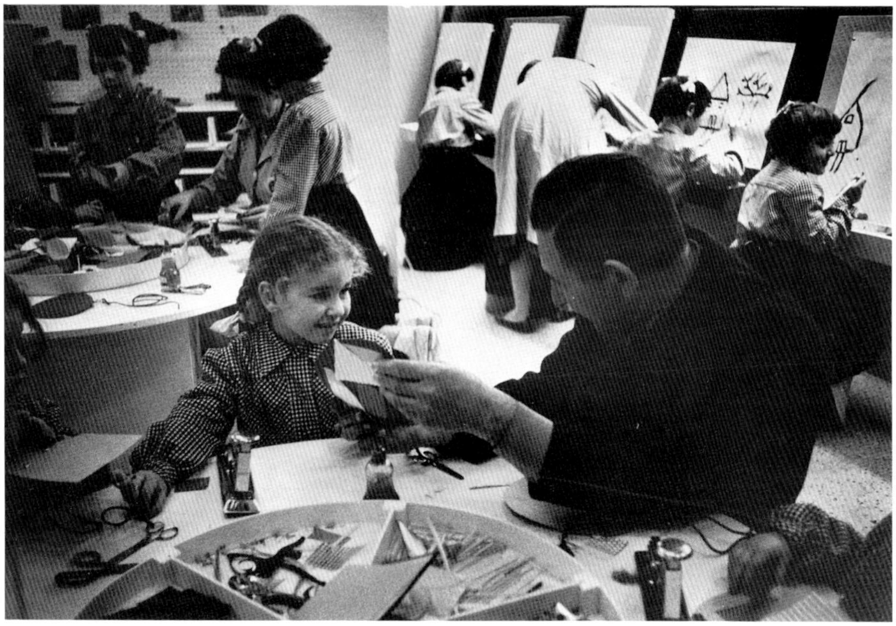

Victor D'Amico with a young student at the collage table, Il Paradisa dei Bambini dal Museum of Modern Art, Milan, 1957

including those on the Art Barge, and the Children's Art Carnival, now an annual event in Harlem.

The 1960s were watershed years for the Museum, as they were for the nation as a whole. Barr retired in 1967, d'Harnoncourt in 1968. As new curatorial staff with graduate degrees in art history joined the Museum, D'Amico and his experiential programs seemed increasingly out of step with their information-based ideas. In 1969, with the Children's Art Carnival well established, D'Amico announced his own retirement. The following year, the People's Art Center was closed by the Museum's Board of Trustees.

•

As we approach the end of the century in which the vast majority of American museums were founded and the professional positions within those institutions came to be defined, the debate over museum education continues. The Museum of Modern Art veered away from the experiential methods of Victor D'Amico a quarter-century ago, having become convinced that making art was not the most direct route to learning to appreciate art made by others. Museum culture since then has generally dictated that education programs focus on the object and what must be known about it in order for it to be appreciated. The current social and political paradigms, however, call into question the role of museums in our society. As funding for the arts grows more precarious, museums across the country are inspired once again to look more closely at their audiences—and potential audiences—in order to understand who they are, where they come from, and what knowledge and experiences they bring with them if they are to design programs that more closely fit their needs.

Although current practices vary significantly from those of D'Amico, some of the ideas he espoused are reemerging in the theory and practice of museum education today. In 1928, Rugg and Shumaker described the essence of creative self-expres-

sion as "concentration upon the object of desire that sets the world aside."[80] D'Amico and his colleagues spent their careers devising methods to induce this experience among their students. In recent years, Mihaly Csikszentmihalyi, of the University of Chicago, has been exploring ways in which museums can create conditions for visitors to have a "flow" experience, "a common experiential state," one "in which people are willing to invest psychic energy in tasks for which extrinsic rewards are absent," "a state of mind that is spontaneous, almost automatic, like the flow of a strong current."[79] Other innovative educators have begun using developmental theories, such as those used by D'Amico decades ago, as a means of designing more appropriate programs for museum audiences. In the late 1980s, Philip Yenawine, then Director of Education at The Museum of Modern Art, began working with educational psychologist Abigail Housen in program development. Housen has developed an empirically-derived theory of aesthetic development based on the cognitive processing of a wide range of viewers as they view works of art. Her theory, coupled with Yenawine's extensive teaching experience, is resulting in a developmental model that has broad implications for program design.

The 1950s were a turning point for museum educational programs in general and for the programs of D'Amico in particular. What began early in the century as a debate between information-based educational practices and progressive ideals came full circle at mid-century. The lessened focus on the individual and the reemergence of knowledge-based practices in education were defined by social and political concerns and reflected in the art of the 1960s. Neither D'Amico nor the Committee on Art Education could accept this challenge to the fundamental beliefs. Those who had been innovators in their time and who had defined some extraordinary moments in art education could not adapt to the demands of a changing world and a changing art scene. Although D'Amico's work has been in eclipse for the past twenty-five years, the lessons to be learned from the past demand a reexamination of the contributions he made to The Museum of Modern Art and to the emerging field of museum education as a whole.

Notes

Thanks to Betsy Barnett, Toby Falk, and the staff of Special Collections at the Milbank Memorial Library of Teachers' College, Columbia University, New York, for research assistance. Special thanks to Amelia Arenas for reading many drafts, and to Howard Conant, Mabel D'Amico, August Freundlich, Jane Gollin, and Muriel Silberstein-Storfer for generously sharing their time and thoughts.

1. Harold Rugg and Ann Shumaker, *The Child-Centered School: An Appraisal of the New Education* (Yonkers-on-Hudson, N.Y., and Chicago: World Book Company, 1928), p. 9.
2. Letter, Rockefeller to D'Amico, September 24, 1951. Courtesy Mabel D'Amico.
3. See Thomas Kuhn, *The Structure of Scientific Revolutions* (1962), International Encyclopedia of Unified Science Series, vol. 2, no. 2 (Chicago: University of Chicago Press, 1970).
4. Arthur Efland, "History of Art Education as Criticism: On the Use of the Past," in *The History of Art Education: Proceedings from the Second Penn State Conference, 1989* (Reston, Va.: The National Art Education Association, 1992), p. 6.
5. Rugg and Shumaker, *The Child-Centered School,* p. 9.
6. Ibid., p. 207.
7. Artemas Packard, "A Report on the Development of The Museum of Modern Art," 1938; typescript, p. 3. The study was conducted in 1935–36; the report was finalized in 1938, but preliminary suggestions were made to the Trustees in January 1936. The Museum of Modern Art Archives: Reports and Pamphlets, Box 3.
8. Ibid., p. 14.
9. Ibid., p. 74.
10. Ibid., pp. 74–75. Packard's position should not be equated with the invectives of the temperamental Dr. Albert C. Barnes of The Barnes Foundation, in Merion, Pennsylvania, who was himself a life-long friend of John Dewey. Barnes's unique application of Dewey's theories became legendary in the art world, and perhaps have done more to undermine a serious reading of the uses of progressive education theories in art education in the first half of the twentieth century than any other single factor. "Based on lengthy and frequent consultations with Dewey, [Barnes] worked out a systematic program of art education . . . and put it into practice. And he merged his two passions [collecting and pedagogy] by establishing the Foundation that still bears his name" (Howard Greenfeld, *The Devil and Dr. Barnes: Portrait of an American Art Collector* [New York: Viking Press, 1989], p. 67). According to Dewey, Barnes's method "was one that he had worked out through many years of personal study and contact with pictures and artists and also the qualities that make painting what it is, so that the ordinary person could be trained to see pictures, and in seeing them feel what there was in them that was of artistic value, and that would also enrich the life of the individual" (ibid., p. 152). Barnes increasingly refused requests from arts professionals and academic groups to view his collection. "He had been hurt and stunned by the ignorance and insensitivity of the men and women who called themselves art critics" (ibid., p. 96), whose virulent response to the exhibition of his collection in 1923 he never forgave. Similarly, his repeated disagreements with academicians led him to believe that "academic groups were inadequately prepared to appreciate the Foundation's collection and were handicapped by what they had been taught in the past, victims of what Barnes called 'intellectual disorder'" (ibid., p. 141).
11. Ibid., p. 20.
12. Ibid., p. 22.
13. Quoted in Frederick M. Logan, *Growth of Art in American Schools* (New York: Harper & Brothers, 1955), pp. 203–06.
14. Packard, "A Report on the Development of The Museum of Modern Art," p. 25.
15. Ibid., p. 15.
16. Ibid., p. 64.
17. Approximately two hundred students per year were enrolled in The Barnes Foundation's tuition-free education classes. The admissions policy was "eccentric," favoring those who lacked formal education and a less professional presentation on their application. Each student attended one session per week. "The five or six members of the faculty who delivered the lectures and led the discussions that followed were all Barnes-trained. . . . Generally the doctor himself conducted one class, on Thursdays. . . . Refusing to rhapsodize poetically over the merits of a work of art and scorning the use of typical art jargon, he spoke in colorful, down-to-earth terms easily understood by his listeners. Frequently he underscored his points by means of unconventional illustrations—sometimes even a piece of music . . . interpreted in a number of ways to demonstrate the possibility of different approaches to a single theme" (Greenfeld, *The Devil and Mr. Barnes,* p. 232).
18. Victor D'Amico, "Report on the Educational Project of The Museum of Modern Art, 1937–1940," The Museum of Modern Art, 1940; manuscript, p. 4. Special Collections, Milbank Memorial Library, Teachers' College, Columbia University, New York.
19. Victor D'Amico, "Creative Art for Children, Young People, Adults, and Schools," *The Bulletin of The Museum of Modern Art* 19 (Fall 1951), p. 12.
20. D'Amico, "Report on the Educational Project," p. 2.
21. Victor D'Amico, "Art for War Veterans," *The Museum of Modern Art Bulletin 12* (September 1945), p. 7.
22. D'Amico, "Creative Art for Children, Young People, Adults, and Schools," p. 7.
23. Victor D'Amico and the Art Committee of the Commission on the Secondary School Curriculum, "The Visual Arts in General Education," Progressive Education Association, 1937; manuscript, pp. 1–2. Courtesy Muriel Silberstein-Storfer.
24. D'Amico, *Experiments in Creative Art Teaching* (New York: The Museum of Modern Art, 1960), p. 16.
25. Ibid., p. 16. When the Museum closed The People's Art Center in 1970, D'Amico and colleague Muriel Silberstein-Storfer continued the parent-child classes at The Metropolitan Museum of Art as "Doing Art Together," which remains a popular program at the museum to this day.
26. "Teaching in Action," summary of the Eighth Annual Conference of the Committee on Art Education held at The Museum of Modern Art, New York, March 24–26, 1950, p. 15.
27. Victor D'Amico, *Experiments in Teaching: A Progress Report on the Department of Education, 1937–1960, The Museum of Modern Art, New York* (Garden City, N.Y.: Doubleday & Company, 1963), p. 42.
28. Ibid., p. 45.
29. Ibid.
30. Ibid., p. 27.
31. Ibid., p. 29.
32. D'Amico, "Creative Art for Children, Young People, Adults, and Schools," p. 10.
33. D'Amico, *Experiments in Creative Art Teaching,* p. 35.
34. Ibid., p. 36. The Carnival was initially open to children of Museum members only, as were the art classes; this policy was changed in the 1950s. In the 1960s, the Carnival was taken to Harlem as an annual summer event sponsored by the Institute of Modern Art, which had assumed responsibility for the Museum's educational programs. When the People's Art Center was closed in 1970, the Children's Art Carnival in Harlem was incorporated as an independent organization. It continues today under the direction of Betty Blayton Taylor, a former colleague of D'Amico.
35. Ibid., p. 34.
36. D'Amico, "Report on the Educational Project," p. 1.
37. Quoted in D. Kenneth Winebrenner, "The Committee at the Crossroads: Reappraisals and Reaffirmations," *NCAE Newsletter* 14 (January 1964), p. 1.
38. Victor D'Amico, "Art, a Human Necessity," address at the 18th Annual Meeting of The National Committee on Art Education, May 7, 1960; manuscript, p. 3. Special Collections, Milbank Memorial Library, Teachers' College, Columbia University, New York.
39. Quoted in Winebrenner, "The Committee at the Crossroads," p. 1.
40. Quoted in August L. Freundlich, untitled manuscript, September 25, 1985, p. 1. Freundlich is a former member of the Committee.
41. Efland, *History of Art Education as Criticism,* p. 6.
42. Victor D'Amico. "Does Creative Art

Education Have a Future?," paper presented at the Conference of the International Society for Education Through Art, Montreal, August 27, 1963; manuscript, p. 6. Special Collections, Milbank Memorial Library, Teachers' College, Columbia University, New York.

43. D'Amico, "Art, a Human Necessity," p. 4.

44. Lois A. Berggren, "Victor D'Amico, His Sources and Influences: The Early Years," master's thesis, Massachusetts College of Art, Division of Art Education Programs, 1984, p. 115.

45. D' Amico, "Art, a Human Necessity," p. 4.

46. "Teaching in Action," summary of the Eighth Annual Conference of the Committee on Art Education, The Museum of Modern Art, New York, March 24–26, 1950, p. 1. The Museum of Modern Art Archives.

47. Russell Lynes, *Good Old Modern: An Intimate Portrait of The Museum of Modern Art* (New York: Atheneum, 1973), p. 171.

48. D'Amico, "Creative Art for Children, Young People, Adults, and Schools," p. 17.

49. Ibid., p. 18.

50. Victor D'Amico, "Point of View: An Occasional Supplement to the Newsletter of the Committee on Art Education" (April 1954), p. 2.

51. *COAE Newsletter* 8 (April 1955), p. 3.

52. *COAE Newsletter* 9 (April 1956), p. 2.

53. Efland, *History of Art Education as Criticism*, p. 2.

54. In all, five conferences were held at locations other than The Museum of Modern Art: Pennsylvania State University at University Park (1956); The University of Michigan at Ann Arbor (1957); The University of Wisconsin at Madison (1959); Ohio State University at Columbus (1961); and The State University of New York at Buffalo (1963).

55. Some of the most significant names include E. M. Benson, the Philadelphia Art Museum; Belle Boas, the Baltimore Museum of Art; William E. Woolfenden, the Detroit Institute of Arts; Kathryn Bloom, The Toledo Museum of Art; Hanna Toby Rose, The Brooklyn Museum; and Gertrude S. Hornung, the Cleveland Museum.

56. "From 1944 to 1952, Kuh organized [educational] exhibitions [at The Art Institute of Chicago] predicated on basic principles of perception that guided the viewer through such varied and unfamiliar visual areas as Cubism, Surrealism, and African art. . ." (Charlotte Moser and Susan F. Rossen, "Primer for Seeing: The Gallery of Art Interpretation and Katharine Kuh's Crusade for Modernism in Chicago," *Art Institute of Chicago Museum Studies* 16, no. 1 [1990], pp. 7–25).

57. Other artists participating in the annual meetings throughout the decade included Will Barnet, Philip Guston, and Robert Motherwell, among others.

58. Robert Iglehart, "The Studio and the Classroom" (1953); quoted in Freundlich, pp. 5–6.

59. "The Art of Teaching Art," digest of the Eighth Annual Conference of the Committee on Art Education, The Museum of Modern Art, New York, March 15–18, 1951, p. 9. The panel member was A. Wellesley Foshay, a professor at Teachers' College, Columbia University, New York.

60. Charles Cook, "Relation of Art Education to Therapy," report on the "Psychology, Psychiatry, and Art Education" seminars at the Eleventh, Twelfth, and Thirteenth Annual Conferences, Committee on Art Education, p. 1. Special Collections, Milbank Memorial Library, Teachers' College, Columbia University, New York.

61. Packard, "A Report on the Development of The Museum of Modern Art," p. 11.

62. Archibald MacLeish, *Art Education and the Creative Process* (New York: The Committee on Art Education of The Museum of Modern Art, 1955), pp. 7, 9.

63. Ibid., p. 6.

64. "Art History—Creative Teaching," seminar bulletin, Thirteenth Annual Conference of the Committee on Art Education, March 14–19, 1955. The Museum of Modern Art Archives.

65. D'Amico, "Does Creative Art Education Have a Future?," p. 7.

66. Victor D'Amico, "Appreciation as an Integral Part of Art Education," n.d.; manuscript, pp. 4–5. Special Collections, Milbank Memorial Library, Teachers' College, Columbia University, New York.

67. Freundlich, p. 14.

68. "The visual arts, through properly directed experiences, can help to develop the visual, the emotional, and the kinesthetic senses, which must be developed along with the verbal and intellectual powers, if an integration of personality is ever to be realized through education" (D'Amico et al., *The Visual Arts in General Education*, pp. 1–2).

69. Packard, "A Report on the Development of The Museum of Modern Art," pp. 10–11.

70. August Freundlich, interview with the author, February 7, 1994. Lowenfeld died in 1960, by which time D'Amico had become less involved with the Committee.

71. See Viktor Lowenfeld, *Your Child and His Art: A Guide for Parents* (New York: Macmillan, 1954), p. 7.

72. Cook, "Relation of Art Education to Therapy," p. 1.

73. Ibid., p. 2.

74. Freundlich, interview with the author, February 7, 1994. Freundlich reports that D'Amico was very uncomfortable at the 1956 conference of the Committee, and recalls hearing him make sarcastic remarks about those who saw evidence of psychological states in children's art, including several of the psychologists who were invited to speak at the seminars on "The Relation of Art Education to Therapy" in 1953, 1954, and 1955.

75. Dorothy Leadbeater, Chairperson, Nominating Committee, "An Open Letter to Members," *COAE Newsletter* 9 (February 1957), p. 3.

76. Victor D'Amico, "20th Annual Conference, 20 Full Years!," *NCAE Newsletter* 13 (March 1962), p. 2.

77. Winebrenner, "The Committee at the Crossroads," p. 4.

78. Freundlich, interview with the author, February 7, 1994.

79. Rugg and Shumaker, *The Child-Centered School*, p. 9.

80. Mihaly Csikszentmihalyi and Kim Hermanson, "What Makes Visitors Want to Learn?," *Museum News* 74, no. 3 (May–June 1995), p. 36.

James Thrall Soby self-styled as a Magritte portrait, which he titled "Author, Traveller, Explorer," 1936

Special Section: James Thrall Soby

James Thrall Soby: Author, Traveler, Explorer

Rona Roob

James Thrall Soby (1906–1979) was one of the pioneering collectors and curators of modern art in America at mid-century, and wrote some of the liveliest art criticism of the period. Along with Alfred H. Barr, Jr., and James Johnson Sweeney, he played a crucial role in shaping the collection of The Museum of Modern Art and in establishing the institution as a leading force in the international art world during the 1940s and 1950s. In the 1930s, he began to assemble a distinguished personal collection that included works by Francis Bacon, Giorgio de Chirico, Joseph Cornell, Matta, Joan Miró, Pablo Picasso, and Yves Tanguy, all of whom became his friends.[1] Soby was a generous, warm man who, with a lighthearted shrug, a turn of phrase, and a laugh, could put things into perspective. Barr, a close friend as well as a colleague, admired Soby's patience, modesty, intelligence, and sense of humor.

Soby in the library designed by Henry-Russell Hitchcock, Farmington, 1938

Soby was born into a comfortable, liberal-minded family in Hartford, Connecticut, at a time when that city was a vigorous commercial, industrial, and cultural center. Once the home of J. P. Morgan, Harriet Beecher Stowe, and Mark Twain, it is the site of the Wadsworth Atheneum, the first incorporated public museum in America, founded in 1842. From 1924 to 1926, Soby attended Williams College in Williamstown, Massachusetts, where he wrote stories, played football, and continued to pursue his interest in literature, leaving before his junior year because he feared he would never be able to pass the required science courses.[2] He attributed the turning point in his "esthetic awareness" to an interest in illustrated books, especially those being published in Paris by Ambrose Vollard. By the fall of 1926, he had decided to go to Paris instead of returning to college.[3]

On this trip Soby bought several illustrated books (those by Pierre Bonnard especially appealed to him), visited art galleries and the Louvre, and attempted to write about French Romantic art. After his return from Paris, he frequented New York galleries, but it was an exhibition at the Wadsworth Atheneum, "Selected Contemporary French Paintings," that inspired him to "take the plunge."[4] Two months after the show closed, in January 1930, he bought his first significant modern paintings, Henri Matisse's *The Red Sofa* (1923) and a Derain landscape of 1925, from the Valentine Gallery in New York.[5]

Soby's art activities in Hartford centered around the Wadsworth Atheneum, where he worked closely as an unsalaried assistant to its brilliant and dynamic director, A. Everett ("Chick") Austin, Jr. With Austin, he organized the first museum show of Surrealist art in the United States in 1931 and, three years later, the first Picasso exhibition ever held in an American museum.[6] Among his many friends in the Hartford area were Archibald MacLeish and Wallace Stevens, the latter among the few American poets who actively admired modern art. James Thurber, Elsa Lanchester, Charles Laughton, Miró, Alexander Calder, Walker Evans,[7] Henry-Russell Hitchcock,[8] and Le Corbusier were but a few of the many cultural figures who were guests in his home.

Soby with his second wife, Eleanor ("Nellie") Howland, in the living room of their Farmington house, 1938

Soby continued to live in Connecticut throughout his life. In August 1935, he moved from West Hartford to Farmington, where he purchased the nineteenth-century Greek Revival Mygatt House, and asked Hitchcock, an architectural historian, to restore the interior and design a gallery wing to accommodate his growing collection; from December 1953 until his death he lived in New Canaan.[9] Beginning in the 1940s, however, and for the next two decades, he also maintained a residence in New York City.

Soby's association with The Museum of Modern Art began in 1937, when he was invited to join its Junior Advisory Committee. His principal roles at the Museum were as a trustee from 1942 to 1949, and as an advisor to the Committee on the Museum Collections from 1940 to 1967. During this time, he recommended the purchase of paintings by Jackson Pollock and Francis Bacon—the first works by these artists to be acquired by a museum.[10] He was appointed to the Acquisitions and Photography committees in 1940, and from 1942 until the end of World War II he directed the Museum's Armed Services Program.[11]

The living room of Soby's New York City apartment, ca. 1943

In January 1943, Soby was named Assistant Director of the Museum by the Board of Trustees; the following October, he was also appointed Director of the Department of Painting and Sculpture, a position he would hold through January 1945 (he would serve as chairman of that department on an interim basis during 1947 and 1957). Later that fall, Soby came to the rescue of Barr, who, in the words of his wife, Margaret Scolari Barr, had been "disestablished from the directorship of the Museum,"[12] his responsibilities having been taken over by "a small committee of trustees."[13] It was Soby who persuaded hesitant or reluctant trustees to support Barr, and he was instrumental in reestablishing Barr as the architect of the Museum's permanent collection.[14] His was "the fist that went into the dike and saved the name and fame of the institution," according to Mrs. Barr.[14]

Soby once defined his and Barr's "life style" as "the love of works of art and the desire to get them for the Museum," and described his close working relationships with Austin and Barr in these terms: "I've been thinking while writing that all my life I've worked better in tandem, for ten years with Austin in Hartford and for twenty-five or more with Alfred at MOMA. I assume I should be ashamed of this fact; I quite bluntly am not and can't be made to be. I think two horses can sometimes pull a wagon faster than one. I've never bothered to ponder the question."[15]

Soby wrote the catalogues that accompanied more than fifteen important exhibitions organized by The Museum of Modern Art, including *Salvador Dali* (1941), *Tchelitchew* (1942), *Romantic Painting in America* (1943), *Georges Rouault* (1945), *XXth Century Italian Art* (1948), *Paul Klee* (1950), *Modigliani* (1951), *Giorgio de*

Chirico (1955), *Yves Tanguy* (1955), *Balthus* (1956), *Juan Gris* (1958), *Jean Arp* (1958), *Joan Miró* (1959), *Bonnard and His Environment* (1964), and *René Magritte* (1965). His books on de Chirico and Miró, along with his working notes and research material on Balthus, Dali, Gris, and Tanguy, are frequently consulted by scholars. In a 1935 review of his *After Picasso*,[16] Hitchcock stated that Soby had achieved "a standard of intelligibility and clarity of statement rare in critical writing on twentieth-century art. . . . His intellectual clarity is infused with a warmth of enthusiasm which in no way confuses his critical determination."[17] These publications, together with articles he wrote as art critic for *The Saturday Review of Literature* from 1946 to 1957 and independently for dozens of other journals and magazines, are models of scholarship informed by a passion for the work of art that was often based on personal acquaintance with the artist. Many years after Soby's death, Mrs. Barr recalled:

The best thing about him was his sense of warm friendship and understanding with artists. They all loved him. He looked with *them at their pictures, understanding and sympathetic to every pulse-beat; they knew he knew and they loved him for it. Unlike Alfred, who was bound to an institution, Jim Soby could analyze, praise, criticize, [or] sympathize, without an official, institutional commitment or responsibility. By 1933, Alfred and I had found already that we could not be simply "pals" with artists. Jim could, and he had a warmth of feeling that made the most disparate painters or sculptors have a feeling of fraternity with him.*[18]

Soby in conversation with an Allied serviceman during a party at The Museum of Modern Art organized as part of the Armed Services Program, 1943

Soby read voraciously and in the 1930s attended lecture series by Erwin Panofsky and Walter Friedlaender offered as part of the Fine Arts Graduate School program of New York University (later the Institute of Fine Arts) and given in the classrooms of The Metropolitan Museum of Art. He earned the esteem of Paul J. Sachs, a professor of art history at Harvard University and a member of the Museum's Board of Trustees, who would later write unabashedly of his admiration for Soby's writings:

There is no mystery about it, for free from all pedantry he does what few closet scholars ever do—he conjures visions with words. He allows us to share his delight in details and he holds us entranced and exhilarated by revealing qualities in works of art that might escape our less practiced vision. Blessed with the observant eye of a true connoisseur he has the rare capacity to express penetrating opinions in words that are never tepid, never casual. . . .

Unlike the other critics of contemporary art, Soby is entitled to our confidence because he makes it crystal clear that he is on terms of intimacy with the art of the past, which for him is not a bulwark against the present but a source of momentum for an understanding of the art of our day.[19]

Barr also admired Soby as an eloquent and independent critic and as an imaginative scholar of "painstaking probity."[20] He believed that Soby's sense of history gave his art criticism perspective and that his experience as a critic, museum man, and collector enhanced his scholarship. For example, Soby's 1955 book on de Chirico was meticulously researched and beautifully written, yet it was his deep understanding of the paintings—an understanding enriched by his ownership of the finest collection of de Chiricos in the world—that gave his analyses such potency. Writing

Photographs taken by Soby in Cremona (left) and Parma (right) while traveling in Italy ca. 1950

in 1961 on the occasion of the exhibition of Soby's collection at M. Knoedler & Co. in New York—a benefit for the Museum's Library—Barr summarized the achievements of his best friend:

Art historians sometimes seem moved as much by intellectual vanity as by love of truth, critics and museum people by partisanship of love of power, collectors by concern for prestige or the values of the art market or simple pride of possession. I do not find these common foibles in James Soby, who as a scholar, critic, museum worker, and collector seems to me inspired primarily by a love of art and a desire to involve others in the same admirable passion. This love and this desire he has brought, and brings, to the service of the Museum of Modern Art in many ways, on many levels and always with skill, devotion, and generosity of spirit. On shoulders such as his the greatness of an institution rests.[21]

Soby wrote easily and quickly (he did his own typing), with a thorough understanding of his role as an art critic:

It seems to me that we pre-empt a function of history when we attempt to decide unreservedly what kinds of art are truly 'modern' and what are static or reactionary . . . the story of Ingres is a case in point. Considered a fussy obstructionist by the rebels of his day, he has been hailed as a revolutionary, along with Cézanne and Seurat, by such pioneers of contemporary art as the cubists and purists . . . even from an advanced viewpoint, the romantic-realist Hopper is as valid a subject for study as Soutine the expressionist. And I speak now not only of intrinsic quality, but of possible meaning for later generations of painters. We are not going to settle in our time the direction art must take; now, as always, good painters will follow divergent paths to conflicting yet equally rewarding goals.[22]

Soby's conversational style and formidable visual memory are apparent in the published writings listed in the accompanying bibliography. His language is simple and direct, and it is a pleasure to see works of art through his words. For example, his description of *Still Life with Old Shoe* (1937), Miró's powerful emotional summary of the Spanish Civil War, is a perfect combination of critical insight and his-

torical research enriched by sensitive first-hand analysis (the painting hung in Soby's home):

For the melancholy protest Miró wished to make against Spain's poverty and suffering, a return to the realism of his early career must have seemed necessary. The colors are dark and lurid. In the sky a ghostly silhouette floats in from the left, the bottle itself casts a heavy shadow and ominous black clouds fill the upper right section. The apple is savagely impaled by the fork, the loaf of bread's carved end becomes a skull, and even the gin bottle with its grimacing letters, GI, seems menaced by the upheld, ragged ends of its own wrapping. The more gentle colors of the old shoe do nothing to obviate its vitality as a symbol of need; the callouses and wrinkles of long wear are effectively defined, and one senses the weariness of the foot it once encased. . . .[23]

In many instances Soby's language is poetic; he once described Brancusi's *Fish* (1930) as being "delicately shaped and swimming in its own other-worldly light."[24]

In 1962, Soby wrote Barr that in the fall he might "begin a book of personal reminiscences about the literary and art worlds which a couple of publishers who somehow read the *Art in America* article I did about collecting have asked me to do. What a horrible thought, except that in another five years I won't be able to remember *anything*."[25] The following winter, he wrote Barr from Sarasota, Florida, to report that he was spending "three hours a day writing an autobiographical piece for Prentice-Hall. . . . I have to do *something*, for God's sake, and I'm afraid winter resorts and I have never been on good terms."[26]

Although they regularly communicated on a variety of matters, it was almost two years before Soby again mentioned the memoir when writing to Barr: "I go crazy when I'm not trying to write something, even though it's a chore. . . . I've decided to take the bull by the horns and try to write a book which I think of calling *Once Over Lightly: Memoirs of the Modern Art World*."[27] Five years later, in November 1969, he sent the Barrs two sample chapters of what he referred to as "this stinking book," exclaiming that the two main difficulties in writing about oneself were "a) to write down what you remember before you forget it; b) to try to decide what might interest someone besides yourself. It's so frighteningly hard not to become enchanted by your own life simply because you've lived it and you have no idea—at least I haven't—whether anyone else will want to listen. This is known as garrulous senility and I *hate* it."[28]

Soby and Picasso at La Californie, Cannes, summer of 1956. Photograph by Margaret Scolari Barr

In April 1971, Soby delivered the typescript to Alfred A. Knopf, expressing concern that the manuscript needed a more logical order.[29] In writing monographs for the Museum, he explained, he had "to stick to chronology and stylistic progression and this made for a built-in order which autobiographical accounts lack—or anyway did for me."[30] A few months later, he decided to dedicate the memoir "To the Memory of My Father"[31] and retitle it *The Changing Stream*, adapting a phrase from Barr's preface for the catalogue of the Museum's tenth-anniversary exhibition, "Art in Our Time": "We are acquiring a collection which will be permanent as a stream is permanent—with a changing content."[32] There is no further correspondence concerning the memoir after 1971, and it remained unpublished at the time of Soby's death in 1979.[33]

In 1980, The Museum of Modern Art received the typescript of the mem-

oir as part of the James Thrall Soby Bequest. In an undated "preface," Soby had written:

I am writing this autobiographical account for two reasons. First, after many years of attempting to do so, I am heartily sick of writing art criticism. Secondly, many of my friends and contemporaries are writing their life stories. Writing mine gives me a chance to say to them, "you be nice to me and I'll be nice to you." This is known as blackmail and I find it the most comforting of sins.[34]

The memoir is excerpted and published here for the first time.

Soby and Nellie at the Lido, Venice, 1937

Notes

The designation *MoMA Archives* refers to The Museum of Modern Art Archives, New York. The complete typescript of Soby's unpublished autobiographical memoir, housed in the Museum Archives, is cited as *Soby memoir*. The memoir is divided into two parts: Part one includes eleven chapters, and part two, chapters twelve through twenty-seven. As each chapter is individually paginated, the designation *2–3*, for example, refers to page three of chapter two. *Bibliog.* indicates the complete bibliography of Soby's published writings that follows on pp. 230–51.

1. When he died in 1979, Soby bequeathed his magnificent collection to The Museum of Modern Art. In June 1985, a second-floor gallery largely devoted to the work of Giorgio de Chirico—an artist whose early work Soby had championed—was dedicated in his honor.
2. See Bibliog. 254, p. 68.
3. Soby memoir, 2–3. Soby writes about his early years, including his family, school experiences, and interest in literature and the visual arts, in the first two chapters of his memoir, which, due to space considerations, are not included among the excerpted portions that follow this essay. In the typescript, he notes that in his room at Williams he hung reproductions and prints, but they did not hold his interest and he quickly tired of looking at them.
4. See Bibliog. 254, p. 69. "Selected Contemporary French Paintings," November 22–December 6, 1929, included works by Christian Bérard, Eugene Berman (lent by Henry-Russell Hitchcock), Georges Braque, de Chirico, André Derain, Charles Dufresne, Raoul Dufy, Jean Fautrier, A. E. Galatin, Moise Kisling, Marie Laurencin, Jean Lurçat, Henri Matisse, Amedeo Modigliani, Pablo Picasso (lent by Paul J. Sachs), Dunoyer de Segonzac, Kristians Tonny (lent by Hitchcock), Maurice de Vlaminck (lent by Mrs. R. Kirk Askew, Jr.), Ossip Zadkine, and Eugene Zak. Wadsworth Atheneum Library, Hartford, Connecticut. This show occurred at the time of The Museum of Modern Art's inaugural exhibition, "Cézanne, Gauguin, Seurat, van Gogh," held from November 8 to December 7, 1929. See also Soby memoir, 4–3.
5. On an invoice dated January 16, 1930, Valentine Gallery to James Thrall Soby, these works are identified as Henri Matisse, *Le Canapé rouge* (1923), and André Derain, *Paysage, ciel bleu* (1925). MoMA Archives: James Thrall Soby Papers, IV.D.1. A photograph of the Matisse found among the Soby Papers identifies it as *Canopé [sic]* Rose and is dated 1921. However, the work to which Soby refers is actually *The Striped Gown* (Barnes Foundation, Merion, Pennsylvania; illus. in Albert C. Barnes, *The Art of Henri Matisse* [New York: Charles Scribner's Sons], no. 914, p. 287). Barnes dated the picture to 1919; Jack Flam confirms that this is probably the correct date, as there is a Bernheim-Jeune photograph of the work (neg. no. 3195) that bears the date May 1920 (Galerie Bernheim-Jeune was Matisse's representative in Paris in the early 1920s).
6. "Newer Super-Realism," held November 10–30, 1931, exhibited the work of Salvador Dali for the first time in America and included works by de Chirico, Max Ernst, André Masson, Joan Miró, and Léopold Survage. The Picasso exhibition marked the opening, on February 6, 1934, of the Avery Memorial, the modern wing of the Wadsworth Atheneum; two days later, the Virgil Thomson–Gertrude Stein opera *Four Saints in Three Acts* had its world première there. These now-famous events attracted distinguished cultural figures from around the world, and were widely reported in the press; Janet Flanner, the brilliant Genêt of *The New Yorker*, referred to Hartford as "that Connecticut Athens" in her "Paris Letter" published in the magazine's March 31, 1934, issue. For excellent descriptions of the occasion and of Hartford in the era of Austin, see *Avery Memorial: Wadsworth Atheneum* (Hartford, Conn.: Wadsworth Atheneum, 1984) and *A. Everett Austin, Jr.: A Director's Taste in Achievement* (Hartford, Conn.: Wadsworth Atheneum, 1958).
7. In 1933, Soby thought that he might become a photographer, and through a mutual friend (probably Chick Austin) asked Lincoln Kirstein whether Walker Evans would take him on as an apprentice for a short time. Evans agreed, and from him Soby learned photographic technique, including distances, angling, lenses, and printing. Although Soby quickly realized that "photography's muse was not for hire" (Bibliog. 184, p. 58), his love of and appreciation for photography were manifest in his activities at The Museum of Modern Art. He was a founding member of the Museum's Photography Committee, organized in November 1940 with David C. McAlpin as chairman; he remained an active member until 1979. His first gift to the Museum consisted of one hundred photographs by Man Ray, given in January 1941, when the Department of Photography was organized formally under the direction of Beaumont Newhall. During World War II, when both McAlpin and Newhall were in the Armed Forces, Soby chaired the department.
8. It is possible that Soby met Hitchcock (1903–1987), the architectural historian and teacher, through Austin, with whom Hitchcock took Paul J. Sachs's famous museum course, "Museum Work and Museum Problems," at Harvard University during the academic year 1926–27. Jere Abbott (future director of the Smith College Museum of Art, Northampton, Massachusetts), R. Kirk Askew (future art dealer and director of the Durlacher Gallery, New York), Alfred H. Barr, Jr. (future director of The Museum of Modern Art), James Rorimer (future director of The Metropolitan Museum of Art), and Walter H. Siple (future director of the Cincinnati Art Museum) also took the course that year.

In addition to the historically significant International Style architecture exhibition that he codirected with Philip Johnson ("Modern Architecture: International Style," MoMA Exh. #15, February 9–March 23, 1932), Hitchcock organized eight other exhibitions for The Museum of Modern Art in the 1930s. Outgoing and noticeable, he loved good food and wine and elegant clothes, and sported a red beard. He is remembered fondly in the memoirs of Virgil Thomson (*Virgil Thomson* [New York: Dalton, 1966]); John Houseman (*Run-Through* [New York: Simon and Schuster, 1972]); and Margaret Scolari Barr ("Our Campaigns," *The New Criterion*, no. 24 [Summer 1987], p. 24), whom he befriended when both were instructors at Vassar College in Poughkeepsie, New York, in 1927–28, before her marriage to Alfred Barr. He subsequently assumed a full professorship at Wesleyan College in Middletown, Connecticut, from 1929 to 1948, and at Smith College from 1948 to 1968. After his retirement from Smith, he taught or lectured at the University of Massachusetts, Amherst College, Yale University, MIT, Cambridge University, and New York University's Institute of Fine Arts, where he was an adjunct professor from 1968 until 1987. See Helen Searing, ed., *In Search of Modern Architecture: A Tribute to Henry-Russell Hitchcock* (New York: The Architectural History Foundation; London and Cambridge, Mass.: The MIT Press, 1982).
9. With his first wife, Elmina ("Mimi") Nettleton, whom he married December 26, 1927, Soby moved in 1931 into a house that had been built for them at 18 Westwood Drive in West Hartford, in the then-popular French Provincial style; here, for the first time, he had adequate wall space to hang his collection of paintings.

Following his divorce from Mimi in 1936, Soby married Mary Eleanor ("Nellie") Howland in New York on February 12, 1938. Nellie Soby knowledgeably and enthusiastically shared her husband's interest in art. She had graduated in 1927 from Mount Holyoke, where she was elected to Phi Beta Kappa in her junior year and took all the art courses she could; from 1934 to 1936 she worked as a secretary to Austin at the Wadsworth Atheneum, leaving to become Barr's secretary at The Museum of Modern Art. She remained with Barr until June 1937, when the Museum moved temporarily from 11 West 53 Street to 14 West 49 Street; she then worked part-time at both the Knoedler and Durlacher galleries, and later worked briefly at the Julien Levy Gallery.

In August 1953, the Sobys purchased the Henry Mygatt House at 29 Mountain Spring Road in Farmington, Connecticut. Built 1837–41, it had neoclassical proportions and a faux-stone wood exterior. Soby commissioned Hitchcock to redesign the interior and to construct a gallery wing where paintings could be hung widely spaced in natural light. Mrs. Barr once described the house as "grand" and the living room area as "ample" and "tall."

The Soby house was considered part of the cultural excitement engendered by Austin's "Hartford renaissance," and apparently many of those who came to visit Austin and the Wadsworth Atheneum also stopped to see Soby's house and collection; such was the case, for example, in October

1935, when Le Corbusier visited the Soby home while in Hartford to deliver a lecture at the Avery Memorial (illus. p. 188).

Soby and Nellie separated and divorced in 1952, and the Soby/Mygatt House was sold in May 1954. (Nellie, who subsequently married John Bunce, continues to live in the Hartford area.) On April 3, 1952, Soby was married for a third time, to Melissa Wadley Childs. In December of the following year, he purchased a residence at 262 Brushy Ridge Road in New Canaan, where he lived until his death in 1979.

10. *The She-Wolf* (1943) by Pollock was purchased in 1944 and Bacon's *Painting* (1946) in 1948.

11. The Museum, being very much of the present, was vehement in its support of the United States war effort. In the spring of 1942, an ambitious Museum Armed Services Program was initiated to provide exhibitions, posters, films, and entertainment facilities for all the Armed Forces and, later, for veterans. As part of the program, thirty-eight contracts for governmental agencies were executed; nineteen exhibitions were sent abroad and twenty-nine were held on the premises, all dealing with the problems and sufferings of the war; enemy propaganda films were analyzed by the Department of Film; Museum facilities were made available free of charge to members of the U.S. and Allied forces; art materials and exhibitions were sent to troops abroad; and therapy was provided for disabled veterans. The programs were terminated in October 1945. See *The Bulletin of The Museum of Modern Art* 9, nos. 3–6 (1942), and 10, nos. 1–3 (1942–43). See also MoMA Archives: Early Museum History, I.3, I.40; Public Information Scrapbooks; and Soby Papers, III.55.3.

12. Margaret ("Marga") Scolari Barr (1901–1987), an art historian and the wife of Alfred Barr, was a brilliant, opinionated woman who cared deeply about the Museum and its future. She helped to establish the Museum Archives program in the 1980s, and frequently discussed Soby with the author. Responding to the author's repeated requests to put her reminiscences in writing, she began compiling notes; those cited herein date from April 1985.

13. MoMA press release no. 55, October 28, 1943. Department of Public Information, The Museum of Modern Art.

14. Margaret Scolari Barr, op. cit. On February 13, 1947, Barr was appointed Director of the Museum Collections and Dorothy C. Miller, Curator. He retired from this position in 1967, Miller in 1969.

15. Letter, Soby to Betsy Jones, May 27, 1970. MoMA Archives: Soby Papers, VII.D.73.

16. See Bibliog. 4.

17. Henry-Russell Hitchcock, "Two Reviews of After Picasso," *The Bulletin of The Museum of Modern Art* 2, no. 8 (May 1935), [p. 3].

18. Margaret Scolari Barr, op. cit.

19. Bibliog. 43, pp. viii, x–xi. Sachs (1878–1965), a founding trustee of the Museum, served on the board from October 1929 to November 1938, when he was elected an honorary trustee.

20. Bibliog. 56, p. 15.

21. Ibid., p. 20. When the author inquired about the great friendship between Barr and Soby, Mrs. Barr responded: "Alfred envied Jim not for his wealth, nor his collection, but because he could be a 'gentleman scholar' and not have to work for a living." Over the years Mrs. Barr frequently remarked that during his lifetime he had completely honest and trusting friendships with only two men: Philip Johnson and Soby.

22. Bibliog. 22, p. 7.

23. Bibliog. 51, pp. 83 and 86.

24. Bibliog. 166, p. 51.

25. Letter, Soby to Barr, n.d. [1962]. The Museum of Modern Art Archives: Alfred H. Barr, Jr., Papers, 1.352. The "article on collecting" that appeared in *Art in America* is a reference to Bibliog. 253.

26. Letter, Soby to Barr, February 23, 1963. MoMA Archives: Barr Papers, 1.352.

27. Letter, Soby to Barr, December 14, 1964. Ibid., 1, item 196.

28. Letter, Soby to Barr and Mrs. Barr, November 22, 1969. Ibid., 1.540.

29. See letter, Soby to Alfred A. Knopf, April 9, 1971. MoMA Archives: Soby Papers, V.66a.

30. Letter, Soby to William A. Koshland, his editor at Knopf, June 16, 1971. Ibid.

31. Bibliog. 166, p. 51. Soby's father, Charles Soby, died of pneumonia in Hartford on December 12, 1921, two days before Soby's fifteenth birthday; see MoMA Archives: Soby Papers, V.66a.

32. *Art in Our Time* (New York: The Museum of Modern Art, 1939), p. 11. This metaphor was used by the Museum's first President, A. Conger Goodyear (1877–1964), eight years earlier in an article titled "The Museum of Modern Art": "The permanent collection will not be unchangeable. It will have somewhat the same permanence that a river has" (see *Creative Art* 10, no. 6 [December 1931], p. 456). For a discussion of changing perceptions of the Museum's collection, see Kirk Varnedoe, "The Evolving Torpedo," pp. 12–73 of the present volume.

33. In the latest letter on the subject in the Museum Archives, Soby wrote Koshland that he wanted the book "to flow easily or let's junk the whole idea" (letter dated July 23, 1971). Perhaps the manuscript did lack "connective tissue," in Koshland's words, but he also informed Soby that everyone at Knopf who had read the chapters was enthusiastic about the book and his writing; see letter, Koshland to Soby, July 21, 1971. All correspondence, MoMA Archives: Soby Papers, V.66a.

34. Ibid.; unpaginated sheet.

Special Section: James Thrall Soby

The Changing Stream

James Thrall Soby

The following excerpts adhere to the order in which they were written by James Thrall Soby. Works of art in Soby's collection that were later given to The Museum of Modern Art as part of the Soby Bequest have been cross-referenced to the appendix that appears on pp. 228–29. Unless otherwise noted, all documentary photographs were taken by Soby, and are courtesy The Museum of Modern Art Archives. Italicized subject headings are Soby's own.

27 Lewis Street

In the very early autumn of 1929, I bought a third interest in the bookshop Edwin Valentine Mitchell had started ten years earlier at 27 Lewis Street in Hartford. . . . It was a beguiling location in downtown Hartford, and doubtless it had been chosen by Edwin Mitchell because it reminded him of places where bookshops were found in London, a city he revered. He had stacked new books from the creaky floors to the high ceilings on the ground floor; upstairs were the diminutive offices and wrapping counter and, later, a rare-book room presided over by a knowledgeable antiquarian, Crampton Johnson. . . .

As I think back on it, Edwin Valentine Mitchell, Inc., was a very good bookshop. Hartford had long since passed its literary prime, of course, though leading writers like Sinclair Lewis lived there for a brief time and the internationally known poet Wallace Stevens was esteemed locally, not as a writer, but as an especially ruthless lawyer at settling insurance claims as a vice-president of the Hartford Accident and Indemnity Company. . . .

Whatever its decline as a literary haven since the days of Mark Twain, Hartford was still known in the trade as "a good book town." There was no real reason why the bookshop shouldn't have prospered. I think it would have if Edwin hadn't had such a passion for publishing books rather than for selling them. This passion had been whetted beyond control the year before I joined the shop. In that year Edwin had published a biography of the great fifteenth-century poet François Villon, written by . . . D. B. Wyndham Lewis (not to be confused with the writer-painter and founder of the Vorticist movement in London, Wyndham Lewis).[1] The book had been selected by the Book-of-the-Month Club and had also sold widely on its own, since Villon was and remains one of literature's most romantic figures. Another factor in the book's success was that only a very few people knew many accurate facts about Villon's bohemian life. Presumably, D. B. Wyndham Lewis did know the facts, though I am not the one to judge. In any case, the book's wild success prompted Edwin to publish a number of other books, some of them written by

himself, which cost far more than they earned.

As a publisher, Edwin took a special delight in issuing books of poetry. . . . I tried and tried to get him to see if any unpublished poems by Wallace Stevens were available. I think Edwin did try once by phone. But Stevens was a gruff, lonely, and difficult man. He almost never came to the bookshop, but he often spent his lunch hours visiting Hartford's extraordinary art museum, the Wadsworth Atheneum, where I was presently to work. Stevens told me once that some of his poems were directly inspired by paintings he'd seen in the Atheneum. Encouraged by this shared interest, I later asked him if he'd like to come to my West Hartford house for a small party in honor of Carl Sandburg. He replied tersely: "I will come only if Archibald MacLeish isn't there." This made things difficult in that MacLeish's wife, Ada, was a Farmington girl adored by everyone in the Hartford area. But I somehow managed, and Stevens sat quietly in a corner while Sandburg strummed on his everlasting guitar.

Chick Austin

I hadn't known Chick[2] in 1928 when he first began to present a series of brilliant exhibitions at the Wadsworth Atheneum, and indeed I'd been abroad much of that year. But in the autumn of 1929 his show "Selected Contemporary French Painting"[3] had left me spellbound and was surely a factor in my decision to buy works by members of the School of Paris. By 1930, I was spending more and more time at the Atheneum and less and less at my bookshop on Lewis Street. Late that year I began taking an active part in the preparation of Chick's forthcoming shows of the neo-Romantics and the Surrealists,[4] I working mainly on catalogues and labels, he handling the shows with his usual rare taste.

Chick Austin and Pavel Tchelitchew in Pompeii, 1937.
Courtesy Tartt Gallery, Washington, D.C.

Russell Hitchcock,[5] Paul Cooley,[6] and I had become his principal allies in the struggle to convert the Atheneum into an important museum and a brilliant showplace for the allied arts. We were joined later by Eleanor Howland,[7] and we were never without the support of such nearby museum directors as Jere Abbott[8] of the Smith College Museum and Agnes Rindge and John McAndrew from Vassar College's faculty.[9] But it was Chick's courage and energy which kept the struggle alive despite public mistrust and trustee caution. . . .

At one point in the early 1930s, Chick and I learned that the great art historian Erwin Panofsky, was giving a series of lectures in New York on the Italian Baroque. The lectures were to be held under the auspices of New York University, and they were to be held once a week. Chick and I promptly enrolled in the course and drove each week to New York. . . .

In addition to his vast erudition, Panofsky possessed a fast and veritable wit. In his opening lecture on the early Flemish painters he began by saying that he had been brought up as a lawyer. He added that that profession had proved too abstract for him to understand, and he had turned to "the factual, precise and tangible study" of art history. I remember even more clearly the night Iris Barry,[10] her husband Dick Abbott,[11] and I took him on his first visit to a New York nightclub. The floor shows were elaborate in those days, and Panofsky stared spellbound at the long row of girls dancing on the stage. Suddenly he whispered to me, "I think the third girl on the left used to be a pupil of mine." I asked him how we could possibly be sure, and he answered quickly, "Go ask her if she knows Dürer's exact birthdate. If she says 'yes,'

she's no pupil of mine." . . .

In 1930 [the year that Soby and Austin began working on the Surrealist show at the Wadsworth Atheneum] . . . Salvador Dali and his countryman, Luis Buñuel, collaborated on what must surely be one of the finest and most scandalous films of its time. This was a full-length film called *L'Age d'or* and was the second film the two men had made together, the first [in 1929] being a short production titled *Un Chien andalou* . . . .

[T]he Avery Memorial Wing of the Atheneum had not yet been built, and there was no other auditorium which could possibly be persuaded to show a film which had caused such a furor in Paris that one of its principal backers, the Vicomte de Noailles, was very nearly excommunicated by the Catholic Church.[12] [In 1932], however, Chick and I decided to show the film privately. . . .

I don't think anyone knows to this day precisely which passages in the film were invented by Dali and which by Buñuel. Nevertheless, my own belief is that Dali contributed the ideas for two major sequences, both especially lurid. In the first, the leading lady commits fellatio on the bare, big toe of a sculpture of the pope. In the second, a group of priests clinging to a rocky hillside are suddenly transformed into praying mantises. The reason I believe in this attribution is that Dali was then obsessed by sexual allusions. Also, he had written, or was about to write, an article in praise of the praying mantis, an insect which has the rather disagreeable habit of killing its mate as soon as its marriage has been consummated. I never got the true story of which of the two men created which parts of the scenario. I couldn't get it even from Luis Buñuel, whom Iris Barry of The Museum of Modern Art's Film Library [later] hired to keep him from starving during World War II,[13] and who spent an hour or so each day in my small office at the Museum telling me what a worthless charlatan Dali was. . . . Buñuel [initially] had come to see me because he knew I'd done Dali's one-man show at the Museum in 1941 [see pp. 196–97 below], and he wanted to protest. But gradually Buñuel and I became friends, and we used to talk endlessly—about everything except the two films he and Dali had made together. He would say crossly, "Dali doesn't understand films at all." Buñuel obviously did and does, and today is honored throughout the civilized world as one of the great filmmakers of our time.

[T]he night we showed *L'Age d'or* my living room was jammed with people sitting on funeral-parlor chairs. The audience seemed spellbound; there was loud applause at the end. Russell Hitchcock . . . had introduced the film with a brilliant speech on the Surrealist aesthetic or anti-aesthetic which ended grandly with the words, "It is that I have already said too much." And then he sat down to watch the film.

The evening went off smoothly with two exceptions. The projectionist became terribly nervous as the film wound on, and kept looking at the front door as though he knew the police would soon arrive and take us all away and his license as a projectionist with us. The second mishap occurred when some of our Catholic friends had become rather tipsy drinking in the bar below the living room. As the Prohibition liquor took hold, they became belligerent and began shouting up the stairs that if we didn't stop the film they would come up and destroy it. Fortunately the winding stairway from the cellar bar was narrow, and it took only one reasonably fat person to block it entirely. I knew we and the film were safe, but the threat-

ened revolt made me angry nevertheless, though I must confess that in general I dislike anti-religious manifestations of any kind. Still, I was fascinated by the imagery of the movie, and I wanted to see it through. All of us did see it to the end, as the battle cries below subsided to faint growls and snarls.

•

I think the two exhibitions on which I worked hardest with Chick were the one called "Literature and Poetry in Painting Since 1850," held at the Atheneum [January 24–February 14, 1933], and the big Picasso retrospective show of 1934, for which I compiled the catalogue.[14] Oddly enough, the former of these two exhibitions was a more difficult and courageous venture than the 1931 exhibition "The Newer Super-Realism," a good part of which had been assembled in New York by Julien Levy's gallery.[15] Besides, as early as 1931, Surrealism had a limited recognition in this country as an avant-garde movement in Paris, though few people here or abroad yet understood that the movement was at first dominated by its literary figures and that André Breton, Paul Eluard, and (for a brief time) Louis Aragon had recruited painters mainly to illustrate their premise. On the other hand, it was sheer heresy in 1933 to suggest that literature and poetry influenced painting after 1850, the approximate date when Courbet's Realism had sought to outlaw all literary, religious, and allegorical subjects in art.

The "Literature and Poetry" show was Chick's idea, as all his shows were. But it was also up my alley in that literature had been my first love, and I was still immersed in it. In any case, Chick, Russell Hitchcock, and I labored long and hard to find literary influence in painting after 1850, though we were aware that a new wave of abstractions in painting was about to hit the shores of England, Europe, and America and was attempting to wipe out the last vestiges of previous literary excursions. The fact is that even some of the most fervently non-objective painters were more deeply influenced by poets and writers in general than they dared admit, since to call a painting "literary" then was to condemn it utterly. The object of the exhibition was perhaps to relieve all the arts of shame in their intimacy. Today, it's hard to believe that such a situation could have existed; today, a leading artist like Francis Bacon openly avows his debt to T. S. Eliot's *The Waste Land*.[16] It would be hard to think of Ben Nicholson, Barbara Hepworth, Sandy Calder, Mondrian, Gabo, or Pevsner making the same admission in 1933.

The Picasso show . . . was sheer delight to work on, but there were days and days when only a handful of people came to see it after the excitement of the opening subsided. I remember how panic-stricken all of us at the Atheneum were when there was some sort of civil uprising in France which threatened our loans from Picasso's dealer in Paris, Paul Rosenberg.[17] And then Rosenberg's telegram arrived, and we all relaxed. The telegram said "Journaux exagérés. Soyez tranquilles." I remember the words because "soyez tranquilles" became a kind of password for the Atheneum's staff. We all needed it; it was a hectic time.

When I look now at the catalogue of the Picasso show on which I worked day and night, it astonishes me that there were so few books on Picasso to which I could give plate references for works not reproduced in our own catalogue. Since 1934 literally hundreds of books and articles on Picasso have been published; then there were very few, and only the first volume of . . . Christian Zervos's *catalogue raisonné* had been issued. . . .

In October 1933, George Balanchine and Vladimir Dimitriev arrived in Hartford to found a ballet company based in the Wadsworth Atheneum. Chick had met them with Lincoln Kirstein and Eddie Warburg[18] at the boat in New York, and there had been some delay in their landing due to passport difficulties. . . . I'd never been interested in ballet and had gone to the now-famous "Ballets 1933" in Paris for the simple reason that I wanted to see the stage sets and costumes by two younger painters I admired, Bérard and Tchelitchew.[19] But Chick, always loyal, told Kirstein flatly that if I didn't attend the discussions about a possible ballet company in Hartford, he wouldn't either, and that settled the matter.

A day or so later I drove Balanchine and Dimitriev around Hartford and West Hartford, looking for a place for them to live. We couldn't find anything they liked, and finally Balanchine in his mild, gracious way told me that what they really wanted was an eighteenth-century apartment. It was rather difficult to explain to him in French that people in Hartford did not build or live in apartments in the eighteenth century. I added that I doubted whether there were any to be found in all America unless a few glorified boarding houses in Boston would come within his definition of an apartment. The two Russians were in a glum mood when I got them back to Chick's office. Their pessimism deepened when an announcement appeared in the local papers that there would be no tuition in the ballet school they proposed to open; this announcement brought . . . a local revolt of dancing teachers against the idea of a ballet school in the Wadsworth Atheneum at which no tuition or fees would be charged. . . .

After discussions, Chick reluctantly agreed with Balanchine, Dimitriev, Kirstein, and Warburg that Hartford was not likely to become a world center of ballet, and the group took off for New York, a city also lacking in eighteenth-century apartments but abounding in eager pupils. In January 1934, they founded there the School of American Ballet, which later developed into the New York City Ballet company, with Balanchine and Lincoln Kirstein still very much in charge. . . .

Henry-Russell Hitchcock, wearing clothes by Larvin, in the library he designed for Soby's Farmington house, summer of 1937; to his right is a photograph of Nellie Soby taken by Man Ray. Courtesy The MIT Press

Love Song to a House

Soon after I'd bought the Farmington house,[20] I discovered that there was a dug well just behind an enlarged dining room and terrace which Russell [Hitchcock had] designed. Since both Russell and I had known and admired Sandy Calder for some years,[21] we decided to ask him to design and make a tall mobile to serve as a well-head [see App. 8]. First Sandy made at home some rough sketches of what it would look like and how it would balance. It was to be about twenty-five feet high, and I think it was the first mobile on that scale Sandy had created. At one end of a long, horizontal metal pole there was a very heavy circular form, at the other a bucket which Sandy told me had been inspired by the elbow pieces on suits of armor he'd seen in the Metropolitan Museum's great collection. In between the large circle and the bucket various other, much smaller circular forms rode vertically and moved around in unpredictable but uncannily precise balance as the big circular form was raised to lower the bucket into the well. It was neither a surprise nor a disappointment to Sandy or me that the bucket seldom hit the well dead center. The real point was that the mobile was gay and hypnotic to watch as the outdoor breezes set it in motion.

•

During the winter of 1936, while Sandy was assembling his mobile on the lawn of the Farmington house and tinkering with its balance, a very different kind of artist was working in the dining room. This was Eugene Berman, whom I'd commissioned to paint a series of five panels for the dining room walls.[22] I'd known "Genia" Berman and admired his pictures for six or seven years, and during that time he'd sent me a number of his pictures in exchange for modest sums of money I sent him at intervals to Paris to help him live and paint. . . .

It was a curious experience having Calder and . . . Berman working at the Farmington house at the same time. They got along perfectly well personally but their backgrounds, preferences, aims, and styles could hardly have been more opposite. Sandy Calder represented the third generation of sculptors in his distinguished family. He is about as American as you can get, especially as to blunt strength and mechanical ingenuity, though he has lived a good part of his life in France. His heroes in the history of art mostly belong to the twentieth century or to pre-Renaissance times, and [the] modern ones he likes are all abstract—Mondrian, Duchamp, and, most notably, Miró, his elder by five years. The work of today's realist artists doesn't trouble him at all; he simply thinks they're wasting their time.

If Calder belongs to the New World wherever he lives, Eugene Berman was reared in and will always belong to the Old. A man of almost scholarly erudition in the art of the past, his taste is rooted in Italy's vast art history, though it encompasses such rather untypical French masters such as the Brothers LeNain and Georges de la Tour. Perhaps since he likes so many seventeenth-century painters, regardless of nationality, it would be more accurate to call him Neo-Baroque than Neo-Romantic. Yet he talks of Uccello and Piero della Francesca more reverently than he does of, say, Bernini or Poussin. The sculpture he collects and displays in his apartment in Rome isn't classical or Baroque but Etruscan and pre-Columbian. The breadth of his taste gives him the kind of support Sandy Calder finds in the very narrowness of his. It's some indication of their conflicting heritages and temperaments surely that Berman admires Sandy's work enormously and Sandy finds Berman's cluttered and useless—"it needs fresh air," Sandy used to say, spinning his big [hat] around like an overheated fan in a tropical saloon.

Henry-Russell Hitchcock, Robert Jacobs, Soby, and Le Corbusier on the roof of Soby's Farmington house, October 1935. Photographer unknown. Courtesy Wadsworth Atheneum Archives

•

I remember . . . when the incomparable architect Le Corbusier came to the house [in 1935] and insisted on clambering up on the roof of the wing . . . which Russell had designed. The lawn then stretched out to the golf course of the Farmington Country Club, and its planting had been handsomely designed by a landscape architect, Christopher Tunnard, then teaching . . . at Yale.[23] But all this verdant splendor meant nothing to Le Corbusier. He stood on the flat roof and said with his usual conviction, "You should make the garden up here on the roof. I will design for you a tree house, with a concrete ramp leading from the roof to the big tulip tree." Whenever I look at the snapshots of the tree's corpse on the ground I wonder about Corbu's practicality; I've never for a moment doubted his genius. . . .

The First Hartford Festival

The first Hartford Festival was given by the Wadsworth Atheneum from February 9 to 16, 1936, in collaboration with the Friends and Enemies of Modern Music.[24]

. . . I wasn't any more interested in music than I am now, and the program

which fascinated me was a program of very early films selected by . . . Iris Barry.[25] Iris had only recently discovered negatives or prints of the films, and they were a superb lot. The earliest was the great fantasy, *A Trip to the Moon,* made by George Méliès in 1902, the latest a film of 1924 called *Entr'acte,* directed by René Clair [who co-wrote the screenplay with] Francis Picabia, with music by Erik Satie. In-between as to date came the 1914 film of Irene and Vernon Castle, dancing the foxtrot, called *The Whirl of Life.* . . .

. . . As usual, I don't remember [the] music even fragmentarily, but I do remember Sandy Calder's stage set [for Satie's *Socrate*], which consisted mainly of a huge brass disk revolving slowly at the back of the stage. The closing performance of that evening was a "Ballet Divertissement," choreographed by the now-famous George Balanchine for Felia Doubrovski and her *corps de ballet,* the music conducted by Alexander Smallens.

The Calders

A few years after I began to work steadily in the Wadsworth Atheneum, Sandy and Louisa Calder . . . bought a small, old farmhouse in Roxbury, Connecticut. Within an astonishingly short time they had converted the interior of the house into a small palace of a special kind, unique in the world. Nearly every accessory in the house, from ashtrays to wire hands which held the toilet paper, [was] made by Sandy himself. Sandy also designed some of the chairs and tables, and everywhere there were cloth objects for every purpose, from pot holders to throw rugs. These were knitted or woven by Louisa or friends in entrancingly bright primary colors. I remember walking into the house for the first time in the early 1930s and literally holding my breath out of pleasure.

Alexander Calder in the kitchen at Farmington, ca. 1957

. . . As a man Sandy is big and strong, yet when he adjusts one of his sculptures he works like a diamond cutter who must make the quick, right move or shatter the rare substance before him. I once had an expert restorer in to adjust the swing of a small beautiful mobile Sandy had given my wife and me. He worked for an hour or more and finally said, "It's impossible; no one can fix it." Then Sandy came over, fussed for a moment with his large hands and the mobile worked like the movements of a fine Swiss watch.

. . . Once in Paris I bought a large Victorian birdcage. I had live birds in it at first and then gave up because the birds were always getting caught in the cage's turrets and could only break free by injuring a leg or wing. So then I had no birds for a while. Sandy came over to Farmington from Roxbury, said an empty birdcage was useless if not sinful and promptly made me a set of new birds from Medaglio D'Oro coffee tins and pipe cleaners. When he was finished in an incredibly short time, he said there should also be birds outside the cage to redress nature's balance and he made me a mobile of finches and doves to flutter around the home of their captive relatives.

Collecting: The Early Years

It was in January 1930 that I decided to buy some paintings by the School of Paris artists whose illustrated books I had admired for some time. I went to the Valentine Gallery in New York and asked its owner, Valentine Dudensing, what pictures by Matisse, Picasso, and Derain he had in stock; he had a good number, and I bought

a smallish Matisse of c. 1923 titled *The Red Sofa* and a Derain landscape of the late 1920s. . . .[27]

I was delighted with my purchases when I got them home and up on the living-room walls of my West Hartford house. I was also scared. I'd never spent more than $1,000 for a painting before, and the Matisse and the Derain cost, respectively, seven and five times that. . . . I didn't then know Chick Austin, but I knew enough about him from his exhibitions to be sure that he, if anyone in Hartford, would give me the moral support I needed badly. I went to his office in the Atheneum and there ensued what for me will always be a golden moment. When I told him the names of the artists whose pictures I'd bought in New York, he quite literally grabbed me by the coat, flung me into his car and we drove off with his customary contempt for speed limits to my West Hartford house. He couldn't have been more excited if the purchases had been his own.[28] From that day on we became close friends. . . .

As the weeks went by, I liked the Matisse more and more, the Derain less. I went on year after year buying more Matisses until I'd owned a total of seven. I didn't have the money to own them all at once; I got them by trading in and out, one for another, until they were all gone, including the best and first one, *The Red Sofa,* which Dr. [Albert C.] Barnes . . . finally bought and hailed in one of his muscle-bound and ponderous articles or books as a top Matisse of its period. . . .[29]

Pierre Bonnard. *Grapes*. 1928. Oil on canvas, 16⅝ x 18¼" (42.2 x 46.4 cm). The Museum of Modern Art, New York. James Thrall Soby Bequest

In retrospect, 1932 seems to me to have been the most reckless and certainly the most frustrating year of my life as a collector. In April I bought Picasso's now-famous *Seated Woman* of 1927 from the Valentine Gallery. It cost $16,000, it scared me to death, and I loved it; it has been my Best Girl ever since. It was "one of the most awe-inspiring of Picasso's figures," as Alfred Barr wrote of it later,[30] and I'm not sure I would have had the courage to buy it if it hadn't been for the enthusiastic moral support of Chick Austin and Jere Abbott. Other people admired the picture but assured me that it was too strong to live with. Even then but with more certainty now, I felt and feel that this is a specious argument. Any collector in the end determines his own span of attention in looking at works of art on his walls. He looks at them when he feels like looking; he looks away when he has had enough temporarily. No one, however hardy, would expect to play Stravinksy's fiercest compositions on the Victrola all his waking hours. . . . The collector's mind has a built-in time switch. There are some weeks when I walk unseeing past the *Seated Woman* and then suddenly I will stare at it constantly, spellbound and proud.

•

In 1932 I was back in Paris for several months and I bought at last my first and only painting by Pierre Bonnard [see App. 7], whose illustrated books I'd admired so much in 1926. I bought it from Bernheim Jeune, a gallery I didn't usually go to unless they were showing Bonnard, Vuillard, or other members of the group who called themselves the "Nabis." I remember being surprised at how high the Bonnard prices were and finally realized that his market was both active and primarily French. In those days Bonnard's pictures rarely appeared in the New York galleries and the only place where they could be seen in quantity was at the Phillips Memorial Gallery in Washington. Mr. Duncan Phillips had bought a good number of very fine ones and I think it was he, in his quiet way, who had first persuaded me that Bonnard was also an absolute master of a curious hide-and-seek iconography which he developed along with his lifelong friend, Vuillard. The elements of this iconography are usu-

ally family or friends, everyday household furnishings and objects, and dogs and cats. These figures and objects are veiled in shimmering color. They are melded into each other with such subtlety of tone and line that very often one discovers their presence only after close study. Bonnard's paintings are sometimes as hard to read on casual glance as the work of the great Cubists, Picasso, Braque, and Gris, and they are, I think, equally beautiful in their quite separate way[s].

•

I think my interest in modern sculpture must have been growing steadily, if unconsciously. As long before as 1930 I had bought two small Maillol bronzes from Ambrose Vollard in Paris.[21] I remember that it had been rather an unpleasant experience because Vollard had been in a disagreeable mood. The visit to his labyrinthine galleries had started badly when he asked me whether I liked Rouault's paintings. At that early point I didn't, though I later liked the early ones very much. I told him so. I remember that I sat for an hour while he glowered at me and mumbled about "les idiots américains." All the time about six of Vollard's cats were walking around, nearer and nearer to a group of fine Renoirs and Cézannes stacked against the wall. Finally one of the cats walked right into one of the canvases, its tail swishing. My temper broke and I said, "Those goddamned cats of yours will ruin the pictures." For once Vollard almost managed a smile, though his expression was remote from helpless mirth. "Cats understand paintings," he said. And then he added crossly, "If you don't like Rouault, the cats certainly understand paintings better than you do." I left in a hurry with my two Maillols in a paper bag.

•

The most important purchase I made in 1933 . . . was not really a purchase at all. At the Marie Harriman Gallery one day in New York I saw a life-size Lehmbruck torso in gray cast stone [see App. 19]. I was determined to have it but didn't have the cash, and I'd been told repeatedly in youth never to borrow anything for any purpose whatever (my father was especially opposed to mortgages and said he preferred to have a veranda on his house). In despair I finally told Mrs. Harriman that I would trade her even—her Lehmbruck for a rather large Matisse of a woman playing a violin at a window, the surrounding wallpaper being purple-and-white stripes.[32] Mrs. Harriman . . . said that I was stark raving mad, since the Matisse was worth four times as much as the Lehmbruck. I assured her that I knew this but I wanted the Lehmbruck; it arrived at my West Hartford house by truck the next day. I've never since had any illusions about my business acumen, and I've never regretted the trade.

. . . I keep wondering whether my sculpture is not the one which appears in photographs of one of Mies van der Rohe's masterpieces, the Tugendhat House, completed in 1930 at Brno, Czechoslovakia. My good friend and neighbor, Philip Johnson, assures me that the Tugendhats were not collectors of painting or sculpture. Nevertheless, Mies may have persuaded them to buy the Lehmbruck or it may have been on loan when the photographs of their house were taken. . . .[33]

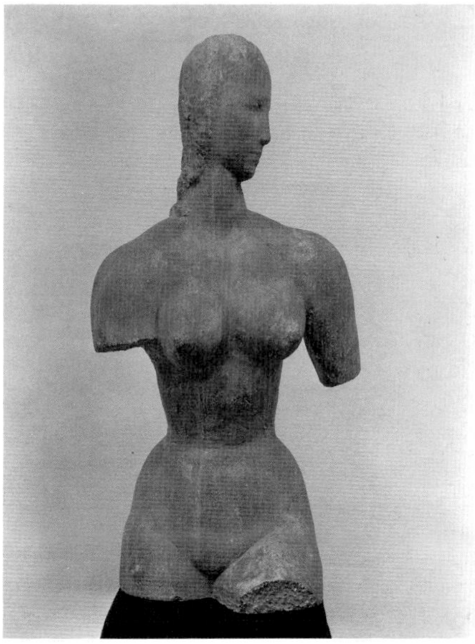

Wilhelm Lehmbruck. *Torso*. 1913–14. Cast stone, 37½ x 18¾ x 14" (95.2 x 47.5 x 35.5 cm). The Museum of Modern Art, New York. James Thrall Soby Bequest

When Chick Austin and I assembled the big Picasso retrospective in the Wadsworth Atheneum [in 1934] . . . we kept staring at two diminutive paintings of the master's neoclassic period, the smaller one [*Nude Seated on a Rock;* App. 31] having been executed in 1921, the larger [*Nude*] in 1922.[34] Both pictures belonged to Picasso himself and he had promised to give them eventually to members of his family, but [he] changed his mind in tribute to our show. We wanted very much to buy

them both, one for the Atheneum, the other for me. I can't remember how we decided which one of the two I would buy, though I think that Chick characteristically gave me the choice. The two little pictures were quite even in quality but I decided on the smaller one and I own it still. It is tempera on wood and it measures [5⅞ x 3⅞] inches; it is therefore about the size of a postcard, though its monumentality and sureness are unbelievable. . . .

I think it was very early in 1935 when I bought my first Miró. It was a small collage, of 1934, of felt and cardboard stuck on a piece of sandpaper. It had been, I thought, the most perfectly resolved of the Miró collages which Pierre Matisse had shown in 1935,[35] and years later Alfred Barr told me that he had thought so, too. . . . The collage had been bought from Matisse by Paul Cooley, a friend of mine since our childhood and a stalwart of the Wadsworth Atheneum in what I call the golden days. . . . It remains one of my favorite Mirós, regardless of size. Everyone tells me it will fall apart one day. But then, indeed, so will I.

Late in 1934 I had begun writing my first book. It was called *After Picasso* and it was published by Dodd, Mead and Edwin Valentine Mitchell in 1935. . . .[36]

The longer I worked on my book the more convinced I became that Giorgio de Chirico in his youth had provided the central starting point both for the reveries of the neo-romantics and for the affronts to logic of the Surrealist painters.[37] The one direction in which he had not affected the latter painters was that of the automatism practiced by Masson, Miró, and others. Otherwise, his influence was everywhere among the neo-Romantics and the Surrealists, especially when younger men like Tanguy and Dali began to make the incredible seem instantly credible through precision of technique. The Surrealists were photographed several times grouped in front of de Chirico's large canvas, *The Enigma of a Day* [App. 10], and they even sent out a questionnaire in which their colleagues were asked to identify objects, phantomic or real, within this picture. The answers were enigmatic, to put it mildly. Oddly enough, de Chirico had become the Surrealist movement's patron saint at almost precisely the moment when his own work had become hopelessly academic. The Surrealists expressed their contempt for their turncoat prophet by publishing a plate of one of de Chirico's classic pictures of the early 1920s and then defacing it with black lines.[38]

It so happened that in 1935, when I was completing my book, Pierre Matisse held in his New York gallery an exhibition of de Chirico's painting of the "metaphysical" period.[39] This period lasted from 1911 to 1917, though in 1919 de Chirico, painting for the first time in artificial light, regained his youthful fervor in a few works like *The Sacred Fish*. . . .[40] I walked back and forth through Pierre's gallery like a man gone crazy with lust and I bought four paintings, including *The Enigma of a Day, The Grand Metaphysical Still Life* [retitled *Great Metaphysical Interior*], *The Duo* [App. 11], and a small still life called *The Faithful Servitor* [App. 14]. I was furious that I couldn't buy more but the only way I could pay for [the] ones I had bought was to sell the beautiful Degas, *Woman Putting on Her Gloves*. I sold the Degas back to Wildenstein, most reluctantly, and waited for Pierre to round up more early de Chiricos. . . .[41]

During the early and mid-1930s the two New York galleries that both Chick Austin and I frequented most were those of Julien Levy and of Durlacher Brothers, the latter gallery owned by R. Kirk Askew, Jr., whom Chick had known at Harvard.

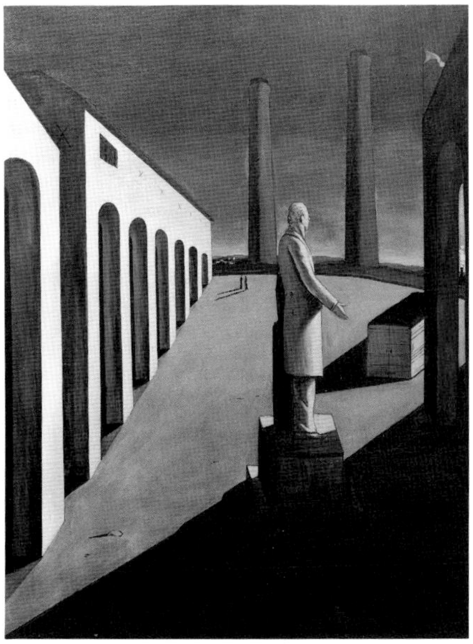

Giorgio de Chirico. ***The Enigma of a Day.*** **1914. Oil on canvas, 6' 1¼" x 55⅛" (185.5 x 139.7 cm). The Museum of Modern Art, New York. James Thrall Soby Bequest**

Giorgio de Chirico. ***Great Metaphysical Interior.*** **1917. Oil on canvas, 37¾ x 27¾" (95.9 x 70.5 cm). The Museum of Modern Art, New York. Fractional gift of James Thrall Soby**

Both galleries were distinguished in very opposite ways. Kirk Askew handled the work of a number of leading contemporary painters, but his main field was the art of the three centuries preceding the nineteenth. I'm not sure how many people understand how important it was to have had in New York a dealer who didn't share the prevailing and ridiculous opinion that all art of consequence began with the Impressionists and Cézanne, as though all artists of earlier periods were of minor consequence and talent. It was always a relief and for me a rare experience to go to Kirk Askew's gallery and see works by Piranesi rather than Picasso, by Guercino rather than Gauguin. No matter how great one's admiration for recent and modern masters is, I think it is always necessary to keep in mind the familiar but easily forgotten adage that [the history of] art is very long indeed. Kirk Askew was and is a scholar as well as a dealer and these two attributes in combination are rare in the commercial art world, especially in New York. . . .

Whereas Askew belonged in taste and heart to many centuries, Julien Levy belonged to only one—our own. He was for a long time the only New York dealer who handled the work of the Surrealists and the neo-Romantics.[42] Indeed, he was as close to being an official Surrealist himself as one could come without signing one of André Breton's guidelines to the Surrealist faith.[43] He spent much of his time in Paris; he was the friend as well as the dealer of many of the younger Parisian artists. Nor did he neglect some of the best younger American painters, sculptors and (a very rare inclusion in the early 1930s in New York) photographers. It was at his various galleries in the 57th Street area that I first saw the paintings of Ben Shahn, the photographs of Atget and Walker Evans and of many other artists whose names now seem secure in art's ever-changing constellation; it was there that I saw Peter Blume's masterwork, *The Eternal City,*[44] and many other works by people of decided originality such as Joseph Cornell, not yet surpassed as the creator of magic objects in the surrealist vein. . . .

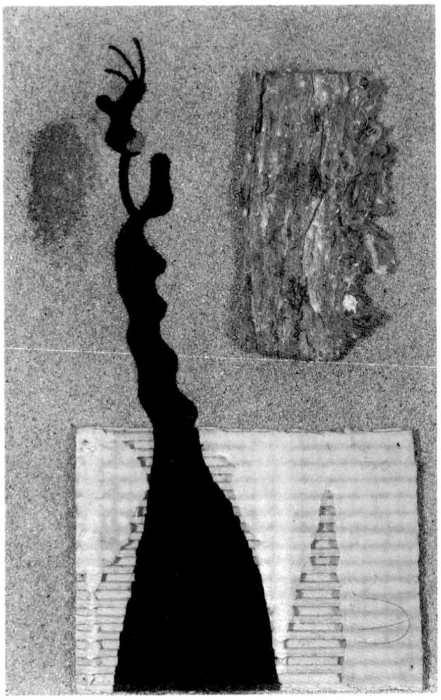

Joan Miró. *Collage*. January 20, 1934. Corrugated cardboard, felt, gouache, and graphite pencil on sandpaper, 14½ x 9¼" (36.9 x 23.6 cm). The Museum of Modern Art, New York. James Thrall Soby Bequest

Collecting: Later Years

[In 1940] two events took place which revived my interest in collecting. The first and more important of these events was that I was made a member of The Museum of Modern Art's Acquisitions Committee, an appointment which so far has lasted more than thirty years. I enjoyed the meetings very much and I couldn't help learning a great deal from Alfred Barr's presentation of works to be considered by the Committee, either as purchases or as gifts. I'd known, of course, that Alfred was the top authority in the international field of modern art and I'd studied carefully his superb catalogues. But listening to him talk informally was a different yet equally rewarding matter. The impact of his knowledge was enough to stun anyone, and it was increased by listening to . . . Dorothy Miller, a true expert in the American field.[45]

I began to realize that there were many facets to the precious and semi-precious jewels in contemporary art's crown and that a good number of these I either hadn't noticed or had passed over too lightly. . . .

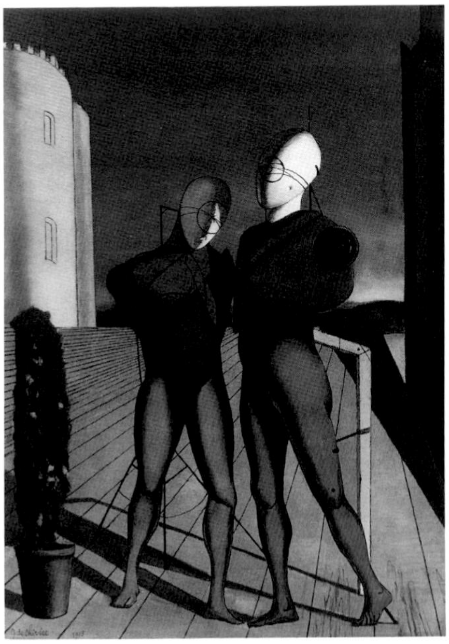

Giorgio de Chirico. *The Duo* (*Les Mannequins de la Tour Rose*). 1915. Oil on canvas, 32¼ x 23¼" (81.9 x 59 cm). The Museum of Modern Art, New York. James Thrall Soby Bequest

The second event which started me buying again was that Pierre Matisse had another show of de Chirico's early works.[46] One would have thought that I'd acquired enough de Chiricos in Pierre's 1935 exhibition to last a lifetime. But I was working in 1940 on the first of two books I did on de Chirico's "metaphysical" paint-

ings,[47] and I probably fell into a trance when trying to describe their importance in my book. In any case, I bought three more paintings out of Pierre's second de Chirico show. One of them was the *Gare Montparnasse* of 1914,[48] identical in size with *The Enigma of a Day* and therefore the second of four large paintings de Chirico did in 1913–14, the other two being in the collections of Walter Arensberg (the Arensberg Collection now belongs to the Philadelphia Museum [of Art]) and Mrs. Wolfgang Schoenborn.[49] The second picture I bought from Pierre's 1940 show was an extremely beautiful still life called *The Amusements of a Young Girl* [App. 13]. It had been painted in 1916 or 1917, when de Chirico was in the Italian Army's mental hospital at Ferrara, and it has that city's magic Castello Estense in its background.[50] My third acquisition was an unusually poetic mannequin picture titled *The Double Dream of Spring*[51] [illus. p. 224].

•

About a year later I sent de Chirico a photograph of *The Double Dream of Spring* through a mutual friend in Rome. I asked the painter to sign the photograph if he'd changed his mind about its authenticity. The photograph came back promptly with de Chirico's signature written all over its face. I thought then and I think now that the *Double Dream* is one of the most romantic in mood of all the de Chirico mannequin pictures. Some years later I gave it to The Museum of Modern Art, which had no paintings in the mannequin series, whereas I had three.[52]

•

As Duncan Phillips once wrote of himself, I was always eager for new sensations in painting. By 1942 Max Ernst had married Peggy Guggenheim,[53] and they were living in a marvelous apartment on the East River in New York. I went to parties there often, and once I took photographs of Max Ernst on the upper terrace, surrounded by his collection of Kachina dolls. Max had long seemed to me one of the most endlessly inventive of all modern artists, and I looked constantly at the new pictures he had in New York. I finally bought one called *Alice in 1941,* painted in 1942 [see App. 17]. It is an imaginary portrait of Max's great friend, Leonora Carrington, a colleague in the Surrealist movement. The picture is partly done in the decalcomania technique of which Ernst was an absolute master. In front of the seated, half-undressed figure in an immense hat are two large birds melded into the rocky landscape. All his life Max has had a special affinity with birds, and I remember that when he first arrived in New York a huge gull flew in his hotel window to keep him company in an alien land. More than that, I have a photograph of Ernst seated in an armchair which had an insanely high back. The photograph was taken by Arnold Newman. Max is smoking and the smoke naturally assumed the form of a bird, what else? It also seems quite in character that *Alice in 1941* was begun in a mountainous part of France where Max had been interned during World War II as an enemy alien. But when he and Peggy Guggenheim were staying in Arizona before coming to New York, the dry hills looked precisely like those he had seen in France during his internment and he finished *Alice in 1941* there, presumably without pause.[54]

•

During my Hartford days I'd become fascinated by the objects Joseph Cornell was creating in the surrealist spirit, and I bought several of them. The finest, I think, was titled *Taglioni's Jewel Casket.*[55] It tells in symbolic terms the story of how the famous ballerina [Marie Taglioni], traveling in winter by sleigh, was held up by bandits, and

Joseph Cornell. *Taglioni's Jewel Casket.* 1940. Wood box containing glass ice cubes, jewelry, etc., 4¾ x 11⅞ x 8¼" (12 x 30.2 x 21 cm). The Museum of Modern Art, New York. Gift of James Thrall Soby

Max Ernst. *Alice in 1941.* 1941. Oil on paper, mounted on canvas, 15¾ x 12¾" (40 x 32.3 cm). The Museum of Modern Art, New York. James Thrall Soby Bequest

in memory of this romantic episode ever afterwards kept her jewels in a case with pieces of ice. I'd bought the Cornell object in 1941 and . . . [in 1953] gave it to The Museum of Modern Art in disgust at my more pragmatic friends who kept pocketing the simulated ice cubes. As works of art, Cornell's objects are in a very high degree. To this day I think him the purest artist our country has produced in the surrealist vein. But Taglioni was by no means the only love of Cornell's febrile imagination. I remember talking to him once about Tamara Toumanova who had come to Hartford to be part of the ill-fated ballet company of Balanchine and Dimitriev in 1933. I was half-way through my summary of Toumanova's great beauty when Cornell put his fingers to his lips and said, "Please talk more softly," he said. "You'll wake her up." I asked where she was and Cornell answered quickly, "She's asleep in my bureau drawer." I don't know why I couldn't stop asking silly questions. But I couldn't, and I said, "Is she alone?" "Of course not," Joseph Cornell answered instantly. "She's with Hedy Lamar." I nodded as though this was the most logical reply in the world but Cornell sensed my skepticism and opened the bureau drawer to show me his somewhat tattered photographs of the two beautiful ladies.

Max Ernst, surrounded by kachina dolls on the terrace of Hale House, the brownstone located on Beekman Place at East Fifty-first Street in Manhattan that he shared with Peggy Guggenheim, ca. 1942

•

My admiration for Yves Tanguy's incredibly single-minded art had been growing steadily with the years and I bought a fairly large painting of his titled *The Furniture of Time* in 1943 [App. 38; illus. p. 196]. It had been painted in 1939 at a French town named Ohemilleux, where a number of Surrealist artists had gathered temporarily and where, according to . . . Tanguy, the English painter Gordon Onslow-Ford had set long, specific hours in which all must paint whether they felt like it or not. It seems likely that Onslow-Ford's insistence on discipline was an inheritance from his years as an extremely brilliant officer in the Royal Navy, a career he gave up without a twinge of regret when he joined the Surrealists.[56] In any case, Tanguy probably worked more regularly then than ever before or after. The result was a new perfection in what I once called "one of his most poetic inventions—the melting of land [into] sky, one image metamorphosed into another, as in the moving-picture technique called lap-dissolve. The fixed horizon was now often replaced by a continuous and flowing treatment of space, and in many paintings of the 1930s and 1940s . . . it is extremely difficult to determine at what point earth becomes sky or whether objects rest on the ground or float aloft. The ambiguity is intensified by changes in the density of the objects themselves, from opaque to translucent to transparent, creating a spatial *double-entendre*."[57]

Yves Tanguy and Joan Miró at Farmington, 1947

•

Of all artists of the post-Picasso generation the one I have long revered most is Joan Miró. . . .

As early as 1941 James Johnson Sweeney[58] and I were directing simultaneous exhibitions [at] The Museum of Modern Art, he of Miró's work, I of Salvador Dali's.[59] When the two shows were nearing completion I found myself spending more time in Jim Sweeney's exhibition than in my own. There was one Miró—the *Still Life with Old Shoe* of 1937[60] [illus. p. 224]—at which I stared day after day. It was a painting in which Miró had reverted to his early, more realistic style in order to express his anguish about the Spanish Civil War. It was also a picture which Jim Sweeney and other leading champions of more abstract forms of art thought at best a courageous mistake.[61] The Surrealists on the other hand admired the picture very

much as so did I. It took me three years of relentless pursuit before Pierre Matisse could persuade its owner—a woman painter from Pennsylvania[62]—to sell me the *Old Shoe,* and she did so then only because she found herself being influenced by Miró's picture. I bought it at once.

I waited even longer before Pierre Matisse cabled me from Paris that he'd decided to sell Miró's *Self-Portrait, I* of 1937–38 [App. 28]. I remember phoning every Western Union office within fifty miles of Farmington until I found one ready and willing to cable to confirm the deal. Luckily Pierre knew how much I wanted the picture since I had made a beeline for it every time I went to his apartment. The picture had been painted in a small Paris flat belonging to a friend of Miró.[63] The room in which he worked on the self portrait for a very long time was extremely small. Miró would work at his easel at one end of the room and look over his shoulder at a round, convex mirror hung on the opposite wall, a fact which undoubtedly accounts for the magnification of his features in the self portrait. In addition to his own visage the portrait contains a virtual anthology of the cryptic and sometimes indefinable forms Miró has used so often in his art. But the picture has little of the bold color on which Miró's fame was first made. When the portrait was completed, Miró therefore had a tracing of it made and began a second, colorful version of the subject. He decided that strong color weakened rather than intensified the image, and he destroyed the second version.[64] One can easily understand his action, since the image's hypnotic intensity depends in good part on what might be called a muted fervor—unlike anything he has sought in any other work. In a sense, both the *Still Life with Old Shoe* and . . . *Self-Portrait, I* are mavericks in Miró's life work. This may or may not be why I admire them so much.

Joan Miró. *Self-Portrait, I.* 1937–38. Pencil, crayon, and oil on canvas, 57½ x 38¼" (146.1 x 97.2 cm). The Museum of Modern Art, New York. James Thrall Soby Bequest

•

What urges collectors on, I suppose, is their incurable conviction that age doesn't dim their eyes. There is plenty of evidence to the contrary, as when one considers the case of even so eminent a collector as Gertrude Stein, who started with Matisse, Picasso and Gris and ended up with Picabia and Sir Francis Rose. But the collecting instinct dies hard and is subject to flare-ups of conviction even in older age. . . .

Salvador Dali

It seems to me unbelievable that of the contemporary artists whose exhibitions I directed at The Museum of Modern Art the easiest to work with was the first—Salvador Dali. I wasn't yet on the staff of the Museum when I did his show in 1941 and I knew little about the complicated mechanics of arranging a show there. I'd known Dali personally since the very early 1930s and I'd seen him again often when he came to New York in 1934. I knew that Dali . . . was easily enraged. Indeed, in 1941, the memory of his fracas with Bonwit Teller two years before was still fresh in mind. There's been so much confusion about the latter incident that it [is] worth reviewing here.

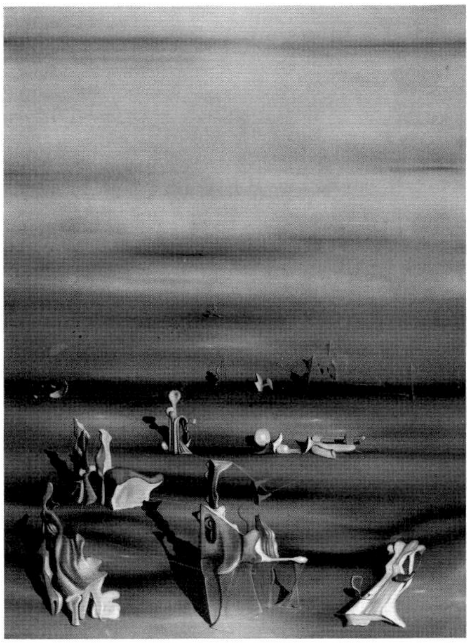

Yves Tanguy. *The Furniture of Time* (*Le Temps meublé*). 1939. Oil on canvas, 46 x 35¼" (116.7 x 89.4 cm). The Museum of Modern Art, New York. James Thrall Soby Bequest

In 1939 Dali had been commissioned by Bonwit's to design two of their [spring] window displays on Fifth Avenue, the themes to be "Night" and "Day."[65] It was understood that he was to be free of censorship and have absolute control of the designs and the materials used. I must say that in promising Dali total control the heads of Bonwit Teller must have been naive, since the artist had been known everywhere for his capacity to shock. Naive or not, the Bonwit people were horrified to

discover that the main element in one of Dali's windows ["Day"] consisted of a large, fur-lined bathtub in which a dozen or more live . . . snakes squirmed and writhed and spilled over the tub's edges. Naturally, important window displays were supposed to halt passersby in envious pleasure; the snakes drove them away in screaming horror.

Bonwit removed the tub and its reptiles as soon as possible, and Dali, inspecting his handiwork later in the day, became so angry that he crashed through the large plate-glass window and was nearly decapitated by a falling sheet of glass.[66] It's often been said that he had alerted the press before making his assault, but I think his rage made him too impatient to summon witnesses and too innocent, then, to know how. . . .

That . . . evening Dali was taken off to jail for trespassing and damaging private property. He was bailed out of jail by his New York dealer, Julien Levy,[67] but for days he sputtered with rage at Bonwit Teller's colossal ignorance of art. Personally I think he had every right to be angry. His action was widely written off as another publicity stunt,[68] but I tend to think that he was defending the right of artists not to have their work tampered with, when it had been agreed that this would not happen. It's also only fair to remember that in 1939 Dali was not the desperate show-off he [would later] become. . . .

Salvador Dali in the backyard at Farmington, 1939

I was nervous at the thought of doing a large, retrospective exhibition of Dali's work in The Museum of Modern Art. I respected that institution greatly. But I had worked there only once and very briefly doing some research on Daumier, an artist I admired, at the request of Alfred Barr, whom I also admired. I'd seen every exhibition held at the Museum since it opened its doors in 1929 and I knew its standards of installation were extremely high. I also knew that I'd had little experience at hanging pictures in a museum, since during my ten years at the Wadsworth Atheneum . . . Chick Austin had always done the installations, while I worked on catalogues and research.

I remember that I asked Monroe Wheeler, then the Museum's Director of Exhibitions and Publications, whether I should ask Dali himself for his ideas on installation. Monroe answered in obvious apprehension that it might be worth a *cautious* try. So I did ask Dali and was astonished by his reply. "Non, non, non," he said in his guttural French. "C'est vous qui dirigez l'exposition. Je vous verrai ou vernissage" ["You are the one who is directing the exhibition. I'll see you at the opening"]. He was true to his word. Not once while the exhibition was being put up on the walls of the Museum did he appear and not once did he object to the installation after he'd seen it on opening night. I often thought of this in later years when I was doing other exhibitions by artists and it was sometimes difficult to keep them from underfoot at all hours of the day and night.

Pavel Tchelitchew

If the [Dali] retrospective . . . was the easiest for me to work on, the most difficult by far was the Tchelitchew show I did the following year. I hadn't expected it to be, since I'd known Pavel ["Pavlik"] Tchelitchew for ten years, he was then living in New York City, and I could go over plans for the exhibition with him nearly every day. Perhaps that's why the exhibition was so hard to do. . . . [U]sually there were numerous other friends in his apartment, from Gypsy Rose Lee to Lincoln Kirstein and Cecil Beaton. . . . More often, however, they were intent on offering me advice

The living room of Soby's Farmington home, spring of 1936. At left, Lehmbruck's *Woman's Head* and Dali's *The Ghost of Vermeer of Delft, which can be used as a table* (1934); on the mantle, two bronzes by Maillol, *Leda* and *Woman Arranging Her Hair*; at center, Bérard's *On the Beach*; at right, Matisse's *The Rose* (1932) and Despiau's *Fillette* (ca. 1904). The andirons were designed for the Sobys by Calder.

The living room of Soby's New York City apartment, ca. 1943. On the walls, clockwise from left: de Chirico's *The Enigma of a Day* and The Duo; Miró's *Portrait of Mistress Mills in 1750;* Peter Blume's *Key West Beach;* Matta's *The Disasters of Mysticism* (1942); and Miró's *Still Life with Old Shoe*. With the exception of the Matta drawing, all works shown are now in the collection of The Museum of Modern Art.

The living room of Soby's New York City apartment, ca. 1943. On the walls, clockwise from left: Miró's *Still Life with Old Shoe;* Klee's *Gifts for I* (ver. 2, 1928); Picasso's *Seated Woman;* and de Chirico's *The Seer, The Enigma of a Day,* and *The Duo*—all now in the collection of The Museum of Modern Art

on what to put in the show and how to hang it. Since I've almost never been able to work on an exhibition or catalogue with someone looking over my shoulder, I finally had to ask Pavlik to please clear the premises until we had the show planned.

Pavlik agreed. We settled down to work and, on my part, to helpless fits of laughter. Among his other virtues and talents, Pavlik was a clown of very high order, with an endless repertory of stories. . . . [One] was about [his] experience in the White Russian Army. His career as a soldier was extremely brief, since his very first day he took off all his clothes, sat in the middle of a snow bank and kept bellowing up at his captain's window, "Please send out some ice; it's terribly warm today." I've never experienced a Russian winter, but I can understand why the captain thought Pavlik better suited to civilian life.

•

The summer reached a miserable climax when Pavlik discovered that in the catalogue for his show I'd said he'd been influenced by the color in the paintings by Matta, his junior by some years. He asked me to change the offending message, and I refused. I like to think that I did so not out of pride but because I really believe that Matta was for a time a sort of Typhoid Mary among artists in New York and not even artists older than he were immune to the virus of his color, particularly if they were his friends, as Tchelitchew was.

. . . Pavlik was a brilliantly nervous man, with a wit as sharp as a razor blade or a viper's tooth, depending on his mood. He was, I think, one of the best draftsmen of our age and some but not all of his paintings were very fine. He wanted desperately to be the Matisse or Picasso of his generation. He never quite made it and so, as Lincoln Kirstein once wrote me, "He died of rage."[69]

And a Dutchman

[W]hen I attended one of my first meetings of The Museum of Modern Art's Acquisitions Committee in 1940, Alfred Barr presented a [Piet] Mondrian painting for the Committee's approval. I remember blurting out that the picture seemed "too antiseptic."[70] There are few words I've uttered before or since which I regret more deeply or have thought more completely misplaced.

A year or so later I clambered up the endless stairs to Mondrian's apartment on East 59th Street.[71] The apartment was very small, consisting of a living room–studio, a bedroom, a bath, and a kitchenette. There was almost no furniture and nearly all of it had been made by the artist himself out of orange crates and other abandoned materials. But the main wall in the living room told an unforgettable story. On it were stuck little cardboard squares and rectangles, painted in primary colors—black, white, red, blue, and yellow. The cardboard pieces had clearly been moved about a great deal, though sometimes only a fraction of an inch, while Mondrian made up his mind slowly what the forms' eventual disposition on a painted canvas would be. The process of choice and placing suddenly seemed to me like an alchemy of an intensely personal and committed kind. Rightly or wrongly I came to believe, and I've believed ever since, that Mondrian's vision had a metaphysical as well as formal basis. . . . I think Mondrian had the kind of transcendental persuasion which Edna St. Vincent Millay tried to express in her famous poem: "Euclid alone has looked on Beauty bare."[72]

I got to know Mondrian best as we sat together on Peggy Guggenheim's admis-

sion juries for her gallery.[73] Mondrian was not an ironic man, as Marcel Duchamp was to the core of his being, and his preferences as a juror were fairly easy to predict. He shifted uneasily in his chair whenever paintings by people who were opening or indirectly his disciples were shown. He liked very much the abstract-expressionist works of men like the then-young Jackson Pollock. I don't think for a moment that pretense of any kind was involved in his choices and I often wondered whether somewhere in his temperament there was a duality of emotion, though God knows it never surfaced in his mature art. And I'm forever puzzled by the fact that while the two greatest painters modern Holland has produced are almost certainly van Gogh and Mondrian, the one was psychotically savage, the other cool and restrained.

•

Mondrian died in February 1944. . . . In that year I was Director of the Painting and Sculpture Department at The Museum of Modern Art and it became my sad duty to ask Jim Sweeney, Harry Holzmann and other closer friends of Mondrian to my office to make funeral arrangements. We all thought the Museum's prestige would be of help in alerting the Dutch Embassy's staff to the fact that their leading contemporary painter had just died and that some gesture should be made to show that the Embassy was aware of this. As I remember it, I had a long and increasingly angry phone conversation before I was connected with an official who claimed to know how important Mondrian had been as a key figure in the evolution of contemporary design, whether in art, architecture, typography or other kinds of visual expression.

At last one of the top men at the Dutch Embassy came to the phone, assured me that he knew all about Mondrian and promised to pay tribute at the latter's funeral.[74] He kept his word, and I wish only that he had kept his silence. He seemed to have Mondrian confused with an academic marine painter by the same or comparable name, and what he said had little to do with Piet Mondrian's extraordinary achievement. I remember that Jim Sweeney, Alfred Barr, and I walked away from the funeral services disgruntled but at least relieved that the death of a major figure in the long, distinguished history of Dutch art had attracted official notice, however misplaced.

Soby at the Shahns' home in the Berkshires, summer of 1947

"The Saturday Review of Literature"

One evening in 1946 I was sitting in the apartment of two of my favorite friends, John Mason Brown and his charming wife, Cassie. Suddenly John turned to me and asked me whether I'd like to do a column on art for the *Saturday Review,* the magazine of which he was one of the most influential editors. I said I'd like to try, but that I couldn't possibly turn out a column each week, since I was still acting as chairman of The Museum of Modern Art's Painting and Sculpture department and very much involved with other chores for [the] Museum. John told me that he would discuss the matter with the *Saturday Review's* editor-in-chief, Norman Cousins, but that he was sure I could work at my own pace, the magazine being eager to cover fields other than literature and music. He promised me a free hand in choosing the artists I felt like writing about, and he and Norman . . . stuck to this agreement during the eleven years I worked for them.

•

I hope the opening chapter in . . . [the 1957 anthology *Modern Art and the New Past*] of my pieces for the *Saturday Review,* will make my meaning obvious. I wrote:

"Whatever may be posterity's verdict on the art created during the first half of our century, there can be no doubt that the period has been extraordinarily rich in reappraisal of the artistic achievements of the past. Our score in this regard is staggering. When one considers the vast amount of material now considered to be of aesthetic, as well as ethnographic, value (the tribal sculpture of Africa and the South Pacific, for instance), when one remembers how many painters are today given top rank instead of their once negligible place, then it becomes apparent that the twentieth century has effected a profound and successful revolution in ways of seeing. Indeed, one of the reasons why some people find modern art difficult is that they apply to it standards of taste which in many cases art historians, no less than living artists, have drastically revised. And the truth is that historians and practicing artists are usually allied, if somewhat unaware, in a common quest."[75]

•

None of the articles was about artists I didn't like because, as I once explained to Geoffrey Hellman of *The New Yorker,* art criticism for me has always been an art of affection. I understand, of course, that someone must help the public separate good art from bad. But this is a task which has never interested me in the slightest, my theory being that talented painters and sculptors need praise far more than artists need blame. Perhaps this is defaulting on the critic's basic responsibility. If so, I plead guilty. I probably wouldn't feel the same way if I were writing about the performing arts, where people need guidance before spending their money for tickets. But painting and sculpture are a more private matter, and I think people should make up their own minds what is or isn't worth their attention. We've all made fun of the old statement about art—"I know what I like." I'm not sure it's as idle a phrase as "I like what someone tells me to like." . . .

Once in a while I now pick up a copy of *Modern Art and the New Past* and look at a few pages warily, as critics often do when confronted with an article written long ago. Many of the pieces I'd like to rewrite. But I don't think I would change much the pieces on Ingres or Alfred Bruyas, the extraordinary man who was the patron of artists as different in temperament and approach as Delacroix and Courbet.

•

From the very beginning, I wanted to write in my column for the *Saturday Review* occasional pieces about photographers. However understanding they are, photographers are usually written about in journals for other photographers or in infrequent museum monographs. Since The Museum of Modern Art had insisted since it opened in 1929 that photography was a valid art medium, I became more and more interested in writing about the subject. The Director of the Museum's Department of Photography was Beaumont Newhall, whose scholarship and high standards of taste were inspirational. I worked with Beaumont on his photography committee from the day I joined the staff. After he went off to the war [in 1942], I worked with his wife, Nancy, whose large exhibition of Paul Strand's photographs remains to this day the finest one-man exhibition of a photographer's work I've ever seen.[76] I wrote about it for the *Saturday Review.*[77]

I'd long been interested in photography's possibilities and as early as 1933; through Lincoln Kirstein's good offices, I was able to take private technical instruction from Walker Evans, whose importance becomes larger every year. Walker was a perfectionist to the core, and I always wonder how he escaped insanity when he

and I were working together developing negatives in a dark-room I had in my Farmington garage. Walker then made large contact prints, and the least speck of dust on a negative would drive him to distraction. I, on the other hand, persisted in smoking cigarettes and dropping ashes all over the place. The expression on Evans' face was formidable to behold when I did so. But after a while he gave up the struggle to reform me, we have remained friends all these years, and together we made some good prints, all from negatives Walker had made during the day, with me peering over his shoulder to learn how his process of selecting and placing images evolved (I never did learn, and now I know that no one can teach anyone how to be a great photographer, just as no one can teach another how to be a great painter). I've never ceased being interested in . . . Evans' work, and naturally I wrote about it for the *Saturday Review,* too.[78] And quite as naturally I wrote about Alfred Stieglitz, the dean of modern American photographers, whose brilliant example can't be left out of any discussion of photography as a serious medium. . . .[79]

There is one admirable modern photographer whom I'd like to mention and whom I also wrote about in the *Saturday Review.*[80] This is the Frenchman, Henri Cartier-Bresson, whose many albums of his prints have made him famous long since. His first one-man show in New York was held in 1933 at Julien Levy's gallery, and I remember vividly the excitement many of us felt at the time.[81] Unlike his elders, especially Stieglitz and Paul Strand, Cartier-Bresson was indifferent to the problem of enriching photography's technique. . . . He seemed intent only on recording scenes which caught his gifted, unorthodox eye. . . . In a *Saturday Review* piece on his work I wrote of him: "Walking the streets with a tiny Leica camera, he had learned to click the shutter with fantastically acute timing, when scenes which interested him reached their psychological climax. . . . Thus if he photographed a child running along a wall in a game of pelota, he did not release the shutter at the instant of most gracious balance, but at the precise second when the child's straining effort and imaginative absorption were so intense as to have an uncanny emotive power. . . ."[82] I went on to compare Cartier-Bresson's interest in asymmetric patterns to those of Degas, obviously inspired by Japanese prints. Cartier-Bresson corrected me sternly the next time I met him in The Museum of Modern Art. "Degas doesn't interest me at all," he said. "It's Poussin whom I adore and study."

Walker Evans, 1934. Courtesy Tartt Gallery, Washington, D.C.

Brancusi

I'd never met Constantin Brancusi on my many visits to Paris before World War II, but after the war I went to see him in his studio on the Impasse Ronsin every time I got to the French capitol. In good part this was because The Museum of Modern Art, like every leading museum in the world, was eager to have a retrospective Brancusi show. Brancusi had seemed the finest sculptor of the post-Rodin generation to most professionals in the art world.

. . . One entered Brancusi's studio by passing through a small courtyard strewn with fragments of sculpture, most of them abandoned by Brancusi himself, a few relics of sculpture from earlier times. Brancusi always opened the studio door to visitors and stood in the doorway, half suspicious, half delighted, and dressed in white from head to foot, with an absurdly small hat perched on his head. And then, when he recognized the visitor as a friend, he would break into a maniacal little jig, waving his arms and saying "come in, come in." Then he would say, "I know what you're

here for. Yes, I would like to come to America. But only if I can travel like King Farouk, with concubines, servants and music and many staterooms. Otherwise I won't come. But sit down and we will have something to eat and drink. You must be tired of standing." "As for me," he added fiercely, "I never get tired. I haven't time to get tired." He thereupon danced another little jig, disappeared for a moment and came back with some cookies and a bottle of very dark liquid. I ate one of the cookies but looked at the drink Brancusi poured for several minutes before I dared take a sip. I knew that Brancusi "cooked" his own brandy over a stove in his studio. I also knew that its strength was lethal. A few weeks before, Brancusi had drunk too much of it, fallen helplessly into a gutter and been carried home by friends who happened to pass by.

•

Brancusi's loathing of other people's photographs of his work was equaled by his dislike of pedestals made by anyone but himself. Some twenty or more years before he had had a one-man exhibition at Joseph Brummer's gallery in New York.[83] I'd seen that show and thought it handsomely installed, as Brummer's exhibitions usually were. But Brancusi was still fuming because one of the plates in the catalogue showed one of his sculptures placed on a simple, low plinth. "Brummer was an exceptional man," Brancusi told me, "but he should have known better than to change the height of a work of mine even by an inch." . . .

Brancusi's temperament as an artist had two boundaries. For convenience they might be called North and South. His pieces in carved wood [are] as aggressive as the North Sea in a gale; his stone and metal pieces [are] as pristine and calm as a becalmed Mediterranean harbor. Of the work in the latter category he talked most about a small piece in polished stone.[84] "This," he said, "is a portrait of a woman so vain that she took a mirror with her even to dinner parties. Her head is bent to catch her reflection as she eats."[85] The thought seemed to delight him and he began to dance again one of his inexplicable little jigs. He ended up standing beside one of his four versions in wood of one of his most famous projects—the *Endless Column.* The tallest of these columns is in metal and stands ninety-eight feet high in the Rumanian town of Tîrgu Jiu, near Brancusi's birthplace.[86] But even the smallest of the "endless columns" is a tour de force of ingenious balance which an engineer like Buckminster Fuller might well envy. They look as though they might topple over and they never do; they are as strong and immovable as the version Brancusi once carved from a live poplar on the estate of a friend. They are rooted not only in a nonexistent earth but in a profound philosophical conviction which nothing can sway. "You see," Brancusi said by way of explanation, "even the Pyramids end somewhere in a point. My columns need not end anywhere but can go on and on."[87] [The] strongest impression I had on my last visit to this studio was the incredibly subtle variety Brancusi was able to give his few preferred subjects—the egg, the bird, the fish, the human head. I realized that this variety had little to do with the basic material he used, whether marble, polished bronze or wood. It was managed by nearly invisible shifts in emphasis on a given form, by changes in scale which many could see but also by alterations of contour and balance which even an expert would find hard to trace or define. I came to the conclusion in the end that Brancusi was one of the last of the true mystics, a fact which his worldliness and rough humor did their best to conceal. More than any artist I've ever known he had an inner life

immune to penetration by the outer world. But he is alive in his sculpture to a degree beyond the reach of aesthetic awareness. I think if I could have only one work of art to live with to comfort by declining years, I would choose his large marble *Fish*,[88] which belongs to The Museum of Modern Art but which swims free in its own other-worldly light.[89]

Two French-Americans

In 1948, after living in this country for nine years, Yves Tanguy became an American citizen. Even though he had been happy during his . . . years in America, it had been an anguished decision for him to make, since he was a Frenchman to the core of his being. He had been born in 1900 in the heart of Paris, at his family's apartment on the Place de la Concorde, near the Ministry of the Marine, in which his father was an administrative official. The lifelong inspiration of his career as an artist had been absorbed during childhood vacations on the Brittany Coast, where he had been equally fascinated by the menhirs and dolmens standing ancient and silent on the fields and by the stones tumbling helplessly on the shore. His incredibly steadfast style as a painter had been formed before he left France in 1939. He was then too old for active military service and indeed had been released from army training in youth because, like Charlie Chaplin [in his] immortal film, *The Gold Rush* [1925], he had persisted in the unmilitary habit of eating his socks.

Unlike Surrealism's overlord, André Breton, Tanguy had no prejudice against the American people or the language they spoke. Whereas Breton, during his wartime years in New York, insisted that no member of his group speak English, which he described as a vulgar and inaccurate tongue, Tanguy made an effort to converse with his neighbors in Woodbury, Connecticut, where he and his beautiful American wife, the painter Kay Sage,[90] had bought a small house in the village and, later on, a larger one on a farm four or five miles north of the town.

•

[T]he process of becoming an American citizen was rather complicated then (even for a Frenchman). It was arranged that I should meet the two Tanguys at the Immigration Office in Waterbury at the unreasonable hour of 8:30 A.M., and be a witness as to Tanguy's general fitness for citizenship and his long residence in this country. All of us arrived promptly, only to be told by the morose official in charge that we were in the wrong office and should have been in Hartford.

I thought Yves would slump to the floor then and there. He had been up all night studying the Constitution, the Bill of Rights, and other key documents of American History on which he knew he would be questioned. He looked extremely haggard, and as we walked sadly out the door, he sighed and said, *"Eh bien, c'est fini."*

I drove back to Farmington, and kept thinking all the way home that never again would Yves be able to memorize the documents he was supposed to know by heart. Back in my former house, I decided in despair that I'd phone my lawyer and lifelong friend, Arthur Shipman, to find out whether Yves could appear at the Hartford Immigration Office soon, before he forgot all he had memorized with such difficulty. By "soon," of course, I meant a week or two, but to my astonishment and relief, Arthur said, "See if you can get the Tanguys up here by late this afternoon, not later than 4 P.M." Yves and Kay arrived in an hour, having driven up on two wheels, with Yves white as a sheet and Kay exuding confidence.

The first questions Yves was asked had to do with a physical description of himself. "What color is your hair?" the official asked. "Blue," Tanguy replied confidently, thinking he'd been asked the color of his eyes. "How tall are you?" was the next question, and Yves, to whom the relationship between metres and inches remained a dubious mystery, replied in a low voice, "Nine feet approximately." I think it was the use of the adverb "approximately" which won the day, for suddenly the official turned to me with a grin and said, "I think your friend will make a very good citizen, I'll O.K. the papers right away." . . .

In 1955, the metamorphosis of Marcel Duchamp from Frenchman into American was a much less harrowing matter. Marcel had spent several years in New York during World War I, knew English perfectly, and was in any case thoroughly imperturbable and worldly-wise. This time the American witnesses were Alfred Barr and myself,[91] [and] the official's questions were answered quickly and accurately by Duchamp, a man of such enigmatic calm that he could have survived the Spanish Inquisition without batting an eye. I remember that Alfred, Marcel, his American wife, Teeny,[92] and I had to wait a very long time in the Immigration Office's bare and gloomy quarters before our turn came. And then it was over as quickly as if Marcel had bought dessert in an automat, and we all walked away, jabbering as if nothing of importance had happened. The transfer of national allegiance can have meant little to Marcel, who had been a citizen of the world for forty years or more and to whom nationality was an accident rather than a religion.

Even so, I often wonder whether the Immigration Officials didn't know that in dealing with Marcel, they were dealing with a man of extraordinary philosophical profundity. Until the last years of his life, he lived in a state of semi-poverty and in New York during World War II supported himself mainly by selling copies of a handsomely-made valise which contained written and illustrated documents leading up to the creation of his masterwork, *The Bride Stripped Bare by her Bachelors, Even.*[93] This very large and heavy work had been painted on glass. The glass had been cracked [in 1927] while being returned from a show at The Brooklyn Museum. . . . Marcel never wavered in his conviction that the resultant cracks had greatly embellished the panel as a work of art. Nevertheless, I was shaking with nerves when I borrowed the Large Glass, as it is commonly called, for The Museum of Modern Art's 15th Anniversary Exhibition, titled *Art in Progress,* in 1944.[94]

I phoned Marcel on the morning we were to move the [work] into its allotted place in the Museum galleries, and asked him if he could please come over and supervise [its] installation. . . . He came at once and sat calmly in a chair smoking his pipe, while the excellent Museum workmen moved the piece into place with dollies and slings. I remember that I was dripping with sweat, thinking that the first accident might have been helpful according to Surrealist thinking, but that a second one would be a disaster. As the slings lifted the Large Glass off its dollies, I heard Marcel grunt quietly and I thought, "Oh my God, something's happened." My eyes were closed tight but I clutched Marcel's arm and managed to say, "What's the matter?" "Nothing," he answered firmly, "I thought for a second it might drop on the workman's foot. It's very heavy you know, and might have broken his toes."

•

I think my most vivid memories of him were the days we were fellow jurors of admission on the shows of younger artists held at Peggy Guggenheim's Art of This Century

gallery. . . . As usually happens on juries, the members sneaked glances at each other to try to discover what their fellows were thinking. With Marcel it was an uphill, if not impossible, subterfuge. To this day I've no distinct impressions as to Marcel's taste and preferences, except that he tended to like pictures which were crudely but convincingly executed—a fact that helps explain his early championship of the American "primitive," Louis Eilshemius. Quite often while we were judging, Marcel would whisper to me, "We must not be too harsh or dogmatic." . . .

As I think back on those exciting occasions at Peggy Guggenheim's gallery, I realize more and more how much she did for the so-called "abstract-expressionist" generation of American painters, especially Jackson Pollock, whom she kept alive and who once painted an entire wall in the foyer of her apartment when he was drunk but nevertheless knew precisely what he was doing and how it should be done.[95] And I think that somehow and quite mysteriously, Marcel Duchamp was one of the central forces behind the extraordinary uprising of American painting during the 1940s and 1950s. He was, in fact, an *eminence grise* but kindly and fertile, rather than vicious.

Left:
Guests at a party held at the Sobys' Farmington home, ca. 1938. From left to right, top row: John Carter and Henry-Russell Hitchcock; middle row: Iris Barry, Ernestine Fantl, and Mr. And Mrs. John Coolidge; bottom row: Helen Austin, Mr. And Mrs. Julien Levy, Nellie Soby, and Dick Abbott.

Right:
Nellie Soby, Iris Barry (kneeling), Dick Abbott, Elsa Lanchester, and Charles Laughton at Farmington, New Year's Eve, 1941. Courtesy Tartt Gallery, Washington, D.C.

Alfred Barr

[The first time I] worked for Alfred on a curatorial matter . . . must have been in the late 1930s, when I was a member of the Museum's Advisory Committee. Alfred asked me to do some research for him on Daumier, I can't remember why, since he'd directed the Corot–Daumier show in the Museum as early as 1930.[96] In any case, I looked up the things he wanted to know, and we walked out of the Museum together for lunch. A young woman with an incredibly active walk (to put it mildly) passed us on the street, and Alfred turned to me and asked, "Wasn't that Georgia Southern?" It was indeed, and I understood why I should have known this pleasurable fact, having gone to a number of burlesque shows in my youth. I couldn't understand why a great scholar like Alfred would know. Ever since, I've accused him of having spent

his time at Harvard ensconced in a front-row seat at the Old Howard Burlesque Theatre in Boston when he was supposed to be attending graduate classes in the fine arts at the Fogg Museum. . . .

[Barr] could never learn to converse . . . easily in French, though he has spent many years of his life traveling abroad, where in most countries English and French will get you around. He does take pride in the fact that he knows some German. I've wondered how much of that difficult language he can speak fluently ever since an evening when . . . Curt Valentin[97] took us and our wives to dinner with a newly arrived friend from Germany. I think the friend was the painter Max Beckmann, but I can no longer be sure. In any case, Alfred sat next to the German friend, and the two men seemed to be jabbering ceaselessly in those harsh sentences which the Germans use to express even the simplest things. He asked no help from his wife, Margaret Scolari Barr, a fluent linguist, and I could have given him none. Besides, he didn't seem to need help. At least I'd thought he didn't until I was walking home with Curt Valentin and told him how impressed I was with the fluency of Alfred's conversation at dinner with Max Beckmann or whoever it was. "Fluency?" said Curt, "My God, my friend just told me he liked Alfred Barr very much but understood only about one in every ten German words he said."

•

Alfred's difficulty in speaking foreign languages once caused a near-panic in Milan in 1948, when our host, Sig. R[omeo] Toninelli,[98] invited to his superb apartment in the old Palazzo Serbelloni all the lenders to the exhibition, *XXth Century Italian Art,* which Alfred and I were assembling.[99] All the guests were Italian, of course, and as a matter of courtesy Alfred felt impelled to ask them in their native tongue why there were so many swifts flying around outside the windows and on the terrace. He asked his Italian wife what the word for swifts was. Marga Barr told him, and somehow on his way to speak to the guests he got the word mixed up with the Italian word for Swiss. Since the Swiss haven't attacked anyone for a very long time, I don't know why his announcement that the Swiss were swarming all over the place caused such pandemonium. But pandemonium it was of a very real kind, and I remember one of the guests coming up to me and saying in an alarmed voice, "Les Suisses sont partout, pourquoi?" It took a long time for the party to calm down and Marga told her husband that if he had to speak a foreign tongue, would he please, for God's sake, stick to German. . . .

The partnership of Alfred and myself as Director and Assistant Director of The Museum of Modern Art began in 1943, and was of short duration, since late in that year both offices were abolished.[100] I've always thought it was a great mistake to have Alfred step down from a job he'd held since the Museum was founded and in which he could easily have served with great distinction for another twenty years. I remember vividly an afternoon in his apartment when Marga Barr and I tried to persuade him to resign and let me resign along with him. . . . I told him that two leading staff members, on the executive rather than the curatorial side, had been undermining him for years with Stephen Clark, then Chairman of the Museum's Board of Trustees.[101] Alfred refused to believe me, though I had plenty of first-hand evidence. He liked one of the two very much personally, and thought the other an able staff member and that was that: his loyalty to them was unshakable and to the Museum, absolute, to the point of self-immolation.

•

[E]xcept for James Johnson Sweeney's brief term as Director of the Painting and Sculpture Department, Alfred and I worked closely together on acquisitions, with incalculable help in the American field from Dorothy Miller. He and I or all three of us lunched together nearly every day, and we combed the market as well as we could, though the number of New York galleries was already beginning to multiply at an amazing rate and there was never time to cover all the exhibitions on view at any time. Today, of course, there are commercial art galleries from one end of Manhattan to the other, or nearly so, and it would take a staff of at least six highly trained scouts to keep track of new shows on display at any given time during the autumn, winter, and spring months. When you compound this situation with visits to the studios of artists who don't have dealers, or to shows held in other cities or towns, the task of keeping abreast of the art market becomes impossible and the tempers of neglected living artists very short indeed.

I've said repeatedly, and I'd like to say once more, that any museum whose principal field is contemporary art faces a grave problem. Such a museum must deal with artists who are often not only still alive and vociferous, but whose wives, children, aunts and third cousins, not to mention friends, are, too. . . .

The third exhibition I did for the Museum was titled *Romantic Painting in America,* and was codirected by Dorothy Miller.[102] It was held in 1943, and Alfred Barr had suggested it to me because he knew I had been working for a number of years on European painting from the late eighteenth century to the advent of Courbet's Realism around 1850. . . . I'd been commissioned to do a book on European Romantic painting, and I'd worked long hours each day on the subject. But I knew scandalously little about Romantic painting in America, though Dorothy knew a great deal and chose the pictures for the show, while I busied myself with the text for the accompanying book. . . . The book and the show got a mixed reception, to say the least. On the one hand, a number of scholars were offended because we hadn't used Romanticism as a circumscribed, chronological term, but as a definition of a spirit underlying the work of a number of earlier and modern painters. . . .[103]

One occasion on which Alfred and I struggled with an unwelcome and difficult problem took place in the spring of 1944. We were then ordered by the officers of the Museum to sell at auction a number of works from the Museum's collection, including a few which were bequests from Miss Lillie P. Bliss, one of the Museum's founders. The auction itself was to be conducted by Parke-Bernet; its catalogue was to be prepared by Alfred and myself. . . .[104]

Before it even began, Frank Crowninshield,[105] sitting next to me, said he thought it was a mistake. I respected Mr. Crowninshield's acumen in such matters, and I began to worry before the first item was sold. I was right to do so. The prices were low even for the dismal spring of 1944, and some fine paintings were lost to the Museum forever, among them a few which should never have been sold at any price, certainly not publicly.

I've never stopped believing that the auction was a serious mistake. I think it cost us some important collections.[106]

•

[T]he Museum of Modern Art has never had a . . . fund for the purchase of works

of art except for Mrs. Simon Guggenheim's large . . . contribution, which was restricted to the acquisition of major paintings and sculptures by the giants in the art of our time.[107] Mrs. Guggenheim was a wonderfully generous and lovable woman, but the only time I can remember her relaxing the rule (which allowed the Museum to acquire a majority of its masterpieces) was when she let us buy a painting of a Cape Cod gas station at night, painted in 1940 by . . . Edward Hopper.[108] The purchase was made in 1943, and at [the] time Hopper's position was nowhere near as exalted as it is today and his prices were astonishingly low, or at least seem so now. But she took the word of Alfred Barr, Dorothy Miller and myself that Hopper was one of America's best twentieth-century painters, and she liked the picture whose title, quite typical of Hopper's love of bluntness and understatement, was *Gas*. We never tried Mrs. Guggenheim's patience again that I can remember, and today I think everyone is glad we didn't.

Giorgio Morandi

I went to see Morandi with an Italian friend in 1949. He lived in a comfortable, bourgeois apartment near the center of [Bologna]. . . . There was no sign anywhere that it was an artist's home until one walked into the small room Morandi used as a studio. There bottles and containers of every kind and substance were lined up on shelves or placed on tables. The surfaces of these objects had often been re-painted by Morandi with simple geometric forms—squares, circles and rectangles, always in soft colors. One sensed the intense meditative and philosophical process through which these objects were arranged in Morandi's paintings. One knew that the slightest shifts in scale, light, color, balance and counter-balance were of the utmost importance to him.[109]

Morandi himself was a tall, solemn, saintly man who talked little and moved about slowly. There was one painting he had just finished which I liked especially [see App. 29], and I asked my Italian friend to find out whether Morandi would sell it to me. The painter nodded and then quoted a price so absurdly low that I blurted out that the Milanese dealers were asking almost precisely one hundred times that much for comparable works. Morandi looked sad and disturbed. "Tell your friend," he said to my companion, "that it makes me nervous to talk about prices. If he keeps on objecting, I'll cut the price in half."

I gave up and walked away with the picture. I felt like a kidnapper, but I was extraordinarily happy with my painting. I have been ever since.

Frank Lloyd Wright and the Hartford Club

In 1949, a large group of Hartford's citizens gathered for luncheon at the Hartford Club in an effort to persuade Frank Lloyd Wright to design a new theatre, the old Parsons Theatre having been torn down some years before and the city left with only the Avery Memorial's small theater and the mammoth stage of the Bushnell Memorial.[110] The latter stage is fine for the concerts for which it had been intended, but it was so big that actors in anything other than a lavish municipal production had to bellow to make themselves heard.

. . .The Master had flown in from Taliesin or one of his other habitual hangouts and had arrived promptly at the Hartford Club wearing a large overcoat and a porkpie hat.

Mr. Wright was in fine form, and all of us present knew we were to be addressed by a very great architect indeed. But I don't think anyone except Helen Austin[111] and myself, seated together at the end of the table, was quite prepared for the kind of speech he would make, both of us having been exposed to his tirades before.

The Master began by addressing the leaders of the business community. He said that he had had long and various dealings with business men and that these dealings had invariably ended up in hopeless compromise from an architect's point of view. The interest of this all-important section of his audience went into a deep freeze immediately, and one could sense that if Hartford got a new theatre by Frank Lloyd Wright, it would be over their dead pocketbooks.

The Master then turned happily to the group from the theatrical world. "I understand," he said, "that some of you object to my having designed the orchestra seats in the shape of a horseshoe." I noticed that Katharine Hepburn's mother [112] and her two beautiful sisters had paled a bit, but they grew paler as he went on in full cry. "I've been going to the theater all my life," the Master said, "and I think it's more interesting to arrange the seats so that one part of the audience can study another part instead of staring at the nonsense going on on the stage." I wished profoundly that Kate Hepburn herself had been present to fell Mr. Wright with a right hook, as she had me in youth in the tunnel we made of autumn leaves.

"De David à Toulouse-Lautrec"

Of all the projects in which I've been involved, none made me more nervous or left me more exhausted than the large exhibition of nineteenth century French masterpieces from American collections held at the Musée de l'Orangerie in Paris during the spring of 1955. The exhibition was titled *De David à Toulouse-Lautrec. . . .*[113]

I . . . worried about how we could install so many different kinds of masterpieces in the Orangerie's rather dark and difficult galleries. I remembered these galleries well, since I'd gone several times over the years to see the late Monet murals on canvas, depicting his lily ponds at Giverny, which his friend, [Georges] Clémenceau, had proudly accepted for the French Government.[114]

•

[While in Paris to install the show] I got a car and a driver to take Dorothy Miller, Sheldon Keck,[115] Porter McCray,[116] my wife [Nellie], and myself up to Giverny to see Monet's studios where the great Impressionist master had painted his late water-lily pictures. Alfred Barr had asked Dorothy and me to see what paintings Monet's son might have left. He didn't think there would be many, though we knew that for thirty years or more there had been only a fitful market for Monet's late pictures, usually thought hopelessly formless. Contrary to our fears, Monet's son had a good number of paintings left, most of them extremely large and some comprising triptychs. Dorothy and I bought what we thought was the best of the triptychs for our Museum and arranged to have it sent back to New York.[117]

. . . I think in retrospect that the purchase was made just in time, because in a year or so the younger abstract painters in New York and Paris rediscovered the late works of Monet's career and were fascinated by the way such real objects as water-lilies and other flowers disappeared and appeared again through mists of light and vaporish colors. As so often happens, the artists' enthusiasm spread to the dealers

and the collectors, and very soon the prices in Paris were extremely high. It remains to be said in fairness, however, that the first Monet of the late period to be bought after thirty years of almost unbroken neglect was acquired by Walter P. Chrysler, Jr., and that it was this picture which persuaded Alfred Barr that we had all vastly underestimated the paintings of Monet's declining years.[118] These paintings had been pushed aside by the re-emphasis on structure of the cubists and by the ferocious use of heavy contours among the Expressionists. They had seemed retarded and spineless to the revolutionary artists of this century's first half and then suddenly they became prophetic of a swift filminess to which a number of today's talented young painters aspire. There is a lesson in this reversal of taste to be learned but very likely only the passage of time once more can make the lesson apply.

Spain, 1960

In June 1960, my wife and I went for the first time to Spain. . . .

It's always better to see a city through an artist's eye, and Miró's eyes had taught us what to look for and cherish in Barcelona's streets, though we were helped enormously by a lifelong friend of Miró's, Joan Prats, a hatmaker by trade and a wonderfully sympathetic man. Prats was not only an early and incessant champion of Miró and his work but also an active leader of the Amigos de Gaudí, a society formed to preserve the architecture of the great architect, Antoni Gaudí. . . . Oddly enough I hadn't first learned about Gaudí through Miró but through an article Salvador Dali wrote in 1933 for the short-lived but remarkable magazine, *Minotaure*. The title of Dali's article was typical of him: it was called "De la beauté terrifiante et comestible de l'architecture 'modern' style."[119] The article was illustrated by *art-nouveau* ornaments and it paid tribute to the genius of Gaudí, a genius which in force and variety of imagination far transcended *art-nouveau*'s expressive limits. It always seems odd to think that Dali's article was published just one year after Henry-Russell Hitchcock and Philip Johnson organized an exhibition of what we all now think of as modern architecture at The Museum of Modern Art and published the first authoritative book on the subject.[120] At first and even second glance Gaudí's fantastically irregular surfaces and use of polychromatic and copious ornament would seem to be the absolute opposite of the bare exteriors and emphasis on pristine design of what we used to call the "international style," with Frank Lloyd Wright a precursor and Mies van der Rohe, Le Corbusier, Gropius and others as its particular heroes. The truth is, however, that Gaudí was too great a figure to be brushed aside as heretical by his more purist successors. It always comes as a start to remember that the enthusiastic foreword to a little monograph on Gaudí was written by Le Corbusier,[121] some of whose later works are not a rejection of Gaudí's effulgence at all. I think especially of the apartment house which Corbusier built at Marseille toward the end of his life. I can't remember the official name of the apartment, but all the taxi-drivers in Marseilles called it "the Fada building."[122] Whether . . . "Fada" means outright loony [its literal translation] or is a vulgarization of "Dada," I just don't know. In any case, like many meaningless words, it says exactly what it's meant to say. It seems appropriate to the work both of Gaudí and the older-age Corbusier.

Summer in Antibes

In the spring of 1961, weary of suitcases, hotels and the other daily nuisances of travel in Europe, my wife and I decided to rent a house for the summer on the French Riviera. . . . We knew the general area because the house was a very short distance away from the Château Grimaldi, later converted into the Musée d'Antibes and now everywhere known as the [Musée Picasso] . . . because of the many pictures the Spanish master painted and left there right after World War II.

•

A totally engaging maid named Marie Lerda came with the premises. . . .

Marie was deeply curious about America, a country she thought of as inhabited exclusively by cowboys, Indians and millionaires—in that order of interest and importance. She grew uncontrollably excited one morning when Romuald Dor de la Souchère [director of the Musée d'Antibes] walked down to our house . . . and announced somewhat glumly that a group of Texans had chartered a plane to make an art tour of Europe and were due at his museum the next morning.

Souchère spoke no English, and he asked me if I would come over and give the Texans a gallery talk. . . . [Marie] wilted when I told her it wasn't at all necessary for me to carry a gun in a holster when talking about art to the Texans.

•

Our first longish excursion in the Citroën was to visit the newly-opened Léger Museum at Biot. For many years I'd been of two minds about [Fernand] Léger's art. I think he was almost never as inspired as a Cubist as Picasso, Braque, and Gris. On the other hand, at intervals throughout his later career he produced certain masterworks like *The Breakfast*[123] and the much later *Three Musicians,* which I once acquired and then found I couldn't afford, though the dealer, Valentine Dudensing, said he would make me a special price because he himself had posed for one of the picture's three figures.[124] Both pictures are now in our Museum, where they belong, and they seem to me more and more impressive. For a long time Léger's paintings struck me as too crude for comfort, but I see now that his bluntness was a very real part of his eloquence as an artist. Several times in his museum at Biot I was struck by the deftness of line and modeling which underlay his massive forms, as though he had been a heavyweight champion who could, when necessary, box like a nimble bantam.

. . . I remembered the first time I'd met Léger, by accident. It was in the very early 1930s, I was living in Paris for a few months and I had with me a long, black Packard roadster, with a special body. It was a handsome car and one day I parked it on the Boulevard St. Germain while I went into a bistro to get a drink. I knew what Léger looked like from photographs and when I came out of the bistro I saw him circling around the Packard in evident admiration. I couldn't resist asking him whether he'd like to drive the car. "Mais oui, mon Dieu!" he said and pumped my hand with his massive paw and off we sped to the Bois de Boulogne, he silent with concentration and I with shyness. He thanked me profusely when we got back and I told him he was an excellent driver, though speed limits, cops and traffic snarls were all things to be disregarded or overcome by sheer speed and power. He remembered the incident several years later when I took him and the Calders to lunch at the old Hotel Heublein in Hartford, where he had come for the Wadsworth Atheneum's Paper Ball.[125] "Do you remember that pedestrian I missed by a foot?" he

asked. I said I did, but, to tell the truth and however callous it sounds, I remember more clearly a truck he missed by an *inch.*

•

Emboldened by my success in managing the Citroën, we made another excursion by car to see a very old friend, . . . Iris Barry, the founder and guiding spirit of the Museum's Film Library. Iris lived in Fayence, a fairly remote hill town north of the Riviera. She lived in a house, on the short main street, which Chick Austin had bought and lent her to live in in her retirement. . . . It had and has no central heating and will always need repairs. Its chief advantage for Iris, so far as I could see, was that it was given her rent-free, it was tranquil except when Chick sent other impoverished friends to visit Iris, and it was not too far from Cannes, where the Film Festival takes place annually.

. . . She was a voracious reader and used to review books for the *Herald-Tribune* and other newspapers. Her wit could be deadly but most often it was softened by laughter. Her accent and character were thoroughly British but her contempt for unnecessary *politesse* was thoroughly American. After all these years I can no longer remember whether it was she or the novelist Stark Young, who once, in the middle of a tiresomely circumspect party, roared out in anguish, "More obscenity, please!" It sounds like Iris.

Balthus at Château de Chassy, near Autun, July 1956

Balthus and Giacometti

One of the strangest friendships in the world of modern art always seemed to me to be that of Balthus Klossowski de Rola, internationally known simply as Balthus, and the . . . Swiss sculptor Alberto Giacometti. Each occupied an exalted, solitary place in our century's art; each was magnificently indifferent to the prevailing tides of taste, style and revolutionary fervor in contemporary painting and sculpture. I would have thought their isolation was all they had in common. On the contrary, their bonds of friendship were many and deep. They saw each other whenever possible, sometimes traveling fairly long distances to do so. Both were relatively silent men but, though I myself was seldom with them together, I've heard many first-hand accounts of how they jabbered like magpies, fought, embraced, quarreled again and always ended in some curious affinity of spirit.

•

I had met and known Giacometti for several years before I knew Balthus. In the very early 1930s Giacometti was close to the Surrealists and I used to meet him with them at the cafes Deux Magots and Flore on the Blvd. St. Germain. I also went several times in those years to the studio on the rue Hippolyte-Maindron in Paris' XIV arrondissement which Giacometti had rented in 1927 and occupied to the end of his life. Nevertheless it was Balthus whom I first got to know well because of an extraordinary picture he'd painted.

The picture, called *The Street* [App. 3], was the first large-scale work of Balthus' career and is an imaginative transcription of a scene on the short rue Bourbon-le-Château in Paris' VI arrondissement. Balthus had painted the picture in 1933 and it had been shown in his first one-man exhibition at Pierre Loeb's Paris gallery the following year. I had seen *The Street* in that show and had never been able to get it out of my mind. A little more than two years later I was again in Loeb's gallery and, to my astonishment, the painting had not yet been sold. I bought it at once, with a vast sigh of relief, having brooded about it almost constantly since 1934.

The fact that *The Street* was almost 6½ by 8 feet in size may have discouraged some possible purchasers. But the chief difficulty, as Pierre Loeb told me frankly, was that the painting's left section included a passage which even the French, usually calm about such matters, found hard to take. The passage shows a young girl being seized by the crotch by a strange . . . young man who has come up behind her, his face taut with easily decipherable excitement. Since the French had been frightened off by this passage, I began to worry about getting the picture through U.S. Customs. But Hartford was then a Port of Entry and I had brought so many modern paintings through Customs there that the officers regarded me as eccentric rather than libidinous, and they let the Balthus through without any fuss of any kind. Indeed, one of these men told me, bless his heart, that this was the first picture I'd sent from Europe which he really liked!

This was not, however, the end of my troubles over *The Street.* I hung the picture proudly on the wall at the end of the living room in my Farmington house. My son, Peter, was then only about four years old and within a month I began getting polite but disturbed phone calls from his friends' parents, asking what on earth kind of picture their children had seen in my house. I tried every explanation and defense I could think of, including the fact that the National Gallery in Washington always had on public view *The Feast of the Gods* by the Italian Renaissance's Giovanni Bellini, which has as explicit if seemingly less aware gestures as that in my Balthus. Perhaps I argued my case badly; perhaps I shouldn't have tried to argue it at all in that sturdily New England community. In any case, the neighborhood clamor didn't subside nor did the number of very small visitors to my living room. . . . I finally decided that it wasn't fair to my small son to have his father thought of as unmoral, if not immoral, and I reluctantly took the picture down and stored it in a fireproof vault I'd built off the garage, where it remained for a number of years.

•

I used to go see Balthus every time I was in Paris, which was almost every year in those days. . . .

It was in the barren studio in the Cours de Rohan that Balthus painted what is to my mind one of the greatest portraits of our century, the *Joan Miró and His Daughter Delores* of 1937–38.[126] I bought this remarkable picture the moment I saw it at Pierre Matisse's gallery, but Pierre phoned me the same afternoon and asked me if I would release it to The Museum of Modern Art because Alfred Barr liked it as much as I did and had even found a donor, a fairly rare occurrence in those earlier days of the Museum's history. It was the first time Pierre and Alfred had asked such a favor of me and I naturally said yes. To this day I can't look at the portrait—and I look at it very often—without wishing it were on my own walls. . . .

The psychological contrast between the somber, dressed-for-the-occasion pose of Miró and the fidgety good manners of his daughter is incredibly real and acute. It is also quite obviously based on fact. For Miró, one of the most delightful visual humorists of our time, is also awed on occasion by his own stupendous talent and puts his best foot forward, so to speak, even though both feet in this portrait are clad in the worn, old shoes of which he is fond. Delores, despite her obvious affection for her father, seems ready to break from Miró's grasp and race around the studio in idle delight. . . .

As the years went by I worried more and more about whether our Museum

Left:
Balthus. *The Street*. 1933. Oil on canvas, 6' 4" x 7' 10" (193 x 238.8 cm). The Museum of Modern Art, New York. James Thrall Soby Bequest

Right:
Detail of *The Street* showing the "offending passage" repainted by the artist in 1956

would be able to exhibit *The Street* when it was finally turned over to that institution at my death. . . . In 1956, Balthus was having a one-man show in Paris[127] and he wrote to ask me whether I'd lend *The Street*. I replied that I would, of course. I added, not as a condition but as a plea, that I was concerned about the picture ever being shown to a large audience in its then-current state. I told Balthus in all frankness that several restorers had offered to "improve" the lurid passage but that I wouldn't let anyone touch the canvas except Balthus himself. I thought this hint would mean the end of a friendship very dear to me. But to my astonishment Balthus replied that he would like to repaint the offending passage. "When I was young I wanted to shock," he wrote. "Now it bores me."[128]

I heard nothing more from Balthus for months after *The Street* had arrived in Paris for his exhibition, and I assumed he'd had a change of heart about making any changes in the composition. But late in the summer of the same year (1956) Alfred Barr, my wife [Melissa], and I stopped off to spend a few days with Balthus at his Château de Chassy, near Autun. We were on our way to Paris from Cannes, and I grew steadily more nervous about what condition *The Street* would be in and thought in my gloomier hours that Balthus had probably painted it out entirely. He must have sensed how apprehensive I was, since he dragged the big picture into the living room at once. The Mongolian boy's hand had been moved very slightly to a less committed position on the young girl's body, though his eyes were tense with the same fever. I think *The Street* is safe now anywhere from Puritanical rage; I've always thought it one of the very great pictures produced by a member of Balthus' generation.

•

I included as many of his works as possible in his one-man exhibition at The Museum of Modern Art in the winter of 1956–57.[129] Their number was restricted by the fact that some were very large in scale because, as Balthus wrote me at the time, "If I have achieved something up to the present it is almost uniquely, I think, in my large paintings."[130] The curious thing is that these big paintings from *The Street* down to its companion piece, *Le Passage du Commerce Saint André* of 1952–54, were all worked on rapidly, though long intervals would intervene when he wouldn't touch the canvases at all. He wrote: "I am always eager not to tire the canvas." He

added, in a sentence his great friend, Giacometti, might have written: "So many painters today have found a trick. I have never been able to find one."[131] I remember clearly that a main difficulty in directing his exhibition at the Museum was to find an adequate number of his marvelous drawings, though I knew many of them existed. Many more no longer did exist. The truth is that he hates nearly all of them, however fine they appear to others. "When I have finished my paintings," he once told me, "I put the drawings for them on the floor and walk on them until they are erased."[132] I saw evidence of this almost criminal practice when I visited him at the Château de Chassy. The room in which he worked had a very old, very rough floor and on it first-rate drawings, nearly illegible except for footprints, were scattered. I got my courage up and scolded him but it did no good, of course.

•

Before his appointment as Director of the French Academy in Rome [in 1941], Balthus spent more and more time at . . . de Chassy, and even telegrams were forwarded to him fairly promptly, I assume from Autun. But Giacometti was almost always in Paris and yet very hard to communicate with except in person. At least he was for me, since my French seems to be instantly soluble in gibberish when I talk on the phone. I remember that once in Paris I had some urgent message for him regarding his forthcoming exhibition at our Museum in New York.[133] I had tried his number at all hours, since I knew he often stayed up all night and slept in the morning and early afternoon. Finally, I was at a party at the apartment of Darthea Speyer, a very dear friend, who was then the brightest light in [the] United States Information Service's otherwise dismal offices, and she offered to try reaching Giacometti by phone for me. . . . I went over to Giacometti's studio, hoping to see a new, large standing figure everyone in Paris had told me was especially marvelous. I saw the sculpture alright; it was lying in plaster fragments on the floor. "There was something wrong with the nose," Giacometti said calmly, "so I destroyed the piece." I knew I shouldn't have said it, but I couldn't resist asking why he couldn't have reworked this small detail and left the six-foot tall figure intact. "No," said Giacometti, "if something goes wrong in a piece of sculpture, you must destroy everything and begin again." He added, "I'm used to beginning again."

. . . He was an artist who worked like one possessed. As I once wrote of him, even his thinnest figures seem large because they "magnetize the surrounding air and light, attracting to themselves an inexplicably poetic nimbus."[134] These figures continue to grow in one's imagination even after the memory of them has begun to dim. . . .

Further Museum Exhibitions[135]

"Ben Shahn"

When, in 1947, The Museum of Modern Art asked me to direct Ben Shahn's retrospective exhibition, I felt a sense of elation which never diminished from the beginning to closing day. . . .[136]

I had heard a great deal about Ben Shahn in 1933 from Walker Evans, who . . . three years before had shared a cabin with . . . Shahn at Truro on Cape Cod. It had been Walker who had taught Shahn to take photographs, primarily as notes for his paintings. And Walker's technical instructions had been simplicity itself, "Set the shutter and the lens and point the camera at anything that pleases you." It sounds

like as simple a recipe as Eastman's famous, "You press the shutter and we'll do the rest." But it wasn't, as anyone who's seen the photographs of Evans and Shahn will know. Both had the all-essential eye of artists.

After I moved to New York in 1942, Shahn and I became close friends. I had met him only briefly at the time of his show at Julien Levy's gallery in New York [in May 1940]. From that show Chick Austin and I had bought for the Wadsworth Atheneum an enchanting small picture called *Vacant Lot;* it shows a solitary young boy practicing baseball against a mammoth, brick wall.[137] From New York it was a fairly easy drive to the house in a New Deal development for garment workers in which Ben Shahn lived to the end of his life. . . .[138]

"Paul Klee"[139]

There is one respect in which Klee remains unrivaled in the art of his own and probably even of earlier times—the direct projection in visual terms, and visual terms alone and unaided, of a fantastically varied humor. . . .

. . . Alfred Barr used to call Klee the great "little master" of our time.[140] And yet if the scale on which he worked was usually small, it had every power of largeness. His favorite symbols—arrow, transmogrified animals, abstract spots and dashes, seemed whispered and yet they echo with grandeur and unfailing authority. There was no such thing as getting used to Klee's vision; it could change and retreat and move forward again without warning signals of any reliable kind. As an artist he could nearly always defeat critics, with their elaborate apparatus of chronology and stylistic analysis. For that ability alone, in this age of pigeon-holed academic certainty, we must be grateful to him. He was like the ultimate magician whose tricks no one could do more than pretend to understand because their inexplicable ingredient was genius, no more and certainly no less.

"Modigliani"[141]

Perhaps there is a note of caution for all art critics in the fact that the first article on a painter or sculptor I ever had published was a bitter attack on the works of Amedeo Modigliani. I no longer have a copy, thank God, but I know it appeared around 1930 in one of the several magazines . . . Edwin Valentine Mitchell published in fairly rapid succession. . . .[142]

I don't think that even when young and very green I disliked Modigliani's drawings; I don't see how anyone could have. But I'd thought his color crude and repetitious and his sculpture over-mannered. I also thought then that his reputation depended to unreasonable extent on the violence of his short, dissipated life and on his amorous conquests. I probably envied both, being a New Englander, and I know I thought this was not the way for an artist or anyone else to behave. Later I began to understand that it was Modigliani's fever, both physical and moral, which gave him his strength. In the 1951 booklet I was able to write with conviction: "It is idle to argue that he might have been a more profound artist had he nursed his energies. Exacerbated nerves were part of his talent's high price."[143]

The miracle is that Modigliani was able to produce so much work in a very short time (mainly from 1915 to 1920). Though no *catalogue raisonné* of Modigliani's work exists,[144] it has been estimated that during those five years, all of them spent in Paris except for a short vacation in the Midi, he completed around 450 paintings and

a little over twenty sculptures, mostly carved in limestone which he soon found easier to cut than marble. There is no accurate way to determine how many drawings he made, since he drew constantly day and night. His fame has long since become international, though for a time his principal enthusiast among Americans was . . . Chester Dale.[145]

. . . I wrote of him in The Museum of Modern Art's publication: "In sculpture as in painting, his sole concern was the human face and figure, and this is true even of those works which seem intended for architectural use—the caryatid and the corbelled head. He dreamed once of working in Carrara's quarries; his instinct was for direct carving rather than modeling in plaster or clay. It may be that this technical preference . . . accounts in part for the nervous vitality of Modigliani's best pieces. They are at any rate exceptionally vigorous, and if we sometimes resent their exaggerations, we know they are alive."[146] . . .

"Yves Tanguy" and "Giorgio de Chirico"

In 1955, the Museum asked me to direct an exhibition of the works of Tanguy and [another of the works of] Giorgio de Chirico.[147] Tanguy's show was, alas, a memorial exhibition; the de Chirico show was held to help promote my book, *Giorgio de Chirico,* which the Museum had just published. Among other reasons for holding the joint exhibition[s] was the fact that, by his own proud admission, Tanguy had decided to become a painter when from a bus window he had seen an early de Chirico painting in the window of Paul Guillaume's gallery.[148] He had jumped off the bus, raced over to peer at the de Chirico and then and there decided not only to become a painter but the kind of painter—of the world of reverie and dreams—he wanted to be.

•

I felt a terrible sadness in doing the Tanguy section of the show, since we had been close friends during his years in America. . . .

Giorgio de Chirico I'd known only slightly and for a short time, when he was living in a brownstone house in New York where Eugene Berman and Léonor Fini also lived. I do remember that he talked learnedly on a variety of subjects relating to art, that he looked disheveled and also imperial, and that he ranted against many of his former colleagues in the School of Paris, most of whom, he said, couldn't even draw. This must have been about 1933, and there was already much of the academician in his character—a not unlikely result of the fact that his own technical training had been unusually thorough and had taken place in Athens and Munich, two cities where the academic tradition was still alive. How the young de Chirico, still in his twenties, can have had the courage to upset these traditions so thoroughly, remains a mystery. The history of hallucinatory inspiration in art is long indeed, of course. Yet a majority of good painters found it a dead end, whereas de Chirico went on to become the most vital, single progenitor of what we now recognize as Surrealist art. And then he became himself an academic painter. The Sur-realists spotted the change first and in 1941 I tried to reinforce their dismay in . . . *The Early Chirico.*[149]

"Balthus"[150]

[Balthus's] works made those of the politically oriented Parisian painters look weak and contrived by comparison. It should be remembered that there was then a spate

of such artists in postwar Europe, especially in Paris, where Communism reached its brief zenith among intellectuals. Today most of these artists have sunk into obscurity or begun to paint the abstract pictures they once thought idle and useless. From the very beginning art has had its own standards of validity and very few painters or sculptors have been able to survive without them.

One thing the Museum's show made crystal clear, I think: that Balthus in his best recent works had become a technical master. In doing so he had naturally sacrificed some of the penetrating crudeness of his early paintings and drawings. But the fire of his solitary temperament still burns through and it is perhaps no accident that he is one of the few younger painters about whom the great Picasso talks with fervor and puzzled admiration. Balthus is a maverick in an era of schools of painting. I find this fact both courageous and a relief. He has had his imitators, of course, as the strong always do. He has had no true rival in diverting art back to paths which once seemed deserted dead ends but on which he found signs of new life and authority.

"Juan Gris"

A number of monographs on modern artists I've written for The Museum of Modern Art have sold out slowly or been reprinted. This is not true of the book I did to accompany the Museum's exhibition of Juan Gris [that] I directed in 1958.[151] I think I still owe the Museum some advance royalties on the book, though I dismiss the Museum's reminders with unpardonable rudeness. The situation still puzzles me. I know that I wrote the Gris monograph with far more enthusiasm that I did the book on Rouault which has gone through several editions. I console myself with the thought that it's far harder to write about ice than fire, though I know that neither word describes adequately the work or temperament of either artist.

. . . It's never true, of course, that everyone is titled to his own opinion, at least where art is concerned. But for me the greatest pictures by Gris are his early, cubist paintings and the totally magnificent collages he did in 1913–14. Since I also prefer early pictures by de Chirico and Rouault to their later works, I suppose this qualifies me as an ambulance chaser of the worst kind, ready to embalm patients before they even get to the hospital. Nevertheless, I go on believing that the creative span of many twentieth-century artists has been unusually short, though I realize that the careers of Matisse, Picasso, Brancusi, and others make my theory seem absurd. For the Romantics, early death solved the problem of sustaining genius over a long period of time. . . . I [do] think [that] many artists go on working long after their point has been made and that only a few add significantly to what they've already said. . . .

"Jean Arp: A Retrospective"

[T]he success of Jean Arp's exhibition[152] in The Museum of Modern Art [in] 1958 was in good measure the result of [Museum Director] René d'Harnoncourt's superb installations.[153] I myself had little to do except write a foreword to the catalogue, which had articles by Arp himself, by his old colleague in the Dada movement, Dr. Richard Huelsenbeck, by the English critic Robert Melville, and by Carola Giedion-Welcker, whose [1958] monograph is a key work on Arp's career. In research for the show I had skilled help from Sam Hunter, then the Department of Painting and Sculpture's Associate Curator, and from Alicia Legg, to my mind one of the absolute

heroines of the Museum's long and at times troubled history.[153]

Arp was accompanied on his trip to America by his extremely efficient secretary, Marguerite Hagenbach, who became his wife soon after their return to Europe. Both Jean and Marguerite Arp came out to visit us in New Canaan, and it was an immense pleasure to be with them. Arp talked so learnedly and gently that it was hard to remember that he had once been a central figure in what remains one of the most violent and subversive movements our century's art has produced. . . .

"Joan Miró"

In 1959, The Museum of Modern Art decided to hold a second large . . . Miró exhibition,[154] and William S. Lieberman and I were appointed codirectors of the show, Bill being at that time Curator of the Museum's Department of Drawings and Prints. The exhibition was a joy to do from beginning to end, except that it was difficult to get Ernest Hemingway's famous early Miró, *The Farm,* out of Castro's Cuba a few days after the revolution [in 1958]. Hemingway was then living in the small Idaho town called Ketchum, a few miles from the elaborate ski resort "Sun Valley." I knew Ketchum well, having been divorced once in Idaho,[164] and I could understand why Hemingway was fond of the surrounding countryside, where fishing and hunting were excellent.

Jean Arp holding the bucket of the Calder mobile in the yard of Soby's house in New Canaan, 1958

Hemingway agreed at once to the loan of *The Farm* but warned me that it would need drastic restoration because it had hung for years in his farmhouse outside Havana, where the dampness was extreme. He was also worried that the authorities of Castro's new government might not allow the picture to leave the country and he asked me to phone him in Ketchum every evening at precisely 7:00 P.M. to let him know what progress I was making. I did so faithfully for about ten days and I was then able to tell him that David Vance [the Museum's Assistant Registrar] . . . was flying to Cuba and had reserved several seats on the return flight so that he could keep the picture near him. Hemingway was delighted, could not have been more cordial during our many phone conversations and told me repeatedly that he didn't care what the restoration costs were, since *The Farm* was his favorite modern picture and had been ever since he won the right to buy it in a crap game with the American writer . . . Evan Shipman.

So far everyone concerned was happy. But when David Vance got on the plane to bring the picture to New York, Castro's police roared onto the field just before take-off, insisted on having *The Farm* unpacked for inspection and finally decided to let . . . Vance depart with the picture safely aboard.[155]

The moment the painting arrived at the Museum, . . . Jean Volkmer, the Museum's able restorer, began working on the canvas.[156] It was a long and difficult job, not only because of the damage from Cuba's tropical weather but because the wooden stretchers were riddled with termites. Jean . . . worked like a slave on the picture for months.

"René Magritte"[157]

Of modern artists whom I misjudged badly in my youth, the one about whom I feel the most repentant is . . . René Magritte. I wrote of him in my first book on art, *After Picasso,* that his paintings "wear thin, like puns too often repeated."[158] I don't understand how I could have been so wrong, since the early 1930s were perhaps the hey-

day of double imagery, that is, imagery wherein a second identity is disguised and left to the observer to discover, as in certain puzzle books for children.

There was nevertheless a fundamental difference between Magritte's dislocation of surface logic and that of the other artists who were fond of ambivalent images. I suppose that the simplest way to explain the difference is that Magritte himself did all the searching for a second meaning in his paintings and stated this meaning clearly and without disguise. For example, he would paint a street scene which to all reasonable intents and purposes should appear in daylight. And then after a moment one realizes with a shock that the sky is that of night and the windows in the houses artificially lighted. He tells bluntly the changed story which sometimes underlies casual observation. In so doing, he suggests a counterlogic which haunts our imagination long after the usual double image has spent its force. His best paintings are the very essence of magic. No one knows precisely how they are done, though technical virtuosity plays a far larger role than I used to think.

•

What impressed me most in working on the Magritte show was the artist's control of the medium. He was not a flashy technician, as Dali had always been. But when he needed to, he could vary his bland surfaces with a rich impasto whose skillful application must be studied closely to make itself apparent. Like Tanguy his career as a painter took its start from a painting by de Chirico—*The Song of Love* (1914)—which he knew only from a reproduction.[159] And like de Chirico he was capable of using both deadpan and richly encrusted passages. I think, for example, that no one can peer for long at his famous *Philosophy in the Boudoir* (1947) without realizing that its sensuality is not a matter of subject-matter alone.[160] The live breasts of the woman stare out from her nightgown on a hanger with the intensity which once frightened Percy Bysshe Shelley on staring at his wife, similarly clothed. And then one realizes how beautifully painted are her shoes on the table before which she stands and how inevitable it is that her toes should protrude from them naked, thus complementing the double-entendre between live model and the hanger on which her nightclothes rest.

There is a final point of originality to be made about Magritte's art. When Dali's giraffes with flaming manes first appeared [in 1937], their outrage to logic was widely hailed in Surrealist circles. Yet as early as 1933, Magritte in several paintings had set fire to a number of supposedly inflammable objects such as metal musical instruments and presented them as though this were an everyday occurrence.[161]

It's not very often on completing an exhibition such as [*René Magritte*] . . . that one wished to see a *catalogue raisonné*. I'm convinced that in Magritte's case such a book would establish him as a central, rather than a peripheral, figure in Surrealist art as a whole. He was a conservative man personally and disliked fanfare. I'd bet that a far more decisive force—the judgment of time—will work on his side.

Notes

For research assistance in the preparation of these notes I wish to acknowledge the thoroughness of my assistant, Leslie Heitzman; the efficiency of Janet Crowley and Rachel Wild; and the kindness of my editor, Barbara Ross. I appreciate the willingness of Nicholas Fox Weber, Director of the Josef and Anni Albers Foundation, and Ann Brandwein and Eugene R. Gaddis of the Wadsworth Atheneum Archives to share their knowledge of cultural activities of the Hartford art community in the 1920s and 1930s.

The designation *MoMA Archives* refers to The Museum of Modern Art Archives, New York; the James Thrall Soby Papers and Alfred H. Barr, Jr., Papers, housed in the Archives, are cited below as *Soby Papers* and *Barr Papers*, respectively. *Bibliog.* indicates the complete bibliography of Soby's published writings that follows on pp. 230–51.

1. Dominic Bevan Lewis, *François Villon: A Documentary Survey* (New York: The Literary Guild of America, 1928).
2. A. Everett Austin, Jr. (1900–1957), was Director of the Wadsworth Atheneum, Hartford, from 1927 to 1944.
3. See n. 4, p. 181.
4. Respectively, "Five Young French Painters" (Christian Bérard, Kristians Tonny, Pavel Tchelitchew, Eugene Berman, and Léonid), April 15–May 16, 1931; and "Newer Super-Realism" (see n. 6, p. 181).
5. See n. 7, p. 181.
6. Paul Whitman Cooley (1907–1974) was a lifelong resident of the Hartford area. He worked as a volunteer assistant to Chick Austin at the Wadsworth Atheneum in 1933 and in 1939 became the owner of the Moyer Gallery in Hartford, specializing in nineteenth-century American paintings and antiques; he also admired modern art and dance. Cooley became a trustee of the Atheneum in 1947 and was an honorary trustee at the time of his death.
7. See n. 9, p. 181.
8. Jere Abbott (1897–1982) was Associate Director of The Museum of Modern Art from 1929 to 1932 and Director of the Smith College Museum of Art, Northampton, Massachusetts, from 1932 to 1946. For the connection between Austin and Abbot, see n. 7, p. 181. Barr and Abbott met in the fall of 1925 at Princeton University, where they were both doing graduate work; see Rona Roob, "Alfred H. Barr, Jr.: A Chronicle of the Years 1902–1929," and Margaret Scolari Barr, "Our Campaigns," in *The New Criterion*, Special Issue (Summer 1987), pp. 7, 10, 12, 14–16, 19, 24, 28.
9. Agnes Rindge (1900–1977) was a professor of art at Vassar College, Poughkeepsie, New York, and an art historian. In 1942, as a member of the Sub-Committee of the Museum's Advisory Committee, she was chosen to review the experimental Educational Project; she was appointed Assistant Executive Vice-President in charge of educational matters the following year; a position she held until June 1943.

John McAndrew (1904–1978) was associated with the Julien Levy Gallery, New York, and Vassar College before serving as Curator in the Museum's Department of Architecture and Industrial Art (after 1940, the Department of Architecture) from 1937 to 1941. During this time he organized and installed the Museum's architecture exhibitions and worked with Barr on other departments' shows; from 1937 to 1939 he represented the Museum as its consultant on the Goodwin/Stone Museum building and was, with Barr, responsible for the design of the first Museum sculpture garden in 1939. He resigned from the Museum in 1941.
10. At the recommendation of Philip Johnson, Iris Barry (1895–1969) was appointed Museum Librarian in August 1933; in July 1935, she helped to establish the Museum's Film Library, of which she was curator until 1946 and Director from 1946 until her retirement in 1951. For Barry's involvement in the development of the Museum's film acquisition and exhibition programs, see Mary Lea Bandy, "Nothing Sacred: 'Jock Whitney Snares Antiques for Museum.' The Founding of the Museum of Modern Art Film Library," pp. 74–103 of the present volume.
11. John E. ("Dick") Abbott (1908–1952) was Director of the Museum's Film Library from 1935 to 1946, Executive Vice-President of the Museum from 1939 until 1943, Museum Secretary from 1946 until his resignation in 1948, and a member of the Board of Trustees from 1940 until his death. In the 1940s, he also served on the Coordination, Executive, and Exhibitions committees.
12. Charles de Noailles had seen Buñuel's *Un Chien andalou* and wanted to help finance the director's next Surrealist film. The day after *L'Age d'or* had its first public showing at the Panthéon theater in Paris, de Noailles was expelled from the Jockey Club, and he later narrowly avoided excommunication (his mother apparently interceded with the Pope on his behalf). The subsequent six-day showing of the film led to a riot at the theater and the censorship of the film. See Luis Buñuel, *My Last Sigh* (New York: Alfred A. Knopf, 1983), pp. 118–19.
13. Buñuel had returned to the United States in 1938. In New York he met his old friend Iris Barry, who offered to help him get a job on Nelson A. Rockefeller's propaganda film committee. Awaiting government authorization for his appointment to the committee, Buñuel edited two German propaganda films that were smuggled into this country by the first secretary in the German Embassy and widely shown, particularly to senators and consulates. He subsequently was offered a position as editor-in-chief at the Museum, selecting anti-Nazi propaganda films and arranging their distribution in North and South America, as well as producing two propaganda films. See ibid, pp. 179–82.
14. This was the first retrospective of the artist's work held in the United States; see n. 6, p. 181. In the exhibition catalogue (*Pablo Picasso* [Hartford: Wadsworth Atheneum, 1934]), Soby's "important share" in its preparation is acknowledged; however, he is not listed as its author.
15. The Julien Levy Gallery opened at 602 Madison Avenue in 1931. It was relocated to 15 East Fifty-seventh Street in 1937, 11 East Fifty-seventh Street in 1942, and 42 East Fifty-seventh Street in 1943, where it remained in operation until April 1949. The "Newer Super-Realism" exhibition at the Wadsworth Atheneum included works by the following Levy Gallery artists: Giorgio de Chirico, Salvador Dali, Max Ernst, Pablo Picasso, Pierre Roy, and Léopold Survage.
16. In a 1979 interview, Bacon said, "I always feel I've been influenced by Eliot. *The Waste Land*, especially, and the poems before it have always affected me very much. . ." (quoted in David Sylvester, *The Brutality of Fact: Interviews with Francis Bacon*, 3rd ed. [London: Thames and Hudson, 1987], p. 152). Bacon's most famous Eliot-inspired painting is *Triptych Inspired by T. S. Eliot's Poem "Sweeney Agonistes"* (1967; Hirshhorn Museum and Sculpture Garden, Smithsonian Institution, Washington, D.C.); in 1982, he painted *A Piece of Waste Land* (private collection). See also Rolf Laessoe, "Francis Bacon and T. S. Eliot," *Hafnia: Copenhagen Papers in the History of Art* 9 (1983), pp. 113–30.
17. In December 1933, Alexandre Stavisky, a Russian émigré involved in the floating of a fraudulent bond issue in Bayonne, fled to escape arrest and, when cornered by authorities, was alleged to have committed suicide. Royalists and fascists stirred up an agitation against the French Republic, echoing the Dreyfus case. It was believed that government officials and politicians were involved and that their guilt was being concealed; the full facts were never made know. In February 1934, serious riots erupted in Paris and other cities throughout France as a result of the "Stavisky case."
18. In addition to their interest in the ballet, Lincoln Kirstein (1907–1996) and his Harvard classmate Edward M.M. Warburg (1908–1992) were early, active participants in The Museum of Modern Art. In April 1930, they were among those young people who were invited by the Museum's Board of Trustees to form a Junior Advisory Committee, the purpose of which was to propose new ideas and provide fresh viewpoints on Museum exhibitions and policies.

In 1932, Kirstein directed the first Museum show to include photographs ("Murals by American Painters and Photographers," MoMA Exh. #16), and in 1933, the first one-man photography exhibition organized by the Modern ("Walker Evans: Photographs of 19th Century Houses," MoMA Exh. #30f). In 1939, he established the Museum Dance Archives (now part of Lincoln Center for the Performing Arts, in New York), and from 1941 until 1943 he was the Museum's consultant on Latin American art.

Warburg was elected a trustee of the Museum in 1932 and an honorary trustee in 1958; he resigned from the board in November 1986. A co-organizer of the Museum's Film Library, he also

served on the Museum's Acquisitions Committee from 1934 to 1936 and again from 1939 to 1942, and on the Policy Committee for the Permanent Collection of Masterworks from 1953 to 1967.

19. As part of the Paris season of the Ballets 1933 at the Théâtre du Champs Elysées, Tchelitchew designed the sets for Balanchine's "Errante" and Bérard the sets for the choreographer's "Mozartiana."

20. See n. 9, p. 181.

21. Beginning in the summer of 1933, Calder (1898–1976) and his wife Louisa (b. 1905) lived in nearby Roxbury, Connecticut.

22. The five dining-room panels were given by Soby to the Wadsworth Atheneum in memory of his father in 1954.

23. Christopher Tunnard (1911–1979), the modernist landscape designer who advocated the use of modern sculpture in gardens, came to the United States from England in 1939 to teach at Harvard's Graduate School of Design, where Walter Gropius had been made dean and where Philip Johnson was in the second year of his academic architectural training; in the 1940s and early 1950s, he taught at Yale University.

24. The Friends and Enemies of Modern Music, Inc. (FEMM), was organized by Chick Austin as a subscription society to introduce contemporary music to Hartford through concerts held in private houses. When the Avery Memorial wing of the Wadsworth Atheneum opened in February 1934, FEMM moved its concerts there and enlarged its scope to include operas and ballets. See Virgil Thomson, "The Friends and Enemies of Modern Music," in *A. Everett Austin, Jr.: A Director's Taste and Achievement* (Hartford, Conn.: Wadsworth Atheneum, 1958), pp. 59–60.

Many forms of contemporary music were represented in the Festival, which included several first performances of musical and ballet works and the showing of early film masterpieces, the latter supplied by the Film Library of The Museum of Modern Art. The Paper Ball, the highlight of the Festival, was a grand procession of 250 people dressed in paper costumes designed by Tchelitchew, Calder, Berman, and students at the Hartford Art School, among others. Tchelitchew decorated the entire court of the Avery Memorial with designs made of newspaper. For "A Nightmare Side Show," the section of the procession in which the Sobys participated, the costumes were designed by Calder "at incredible speed. . . . Sandy had brought with him only huge sheets of brown wrapping paper, staplers, scissors, needles and strong thread. Yet it seemed to me that at one moment I looked around at old friends, at the next to see the house swarming with tigers, elephants and other jungle beasts" (Soby memoir, 7–5). Pierre and Alexina Matisse, the Calders, Kirk Askew, and Henry-Russell Hitchcock were all members of the Soby "menagerie."

25. "Early Masterpieces of Cinematographic Art," shown Sunday, February 9, 1936.

26. *Entr'acte* was originally commissioned by Rolf de Maré to serve as an intermission (entr'acte) for the Ballets Suédeis at the Théâtre du Champs Elysées in Paris. Picabia, Satie, Marcel Duchamp, Man Ray, and Georges Auric, among others, performed in the 22-minute film.

27. See n. 5, p. 181.

28. Austin exhibited works from Soby's collection at the Wadsworth Atheneum on two occasions: "Contemporary Paintings," November 16–30, 1930; and "Modern Paintings and Drawings," in June 1931.

29. See n. 5, p. 181. In the Barnes/Matisse literature, Dr. Barnes refers to this work only in connection with other pictures and does not single it out as "a top Matisse of its period." As Barnes's prose style is usually formal and staid, it is possible that Soby was paraphrasing a remark made by Barnes.

30. Alfred H. Barr, Jr., *Picasso: Forty Years of His Art* (New York: The Museum of Modern Art, 1939), p. 134.

31. The larger of the two sculptures, *Leda* (ca. 1902), 11⅛" (28.3 cm) high, entered the Museum Collection as part of the Soby Bequest in 1979; see App. 24. *Woman Arranging Her Hair* (ca. 1898), 10¾" (27.3 cm) high, was also bequeathed to the Museum, but, following the terms of Soby's will, is now in the collection of the Wadsworth Atheneum; see Bibliog. 56, p. 51.

32. According to Andrea Farrington of the Pierre Matisse Foundation, it is probable that Soby is referring here to Matisse's *Jeune Femme jouant du violon devant la fenêtre ouverte* of 1923, now in the collection of the National Gallery of Art, Washington, D.C.

33. The Lehmbruck *Torso* appears in a photograph of Mies van der Rohe's Ernst and Grete Tugendhat House in Brno, completed in 1930 (see illus. below). The sculpture had already been used by Mies and Lilly Reich in their "Living Area of Plated Glass," an exhibit in the 1927 Werkbund exhibition "The Dwelling" in Stuttgart (courtesy Pierre Adler, Mies van der Rohe Archives, The Museum of Modern Art). It is unclear whether Soby's *Torso*, formerly in the collection of Dr. Gottlieb Reber of Lausanne and acquired by Soby in 1933, is the same as that photographed in the Tugendhat House in 1930. The 1961 catalogue of the Soby collection refers to three versions: Soby's cast-stone version, which in 1933 belonged to the Marie Harriman Gallery in New York; a bronze version in the Lehmbruck Museum in Duisburg; and a smaller cast-stone model (location unknown). See Bibliog. 56, p. 51.

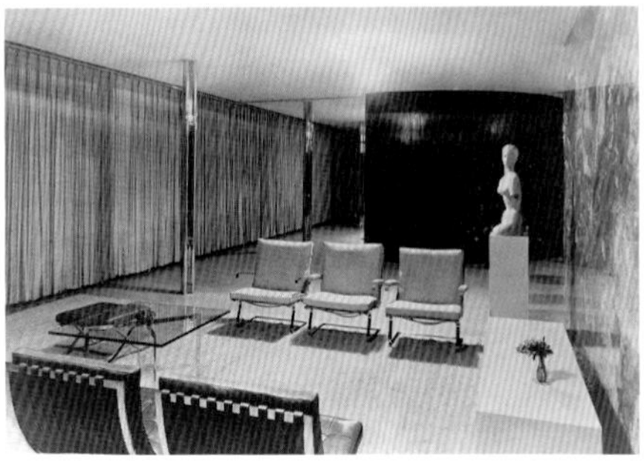

The living room of the Tugendhat House, Brno, Czechoslovakia, 1930. Lehmbruck's *Torso* is at far right.

34. *Nude Seated on a Rock*, purchased by Soby in 1935, entered the Museum Collection in 1979 as part of the Soby Bequest; see App. 31. *Nude* (1922), oil on wood, 7½ x 5½" (19 x 14 cm), was purchased by the Wadsworth Atheneum.

35. "Joan Miró, 1933–1934," Pierre Matisse Gallery, January 10–February 9, 1935.

36. See Bibliog. 4.

37. See Bibliog. 7.

38. The defaced photograph of de Chirico's *Orestes and Electra* (1923; private collection) was published in *La Révolution Surréaliste*, no. 6 (March 1, 1926), p. 32.

39. The Pierre Matisse Gallery held its first de Chirico show November 19–December 21, 1935, followed by exhibitions in 1940, 1941, and 1943.

40. Giorgio de Chirico, *The Sacred Fish*. 1919. Oil on canvas, 29½ x 24⅜" (74.9 x 61.9 cm). The Museum of Modern Art, New York. Acquired through the Lillie P. Bliss Bequest, 1949.

41. *Woman Putting on Her Gloves* (1974–75) was purchased from the Wildenstein Gallery in 1931. Soby resold the work to Wildenstein in 1936.

42. In the period 1931–49, the Julien Levy Gallery exhibited both Surrealist and neo-Romantic works by Bérard, Berman, de Chirico, Jean Cocteau, Joseph Cornell, Dali, Duchamp, Max Ernst, Leonore Fini, Léonid, René Magritte, Man Ray, Matta, Joan Miró, Richard Oelze, Picasso, Roy, Yves Tanguy, and Tonny; see Julien Levy, *Memoir of an Art Gallery* (New York: G. P. Putnam and Sons, 1977), pp. 296–312. The Durlacher Gallery only began to show modern art in the mid 1940s.

43. Soby is referring here to André Breton's *Manifesto of Surrealism* (1924) and *Second Manifesto of Surrealism* (1930).

44. Peter Blume. *The Eternal City*. 1934–37; dated on painting 1937. Oil on composition board, 34 x 47⅞" (86.4 x 121.6 cm). The Museum of Modern Art, New York. Mrs. Simon Guggenheim Fund, 1942.

45. Dorothy C. Miller is perhaps best known for a series of six exhibitions, held between 1942 and 1963, in which she introduced contemporary American artists to the Museum public in an original format. Unlike the usual large group show, Miller limited the number of artists, representing each by a body of work installed in a separate small gallery. Miller was receptive to new styles and trends in art, and stylistic diversity was an important feature of her "Americans" exhibitions.

Miller has been associated with the Museum in various capacities since she joined the staff in October 1934 as Assistant to the Director. In the Department of Painting and Sculpture, she served as Assistant Curator, from 1935 to 1941; Associate Curator, from 1941 to 1943; and Curator, from 1943 to 1947. As Curator of Museum Collections from

1947 to 1967, she worked closely with Barr to expand the Museum's holdings. She held the title of Senior Curator from 1968 until her retirement in June 1969. In March 1984, Miller was elected an honorary trustee of the Museum, and continues to serve the Museum in that capacity.

46. See n. 39 above; the second de Chirico exhibition was held at the gallery October 22–November 23, 1940.

47. See Bibliog. 7 and 37.

48. Giorgio de Chirico. *Gare Montparnasse (The Melancholy of Departure).* 1914. Oil on canvas, 55⅛" x 6' ⅝" (140 x 184.5 cm). The Museum of Modern Art, New York. Gift of James Thrall Soby, 1969.

49. The two paintings to which Soby refers are *The Soothsayer's Recompense* (1913; The Philadelphia Museum of Art, Louise and Walter Arensberg Collection) and *Ariadne* (1913; The Metropolitan Museum of Art, New York).

50. De Chirico was stationed in Ferrara as a soldier in the 27th Infantry Regiment from 1915 to 1917; he continued to paint while in the army and took advantage of the relative quiet of a nearby convalescent home to work on his metaphysical paintings.

51. Giorgio de Chirico. *The Double Dream of Spring.* 1915. Oil on canvas, 22⅛ x 21⅜ (56.2 x 54.3 cm). The Museum of Modern Art, New York. Gift of James Thrall Soby, 1957. (Illus. above.)

52. In addition to *The Double Dream of Spring,* Soby donated to the Museum his two other paintings from the mannequin series, *The Duo* and *The Seer,* both of 1915; see App. 11 and 12. *The Double Dream of Spring* is a companion piece to these paintings.

53. Ernst and Guggenheim were married in 1941 and divorced in 1943. (Ernst had met Dorothea Tanning in December 1942; they married in 1946.)

54. See Bibliog. 56, p. 43.

55. Joseph Cornell. *Taglioni's Jewel Casket.* 1940. Wood box containing glass ice cubes, jewelry, etc., 4¾ x 11⅞ x 8¼" (12 x 30.2 x 21 cm). The Museum of Modern Art, New York. Gift of James Thrall Soby, 1953.

56. Gordon Onslow-Ford (b. 1912), an English painter, met André Breton in 1938 and was among the last painters to join the Surrealist group. In 1940, he fled Paris for New York, where he gave a series of lectures on Surrealism at the New School for Social Research. He collected paintings by de Chirico, as mentioned in a letter to Soby of October 29, 1940 (MoMA Archives: Soby Papers, App. III.B.1.C). Onslow-Ford moved permanently to the United States in 1947, becoming an American citizen in 1952; he currently lives and paints in Northern California.

57. See Bibliog. 40, p. 18.

58. James Johnson Sweeney (1900–1986) served as Director of the Department of Painting and Sculpture at the Museum from January 1945 until his resignation in September 1946. He became associated with the Modern in the early 1930s as a member of the Junior Advisory Committee, and subsequently directed and wrote the catalogues for numerous Museum exhibitions; they include *African Negro Art* (1935), *Joan Miró* (1941), *Paul Klee* (1941), *Alexander Calder* (1943), *Stuart Davis* (1945), and *Mondrian* (1945).

59. See Bibliog. 8.

60. Joan Miró. *Still Life with Old Shoe.* 1937. Oil on canvas, 32 x 46" (81.3 x 116.8 cm). The Museum of Modern Art, New York. Gift of James Thrall Soby, 1969. (Illus. above.)

61. Sweeney wrote: "This strange isolated work was perhaps an unconscious token of his sympathy for the poverty and suffering so acute at this period in the world of his boyhood. But if his conscience was in the effort, certainly his heart was not" (James Johnson Sweeney, *Joan Miró* [New York: The Museum of Modern Art, 1941]), p. 68.

62. The "woman painter" was Mrs. Earle C. Miller, of Downington, Pennsylvania.

63. Miró began work on *Self-Portrait, I* in mid-October 1937 in an apartment at 98, boulevard Auguste Blanqui, Paris, where he used one room as a studio; the painting was completed in late March 1938. See Anne Umland, compiler, "Chronology," in Carolyn Lanchner, *Joan Miró* (New York: The Museum of Modern Art, 1993), entries for 1937 ("Before March 7") and 1938 ("Late March?"), p. 333.

64. Ibid., p. 358, n. 591.

65. See Salvador Dali, *The Secret Life of Salvador Dali,* trans. Haakon M. Chevalier (New York: Dial Press, 1942), pp. 371–76; and *Salvador Dali: Retrospective 1920–1980* (Paris: Centre Georges Pompidou, Musée National d'Art Moderne, 1980), vol. 2, *La Vie publique de Salvador Dali,* pp. 74–75.

66. Press reports and the artist's own published reminiscences indicate that it was an enraged Dali who, on March 17, 1939, deliberately overturned the bathtub, inundating the display area with water and breaking the plate-glass window. However, there is no mention of "reptiles" in the astrakhan-lined bathtub in the account published in the *Daily News* (New York), March 17, 1939, or in Dali's autobiography (see *The Secret Life of Salvador Dali,* pp. 372–75).

67. In his memoirs, Dali wrote that he declined being released immediately on bail and chose to remain in jail for a short time until the case was taken care of. See ibid., p. 375; and Levy, *Memoir of an Art Gallery,* pp. 197–99.

68. A Dali exhibition was scheduled five days later at the Julien Levy Gallery, March 21–April 1, 1939.

69. In reply to a query dated August 30, 1995, Kirstein stated that he no longer has a copy of this letter.

70. Soby is perhaps referring to *Composition, II* (1929), oil on canvas, 15⅞ x 12⅝" (40.3 x 30.1 cm), which was accepted by the Museum at its June 10, 1941, Acquisitions Committee Meeting as a gift of Philip Johnson.

71. Mondrian occupied his studio at 15 East Fifty-ninth Street from October 1943 until his death in February 1944.

72. Edna St. Vincent Millay, "Euclid alone has looked on Beauty bare" (1923).

73. The Art of This Century Gallery was located at 30 West Fifty-seventh Street, New York, from 1943 to 1947. Peggy Guggenheim began choosing juries to select works for her exhibitions after Herbert Read conceived the idea of holding a spring salon in London in 1939; in addition to Soby and Mondrian, Barr, Sweeney, Breton, Duchamp, Max Ernst, Jimmy Ernst, and Howard Putzel were among the jurors.

74. Barr delivered the eulogy at this memorial service on February 3, 1944; excerpts were published in "Memorial Service," *Knickerbocker Weekly* 51, no. 3 (February 1944), p. 23. According to *The New York Times,* February 4, 1944, Tony Elink Schurman, consul general of the Netherlands, also spoke, and "over two hundred artists, writers and art connoisseurs" attended (MoMA Archives: Public Information Scrapbooks, General L [MF39;419]). See Bibliog. 19.

75. See Bibliog. 43, pp. 3–4.

76. *Paul Strand* (MoMA Exh. #286, April 25–June 10, 1945) was organized by Nancy Newhall (1908–1974), at the time Acting Curator in the Department of Photography; see Newhall, *Paul Strand: Photographs, 1915–1945* (New York: The Museum of Modern Art, 1945).

77. See Bibliog. 165.

78. See Bibliog. 167 and 183.

79. See Bibliog. 70.
80. See Bibliog. 77 and 165.
81. See Peter Galassi, *Henri Cartier-Bresson: The Early Work* (New York: The Museum of Modern Art, 1987), p. 18.
82. Bibliog. 77, p. 33.
83. The Brummer Gallery was then located at 27 East Fifty-seventh Street. An exhibition of Brancusi's work organized by Marcel Duchamp was held there November 17–December 15, 1926.
84. Margit Rowell, Chief Curator of the Museum's Department of Drawings, has suggested that Soby is referring here to Brancusi's *Princess X* of 1915, a white marble column, 22" (55.9 cm) in height, now in the collection of the Sheldon Memorial Art Gallery, University of Nebraska, Lincoln; see *Constantin Brancusi: 1876–1957* (Paris: Centre Georges Pompidou, Musée National d'Art Moderne; Philadelphia: Philadelphia Museum of Art, 1995), p. 138.
85. Bibliog. 166, p. 50.
86. Constantin Brancusi. *La Colonne sans fin [The Endless Column]*. 1937. Gilt steel, 97' 6" (30 m) high. Brancusi began producing his "endless columns" in 1918; the Tîrgu Jiu column was commissioned in 1935 to commemorate the fallen heroes of World War I.
87. Quoted in Bibliog. 166, p. 50.
88. Constantin Brancusi. *Fish*. 1930. Gray marble, 21 x 71 x 5½" (53.3 x 180.3 x 14 cm); on three-part pedestal of marble, 5⅛" (13 cm) high, and two limestone cylinders, 13" (33 cm) and 11" (27.9 cm) high x 32⅛" (81.5 cm) diameter at widest point. The Museum of Modern Art, New York. Acquired through the Lillie P. Bliss Bequest, 1949.
89. Bibliog. 166, p. 51.
90. On Kay Sage, see Bibliog. 31, 52, 63, and 153. Soby was the executor of the Kay Sage Estate.
91. Barr and Soby accompanied Duchamp to the Naturalization Division of the Immigration and Naturalization Service on March 9, 1954, to file the petition for his final citizenship papers. Eighteen months later, having heard nothing, Barr prevailed upon Nelson Rockefeller to intercede on Duchamp's behalf, and citizenship was granted on December 30, 1955. See Barr/Rockefeller correspondence, especially letter of November 2, 1955, Barr to Rockefeller; MoMA Archives: Barr Papers, 1.273.
92. Alexina Sattler Matisse Duchamp (1906–1995), known as Teeny, was married to Pierre Matisse from 1929 until their divorce in 1949; they had three children, Paul, Jacqueline, and Peter. She was married to Marcel Duchamp from 1954 until his death in 1968.
93. Duchamp's *La Mariée mise á nu par ses célibataires, même* (1915–23) consists of oil, varnish, lead foil, lead wire and dust on glass panels, each mounted between two glass panels mounted within a wood-and-steel frame; it measures 109¼ x 69¼" (277.5 x 175.8 cm) overall. The work entered the collection of The Philadelphia Museum of Art in 1953 as part of the Katherine S. Dreier Bequest.
94. "Art in Progress: A Survey Prepared for the Fifteenth Anniversary of The Museum of Modern Art, New York," was a multidepartmental exhibition, and each section had its own director: "Painting and Sculpture" (May 24–October 15), was directed by Soby; "Design for Use" (May 24–October 22), by Serge Chermanyeff; "Built in U.S.A." (May 24–October 22), by Elizabeth Mock; "Dance and Theatre Design" (May 24–September 17), by George Amberg; "Posters" (May 24–September 17), by Monroe Wheeler; "Photography" (May 24–September 17), by Nancy Newhall; "Circulating Exhibitions" (May 24–September 24), by Elodie Courter; "Educational Services" (May 24–September 10), by Victor d'Amico; and "Film Library" (May 24–September 17), by Iris Barry. See also Bibliog. 13.
95. Guggenheim commissioned Pollock to paint *Mural*—the title given to the painting by Lee Krasner at the time it was executed in either December 1943 or early January 1944—for the first-floor entrance hall of the duplex apartment she then shared with the writer Kenneth McPherson at 155 East Sixty-first Street. Duchamp advised her that it be painted on canvas so that it could later be moved, and he supervised its installation. Executed in oil and measuring 7' 11¾" by 19' 9½" (243.2 by 603.3 cm), *Mural* was donated by Guggenheim to the University of Iowa Museum of Art, Iowa City, in 1948. See Peggy Guggenheim, *Out of This Century: Confessions of an Art Addict* (New York: Universe Books, 1979), pp. 295–96. See also Francis V. O'Connor and Eugene V. Thaw, eds., *Jackson Pollock: A Catalogue Raisonné of Paintings, Drawings and Other Works* (New Haven, Conn., and London: Yale University Press, 1978), cat. no. 102, pp. 94–96; and Robert Hobbs and Frederick Woodard, eds., *Human Rights/Human Wrongs: Art in Social Change* (Iowa City: University of Iowa Museum of Art, 1986), pp. 111–45.
96. "Corot, Daumier, Museum of Modern Art Eighth Loan Exhibition," was held at 730 Fifth Avenue, New York, October 15–November 23, 1930.
97. Curt Valentin (1902–1954) began his career as a dealer in modern art in Berlin, first working for himself and then, in 1934, joining Karl Buchholz's gallery in Hamburg. In 1937, Valentin emigrated to the United States, opening a gallery in New York called The Buchholz Gallery; in 1951, it became the Curt Valentin Gallery. In addition to being one of the foremost modern art dealers in New York, Valentin also published limited-edition books in which the writings of poets and novelists were illustrated by a contemporary artist. See Bibliog. 154.
98. Romeo Toninelli (d. 1979) of Milan was an industrialist, publisher, art dealer, and collector of twentieth-century Italian art in general and Futurist art in particular. When he visited the Museum in 1946, he found Italian painters of this century (with the exceptions of de Chirico and Modigliani, who were presented in connection with the French) almost totally ignored. He asked to speak with Monroe Wheeler, then Director of Exhibitions and Publications, and proposed a show of modern Italian art. A second meeting, involving Nelson Rockefeller (then President of the Museum), Barr, and Soby, ensued, and in the summer of 1948, the Barrs and the Sobys traveled to Italy to assemble the exhibition "XXth Century Italian Art" (MoMA Exh. #413; see Bibliog. 26).
99. See Bibliog. 26.
100. See p. 176.
101. In a letter of March 7, 1971, to Russell Lynes (then working on his book *Good Old Modern: An Intimate Portrait of the Museum of Modern Art* [New York: Atheneum, 1973]), Soby wrote: "Since Dick [John Abbott] is now dead, I can tell you that he and Frances Hawkins—a very bright but terribly neurotic woman—were in great part responsible for Alfred's temporary downfall. Yet Alfred would never hear a word against Dick, though he must have known that Dick and Hawkins were constantly bombarding him to Clark; I heard them do it a number of times and balled [sic] them out for it. It's true that Alfred and Monroe [Wheeler] didn't get along very well in the earlier years. . . ." MoMA Archives: Soby Papers, V.66a. Hawkins was appointed Acting Secretary of the Museum in March 1940 and was soon made Secretary; she resigned in January 1945, apparently because she did not like working with Stephen C. Clark (1882–1960), a founding trustee and chairman of the Museum's board from 1939 to 1946. (Clark, a member of the Acquisitions Committee—later the Committee on Museum Collections—throughout the 1940s, was also a core member of the Policy Committee for the Permanent Collection of Masterworks from 1953 to 1967; after resigning from the Museum's board, Clark became increasingly active at The Metropolitan Museum of Art, a major beneficiary of his important collection.) For a description of Abbott's activities at the Museum, see n. 11 above.
102. See Bibliog. 11.
103. For critiques of the exhibition, see MoMA Archives: Public Information Scrapbooks, 46A [MF13; 96].
104. See Bibliog. 12.
105. Frank Crowninshield (1872–1947), editor of *Vanity Fair*, was a founding trustee of the Museum, serving from October 1929 until May 1935; he was elected an honorary trustee in 1935, a position he held until his death in 1947. See Geoffrey T. Hellman, "Profiles: Last of the Species [Frank Crowninshield]," *The New Yorker* 18, no. 31 (September 19, 1942), pp. 22–33; 18, no. 32 (September 26, 1942), pp. 24–31.
106. "As a result of the sale, Lewisohn would in time change his will and bequeath his paintings to the Metropolitan Museum, where they now hang in the André Meyer Gallery" (Margaret Scolari Barr, op. cit., p. 73).
107. Olga Hirsch Guggenheim (1877–1970) became associated with The Museum of Modern Art on December 6, 1937, when she donated the funds for the Museum's purchase of Picasso's *Girl Before a Mirror* (1932). As Margaret Scolari Barr wrote, this was "the first pearl in the brilliant neck-

lace of gifts that bear her name" (ibid., p. 50). In October 1940, Mrs. Guggenheim became a trustee of the Museum and a member of its Acquisitions Committee, and in 1941 she established the Mrs. Simon Guggenheim Fund, to be used for the purchase of "masterworks." (The Museum's first—and unrestricted—purchase fund was the Mrs. John D. Rockefeller, Jr. Purchase Fund, established in January 1938 by Abby Aldrich Rockefeller and Nelson Rockefeller.)

108. Edward Hopper. *Gas.* 1940. Oil on canvas, 32¼ x 40⅛" (81.9 x 101.9 cm). The Museum of Modern Art, New York. Mrs. Simon Guggenheim Fund, 1943.

109. Soby became familiar with Morandi's work while assembling the exhibition "Twentieth Century Italian Art" with Alfred Barr in 1948. Though Soby once dismissed Morandi as a painter of "limited iconography" (Soby memoir, 21–1), he later realized "that Morandi was not simply a painter of bottles and occasional landscapes but a man intent on exploring subtle equations of forms, placing, and atmospheric effects. It was as though he, like Chardin, had found the external world hopelessly convoluted and had preferred to stare endlessly at simple objects on a studio table, separating their volumes and color and then interlocking them again through an alchemy he alone understood" (ibid., 21–2).

110. The plans and model for The New Theatre designed by Wright were exhibited at the Wadsworth Atheneum January 26–February 27, 1949; see exhibition pamphlet, MoMA Archives: Soby Papers, V.66a.

111. Helen Austin (1898–1986) had a direct connection with the Museum in that her brother, Philip Lippincott Goodwin (1885–1958), was the Museum's first architect. Goodwin was elected to the board in 1934 and served as its Vice Chairman from 1946 to 1950. He was Chairman of the Department of Architecture from 1940 to 1948 and a member of the Committee on the Museum Collections from 1937 to 1939 and again from 1950 to 1958.

112. Soby and Thomas Hepburn, elder brother of the actress Katharine, were good friends at the Kingswood School in Hartford; Soby knew the entire Hepburn family, who moved to Hartford in 1905.

113. See Bibliog. 39.

114. Georges Clemenceau (1841–1929), former Premier of France and longtime friend of Monet, was present at the official opening of the artist's *Grandes Décorations (Water Lilies)* at the Orangerie on May 17, 1926.

115. Sheldon Keck (1910–1993) and his wife Caroline (b. 1908) were pioneers in the art and science of painting conservation. They worked as consulting conservators to The Museum of Modern Art and many other institutions during their careers, in addition to lecturing and writing on conservation issues.

116. Porter McCray (b. 1908) was Director of Circulating Exhibitions at the Museum from 1947 through 1950; after a brief leave of absence, he was appointed the first director of the Museum's International Program, serving from 1952 to 1961. He was a member of the Board of Trustees from 1957 to 1966, and continues his association with the Museum as an honorary member of The International Council.

117. Claude Monet. *Water Lilies (Les Nymphéas).* ca. 1925. Oil on canvas, 6' 6¾" x 18' 5½" (200 x 562.5 cm). The Museum of Modern Art, New York. Mrs. Simon Guggenheim Fund.

Monet's *Water Lilies* was purchased by the Museum from Michel Monet, the artist's son, in April 1955 and was destroyed in the fire in the Museum galleries on April 15, 1958. Barr decided to replace the painting with another Monet of similar size. Miller contacted the Paris art dealer Katia Granoff, from whom Barr purchased the triptych that now hangs in the Museum galleries. See Rona Roob, "From the Archives: Fire and Water Lilies," *Museum of Modern Art Members Quarterly,* no. 7 (Spring 1991), pp. 24–25.

118. Claude Monet. *Nymphéas.* ca. 1920–26. Oil on canvas, 80½" x 7' 4" (204.4 x 602.6 cm). Walter P. Chrysler, Jr., purchased the work from Sorel Roussel in 1954.

119. Salvador Dali, "De la Beauté terrifiante et comestible, de l'architecture modern style," *Minotaure* 3–4; Editions Albert Skira; 69–76.

120. The exhibition was titled "Modern Architecture: International Exhibition" (MoMA Exh. #15, February 9–March 23, 1932) and was accompanied by a book of the same title; see Alfred H. Barr, Jr., Henry-Russell Hitchcock, and Philip Johnson, *Modern Architecture: International Exhibition* (New York: The Museum of Modern Art, 1932).

121. Le Corbusier, *Gaudí* (Barcelona: Editorial R. M., 1958).

122. Soby is referring here to L'Unité d'Habitation (built 1947–52), located on the avenue Michelet, Marseilles.

123. Fernand Léger. *Le Petit Déjeuner [The Breakfast].* Before 1935. Oil on canvas, 36¼ x 27½" (92 x 65 cm). Musée National d'Art Moderne, Centre Georges Pompidou, Paris.

124. Fernand Léger. *Three Musicians.* 1944 (after a drawing of 1924–25; dated on canvas 24–44). Oil on canvas, 68½ x 57¼" (174 x 145.4 cm). The Museum of Modern Art, New York. Mrs. Simon Guggenheim Fund, 1955.

125. The exhibition "Fernand Léger: Paintings and Drawings" (MoMA Exh. #42a) was held in New York from September 30 to October 24, 1935; it is probable that Léger, who attended the exhibition, later traveled to Hartford to visit the Atheneum's "Abstract Art" exhibition, which ran from October 22 to November 17, 1935. On December 7, 1935, *The Hartford Courant* published a photograph of Léger with Alexander and Louisa Calder in the Atheneum galleries; he is not, however, listed as a participant in the Hartford Festival program.

126. Balthus. *Joan Miró and His Daughter Dolores.* 1937–38. Oil on canvas, 51¼ x 35" (130.2 x 88.9 cm). The Museum of Modern Art, New York. Abby Aldrich Rockefeller Fund, 1938.

127. The exhibition was held at the Galerie Beaux-Arts, Paris, in March 1956. Soby's letter to Balthus of October 28, 1955, indicates that it was Soby who offered the painting for the Paris show: "Pierre [Matisse] tells me that you are having a retrospective exhibition in Paris this winter. If you would like to have *La Rue* in the exhibition, by all means do so. . . ." MoMA Archives: Soby Papers, IV.C.1.

128. Concerned that the French Customs officials would not permit the reentry of *La Rue* into France, Soby asked the conservators Sheldon and Caroline Keck to advise him as to methods of camouflage. They overpainted the offending area with watercolor, so that it could be easily and safely removed by Balthus when the painting reached France. Pierre Matisse acted as intermediary between Soby and the artist, arranging for the painting to be sent from Paris "to Chassy where Balthus plans to operate on the offending parts! T[o] tell you the truth he does not quite know how he is going to do it and it will probably require quite a bit of thought" (letter, Pierre Matisse to Soby, June 21, 1956; MoMA Archives: Soby Papers, I.7.2).

On June 20, 1956, Balthus wrote to Soby, "It was a strange feeling, after so many years, to see this picture again which I painted when I was little over twenty. I succeeded only in the last few days to change the objectionable gesture of the boy—a rather difficult affair, the whole picture having been built up mathematically. As I told P.M. [Pierre Matisse] I accepted to reconsider the matter as I do not think—and never thought—that the real interest, if any, was residing *there.* It was rather done in a mood of youthful desire to provoke, at a time one still believed in scandal. Today scandal is just worn out as an old shoe." Soby was thoroughly pleased with the changes made, writing to Balthus on August 20, 1956, "I am everlastingly grateful for your repairs on *La Rue.* I know it must have been a struggle and I greatly appreciate it." MoMA Archives: Soby Papers, I.7.2.

For additional correspondence concerning the artist's repainting of the picture, see MoMA Archives: Soby Papers, IV.C.1 and I.7.2, particularly correspondence in the latter file from Pierre Matisse to Soby dated June 21 and July 1, 1956.

129. See Bibliog. 42.

130. Letter, Balthus to Soby, September 4, 1956: ". . . car si j'ai realisé quelque chose à présent, c'est, je crois, presque uniquement dans mes grandes tableaux." MoMA Archives: Soby Papers: I.7.2.

131. Quoted in Bibliog. 42, pp. 5–6. In fact, Soby's Balthus exhibition at the Museum included a number of drawings from the Wuthering Heights series.

132. Quoted in Bibliog. 42, p. 4.

133. See Bibliog. 42.

134. Bibliog. 163, p. 36.

135. In addition to the exhibitions mentioned

below, Soby was involved in organizing the retrospective "Georges Rouault: Paintings and Prints" for The Museum of Modern Art in 1945 (see Bibliog. 16). Soby's opinion of Rouault was mixed. With few exceptions, he found the artist's "repetitions . . . monotonous, especially in pictures executed in his later years." He came to believe that Rouault "was a great painter only from roughly 1903 to the end of World War I" and "thereafter became at his best a superb printmaker." Soby was puzzled by the veneration accorded Rouault after the war: "I couldn't understand . . . why admiration for him should have made these [American] collectors dismiss as charlatans Rouault's peers in the School of Paris, especially Picasso. . . . Rouault was incense, Picasso quicksilver, and I preferred the latter substance." See Soby memoir, 21–1 through 21–3.

136. See Bibliog. 18.

137. Ben Shahn. *Vacant Lot.* 1940. Tempera on board, 19 x 23" (48.2 x 63.4 cm). Wadsworth Atheneum, Hartford. Summer Fund, 1941.

138. In 1938, Shahn settled in a Federal housing development in Roosevelt, New Jersey, where he had completed a fresco in the community center as part of a Farm Security Administration project; the development village had been designed as a cooperative commune for laborers from New York's Lower East Side.

Soby was an avid supporter of Shahn and wrote extensively about his work; see Bibliog. 18, 33, 34, 44, 45, 58, 59, 223, 225, 226, and 227.

139. See Bibliog. 25.

140. Barr met Klee on December 7, 1929, in the course of a four-day visit to the Dessau Bauhaus while on sabbatical from Wellesley College, where he was an associate professor; see MoMA Archives: Barr Papers, 9.F.71.

141. See Bibliog. 28.

142. See Bibliog. 192.

143. Bibliog. 28, p. 8.

144. A catalogue raisonné of Modigliani's works has since been published; see Christian Parisot, *Modigliani: Catalogues raisonnés*, eds. Giorgio and Guido Guastalla (Livorno: Graphis Arte, 1990–91).

145. Chester Dale (1883–1962) was a trustee of The Museum of Modern Art from 1929 to 1931. However, from the time the National Gallery of Art opened in Washington, D.C., in 1941, Dale was one of its most ardent, and generous, supporters. He became a trustee of that institution in 1943 and served as its president from 1955 until his death in 1962, when his collection of over two hundred and fifty paintings, sculptures, prints, and drawings was bequeathed to the Gallery (in addition to the sixty-three works given during his lifetime) and a museum scholarship fund was established for study abroad.

146. Bibliog. 28, p. 11.

147. These were two exhibitions that ran concurrently, from September 6 to October 30, 1955; each was assigned its own exhibition number by the Museum Registrar. See Bibliog. 38 and 40.

148. The Galerie Paul Guillaume was located at 6, rue de Miromesnil, Paris.

149. See Bibliog. 7. Elsewhere in his memoir, Soby comments that the book "naturally infuriated de Chirico, who calls himself our century's greatest artist and includes his wife, Isabella Far, as the century's greatest philosopher," and wishes them luck "in their self-appointed majesty"; however, he concludes, "De Chirico created from 1911 [to] 1919 what I will always think of as among the greatest works of art of our time" (Soby memoir, 22–16).

150. See Bibliog. 42.

151. See Bibliog. 47.

152. See Bibliog. 48.

153. Alicia Legg (b. 1915) served in various capacities at the Museum from 1949 until her retirement in 1987, including that of Associate Curator in the Department of Painting and Sculpture, from 1951 to 1979; and as Curator of Painting and Sculpture, from 1979 to 1987.

154. The exhibition was organized by William Lieberman, with a catalogue by Soby; see Bibliog. 51.

155. Barr and Soby hoped that the Museum would be the ultimate recipient of *The Farm.* Hemingway, when he visited the Museum in October 1957, had told Barr that it was "by far the greatest of Miró's early paintings." During that conversation, Hemingway implied that he was seriously considering giving the painting to the Museum and, again according to Barr's account, his wife Mary also seemed agreeable. See letter, Barr to Soby, October 2, 1957; MoMA Archives: Soby Papers, I.27.5.

The picture was in Hemingway's home in Havana when the political situation deteriorated in late 1958, making a journey to New York complicated. The "wall-to-wall" insurance coverage against *all* risks—including war, civil disturbance, and rioting—was difficult to obtain, and transportation of the picture between Havana and New York was problematic. It took Vance several days to secure permission to leave Cuba with the painting. He arrived in New York on February 7, 1959, in time for the painting's inclusion in the Miró exhibition that opened on March 19 (MoMA Exh. #641).

Hemingway died in 1961. *The Farm* remained on extended loan to the Museum from September 15, 1959, until January 17, 1964, when it was returned at Mary Hemingway's request to her apartment in New York. Despite Barr's hope that the picture would enter the Modern's collection, it was bequeathed by Mary to the National Gallery of Art in Washington, D.C. See letter dated December 19, 1963, from Alfred Rich, Mary's lawyer, to Richard H. Koch, the Museum's General Counsel and Director of Administration, enclosing Mary's letter to the Museum of December 16, 1963, in which she requested the return of the painting; MoMA Archives: Soby Papers I.27.5.

156. Jean Volkmer (b. 1920) began working at the Museum in March 1943 as a designer in the Department of Exhibitions. In 1954, with Dorothy Miller's help, she began an apprenticeship with the independent conservators Sheldon and Caroline Keck; the Kecks frequently did conservation work for the Modern, which then did not have an on-site facility. As a direct result of the fire in the Museum galleries in April 1958, a fully equipped in-house conservation and restoration laboratory was opened the following October, and Volkmer, then Coordinator of Exhibitions, was appointed Museum Conservator. She retired from the Museum as Chief Conservator in December 1982. See MoMA Archives: Jean Volkmer Oral History.

157. See Bibliog. 62.

158. Soby was mistaken: He never mentioned Magritte in *After Picasso.* However, in *The Early Chirico* (1941) he included this remark in a discussion of the influence of de Chirico's work on Magritte, who knew de Chirico's early work from the collection of the Belgian collector René Gaffé; see Bibliog. 7, pp. 94–95.

159. Giorgio de Chirico. *The Song of Love.* 1914. Oil on canvas, 28¾ x 23⅜" (73 x 59.1 cm). The Museum of Modern Art, New York. Nelson A. Rockefeller Bequest, 1979.

160. René Magritte. *La Philosophe dans le boudoir (Philosophy in the Boudoir).* 1947. Oil on canvas, 31½ x 23⅞" (80 x 60 cm). Private collection.

161. Magritte depicted a flaming "tuba" in *The Ladder of Fire, I,* of 1933: "[T]he blaze was hard to extinguish as an imaginative way of enlivening contours. It soon spread to the gawky necks of Salvador Dali's giraffes" (Bibliog. 62, p. 13). Giraffes with flaming manes appear in Dali's *Portrait of Harpo Marx, Dinner in the Desert Lighted by Giraffes on Fire, The Burning Giraffe,* and *The Invention of the Monsters,* all painted in 1937.

Appendix: The James Thrall Soby Bequest

Following is a listing of the forty-one paintings and sculptures included in the James Thrall Soby Bequest to The Museum of Modern Art in 1979. Works on paper in the bequest are not included; neither, of course, are works in any medium given by Soby to the Museum in his lifetime.

The works are arranged alphabetically by artist and chronologically for the works of each artist. Dimensions are given in feet and inches, followed by centimeters, height preceding width preceding depth.

1. Francis Bacon. *Study of a Baboon.* 1953. Oil on canvas, 6' 6¾" x 54⅛" (198.3 x 137.3 cm)
2. Francis Bacon. *Study for Portrait, Number IV (after the life mask of William Blake).* 1956. Oil on canvas, 24⅛ x 20" (61.1 x 50.8 cm)
3. Balthus (Baltusz Klossowski de Rola). *The Street.* 1933. Oil on canvas, 6' 4¾" x 7' 10½" (195 x 240 cm)
4. Eugene Berman. *The Cart.* 1930. Oil on composition board, 45½ x 35½" (115.6 x 90.2 cm)
5. Eugene Berman. *Memory of Ischia.* 1931. Oil on canvas, 40 x 31¾" (101.4 x 80.5 cm)
6. Peter Blume. *Key West Beach.* 1940. Oil on canvas, 12 x 18" (30.3 x 46 cm)
7. Pierre Bonnard. *Grapes.* 1928. Oil on canvas, 16⅝ x 18⅜" (42.2 x 46.4 cm)
8. Alexander Calder. *Well Sweep.* 1935. Standing mobile: steel and painted stainless steel, 22' (670.6 cm)
9. Alexander Calder. *Swizzle Sticks.* 1936. Mobile relief: wire, wood, and lead against painted plywood panel; overall, 56⅜ x 45⅝ x 48½" (143.2 x 105.8 x 123.1 cm) (variable)
10. Giorgio de Chirico. *The Enigma of a Day.* 1914. Oil on canvas, 6' 1¼" x 55" (185.5 x 139.7 cm)
11. Giorgio de Chirico. *The Duo (Les Mannequins de la Tour Rose).* 1915. Oil on canvas, 32¼ x 23¼" (81.9 x 59 cm)
12. Giorgio de Chirico. *The Seer.* 1915. Oil on canvas, 35½ x 27½" (89.6 x 70.1 cm)
13. Giorgio de Chirico. *The Amusements of a Young Girl.* 1916? Oil on canvas, 18¾ x 16" (47.5 x 40.3 cm)
14. Giorgio de Chirico. *The Faithful Servitor.* 1916 or 1917. Oil on canvas, 15⅛ x 13⅝" (38.2 x 34.5 cm)
15. Salvador Dali. *Debris of an Automobile Giving Birth to a Blind Horse Biting a Telephone.* 1938. Oil on canvas, 21½ x 25⅝" (54.5 x 65.1 cm)
16. Jean Dubuffet. *My Cart, My Garden (Mon Char, mon jardin)* from the Charrettes, jardins, personnages monolithes series. 1955. Oil on canvas, 35⅛ x 45¾" (89.2 x 115.9 cm)
17. Max Ernst. *Alice in 1941.* 1941. Oil on paper, mounted on canvas, 15¾ x 12¾" (40 x 32.3 cm)
18. Alberto Giacometti. *Tall Figure.* 1949. Painted bronze, 65⅜ x 6½ x 13½" (166 x 16.5 x 34.2 cm)

19. Wilhelm Lehmbruck. *Torso.* 1913–14. Cast stone, 37½ x 18¾ x 14" (95.2 x 47.5 x 35.5 cm)
20. Léonid (Léonid Berman). *Mussel Gatherers at High Tide (Les Bouchots à marée haute).* 1937. Oil on canvas, 21¼ x 31⅞" (54 x 81 cm)
21. Léonid. *The Quarriers (Les Carriers).* 1930. Oil on canvas, 10¾ x 16¾" (27.1 x 41.4 cm)
22. Loren MacIver. *Tree.* 1945. Oil on canvas, 40 x 26" (101.5 x66 cm)
23. Loren MacIver. *Skylight.* 1948. Oil on canvas, 40¼ x 48⅛" (102 x 122.1 cm)
24. Aristide Maillol. *Leda.* 1902. Bronze, 11⅛ x 5⅞ x 5½" (28.1 x 14.7 x 14 cm)
25. Marino Marini. *Dancer.* 1948. Bronze (cast 1949), 69½ x 23 x 11" (176.5 x 58.1 x 27.8 cm)
26. Matta (Roberto Sebastián Antonio Matta Echaurren). *Here, Sir Fire, Eat!* 1942. Oil on canvas, 56⅛ x 44⅛" (142.3 x 112 cm)
27. Joan Miró. *Portrait of Mistress Mills in 1750.* 1929. Oil on canvas, 46 x 35⅛" (116.7 x 89.6 cm)
28. Joan Miró. *Self-Portrait, I.* 1937–38. Pencil, crayon, and oil on canvas, 57⅛ x 38⅛" (146.1 x 97.2 cm)
29. Giorgio Morandi. *Still Life.* 1949. Oil on canvas, 14¼ x 17¼" (36 x 43.7 cm)
30. Isamu Noguchi. *Mitosis.* 1962. Bronze (cast 1962) in two parts, overall 14½ x 22¼ x 16½" (36.8 x 56.5 x 41.8 cm)
31. Pablo Picasso. *Nude Seated on a Rock (Baigneuse).* 1921. Oil on wood, 6¼ x 4⅜" (15.8 x 11.1 cm)
32. Pablo Picasso. *The Sigh.* 1923. Oil and charcoal on canvas, 23¾ x 19¾" (60.3 x 50.2 cm)
33. Henri Rousseau. *The Goatherd.* 1905. Oil on canvas, 18¼ x 22⅞" (46.2 x 57.9 cm)
34. Kay Sage. *Watching the Clock.* 1958. Oil on canvas, 14 x 14" (35.6 x 35.6 cm)
35. Ben Shahn. *Liberation.* 1945. Tempera on cardboard mounted on composition board, 29¾ x 40" (75.6 x 101.4 cm)
36. René Pierre Tal-Coat. *Blue Vase.* N.d. Oil on canvas, 5¾ x 7¼" (14.5 x 18.3 cm)
37. Yves Tanguy. *The Mood of Now (L'Humeur du temps).* 1928. Oil on canvas, 39½ x 28⅞" (100.1 x 73.3 cm)
38. Yves Tanguy. *The Furniture of Time (Le Temps meublé).* 1939. Oil on canvas, 46 x 35¼" (116.7 x 89.4 cm)
39. Pavel Tchelitchew. *Madame Bonjean.* 1931. Oil on canvas, 51¼ x 38⅛" (130.1 x 96.7 cm)
40. Pavel Tchelitchew. *Leaf Children.* 1940. Oil on canvas, 16½ x 14½" (41.7 x 36.7 cm)
41. Esteban Vicente. *Bridgehampton Rose.* 1970. Oil on canvas, 60⅛ x 48" (152.7 x 122 cm)

Special Section: James Thrall Soby

A Bibliography of the Published Writings of James Thrall Soby

Compiled by Rona Roob

This bibliography lists 258 published writings by James Thrall Soby, arranged chronologically in three categories:

I. Books and Exhibition Catalogues
II. The Saturday Review of Literature
III. Other Periodicals

Soby's writings span a period of fifty-five years: the earliest, a short story, was written when he was a student at Williams College in 1926; the latest, a brief reminiscence of a visit with Giorgio Morandi, was published by the Arts Council of Great Britain in 1970. Of the sixty-six books and exhibition catalogues in Category I, thirty-six were written for The Museum of Modern Art between 1941, the year before Soby joined the Museum's Board of Trustees, and 1966, one year before he resigned as Chairman of the Museum Collections Committee. Soby was also a founding member of the Museum's Photography Committee, and eleven of these entries concern that art form. In addition to writing 121 articles for *The Saturday Review of Literature* between 1946 and 1965, he contributed articles to forty-one different periodicals, only half of which could be considered strictly art publications.

This bibliography does not reflect Soby's important contribution to the *Magazine of Art*, where he served on the editorial board from 1945 to 1953 and as Acting Editor from 1950 to 1951, nor does it include unpublished materials in the public domain that are available in The Museum of Modern Art Archives: a lecture on twentieth-century Italian painting and sculpture, given to members of the Museum's Junior Council on February 8, 1949, and to the Fairfield County, Connecticut, Smith College Club on March 6, 1956; a paper titled "Some Thoughts on American Art and Artists Abroad," presented by Soby at the Institute of International Education Conference on Exchange in the Arts in New York, October 4 and 5, 1956; a manuscript with the working title of "French Painting 1800–1850," prepared for a proposed Museum publication in 1959; a lecture on Ben Shahn delivered at the Philadelphia Museum of Art on November 6 and 7, 1961; and a discussion with Alfred H. Barr, Jr., taped on October 29, 1952, at the time of John Rewald's *Les Fauves* exhibition at The Museum of Modern Art.

The wording of each entry is recorded as it appears in the original publication. Brackets indicate bibliographic information obtained from outside sources. Arno Press publications were reprinted from the first editions unless otherwise noted. Exhibitions organized by The Museum of Modern Art are indicated by the abbreviation *MoMA Exh.,* followed by the number assigned to the exhibition by the Museum Registrar. *C/E* refers to the circulating version of an exhibition organized by the Department of Circulating Exhibitions between 1933 and 1969; *ICE* denotes an International Circulating Exhibition—that is, an exhibition organized under the auspices of the International Council of the Museum of Modern Art— whereas *SP-ICE* identifies Special Projects International Circulating Exhibitions, such as competitions and the United States' representation at recurring international exhibitions (see, for example, Bibliog. 38). A Circulating Exhibition did not necessarily replicate the version shown at the Museum.

All of the items cited are available in The Museum of Modern Art Archives.

R.R.

I. Books and Exhibition Catalogues

1. Introduction. In Scott, Sir Walter. *Wandering Willie's Tale*, pp. 9–12, 15–16. Edward Valentine Mitchell, 1929.

2. Soby, ed. *The Booklover's Diary*. Hartford: Edward Valentine Mitchell; New York: Dodd, Mead & Company, 1930. A handbook of literary information, with blank pages for readers to record their impressions.

3. *Photographs by Man Ray 1920 Paris 1934*. Hartford: James Thrall Soby, 1934. Reprinted as *Photographs by Man Ray: 105 works, 1920–1934*. New York: Dover, 1979. Includes one page of text in English and French by each of the following: Man Ray, Paul Eluard, André Breton, and Tristan Tzara; and one page of text in German and English by Rrose Sélavy (Marcel Duchamp).

4. *After Picasso*. Hartford: Edwin Valentine Mitchell; New York: Dodd, Mead & Company, 1935. According to Soby, this was "the first book in English on surrealism and neo-romanticism"; in it he discusses "the reaction of the Neo-Romantics and the Surrealists against the Cubists' principle of 'painting as architecture.'"

5. [Foreword.] In *Balthus: Paintings*. Unpaginated. New York: Pierre Matisse, [1938]. Catalogue of the first Balthus exhibition held outside France, at the Pierre Matisse Gallery, New York, March 21–April 16, 1938.

6. Preface. In *Eugene Berman: Catalogue of the Retrospective Exhibition of His Paintings, Drawings, Illustrations and Designs Organized by The Institute of Modern Art, Boston, October 1941 Through May 1942*, pp. 10–13. Boston: The Institute of Modern Art, 1941.

7. *The Early Chirico*. New York: Dodd, Mead & Company, 1941. Substantially revised in 1955; see Bibliog. 38.

8. *Paintings, Drawings, Prints: Salvador Dali*. New York: The Museum of Modern Art, 1941. Second edition, revised, 1946. Reprinted as *Salvador Dali*. New York: Arno Press, 1969. Catalogue of MoMA Exh. #158, November 19, 1941–January 11, 1942; circulated as C/E II.1/50(1).

9. "Europe." In *Artists in Exile*. Unpaginated. New York: Pierre Matisse, 1942. Catalogue of an exhibition of works by fourteen European artists who resided in the United States during World War II, held at the Pierre Matisse Gallery, March 3–28, 1942.

10. *Tchelitchew: Paintings, Drawings*. New York: The Museum of Modern Art, 1942. Reprint edition. New York: Arno Press, 1972. Catalogue of MoMA Exh. #203, October 28–November 29, 1942.

11. With Miller, Dorothy C. *Romantic Painting in America*. New York: The Museum of Modern Art, 1943. Reprint edition. New York: Arno Press, 1969. Catalogue of MoMA Exh. #246, November 17, 1943–February 6, 1944; circulated as C/E II.1/99(1). See also Bibliog. 207.

12. Foreword. In *Notable Modern Paintings & Sculptures: Including Important Works by Corot, Cézanne, Picasso and Matisse: Property of The Museum of Modern Art: With Additions from Members of the Museum's Board of Trustees*

and Advisory Committee. Unpaginated. New York: Parke–Bernet Galleries, 1944. Catalogue of sale no. 567, May 11, 1944. Formally cited and catalogued as *Modern Paintings & Sculptures: Including Works by Cézanne, Seurat, Matisse, Picasso, Derain, Despiau, Maillol, Marie Laurencin, Modigliani, Braque, Chagall and other artists including Corot: A Small Group of African Sculptures: Property of The Museum of Modern Art, With Additions from the Members of the Museum's Board of Trustees and Advisory Committee.* The foreword text was entered in the Museum Trustee minutes of March 9, 1944, as having been written by Soby.

13. "Painting and Sculpture." In *Art in Progress: A Survey Prepared for the Fifteenth Anniversary of The Museum of Modern Art*, p. 11. New York: The Museum of Modern Art; 1944. Catalogue of MoMA Exh. #258a, May 24–October 15, 1944.

14. Introduction. In *Contemporary British Artists.* Unpaginated. New York: Buchholz Gallery/Curt Valentin, 1945. Catalogue of exhibition at the Buchholz Gallery, March 27–April 14, 1945; see also Bibliog. 214.

15. Acknowledgments. In *The Prints of Paul Klee,* [pp. i–xv]. New York: Curt Valentin, 1945. Second edition. New York: The Museum of Modern Art, 1947.

16. *Georges Rouault: Paintings and Prints.* New York: The Museum of Modern Art, February 1945. Second edition, June 1945. Third edition, 1947. Reprint from third edition. New York: Arno Press, 1972. Catalogue of MoMA Exh. #284, April 4–June 3, 1945.

17. "Jacques-Louis David." In *Sculpture by Houdon/Paintings and Drawings by David.* Unpaginated. New York: Caxton, 1947. Catalogue of exhibition held at The Century Association, New York, February 19–April 10, 1947.

18. *Ben Shahn.* The Penguin Modern Painters series, edited by Sir Kenneth Clark; Alfred H. Barr, Jr., ed., U.S. edition. West Drayton, Middlesex: Penguin Books, Limited; New York: The Museum of Modern Art, 1947. Catalogue of MoMA Exh. #358, September 30, 1947–January 4, 1948; circulated as C/E II.1/100(9). See also Bibliog. 223.

19. "Max Beckmann." In *Beckmann.* New York: Buchholz Gallery/Curt Valentin, 1947, [pp. 1–4]. Catalogue of exhibition held at the Buchholz Gallery, November 17–December 6, 1947; reprinted in Bibliog. 22.

20. *The Museum of Modern Art.* [New York: The Museum of Modern Art, 1947]. Based on Bibliog. 216.

21. [Introduction.] In *New York Private Collections.* Unpaginated. New York: The Museum of Modern Art, 1948. Catalogue of MoMA Exh. #381, July 20–September 12, 1948. Soby wrote that this was the "second in a series of exhibitions [of modern art] . . . owned by collectors in New York State"; the first was "Paintings from New York Private Collections" (MoMA Exh. #325, July 2–September 22, 1946).

22. *Contemporary Painters.* New York: The Museum of Modern Art, 1948. Reprint edition. New York: Arno Press, 1966. Soby dedicated this book of essays to Alfred H. Barr, Jr., and Dorothy C. Miller; see also Bibliog. 19, 222, 230.

23. "Le Corbusier the Painter." In Papadaki, Stamos, ed. *Le Corbusier: Architect, Painter, Writer*, pp. 115–32. New York: The Macmillan Company, 1948.

24. [Introduction.] In *Mural-Scrolls*. Unpaginated. New York: Katzenbach and Warren, Inc., 1948. A brochure introducing limited-edition mural-scrolls designed by Henri Matisse, Matta, Joan Miró, and Alexander Calder and silkscreened onto wallpaper.

25. *Paintings, Drawings and Prints by Paul Klee from the Klee Foundation, Berne, Switzerland, with Additions from American Collections*, pp. 7–10. New York: The Museum of Modern Art, 1949. Catalogue of MoMA Exh. #433, December 20, 1949–February 19, 1950; circulated as C/E II.1/68(5).

26. Foreword, Acknowledgments, "The *Scuola Metafisica*," "Amedeo Modigliani," and "Painting and Sculpture Since 1920." In Soby and Barr, Alfred H., Jr. *XXth Century Italian Art*, pp. 5, 6, 17–34. New York: The Museum of Modern Art, 1949. Reprint edition. New York: Arno Press, 1972. Catalogue of MoMA Exh. #413, June 28–September 18, 1949; see also Bibliog. 235.

27. *Marino Marini*. New York: Buchholz Gallery/Curt Valentin, 1950. Unpaginated. Catalogue of exhibition held at the Buchholz Gallery, February 14–March 11, 1950; reprinted in Bibliog. 29.

28. [Introduction.] In *Modigliani: Paintings, Drawings, Sculpture*, pp. 9–15. New York: The Museum of Modern Art, 1951. Published in collaboration with the Cleveland Museum of Art. Second edition, 1954. Third edition, revised, 1963. Reprint edition. New York: Arno Press, 1972. Catalogue of MoMA Exh. #474, April 10–June 10, 1951; see Bibliog. 119.

29. "Marino Marini." In *Marino Marini: Sculpture and Drawings*. Unpaginated. London: The Hanover Gallery, 1951. Catalogue of exhibition held at The Hanover Gallery, May 8–June 16, 1951; see Bibliog. 27.

30. "Postwar Painting: In the Shadow of 'Guernica.'" In *America and the Mind of Europe*, pp. 105–15. Introduction by Lewis Galantière. London: Hamish Hamilton Ltd., 1951. A collection of articles that originally appeared as a special issue of *The Saturday Review of Literature* devoted to the theme "America and the Mind of Europe: Mid-Century"; see Bibliog. 115.

31. *Kay Sage*. Rome: Galleria dell'Obelisco, 1953. Unpaginated. Catalogue of exhibition held at the Galleria dell'Obelisco, March 1953; text in Italian and English; reprinted in Bibliog. 52.

32. Foreword. In *17 East Hampton Artists*. Unpaginated. East Hampton, N.Y.: Guild Hall, 1953. Catalogue of exhibition held at Guild Hall, July 25–August 15, 1953.

33. "Ben Shahn." In *2 Pittori, de Kooning, Shahn; 3 Scultori, Lachaise, Lassaw, Smith: Esposizione organizzata dal Museum of Modern Art, New York, XXVII Biennale Venezia, 1954*. Unpaginated. New York: Marchbanks Press, June 1954. Catalogue of ICE #F–23–54, printed for the Museum's Trustees; see also Bibliog. 34.

34. "Ben Shahn." In *XXVII Biennale di Venezia Catalogo*, pp. 388–89. Venice: Alfieri, 1954.

35. [Selected descriptive entries.] In Barr, Alfred H., Jr., ed. *Masters of Modern Art*, pp. 105, 115, 128, 134–135. New York: The Museum of Modern Art, 1954. Second edition, 1955. Third edition, revised, 1958. Foreign-language editions: French, 1955; German, 1956; Spanish, 1955; Swedish, 1956.

36. "Homage to Bruyas." In *Saturday Review Reader No. 3*, pp. 89–91. New York: Bantam, 1954. Reprint of Bibliog. 142.

37. Foreword. In "15 Paintings by French Masters of the Nineteenth Century Lent by the Louvre and the Museums of Albi and Lyon." *The Museum of Modern Art Bulletin* 22, no. 3 (Spring 1955): 5–8. Reprint edition. New York: Arno Press, 1967. This issued of the *Bulletin* served as the catalogue for "15 Paintings by French Masters of the Nineteenth Century" (MoMA Exh. #572, February 25–April 24, 1955).

38. *Giorgio de Chirico*. New York: The Museum of Modern Art, 1955. Reprint edition. New York: Arno Press, 1966. Published to coincide with "Giorgio de Chirico" (MoMA Exh. #583, September 6–October 30, 1955). Soby was preoccupied with this revision of his earlier de Chirico text (see Bibliog. 7) "at intervals since 1945."

39. Foreword. In *De David à Toulouse-Lautrec: Chefs-d'oeuvre des collections américaines*, [pp. 17–24]. Paris: Musée de l'Orangerie, 1955. Catalogue of SP–ICE #7–54, an exhibition held at the Orangerie April 20–July 5, 1955, for which Soby served as Chairman of the Selection Committee. The text of his English-language "Foreword" appears in French translation as the "Introduction" [pp. 25–33]; reprinted in Italian translation, with illustrations, as Bibliog. 248.

40. *Yves Tanguy*. New York: The Museum of Modern Art, 1955. Reprint edition. New York: Arno Press, 1972. Catalogue of MoMA Exh. #584, September 6–October 30, 1955; the exhibition was directed by Soby.

41. *Paintings from The Museum of Modern Art*. The Metropolitan Museum of Art Miniatures Series II: Expressionism, Impressionism, Surrealism. New York: The Metropolitan Museum of Art, 1956.

42. *Balthus: The Museum of Modern Art Bulletin* 24, no. 3 (1956): 3–9. New York: The Museum of Modern Art, 1956. Reprint edition. New York: Arno Press, 1967. This issue of the *Bulletin* served as the catalogue for "Balthus" (MoMA Exh. #611, December 19, 1956–February 3, 1957), the first exhibition of the artist's work to be held in a museum.

43. *Modern Art and the New Past*. Norman, Okla.: University of Oklahoma Press, 1957. Italian translation, *L'Arte moderna e il suo recente passato*. Rome: Toninelli Editore, 1972. A collection of articles that originally appeared in *The Saturday Review*, with an introduction by Paul J. Sachs; the foreign-language edition includes illustrations.

44. *Ben Shahn: His Graphic Art*. New York: George Braziller, Inc., 1957.

45. "Charles Demuth," "Man Ray," "Ben Shahn," "Grant Wood," "Rico Lebrun," "Stuart Davis," "Peter Blume," "Willem de Kooning," and "Jackson Pollock." In Baur, John I. H., ed. *New Art in America: Fifty Painters of the 20th Century*, pp. 50–55, 88–91, 118–23, 134–37, 172–76,

182–87, 203–08, 232–41. Greenwich, Conn.: New York Graphic Society; New York: Frederick A. Praeger, 1957.

46. "A. Everett Austin, Jr. and Modern Art." In *A. Everett Austin, Jr.: A Director's Taste and Achievement*, pp. 27–32. Hartford, Conn.: Wadsworth Atheneum, 1958.

47. *Juan Gris*. New York: The Museum of Modern Art, 1958. Published in collaboration with The Minneapolis Institute of Arts, the San Francisco Museum of Art and the Los Angeles County Museum. Reprint edition. New York: Arno Press, 1980. Catalogue of MoMA Exh. #630, April 8–15, 1958, and May 12–June 1, 1958; the exhibition was interrupted by a fire that occurred in the Museum galleries on April 15, 1958, and caused the Museum to suspend its programs temporarily.

48. Acknowledgments and "Introduction: The Search for New Forms." In Soby, ed. *Arp*, pp. 6–11. New York: The Museum of Modern Art, 1958. Reprint edition. New York: Arno Press, 1980. Catalogue of the exhibition "Jean Arp: A Retrospective" (MoMA Exh. #631, October 8–November 30, 1958).

49. [Foreword.] In *Guttuso: April 7 to April 28, 1958, ACA Gallery and Heller Gallery*, pp. 3–6. Geneva and Rome: Editions Internationales, [1958].

50. Introduction. In *Recent Sculpture U.S.A.: The Museum of Modern Art Bulletin* 26, no 3 (Spring 1959): unpaginated. Reprint edition. New York: Arno Press, 1967. This issue of the *Bulletin* served as the catalogue of "Recent Sculpture U.S.A" (MoMA Exh. #644, May 13–August 16, 1959); the exhibition and its subsequent tour were sponsored by the Museum's Junior Council.

51. *Joan Miró*. New York: The Museum of Modern Art, 1959. Reprint edition. New York: Arno Press, 1980. Spanish edition, revised, Rio Piedras: Universidad de Puerto Rico, 1960. Issued as an independent publication at the time of the retrospective "Joan Miró" (MoMA Exh. #641, March 19– May 10, 1959).

52. *Kay Sage: Retrospective Exhibition 1937–1958*. New York: [Catherine Viviano], 1960. Unpaginated. Catalogue of exhibition held at the Viviano gallery, April 5–30, 1960; see Bibliog. 31.

53. "Presentazione." In *Arte italiana del XX secolo de collezioni americaine*, pp. 16–18, 21–23. Milan: "Silvana" Editorale d'Arte, 1960. Catalogue of SP–ICE #22–58, organized for showings at the Palazzo Reale, Milan, April 30–June 26, 1960, and the Galleria Nazionale d'Arte Moderna, Rome, July 16–September 18, 1960; separate catalogues were issued for each venue. Also shown at the Santini Brothers Warehouse, New York, October 24–26, 1960.

54. Foreword. In Liberman, Alexander. *The Artist in His Studio*. Unpaginated. New York: The Viking Press, 1960.

55. Foreword. In *The Colin Collection: Paintings, Watercolors, Drawings and Sculpture*. Unpaginated. New York: Knoedler, 1960. Catalogue of exhibition held at M. Knoedler & Co., April 12–May 14, 1960, organized to ben-

efit the hospitalized veterans' service of the Musicians' Emergency Fund.

56. "The Museum's Library" and "Catalogue with Notes." In *The James Thrall Soby Collection of Works of Art Pledged or Given to The Museum of Modern Art*, pp. 6, 13, 21–68. New York: The Museum of Modern Art, 1961. Catalogue of exhibition held at M. Knoedler & Co., February 1–March 4, 1961, held to benefit the Museum's Library.

57. Foreword. In *Rico Lebrun: Drawings*. Berkeley and Los Angeles: University of California Press, 1961.

58. With Constantine, Mildred. *Ben Shahn: Graphics*. Zagreb: Galerija Suvremene Umjetnosti, 1962. Catalogue of ICE #F–68–61.

____. See Bibliog. 258, also written at this time.

59. *Ben Shahn: Paintings*. New York: George Braziller, Inc., 1963.

60. Introduction. In Soby; Elliott, James; and Wheeler, Monroe. *Bonnard and His Environment*, pp. 9–13. New York: The Museum of Modern Art, 1964. Published in collaboration with the Los Angeles County Museum of Art and The Art Institute of Chicago. Catalogue of MoMA Exh. #749, October 7–November 29, 1964.

61. "The Collections." In *The Museum of Modern Art: A Pictorial Chronicle*, [p. 40]. New York: Art in America Company, Inc., 1964. Reprint edition, with updated information, 1965. See also Bibliog. 257.

62. Acknowledgments (with Seitz, William C.) and untitled text. In *René Magritte*, pp. 6, 7–19. New York: The Museum of Modern Art, 1965. Published in collaboration with the Rose Art Museum, Brandeis University; The Art Institute of Chicago; The University Art Museum, the University of California at Berkeley; and the Pasadena Art Museum. Catalogue of MoMA Exh. #782, December 15, 1965–February 27, 1966.

63. "Kay Sage." In *A Tribute to Kay Sage: 1898–1963*. Unpaginated. Waterbury, Conn.: Mattatuck Museum, 1965 (Publication no. 35).

64. Introduction. In Barr, Alfred H., Jr.; Soby; and Lippard, Lucy R., *The School of Paris: Paintings from the Florene May Schoenborn and Samuel A. Marx Collection*, pp. 7–9. New York: The Museum of Modern Art, 1965. Published in collaboration with The Art Institute of Chicago, the City Art Museum of St. Louis, the San Francisco Museum of Art, and the Museo de Arte Moderno, Mexico City. Catalogue of MoMA Exh. #779, November 2, 1965–January 2, 1966; circulated as SP–ICE #35-65.

65. Introduction. In *Balthus: An Exhibition Circulated by The Museum of Modern Art*. Unpaginated. [New York: The Museum of Modern Art, 1966]. A broadside for a Museum of Modern Art Circulating Exhibition (C/E 65–5).

66. "A Visit to Morandi." In Davison, Elizabeth, ed. *Giorgio Morandi: An Exhibition of Paintings, Watercolours, Drawings and Etchings Organized by the Arts Council of Great Britain*, pp. 5–6. London: [The Arts Council], 1970. Catalogue of exhibition held at the Royal Academy of Arts, London, December 5, 1970–January 17, 1971; and the Musée National d'Art, Paris, February 9–April 12, 1971.

II. *The Saturday Review of Literature*

The Saturday Review of Literature began weekly publication in 1924. Its title was changed in 1952 to *Saturday Review*. From May 1946 through November 1957, Soby regularly wrote the column "The Fine Arts," which appeared monthly in the magazine; additionally, from 1958 through 1965 he contributed five full-length articles. Unless otherwise noted, all writings cited in this section originally appeared in the "Fine Arts" column.

67. "Collecting Today's Pictures." *SRL* 29, no. 21 (May 25, 1946): 42–44.

68. "To the Ladies." *SRL* 29, no. 27 (July 6, 1946): 14–15. Commentary on "Georgia O'Keeffe" (MoMA Exh. #319, May 14–August 25, 1946), and on women artists in general; see also Bibliog. 136.

69. "Writer vs. Artist."*SRL* 29, no. 33 (August 17, 1946): 24–26. Addresses the inability of the writer to deal with contemporary art, using Evelyn Waugh's *Brideshead Revisited* (1945) and Edmund Wilson's *Memoirs of Hecate County* (1946) as examples.

70. "Alfred Stieglitz." *SRL* 29, no. 39 (September 28, 1946): 22–23. An appreciation of Stieglitz written shortly after the artist's death on July 13, 1946.

71. "Art in Paris." *SRL* 29, no. 42 (October 19, 1946): 34–36.

72. "Temptation of Saint Anthony." *SRL* 29, no. 46 (November 16, 1946): 42–44. Concerns an exhibition of the same title held at M. Knoedler & Co. in the fall of 1946. Eleven artists were asked to submit renderings on this theme to be used in a motion picture of Guy de Maupassant's *Bel Ami* (1946). Max Ernst won the competition, which was judged by Alfred H. Barr, Jr., Marcel Duchamp, and Sidney Janis; reprinted as Bibliog. 221.

73. "Art in England Today." *SRL* 29, no. 49 (December 7, 1946): 76–79 (Christmas Book Number).

74. "Museum Curators and the Literary Graces." *SRL* 30, no.1 (January 4, 1947): 28–29. Written in response to an article by William G. Dooley titled "Double-Talk in the Museum World," which appeared in *The New York Times Book Review* the previous fall; Soby praises the writing accomplishments of New York area museum professionals and refutes Dooley's contention that such writing is "incoherent, pompous and complicated."

75. "Slighted Fields and Familiar Ground." *SRL* 30, no. 5 (February 1, 1947): 28–29. A discussion of recently published art books dealing with familiar periods as well as less popular ones; see also Bibliog. 80.

76. "Second Look at Paris." *SRL* 30, no. 9 (March 1, 1947): 29–30. A review of an exhibition of works produced by younger French painters, held at the Whitney Museum of American Art, New York; see also Bibliog. 89.

77. "A New Vision in Photography."*SRL* 30, no. 14 (April 5, 1947): 32–34. The "Henri Cartier-Bresson" retrospective (MoMA Exh. #343, February 4–April 6, 1947; C/E II.1/44[3]), organized by Lincoln Kirstein and Beaumont Newhall, is discussed.

78. "History of a Picture." *SRL* 30, no. 17 (April 26, 1947): 30–32. An examina-

tion of public reaction to Peter Blume's *South of Scranton* in 1934, the year it was painted, prompted by criticism of a collection of contemporary American paintings purchased by the U.S. Department of State in 1947.

79. "Gertrude Stein and the Artists." *SRL* 30, no. 21 (May 24, 1947): 34–36. Concerns an exhibition of Stein's bequest of her "literary remains" at the Sterling Memorial Library, Yale University, New Haven, Connecticut.

80. "Neglected Artists." *SRL* 30, no. 26 (June 28, 1947): 26–27. A discussion of artists and art fields not sufficiently studied; see also Bibliog. 75.

81. "Philadelphia's Private Array." *SRL* 30, no. 31 (August 2, 1947): 25–26. Soby comments on the Philadelphia Museum of Art's "Masterpieces of Philadelphia" exhibition.

82. "Washington Allston, Eclectic." *SRL* 30, no. 34 (August 23, 1947): 28–29. A review of the Allston exhibition organized by the Detroit Institute of Arts and the Museum of Fine Arts, Boston.

83. "A Salvo to Recent Art Books." *SRL* 30, no. 44 (November 1, 1947): 40–41.

84. "Life Magazine Stoops to Conquer." *SRL* 30, no. 49 (December 6, 1947): 34, 93 (Christmas Book Number). A condemnation of *LIFE* magazine's treatment of Picasso in an article published in the October 13, 1947, issue.

85. "Iron Lungs for Genius." *SRL* 31, no. 4 (January 24, 1948): 36–37. A comparison of the work of Albert Pinkham Ryder, exhibited at the Whitney Museum of American Art, New York, in January 1948, and that of Frederick Edwin Church.

86. "The Case of Ingres." *SRL* 31, 13 (March 27, 1948): 32–34. A discussion of Jean-Auguste-Dominique Ingres, with a mention of Jean Cassou's "new . . . little volume" on the artist (*Ingres* [Brussels: Editions de la Connaissance, 1947]).

87. "The Worth While and the Extravagant." *SRL* 31, no. 18 (May 1, 1948): 32–33. Soby laments England's neglect of some of its "minor masters" and comments on recently published English and European art books.

88. "The Venice Biennial." *SRL* 31, no. 32 (August 7, 1948): 30–32. A review of the Italian section of the XXIV Biennale di Venezia, with emphasis on the work of Carlo Carrà, de Chirico, Giacomo Manzù, Marini, Morandi, and others.

89. "Report on Paris." *SRL* 31, no. 33 (August 14, 1948): 25–26. Writing from Paris, Soby expresses regret that the exhibition "Second Look at Paris," held at the Whitney Museum of American Art the previous spring, did not include works by Balthus; see also Bibliog. 76.

90. "Challenging the Lambent, Languorous Pitchmen." *SRL* 31, no. 41 (October 9, 1948): 44–46. An overview of art books published in America in 1948.

91. "The Importance of Collage." *SRL* 31, no. 45 (November 6, 1948): 36–37. A discussion of "Collage" (MoMA Exh. #385, September 21–December 5, 1948).

92. "For an Artful Christmas." *SRL* 31, no. 49 (December 4, 1948): 50–52, 66

(Christmas Book Number). Recommendations of recently published art books as Christmas gifts.

93. "Gruenewald and the Moderns." *SRL* 32, no. 5 (January 29, 1949): 32–33. A consideration of modern painters' attraction to the work of the sixteenth-century painter Mathias Grünewald, prompted by the publication of *The Drawings of Mathis Gothart Nithart, Called Gruenewald* (New York: H. Bittner & Co., 1948).

94. "Realism—Macchiaioli Style." *SRL* 32, no. 10 (March 5, 1949): 28–29. A discussion of the New York gallery Wildenstein & Co.'s exhibition of nineteenth-century Italian painting featuring the Macchiaioli, a group formed mid-century that proclaimed everyday reality as the subject of their art.

95. "Death of a Prodigal." *SRL* 32, no. 14 (April 2, 1949): 30–32. The "prodigal" was Christian Bérard, who died on February 12, 1949.

96. "Art as Propaganda." *SRL* 32, no. 19 (May 7, 1949): 30–31. A review of *Pageant Master of the Republic* (Lincoln, Nebr.: University of Nebraska, 1949), David L. Dowd's monograph on Jacques-Louis David.

97. "A Going in the Mulberry Trees." *SRL* 32, no. 27 (July 2, 1949): 30–31. Criticism of a speech before the U.S. House of Representatives by Congressman George A. Dondero, in which he attacked modern art as being "Communistic." The speech was entered in the *Congressional Record* of March 11, 1949.

98. "Does Our Art Impress Europe?" *SRL* 32, no. 32 (August 6, 1949): 142–49 (25th Anniversary Issue). From the Contents page: ". . . after examining the factors tending to restrict American art to a peripheral importance, [Soby] argues for a national Secretaryship of the Arts."

99. "The Rose Horse of Trajan." *SRL* 32, no. 36 (September 3, 1949): 29–30. A discussion of Eugène Delacroix's contribution to the origins of modern art.

100. "The Object Disappears." *SRL* 32, no. 40 (October 1, 1949): 35–36. Soby traces the disappearance of the object in painting, from the time of Jacques-Louis David and Antoine-Jean Gros, with emphasis on Gustave Courbet's contribution.

101. "The French Art Shows." *SRL* 32, 45 (November 1949): 30–31. Written from Paris.

102. "Among Others, Marino Marini, Who Lives in Milan." *SRL* 32, no. 49 (December 3, 1949): 64–66 (Christmas Book Number). An overview of contemporary Italian art, written from Rome.

103. "Modern Religious Art." *SRL* 33, no. 1 (January 7, 1950): 35–36.

104. "Artist Lost and Found: Georges de la Tour." *SRL* 33, no. 4 (February 4, 1950): 34–35.

105. "Arrested Time by Edward Hopper." *SRL* 33, no. 9 (March 4, 1950): 42–43. A defense of Hopper against criticism by abstract art's formalist supporters, inspired by the Hopper retrospective at the Whitney Museum of American Art.

106. "Vienna's Wonders on Display."*SRL* 33, no. 13 (April 1, 1950): 40–41. A

review of the exhibition "Art Treasures from the Vienna Collections" at the Metropolitan Museum of Art, New York.

107. "A Case of Mistaken Identity." *SRL* 33, no. 18 (May 6, 1950): 66–68. Concerns an exhibition of the works of John Frederick Peto, an artist whose work was often attributed to William Michael Harnett, at the Smith College Museum of Art, Northampton, Massachusetts. Soby praises Alfred Frankenstein of *The San Francisco Chronicle*, whose investigation of misattributed works made the show possible.

108. "Fare on Fifty-seventh Street." *SRL* 33, no. 22 (June 3, 1950): 34–36. Includes comments on various New York gallery shows held January–May 1950.

109. "Modern Artists and the Analyst's Couch." *SRL* 33, no. 26 (July 1, 1950): 38–39. A review of two books concerning psychoanalysis and art: Dr. Lionel Goitein's *Art and the Unconscious* (New York: United Book Guild, 1948) and Dr. Daniel E. Schneider's *The Psychoanalyst and the Artist* (New York: Farrar, Straus, 1950).

110. "Edvard Munch." *SRL* 33, no. 31 (August 5, 1950): 34–35. A discussion of paintings and prints by Munch on view at the Museum June 30–August 13, 1950 (MoMA Exh. #450), an exhibition organized by the Institute of Contemporary Art in Boston.

111. "Student Art at the Addison Gallery." *SRL* 33, no. 35 (September 2, 1950): 38–39. The Addison Gallery of American Art is located in Andover, Massachusetts; in 1950 its director was Bartlett Harding Hayes.

112. "Guillaume Apollinaire: The Wedding of the Arts." *SRL* 33, no. 40 (October 7, 1950): 66–68. A discussion of Apollinaire and recently published selections of his writings, including Roger Shattuck's *The Selected Apollinaire Writings* (New York: New Directions, 1950) and several editions of *Les Peintres Cubistes* (Paris), originally issued in 1913.

113. "A Bucolic Past & a Giddy Jungle." *SRL* 33, no. 44 (November 4, 1950): 40–41. Concerns the documentary film *Grandma Moses* (1950), written and narrated by Archibald MacLeish.

114. "What's New & Renewed." *SRL* 33, no. 48 (December 2, 1950): 74, 76. A review of the "1950 Annual Exhibition of Contemporary American Sculpture, Watercolors and Drawings" at the Whitney Museum of American Art.

115. [Article.] "Postwar Painting: In the Shadow of 'Guernica.'" *SRL* 34, no. 2 (January 13, 1951): 64–67, 96. In this issue, subtitled "America and the Mind of Europe: Mid-Century," Soby discusses reactions to Picasso's *Guernica* in England, Italy and France. Reprinted in Bibliog. 30.

116. "Bellicose Fish and a Steady Pulse." *SRL* 34, no. 5 (February 3, 1951): 28–29. A discussion of "Abstract Painting and Sculpture in America" (MoMA Exh. #466, January 23–March 25, 1951) and the catalogue by exhibition organizer Andrew Carnduff Ritchie; circulated as C/E II.1/32(4).

117. "A 'David' Reattributed." *SRL* 34, no. 9 (March 3, 1951): 42–43. Report on Charles Sterling's discovery that the portrait of Mlle. Charlotte du Val d'Ognes was painted not by Jacques-Louis David but by Mme. Constance

Marie Charpentier. Sterling was on the staff of The Metropolitan Museum of Art as Foreign Advisor to the Department of Paintings.

118. "Masterpieces of Drawing." *SRL* 34, no. 14 (April 7, 1951): 44–45. Includes a reference to *The Pocket Book of Great Drawings* (New York: Washington Square Press, 1951), by Paul J. Sachs.

119. "Amedeo Modigliani." *SRL* 34, no. 18 (May 5, 1951): 34–35. Written as a foreword to the catalogue of "Amedeo Modigliani" (MoMA Exh. #474, April 10–June 10, 1951); see also Bibliog. 28.

120. "Piero della Francesca." *SRL* 34, no. 22 (June 2, 1951): 36–37. A review of Sir Kenneth Clark's *Piero della Francesca* (New York: Oxford University Press, 1951).

121. "Delacroix and Daumier." *SRL* 34, no. 27 (July 7, 1951): 36–37. Concerns an exhibition of the artists' works at Wildenstein & Co.

122. "The Karolik Collection at Boston." *SRL* 34, no. 40 (October 6, 1951): 52–53 (Fall Book Number). A review of an exhibition of the Karolik Collection at the Museum of Fine Arts, Boston, and the accompanying catalogue.

123. "James Ensor." *SRL* 34, no. 44 (November 3, 1951): 40–42. A review of "James Ensor" (MoMA Exh. #491, September 25–October 28, 1951).

124. [Article.] "A Reply to Mr. Benton." *SRL* 34, no. 50 (December 15, 1951): 11–14. Written in response to an article by Thomas Hart Benton, "What's Holding Back American Art?," which also appears in this issue. Benton's article, which was adapted from his autobiography, expresses the need for Regionalist art in America.

125. "Matisse Reconsidered." *SRL* 35, no. 1 (January 5, 1952): 34–35. Includes Soby's reactions as a collector to Matisse's painting, with comments on the retrospective "Henri Matisse" (MoMA Exh. #492, November 13, 1951–January 13, 1952; circulated as C/E II.1/74[1]), organized by Alfred H. Barr, Jr.

126. "Chicago's Art Institute." *SR* 35, no. 5 (February 2, 1952): 40–41. An appreciation of the Art Institute's collection of late–nineteenth-century painting.

127. "A Letter from the National Sculpture Society." *SR* 35, no. 9 (March 1, 1952): 52–53. Soby criticizes as "arrant nonsense" a letter written by the National Sculpture Society to The Metropolitan Museum of Art concerning its "American Sculpture" exhibition held in the winter of 1951–52.

128. "The Case of Dr. Barnes." *SR* 35, no. 14 (April 5, 1952): 44–45. Written in support of opening the collection of the Barnes Foundation, in Merion, Pennsylvania, to the public; its founder, Dr. Albert C. Barnes, died in 1951.

129. "Upsurge in Painting." *SR* 35, no. 23 (June 7, 1952): 38–39. A reflection on recent trends in Canadian painting as discussed by Graham McInnes in *Canadian Art* (Toronto: MacMillan Company of Canada, 1950).

130. "The Prophetic Painter." *SR* 35, no. 27 (July 5, 1952): 34–35. Addresses the possibility of prophetic meaning in modern painting, specifically in de Chirico's *Portrait of Apollinaire* (1914) and Umberto Boccioni's *The City Rises* (1910).

131. "The State of Collecting." *SR* 35, no. 31 (August 2, 1952): 38–39. Concerns "What Businessmen Collect," an exhibition at East Hampton's Guild Hall.

132. "The Unaging Frank Lloyd Wright." *SR* 35, no. 40 (October 4, 1952): 58–59. A review of *Taliesin Drawings: Recent Architecture of Frank Lloyd Wright*, by Edgar Kaufmann, Jr. (New York: Wittenborn, Schultz, 1952).

133. "From David to Delacroix." *SR* 35, no. 44 (November 1, 1952): 44–45. Concerns the reissue of Dr. Walter F. Friedlander's *David to Delacroix*, translated by Robert Goldwater (Cambridge, Mass.: Harvard University Press, 1952).

134. "Whitney Annual." *SR* 35, no. 49 (December 6, 1952): 60–61 (Christmas Book Number).

135. "De Stijl." *SR* 36, no. 2 (January 10, 1953): 42–43. A discussion of the multiple contributions of the Netherlands to the evolution of modern art, with comments on the 1952 survey "De Stijl" (MoMA Exh. #527, December 16, 1952–February 15, 1953; circulated as II.1/50[9]).

136. "Again, to the Ladies!" *SR* 36, no. 6 (February 7, 1953): 50–51. Concerns an exhibition of the work of Loren MacIver and I. Rice Pereira at the Whitney Museum of American Art; see also Bibliog. 68.

137. [Article.] "Painting & Sculpture." *SR* 36, no. 11 (March 14, 1953): 19, 60–61. In the section titled "The Postwar Generation in Arts & Letters," Soby discusses the rise of sculpture and the New York School of painting in postwar American art.

138. "Resurrection of a Museum." *SR* 36, no. 14 (April 4, 1953): 69–70 (Annual University Press Issue). Concerns an exhibition of works from the permanent collection of the Solomon R. Guggenheim Museum, New York, directed by James Johnson Sweeney.

139. "Miracle at Genoa." *SR* 36, no. 23 (June 6, 1953): 42. Concerns the reinstallation of the collection in the Palazzo Bianco by Dr. Caterina Marcenaro, Director of Fine Arts for the Commune of Genoa.

140. "Paris Art Scene." *SR* 36, no. 27 (July 4, 1953): 39. Written from Paris.

141. "The Museum of Albi." *SR* 36, no. 31 (August 1, 1953): 33–34. Concerns the permanent installation of Henri de Toulouse-Lautrec's work at the Palais de la Berbie in Albi.

142. "Homage to Bruyas." *SR* 36, no. 36 (September 5, 1953): 34–35. A description of the collection of the nineteenth-century art patron Alfred Bruyas at the Fabre Museum in Montpellier, which Soby visited in the summer of 1953; reprinted in Bibliog. 36.

143. [Article.] "Renaissance on the Riviera." *SR* 36, no. 43 (October 24, 1953): 47–48. Soby attributes the "magnificent creative activity in the fine arts" in this area to the postwar achievements of Picasso, Matisse, and Le Corbusier.

144. "Mr. Francis Bacon." *SR* 36, no. 45 (November 7, 1953): 48–49. A review of the artist's first one-man exhibition outside of London, which opened at Durlacher Brothers in New York on October 20, 1953.

145. "'Gangster's Funeral.'" *SR* 36, no. 49 (December 5, 1953): 57–58 (Christmas

Book Number). Concerns the 1953 painting of the same title by Boston artist Jack Levine.

146. "Younger European Painters." *SR* 37, no. 1 (January 2, 1954): 61–62. Soby comments on the exhibition of contemporary European painting at the Solomon R. Guggenheim Museum.

147. "The Care and Feeding of Pictures." *SR* 37, no. 6 (February 6, 1954): 31–32. A discussion of "Take Care," the Brooklyn Museum exhibition concerned with the preservation of pictures, organized by the Museum's conservators, Caroline and Sheldon Keck. Included is a mention of *How to Take Care of Your Pictures* (1954), a booklet written by Caroline Keck and published jointly by the Brooklyn Museum and The Museum of Modern Art.

148. "Edouard Vuillard." *SR* 37, no. 10 (March 6, 1954): 37–38. A discussion of the Vuillard retrospective at the Cleveland Museum of Art organized in collaboration with and later shown in New York at The Museum of Modern Art (MoMA Exh. #555, April 6–June 6, 1954), and the accompanying monograph by Andrew Carnduff Ritchie.

149. "Man in the Frock Coat." *SR* 37, no. 14 (April 3, 1954): 56–57. "Editor's Note: The following article is based on a chapter in Mr. Soby's 'Giorgio de Chirico,' to be published by the Museum of Modern Art next autumn" (see Bibliog. 38); excerpted in Bibliog. 248. Soby attributes de Chirico's inspiration for the motif of the statue of the man in the frock coat to a statue of the Italian philosopher Giovanni Battista Bottero in the Largo Quattro Marzo in Turin.

150. "Edward VII's Americans." *SR* 37, no. 19 (May 8, 1954): 37–38. A review of an exhibition of the work of John Singer Sargent, James Abbott McNeill Whistler, and Mary Cassatt organized by The Art Institute of Chicago and shown at The Metropolitan Museum of Art, with commentary on the accompanying publication by Frederick A. Sweet.

151. "Manet and His Contemporaries." *SR* 37, no. 27 (July 3, 1954): 28–29. Inspired by George Heard Hamilton's *Manet and His Critics* (New Haven, Conn.: Yale University Press, 1954).

152. "The Mannerist Movement." *SR* 37, no. 32 (August 7, 1954): 33–34. A discussion of *Pontormo to Greco*, published in 1954 by the John Herron Art Institute, Indianapolis, in conjunction with their exhibition on sixteenth-century mannerism. Soby's emphasis is on the preface by the Institute's director, Walter Friedlander.

153. "Double Solitaire." *SR* 37, no. 36 (September 4, 1954): 29–30. In this review of concurrent retrospective exhibitions of Yves Tanguy and his wife Kay Sage at the Wadsworth Atheneum in Hartford, Connecticut, Soby defends a critic's right to judge the work of artists who are also his friends.

154. "Death of a Valiant." *SR* 37, no. 40 (October 2, 1954): 48–50. A tribute to Curt Valentin, who died August 19, 1954.

155. "The Arensberg Collection." *SR* 37, no. 45 (November 6, 1954): 60–61. Concerns the Arensberg Collection at the Philadelphia Museum of Art, with emphasis on the works of Marcel Duchamp and Constantin Brancusi.

156. "Hemingway and Painting." *SR* 37, no. 49 (December 4, 1954): 60–61. Soby viewed Hemingway as the only important American writer to whom painting was meaningful.

157. "Bullish Days in the Art Market." *SR* 38, no. 2 (January 8, 1955): 36–37.

158. "American Art Marts." *SR* 38, no. 6 (February 5, 1955): 34–35. A discussion of the international market for American art.

159. "Non-Abstract Authorities." *SR* 38, no. 17 (April 23, 1955): 52–53. Painter Grace Hartigan and sculptor Elbert Weinberg are the two "non-abstract authorities" to whom the title refers.

160. "Reg Butler and Francis Bacon." *SR* 38, no. 19 (May 7, 1955): 60–62.

161. "The New Decade." *SR* 38, no. 23 (June 4, 1955): 34–35. A review of "The New Decade: 22 European Painters and Sculptors" (MoMA Exh. #579, May 10–August 7, 1955; circulated as C/E II.1/85[5]), an exhibition of postwar European art organized by Andrew Carnduff Ritchie, and the accompanying catalogue.

162. "Collector's Choice." *SR* 38, no. 27 (July 2, 1955): 34–35. A review of "Paintings from Private Collections" (MoMA Exh. #580, May 31–September 7, 1955).

163. "Alberto Giacometti." *SR* 38, no. 32 (August 6, 1955): 36–37. Concerns Soby's visit with the artist in his Paris studio.

164. "Interview with Larry Rivers." *SR* 38, no. 36 (September 3, 1955): 23–24.

165. "Two Contemporary Photographers." *SR* 38, no. 45 (November 5, 1955): 32–33. A discussion of the work of Paul Strand and Henri Cartier-Bresson.

166. "Constantin Brancusi." *SR* 38, no. 49 (December 3, 1955): 50–51 (Christmas Book Number). A description of the sculptor's Paris studio and an exhibition of his work at the Solomon R. Guggenheim Museum.

167. "Baron Gros." *SR* 39, no. 2 (January 14, 1956): 34–35. A review of an exhibition of Antoine-Jean Gros's work, which Soby had recently seen at the Jacques Seligmann Gallery, New York.

168. "Walker Evans." *SR* 39, no. 7 (February 18, 1956): 28–29. Evans was one of four photographers included in "Diogenes with a Camera III" (MoMA Exh. #596, January 17–March 18, 1956), organized by Edward Steichen.

169. "Arthur Dove and Morris Graves." *SR* 39, no. 14 (April 7, 1956): 32–33. A review of the Dove exhibition at the Downtown Gallery, New York, and the Graves exhibition at the Whitney Museum of American Art.

170. "Suggestions and Symbols." *SR* 39, no. 18 (May 5, 1956): 11–12. Under the heading "Freud's 100th Birthday" and the subheading "Freud and Modern Art," Soby discusses the psychoanalyst's influence on twentieth-century artists.

171. "Twelve Americans." *SR* 39, no. 23 (June 9, 1956): 34–35. A review of "Twelve Americans" (MoMA Exh. #604, May 30–September 9,1956), organized by Dorothy C. Miller.

172. "An Afternoon with Picasso." *SR* 39, no. 35 (September 1, 1956): 28–29. Soby describes his visit to Picasso's studio at Cannes, accompanied by his wife,

Melissa; Alfred H. Barr, Jr.; and Margaret Scolari Barr.

173. "English Contemporary Art." *SR* 39, no. 40 (October 6, 1956): 43–44.

174. [Book review]. "The Artist at Seventy-five." *SR* 39, no. 48 (December 1, 1956): 26–27. Concerns Roland Penrose's *Portrait of Picasso* (London: Lund Humphries/ICA, 1956).

175. "The Ringling Art Museum." *SR* 40, no. 1 (January 5, 1957): 30–31. A description of the John and Mable Ringling Art Museum in Sarasota, Florida and the achievements of his friend and mentor A. Everett Austin, Jr. as Director.

176. "Minneapolis's Treasures." *SR* 40, no. 5 (February 2, 1957): 28–29. A review of an exhibition of twenty-five works from the Minneapolis Institute of Arts, held at M. Knoedler & Co.

177. "Two Masters of Expressionism." *SR* 40, no. 9 (March 2, 1957): 28–29. Concerns an exhibition of Egon Schiele's watercolors and drawings at the Galerie St. Etienne, New York, and "The Graphic Work of Edvard Munch" (MoMA Exh. #614, February 6–March 3, 1957; circulated as C/E II.1/62[11] and ICE# D–11–56).

178. "Art on TV." *SR* 40, no. 15 (April 13, 1957): 29–30. Addresses the popularity of art as a subject for television, centering on two broadcasts: Claudette Colbert's "One Coat of White" (CBS, February 21, 1957) and Robert Montgomery's "Reclining Nude" (an adaptation of a Broadway show; NBC, February 25, 1953).

179. "The Pulitzer Collection." *SR* 40, no. 19 (May 11, 1957): 29–30. The title refers to an exhibition originally organized as a benefit for the Fogg Art Museum, Harvard University, Cambridge, Massachusetts. Soby waxes enthusiastically over the selected works later shown in New York at M. Knoedler & Co.

180. "Pablo Picasso." *SR* 40, no. 23 (June 8, 1957): 28–29. A review of "Picasso: 75th Anniversary Exhibition" (MoMA Exh. #619, May 4–August 25, 1957), organized and with a catalogue by Alfred H. Barr, Jr.

181. "Interview with Grace Hartigan." *SR* 40, no. 40 (October 5, 1957): 26–27.

182. "Stuart Davis." *SR* 40, no. 45 (November 9, 1957): 32–33. Concerns the Davis exhibition at the Whitney Museum of American Art, with a catalogue by H. H. Arnason.

183. "Giorgio Morandi." *SR* 41, no. 1 (January 4, 1958): 23–24. An appreciation of the artist.

184. [Article.] "The Muse Was Not for Hire." *SR* 45, no. 38 (September 22, 1962): 57–58. In the section titled "Creative Vision: Six Decades of the Photographer's Art," Soby reminisces on what Walker Evans's work meant to him and others during the Depression.

185. [Book review.] "Prophet in His Own Country." *SR* 46, no. 44 (November 2, 1963): 21. In the section titled "The Creative Artist," Soby reviews Francis Steegmuller's *Apollinaire: Poet Among the Painters* (New York: Farrar, Strauss, 1963).

186. "About the Cover." *SR* 47, no. 46 (November 14, 1964): 63. Excerpt concerning de Chirico's *Nostalgia of the Infinite* (1913–14?; dated on painting 1911), which originally appeared on pp. 134–35 of *Masters of Modern Art*, edited by Alfred H. Barr, Jr. (New York: The Museum of Modern Art: 1954).

187. [Book review.] "Through Snowden's Lens." *SR* 48, no. 50 (December 11, 1965): 34. A review of *Private View* (London: Nelson, [1965]), a book of photographic portraits of contemporary English artists by Lord Snowden (Antony Armstrong-Jones), with foreword by John Russell and text by Bryan Robertson.

III. Periodicals

Unless otherwise noted, the place of publication for all periodicals cited is New York, New York.

188. "The Middle Fate." *The Williams Graphic* (Williamstown, Mass.) 7, no. 1 (April 1926): 7–8, 10, 28. A short story written for the literary magazine of Williams College.

189. "Voyage of Fancy." *The Williams Graphic* (Williamstown, Mass.) 7, no. 1 (April 1926): 26. A poem about a work by Maxfield Parrish.

190. "The New Arrivals." *The Williams Graphic* (Williamstown, Mass.) 7, no. 2 (May 1926): 8–9. A short story.

191. "Derain and the French Tradition." *Fifth Floor Window* 3 (April 1931): unpaginated.

192. "Modigliani." *Fifth Floor Window* 4 (May 1931): unpaginated.

193. "Since Picasso: The Revolt of the Young Romantics." *The Literary Observer* (Hartford, Conn.) 1, no. 1 (April–May 1934): 14–15, 20.

194. "Waving the Swastika for American Art." *The Literary Observer* (Hartford, Conn.) 1, no. 2 (June–July 1934): 47–48.

195. "Modern Photography." *The Literary Observer* (Hartford, Conn.) 1, no. 3 (August–September 1934): 67–68.

196. "The Ear of Vincent Van Gogh." *The Literary Observer* (Hartford, Conn.) 1, no. 4 (October–November 1934): 101.

197. "The Literary Surrealists: The Art of Invective and Abuse." *The Literary Observer* (Hartford, Conn.) 1, no. 6 (February–March 1935): 169. An appraisal of selected contributions made to *La Révolution Surréaliste* (Paris) between 1924 and 1929.

198. "The Light Fantastic Show." *Town and Country* 91, no. 4170 (December 1936): 68–71, 166 (90th Anniversary Issue). Concerns the year's exhibitions of Surrealist art and reaction to the movement in London and New York.

199. "Picasso: A Critical Estimate." *Parnassus* 11, no. 8 (December 1939): 8–12.

200. "Notes on Documentary Photography: A Collector of Modern Art and Modern Photography Appraises the Documentarians, Their Work and Aims." *U.S. Camera Magazine* 1, no. 12 (November 1940): 38, 73–74. Soby

is the collector to whom the subtitle refers.

201. "The Art of Poetic Accident: The Photographs of Cartier-Bresson and Helen Levitt." *Minicam Photography* 6, no. 7 (March 1943): 28–31, 95.

202. "In Defense of Modern Art as a Field for Research." *College Art Journal* 1, no. 3 (March 1942): 63–65. Refers to articles by Alfred H. Barr, Jr., and Frank J. Mather, Jr., in *College Art Journal* 1, no. 1 (January 1942): 3–6 and *College Art Journal* 1, no. 2 (February 1942): 31–33.

203. "Return to the North." *View*, Series 2, no. 2 (May 1942): unpaginated [Yves Tanguy/Pavel Tchelitchew number]. Reprint edition. Nendeln/Liechtenstein: Kraus, 1969.

204. "Peter Blume's 'Eternal City.'" *The Bulletin of The Museum of Modern Art* 10, no. 4 (April 1943): 1–6. Reprint edition. New York: Arno Press, 1967.

205. "New Acquisitions in American Paintings." *The Bulletin of The Museum of Modern Art* 11, no. 4 (February–March 1944): 1–5. Reprint edition. New York: Arno Press, 1967. See also Bibliog. 206, 242.

206. "Acquisitions Policy of The Museum of Modern Art: Painting and Sculpture." *The Museum News* 22, no. 4 (June 1944): 7. See also Bibliog. 205, 242.

207. [Letter to the editor.] "What Is 'Romanticism'?" *Magazine of Art* (Washington, D.C.) 37, no. 2 (February 1944): 77–78. Concerns Romanticism as defined in the exhibition "Romantic Painting in America" (see Bibliog. 11).

208. "Romantic Painting in America: The *Journal* inaugurates a Series of Exceptional Pictures by American Artists." *Ladies' Home Journal* 61, no. 9 (September 1944): 22–23.

209. "The Collection of the Museum of Modern Art: Four Basic Policies." *Art in America* 32, no. 4 (October 1944): 230–235. A special issue focusing on American art collections.

210. "The Personality of Eugène Delacroix." *Magazine of Art* (Washington, D.C.) 37, no. 8 (December 1944): 282–86.

211. "Marcel Duchamp in the Arensberg Collection." *View*, series 5, no. 1 (March 1945): 11–12 (Marcel Duchamp number). Reprint edition. Nendeln/Liechenstein: Kraus, 1969.

212. [Letter to the editor.] *Art News* 44, no. 5 (April 15–30, 1945): 4. A defense of recent Museum of Modern Art acquisitions against editorial criticism by *Art News;* included in the Museum Trustee minutes of March 29, 1945.

213. [Book review.] *The Art Bulletin* 27, no. 2 (June 1945): 157–58. A review of Edgar P. Richardson's *American Romantic Painting* (New York: Weyhe, 1944).

214. "Notas sobre la pintura inglese de nuestros dias." *La Revista Belga* (New York: Belgian Office for Latin America) 2, no. 10 (October 1945): [28–32], 33, [34–37], 38. Spanish translation of Bibliog. 14.

215. "Italy: Two Movements and Two Paintings." *Magazine of Art* (Washington, D.C.) 39, no. 2 (February 1946): 49–51, 76–79. Concerns Boccioni's *States*

of Mind, I: Leave Taking (1911) and de Chirico's *The Melancholy of Departure* (1914), Futurism, and "pittura metafisica."

216. "The Museum of Modern Art." *Transatlantic*, no. 34 (June 1946): 12–33. See also Bibliog. 20, 220.

217. [Letter to the editor.] "Chirico v. Chirico." *Time* 48, no. 12 (September 1946): 11, 16. A defense of de Chirico against "all comers, including his aging . . . rather wonderful self."

218. "An Art Program for New York State." *Magazine of Art* (Washington, D.C.) 40, no. 1 (January 1947): 29–30.

219. [Letter to the editor.] "Sculptor Henry Moore." *Life* 22, no 6 (February 10, 1947): 4, 10. Soby defends Moore against his critics, praising his "clarity and eloquence."

220. "The Museum of Modern Art." *The Bulletin of The Museum of Modern Art* 14, no. 2 (February 1947): 1–16. Reprint edition. New York: Arno Press, 1967. Soby explains the educational mission of The Museum of Modern Art; see also Bibliog. 216.

221. "The Temptation of Saint Anthony." *Film and Radio Guide* (Newark, N.J.) 13, no. 5 (February 1947): 17–19. See also Bibliog. 72.

222. "Matta Echaurren." *Magazine of Art* (Washington, D.C.) 40, no. 3 (March 1947): 102–06. Reprinted in Bibliog. 22.

223. "Ben Shahn." *The Bulletin of The Museum of Modern Art* 14, no. 4–5 (Summer 1947). Reprint edition. New York: Arno Press, 1967. A special issue of the Museum *Bulletin* devoted to the Shahn retrospective exhibition, intended as a supplement to the monograph on the painter published by Penguin Books (see Bibliog. 18).

224. "The Younger American Artists." *Harper's Bazaar*, no. 2829 (September 1947): 194–97.

225. "Ben Shahn and Morris Graves." *Horizon* (London), no. 93–94 (October 1947): 48–57. Special issue, "Art on the American Horizon," edited by Cyril Connolly.

226. "Ben Shahn." *'48* 2, no. 1 (January 1948): 73–79.

227. "Ben Shahn." *Graphis: International Journal for Graphic and Applied Art* (Zurich) 4, no. 22 (March–April 1948): 102–04. Text also in German (pp. 104–05, 189) and in French (107, 188–89).

228. "The Constructivist Brotherhood." *Art News* 47, no. 1 (March 1948): 22–25, 57–59. Concerns Naum Gabo and Antoine Pevsner, whose works were on view at the Museum in the exhibition "Gabo–Pevsner" (MoMA Exh. #369, February 10–April 25,1948).

229. "Last of the Impressionists: Pierre Bonnard." *Town and Country* 102, no. 4308 (May 1948): 70–71, 90, 92, 94.

230. "Three Artists Who Are Humourists: Klee, Miró, Calder." *Vogue* 111, no. 8 (May 1, 1948): 178, 181–82. Reprinted in Bibliog. 22.

231. "Five Modern Italian Artists." *Vogue* 111, no. 18 (November 1, 1948): 190–92. Soby briefly discusses Renato Guttuso, Manzù, Marini, Morandi, and

Giuseppe Santomaso.

232. "Inland in the Subconscious: Yves Tanguy." *Magazine of Art.* (Washington, D.C.) 42, no. 1 (January 1949): 2–7.

233. "T. Cole: Reviving an Ancestor." *Art News* 47, no. 9 (January 1949): 26–29, 58.

234. "A Symposium: The State of American Art." *Magazine of Art* (Washington, D.C.) 42, no. 3 (March 1949): 98–99. Soby was one of sixteen writers and critics who were asked to comment in this issue on current trends in American art.

235. [Letter to the editor.] *New York Herald Tribune*, July 31, 1949, sect. 5: 5 Soby explains that the omission of works by Guillermo Meissner from The Museum of Modern Art's "XXth Century Italian Art" exhibition (see Bibliog. 26) was not deliberate.

236. "Léonid." *Horizon* (London) 20, no. 119 (November 1949): 330–38.

237. "A Symposium: Government and Art." *Magazine of Art* (Washington, D.C.) 43, no. 7 (November 1950): 244–47. Written in favor of Federal support for the arts.

238. [Editorial.] "New Climate for British Art." *Magazine of Art* (Washington, D.C.) 44, no. 1 (January 1951): 4. Soby was appointed Acting Editor of the *Magazine of Art* in December 1950; this was his first editorial for the magazine.

239. "Boccioni à New-York." *La Fiera letteraria* (Rome) 9, no. 7 (February 14, 1954): 7.

240. "Eugene Berman Panels: Gift of James T. Soby in memory of his father Charles Soby." *Wadsworth Atheneum Bulletin* (Hartford, Conn.), series 2, no. 50 (October 1954): 1.

241. "The Eastern Seaboard: New York City—Art Capital." *Art in America* 42, no. 1 (Winter 1954): 11.

242. "Recent Acquisitions of The Museum of Modern Art, New York." *The Studio* (London and New York) 148, no. 741 (December 1954): 161–71. See also Bibliog. 205, 206.

243. "Foreword . . . New Talent in the U.S.A." *Art in America* 43, no. 1 (February 1955): 12–13.

244. "Documents: 'Collecting: A Critic's View.'" *Arts Digest* 29, no. 15 (May 1, 1955): 14, 32. Text of a lecture delivered at the American Federation of Arts' 45th Anniversary national convention in New York.

____. See Bibliog. 37, also written at this time.

245. "The Painting of John Marin." *Perspectives USA* 11 (Spring 1955): 48–53. Also issued in French translation (see Bibliog. 247).

246. "The Landscape of Yves Tanguy." *Fashion and Travel* 12, no. 3 (1955).

247. "La Peintre de John Marin." *Profils* (Paris), no 11 (Spring 1955): 145–51. See also Bibliog. 245.

248. "Capolavori di oltre atlantico." *L'Illustrazione Italiana* (Milan) 82, no. 6 (June 1955): 47, [48–51], 52. See also Bibliog. 39.

249. [Letter to the editor.] "Work of Fernand Léger." *The New York Times*, August 27, 1955, sect. 1: 14. Soby objects to misstatements in *The Times*'s obituary on Léger.

250. "De Chirico: Case History of the Metaphysician." *Art News* 54, no. 5 (September 1955): 32–35. Includes excerpts from Bibliog. 149.

251. "Un Demi-siècle d'art aux États-Unis: La Peinture américaine moderne et Paris." *Cahiers d'art 1955* (Paris: Editions "Cahiers d'art") 30 (1956): 21–24.

252. "Matta." *Salamander* (Copenhagen) 2 (1955): 5–11.

___. See Bibliog. 42, also written at this time.

253. [Editorial.] "American Trends in Collecting." *Art in America* 46, no. 2 (Summer 1958): 10–11.

254. "Genesis of a Collection." *Art in America* 49, no. 1 (February 1961): 68–81. An autobiographical essay by Soby, published to coincide with the exhibition of his collection at M. Knoedler & Co. See also Bibliog. 56.

255. "Jazz: An Intimate View of This Most Colorful Aspect of American Cultural Life." *Art in America.* 51, no. 4 (August 1963): 134–39. Illustrated with seven photographs by Lee Friedlander.

256. [Letter to the editor.] With Barr, Alfred H., Jr. *Art in America* 51, no. 5 (October 1963): 143. Soby and Barr defend the integrity of Ad Reinhardt's painting; written in response to an article by Ralph F. Colin, a Museum Trustee, who accused the artist of being a "fake."

257. "The Collections." *Art in America* 52, no. 1 (February 1964: 40. Included as part of Geoffrey Hellman's article "Profile of a Museum." Reprinted in Bibliog. 61.

258. "A Trail of Human Presence: On Some Early Paintings of Francis Bacon." *MoMA Members' Quarterly* [The Members' Quarterly of The Museum of Modern Art] 2, no. 4 (Spring 1990): 8–13. Excerpted from an unpublished text completed by Soby in 1962, with an introduction by Rona Roob.

Photograph Credits

Acquavella Galleries, Inc., New York: 124. Oliver Baker, courtesy The Museum of Modern Art, New York: 192 bottom, 193 bottom. The Barnes Foundation, Merion, Pennsylvania: 106 right. Mabel D'Amico, courtesy The Museum of Modern Art, New York: 159 top left. Department of Film and Video, The Museum of Modern Art, New York: 83, 87, 89, 95, 99. Department of Painting and Sculpture, The Museum of Modern Art, New York: 109, 126. David Gahr: 142. Peter A. Juley & Son, courtesy The Museum of Modern Art, New York: 42 middle. Kate Keller, courtesy The Museum of Modern Art, New York: 44 bottom, 190. Carl Klein Studios, courtesy The Museum of Modern Art, New York: 191. James Mathews, courtesy The Museum of Modern Art, New York: 129. The Metropolitan Museum of Art, New York: 30 top left, 30 top right, 30 bottom right, 42 top, 63. The Museum of Modern Art, New York: 16, 19, 24 left, 35 bottom left, 91, 123 left, 132 left, 132 right, 134, 135, 140, 155, 156 left, 156 right, 157 top, 157 bottom, 158 right, 165 top, 165 bottom, 167. The Museum of Modern Art Archives, New York: 12, 20, 26, 50–62, 174, 175, 176 top, 176 bottom, 177, 178 left, 178 right, 179, 180, 189, 195 top, 195 bottom, 197, 198 top, 198 middle, 198 bottom, 200, 206 left, 213, 220, 223. The Museum of Modern Art Film Stills Archive, New York: 74, 76, 77, 79, 82, 84, 85, 86, 88, 92, 94, 96. Paul Parker, courtesy The Museum of Modern Art, New York: 18. Rolf Petersen, courtesy The Museum of Modern Art, New York: 35 top left, 106 left, 121. © PHOTO R.M.N. Photo Routhier, courtesy The Museum of Modern Art, New York: 215. Special Collections, Milbank Memorial Library, Teachers' College, Columbia University, New York: 150, 159 bottom. Arline Strong, courtesy The Museum of Modern Art, New York: 158 left. Soichi Sunami, courtesy The Museum of Modern Art, New York: 24 right, 27, 30 bottom left, 35 bottom right, 35 top right, 42 bottom, 44 top, 44 middle, 46, 113, 115, 123 right, 130, 136 top, 136 bottom, 137, 138, 192 top, 193 top, 194 top, 194 bottom, 196 top, 196 bottom, 215, 224 Left, 224 right.The Tate Gallery, London: 125, 141. © Michael Vaccaro: 105. Vanderveen, courtesy The Museum of Modern Art, New York: 159 top right, 170. Washburn Gallery, New York: 81

Contributors

Mary Lea Bandy is Chief Curator of the Department of Film and Video

James Leggio is Senior Editor at Harry N. Abrams, Inc., New York

Carol Morgan is the former Acting Director of the Department of Education

Rona Roob is Museum Archivist

Kirk Varnedoe is Chief Curator of the Department of Painting and Sculpture

A Note to Contributors

Studies in Modern Art publishes scholarly articles focusing on works of art in the collection of The Museum of Modern Art and on the Museum's programs. It is issued annually, although additional special numbers may be published from time to time. Each number deals with a particular topic. A list of future topics may be obtained from the journal office.

Contributors should submit proposals to the Editorial Committee of the journal by January 1 of the year preceding publication. Proposals should include the title of the article; a 500-word description of the subject; a critical appraisal of the current state of scholarship on the subject; and a list of works in the Museum's collection or details of the Museum's program that will be discussed. A working draft of the article may be submitted as a proposal. The Editorial Committee will evaluate all proposals and invite selected authors to submit finished manuscripts. (Such an invitation will not constitute acceptance of the article for publication.) Authors of articles published in the journal receive an honorarium and complimentary copies of the issue.

Please submit all inquiries to:

Studies in Modern Art
The Museum of Modern Art
11 West 53 Street
New York, New York 10019

Trustees of The Museum of Modern Art

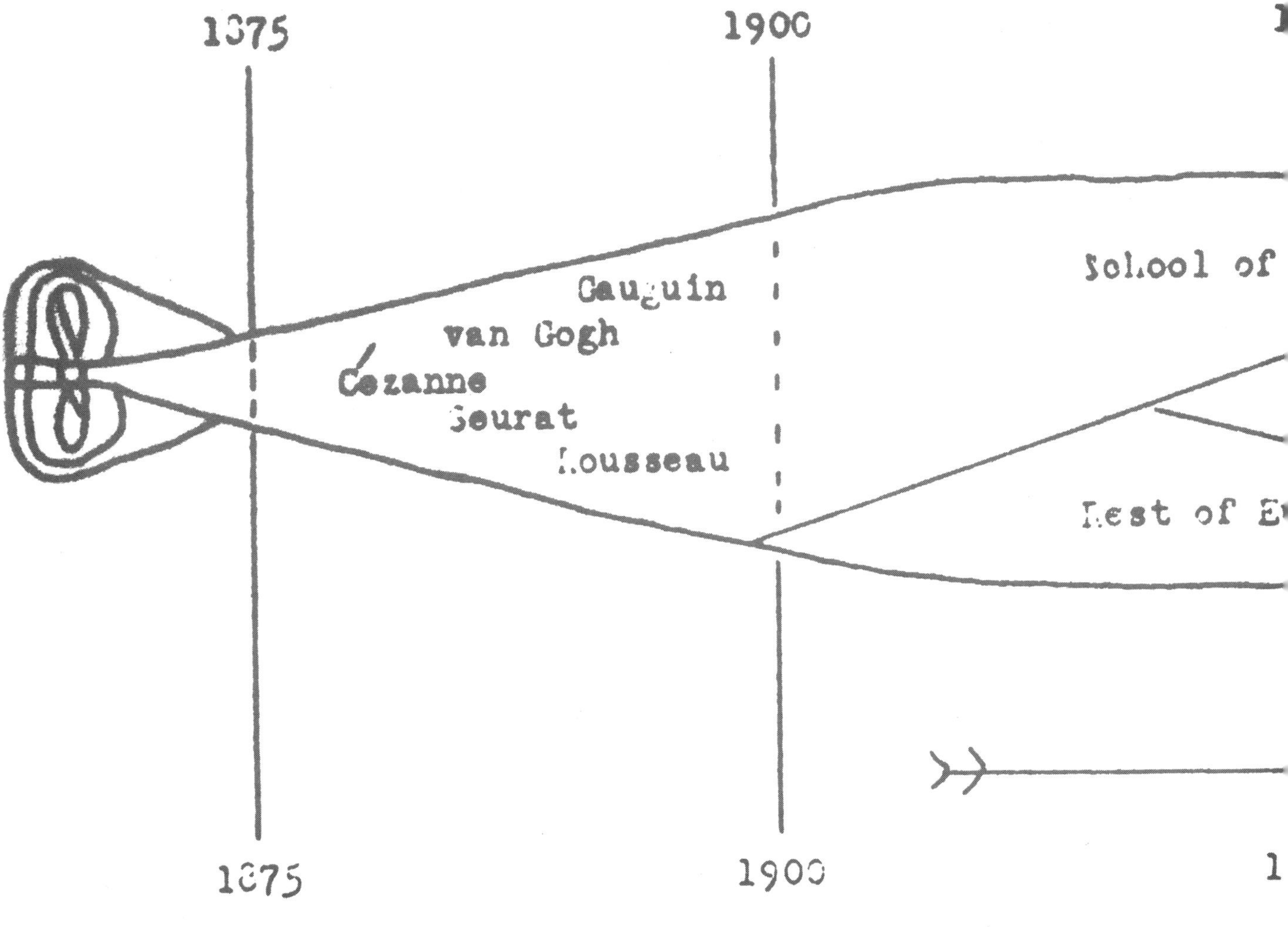
1875
1900
Gauguin
van Gogh
Cezanne
Seurat
Rousseau
School of
Rest of E
1875
1900